EASY ACCESS
TO NATIONAL PARKS

Wendy Roth and Michael Tompane

EASY
ACCESS
TO
NATIONAL
PARKS

THE SIERRA CLUB GUIDE FOR
PEOPLE WITH DISABILITIES

Sierra Club Books   *San Francisco*

The Sierra Club, founded in 1892 by John Muir, has devoted itself to the study and protection of the earth's scenic and ecological resources — mountains, wetlands, woodlands, wild shores and rivers, deserts and plains. The publishing program of the Sierra Club offers books to the public as a nonprofit educational service in the hope that they may enlarge the public's understanding of the Club's basic concerns. The point of view expressed in each book, however, does not necessarily represent that of the Club. The Sierra Club has some sixty chapters coast to coast, in Canada, Hawaii, and Alaska. For information about how you may participate in its programs to preserve wilderness and the quality of life, please address inquiries to Sierra Club, 730 Polk Street, San Francisco, CA 94109.

Copyright © 1992 by Wendy Roth and Michael Tompane
All rights reserved under International and Pan-American Copyright Conventions. No part of this book may be reproduced in any form or by any electronic or mechanical means, including information storage and retrieval systems, without permission in writing from the publisher.

Wherever we go and whatever we do, we are all responsible for our own actions and safety. The authors and publisher shall not be responsible and disclaim any liability for injury, loss, or inconvenience sustained by any person resulting from the use of the information contained in this guide.

LIBRARY OF CONGRESS CATALOGING IN PUBLICATION DATA

Roth, Wendy, 1952–
    Easy access to national parks: a Sierra Club guide for people with disabilities/ by Wendy Roth and Michael Tompane.
      p. cm.
    Includes bibliographical references and index.
    ISBN 0-87156-620-6
    1. National parks and reserves — United States — Guide-books.
    2. United States — Description and travel — 1981- — Guide-books.
    3. Parks — United States — Access for the physically handicapped — Guide-books. I. Tompane, Michael, 1951-   II. Sierra Club.
III. Title.
E160.R5 1992
917.304′928′087 — dc20   91-34274
                                          CIP

Production by Robin Rockey
Cover design by Laurie Dolphin
Book design by Abigail Johnston
Set in ITC New Baskerville by Classic Typography
Maps by Tim Krasnansky
Map graphics done on Apple Macintosh computers

Printed on acid-free paper containing a minimum of 50% recovered waste paper, of which at least 10% of the fiber content is post-consumer waste.

10 9 8 7 6 5 4 3 2 1

TO OUR FATHERS,
JERROLD ROTH AND EUGENE TOMPANE,
WHO, IN ADDITION TO EVERYTHING ELSE,
INTRODUCED EACH OF US TO
THE NATIONAL PARKS

CONTENTS

III · A T A G L A N C E

PREFACE

O n a recent vacation, we visited three inspiring national parks — Bryce Canyon, Zion, and the Grand Canyon. How much better our trip would have been had we known earlier about the excellent wheelchair accessibility at Bryce Canyon and Zion and the minimal opportunities at the Grand Canyon's North Rim. We asked ourselves: Why not write a guide for everyone on the accessibility of all the greater national parks? As the idea jelled during our drive home through the Mojave Desert, an amazing display of ball, sheet, horizontal, and vertical bolts of lightning illuminated the sky before our windshield. Lasting for hours, the storm seemed to affirm the significance of our intentions. *Easy Access to National Parks* resulted from this idea.

Through our preliminary research, we found that the National Park Service provides useful printed visitor guides regarding accessibility for some parks, but other parks had little or no information. What *was* available may not have been complete or up-to-date. We needed additional information and felt other park visitors would as well.

The National Park Service administers more than 350 sites in the United States: small historical sites, battlefields, monuments (both historical and natural), and river, lake, and seashore recreation areas, as well as the larger, well-known areas with their tremendous natural beauty designated by Congress as national parks. These larger parks are informally referred to as the greater national parks. We decided to visit firsthand as many of them as we could.

While researching the parks on-site, we produced an educational video program, called *Easy Access National Parks*, featuring people with various disabilities enjoying accessible park trails and several backcountry experiences at selected national parks. For more information about the video program, call Questar Video 800-633-5633.

With the passage of the Americans with Disabilities Act (ADA) in 1990, this society has officially recognized the rights of people with disabilities to equal access opportunities in the United States. The National Park Service has long been at the forefront of making opportunities accessible for people with disabilities and was the first federal agency to make accessibility a matter of policy. Although the parks have been working for many years to improve access, we and most park personnel agree that much remains to be done.

In the process of putting this book together, we set out to discover accessible areas in the national parks, and in so doing we received an informal education in accessibility requirements. Michael used his background as a building contractor to learn, interpret, and apply accessibility codes and guidelines. We used park trails and facilities, often inviting other persons with disabilities to accompany us in an effort to evaluate park opportunities. The results we report in this guide are based on firsthand experiences, interviews with park personnel, park self-evaluations, and responses to our written questionnaires.

In several parks, families with young children and seniors stopped to ask us where we had found accessible park activities. These people made us aware of the common access needs for those using wheelchairs or pushing strollers and for others who do not want strenuous hikes. Laughingly, we began to say Easy Access was in search of trails for tots and wheels. We found that if trails and facilities did not meet legal accessibility standards, people with disabilities and others could increase their own access to the parks with appropriate preparations, expectations, and assistance. We noted alternative means of park exploration such as boating, horseback riding, and assisted touring as we encountered them.

In the past, able-bodiedness has incorrectly been used as a yardstick of humanness, but people with disabilities are no less human than people who are not disabled. In fact, everyone is disabled at some time in their lives, whether through injury or sickness or because of youth or natural aging. People with disabilities form the only minority group anyone can join at anytime, and everyone who is not disabled is only temporarily able-bodied.

With these considerations in mind, we have chosen to use in our text the term *nondisabled* to mean persons who are temporarily able-bodied. We do this to suggest that neither persons with disabilities nor nondisabled persons are the norm. Likewise, we strive to use language that does not stereotype anyone.

The Easy Access Project has become a catalyst for concrete changes to enhance access in the parks for people with disabilities. The National Park Foundation enthusiastically formed the Easy Access Challenge, a national volunteer effort to improve national park recreational opportunities for people with disabilities. The Telephone Pioneers of America, a premier industry-based service organization of volunteers, has joined the Challenge and is already involved in improving park trails and programs. Director James Ridenour recently continued the National Park Service's commitment to improving outdoor recreational opportunities for people regardless of disability, "by working with such groups as the Telephone Pioneers of America. . . . We will be expanding hiking-biking trails, campgrounds, boating, cross-country skiing, and swimming opportunities at a number of our national parks as a result of this initiative."

We hope the Easy Access Challenge will make a contribution to barrier-free parks. One measure of this group's success is that *Easy Access to National Parks* will miss references to some new and future accessible opportunities in the parks as our book goes to print.

While we strongly endorse the improvement of accessibility, some misuse the issue to advocate developments that are destructive to wilderness. We believe the role of the national parks is to restore or augment everyone's appreciation of nature. This is a heritage to be enjoyed and preserved for now and for future generations.

Our last research trip was to Sequoia and Kings Canyon national parks. We had intended to drive directly to our home in Los Angeles, but the friends with whom we visited these last two parks took us on an unexpected detour. Again we found ourselves crossing the Mojave Desert. As the full moon rose over the desert, we realized this was the end of our journeys to the parks, at least for this project. Then lightning began. The storm was distant and less dramatic, yet no less significant in our minds and hearts than the one at the inception of *Easy Access*.

ACKNOWLEDGMENTS

This book could not have been completed without the tremendous support of many individuals, foundations, and corporations who generously gave their time, information, expertise, and contributions. The National Park Service eagerly welcomed and fully cooperated with the project, lending knowledge and advice in the field. We wish to thank everyone who helped us in this endeavor.

Our special gratitude goes to the National Park Foundation. Alan A. Rubin, its president, has been a constant source of encouragement and dedication in helping us to make this project happen. National Park Foundation staff, particularly Mary Hewes, Andrea Talentino, and Christopher Jerussi, were instrumental with their able assistance. John L. Bryant, Jr., past president of the foundation, was an early champion of Easy Access National Parks, and we will always be grateful to him.

Our editor, Jim Cohee, recognized the value of this project from its inception and encouraged us throughout as we sought nationwide support. His ideas and contributions during the writing and production of this book have been invaluable.

We will always fondly remember the assistance of those who devoted their vacations to help us on our survey trips: Dick Roth and Char Curtiss Roth at Olympic, Yosemite, and Rocky Mountain national parks; Enid Roth at Mt. Rainier, North Cascades, and Acadia national parks; Virginia Kamsky and P. D. Fyke at Shenandoah, Sequoia, and Kings Canyon national parks; and Dana Mathews at Sequoia National Park. John Livzey and Dana Mathews generously gave us their time in Yosemite National Park. Eugene and Mary Beth Tompane made our visit to Hawaii Volcanoes National Park possible. Their love and support will always be appreciated.

Phil Donahue and Marlo Thomas have been avid supporters throughout this undertaking. Phil's enthusiasm and excellent advice concerning this project and its efforts to improve the awareness of accessibility in the national parks have been invaluable.

We are indebted to Douglas Martin, Ph.D., California Coalition for Access, and Paul Longmore, Ph.D., visiting assistant professor of history at Stanford University and coeditor of *Unhandicapping Our Language,* who have provided us with important and continuous counsel concerning people with disabilities. Stanley van den Noort, M.D., has also always been there for us.

This project would not have been possible without generous financial contributions from Ella Lyman Cabot Trust, Firestone Trust Fund, Horace W. Goldsmith Foundation, Walter J. and Elise Haas Foundation, W. K. Kellogg Foundation, Kraft General Foods Foundation, Margaret T. Morris Foundation, and the Dr. Scholl Foundation.

Richard Menschel and Eugene Polk have been particularly instrumental in making this project viable.

We are also thankful to Susan and Theo Cherbuliez, Phil Donahue, and Esta and Harold Epstein, Allan Esses, Mollie Himmelfarbe, John and Anne Nevin, Maureen and John Nunn, Phyllis Roth-Feigenbaum, Betsy and Buzz Schmidt, and anonymous donors.

Our appreciation goes to both Nina Zolt, attorney-at-law, and Chuck Jones, executive director, Southern California Ecumenical Council.

Materials furnished by Eastman Kodak, Invacare, and Sony Magnetic Tape Division were greatly appreciated, as was in-kind support from Joe Wojcich at Tempe Camera Repair, TW Recreational Services, and Yosemite Park and Curry Company.

The National Park Service has been wonderfully supportive throughout the research and writing of this book. David C. Park, chief, Special Programs and Population Branch, and Kay Ellis, recreation specialist, are among the most knowledgeable concerning outdoor recreational accessibility and have been a great help to us. We also want to thank Jack Morehead, formerly associate director, Operations; Michael Paskowsky, interpretive planner, Harpers Ferry Center; Linda Meyers, Division of Publications, Harpers Ferry Center; and Rene Minick, Lands Division, Washington Office.

Many park personnel contributed to *Easy Access to National Parks,* and we developed great respect for their abilities. Any credit to us for this work belongs to them as well. Those who were particularly significant include: Diane Allen, Arches NP; Joe Arnold, Jr., Rocky Mountain NP; Ross Balch, Everglades NP; Joe Ballard, Lake Clark NP; Shirley Beccue, Acadia NP; Warren Bielenberg, Midwest Region; Eric Becker, Chaco Culture NHP; Carol Bourneman, Voyageurs NP; Kent Bullard, Channel Islands NP; Bob Butterfield, Denali NP; Stanley G. Canter, Great Smoky Mountains NP; Danny Cantu, Carlsbad Caverns NP; Sonya Capek, Yellowstone NP; Manny Cortez, Carlsbad Caverns NP; Rod Dean, Big Bend NP; Jim Dougan, Voyageurs NP; Bill Ehorn, Redwood NP; Steve Eide, Yellowstone NP; Janet Ellis, Yellowstone NP; William Elms, Carlsbad Caverns NP; Jon Erickson, Hawaii Volcanoes NP; Lawrence Feser, Lassen NP; Frank Fiella, Wrangell-St. Elias NP; Don Fiero, Mesa Verde NP; Peter Fitzmaurile, Kenai Fjords NP; Larry Frederick, Canyonlands NP; Bill Gardener, Voyageurs NP; Lisa Gardiner, Biscayne NP; Tim Glass, Channel Islands NP; Robin Gregory, Grand Teton NP; Pete Hart, Theodore Roosevelt NP; Dennis Holden, Glacier NP; Tim Jarrel, Hot Springs NP; Bruce Kaye, Guadalupe Mountains NP; Kevin Kennedy, Okanogan NP; Christopher Kishiyama, Rocky Mountain NP; Sandy Kogel, Denali NP; Loren E. Lane, Mt. Rainier NP; Terry Lindsey, Shenandoah NP; Bill Link, Isle Royale NP; Sue McGill, Bryce Canyon NP; Robert Mack, Capitol Reef NP; Terry Maze, Petrified Forest NP; Jim Martin, Hawaii Volcanoes NP; John Miele, Crater Lake NP; John Morris, Lake Clark NP; Irv Mortenson, Badlands NP; Uwe Nehring, North Cascades NP; David Nemeth, Katmai NP; Phil Noblitt, Blue Ridge Parkway; Robyn Nolen, Shenandoah

NP; Kit Osterling, Big Bend NP; Bruce Reed, Guadalupe Mountains NP; Mary Reed, Redwood NP; Warren Rigby, Kobuk Valley NP; Mary Risser, Grand Teton NP and Yosemite NP; Jeff Samco, Yosemite NP; James Sanders, Biscayne NP; Terry Saunders, Great Basin NP; Jay Schuler, Badlands NP; Kim Sikoyak, Haleakala NP; Nelson Siler, Sequoia NP and Kings Canyon NP; Michael Smithson, Olympic NP; Ron Sutton, Gates of the Arctic NP; Bill Swift, Wind Cave NP; Kent Taylor, Crater Lake NP; Paul Thomas, Virgin Islands NP; Karen Wade, Guadalupe Mountains NP; Kathy Wagner, Shenandoah NP; James Weatherill, Grand Canyon NP; Mark Wellman, Yosemite NP; Larry T. Wiese, Zion NP; Chris Williams, Lassen NP; Lois Winter, Mammoth Cave NP; and Linda Z. Wright, Rocky Mountain NP. We may have mistakenly omitted a few names, and for that we apologize.

During our visits to the parks, many individuals with various disabilities met us and shared their insights into the accessibility of park trails and facilities: Dannie and Doreen Allocco, David Blair, Bill Boharsky, Ted and Sallie Brodis, Jim Butler, Carrie Dalton, Barbara Johnson, Lary and Alan Leby, Peter Mannheimer, Alan Parker, Richard and Priscilla Rhine, Diana Richardson, David Robinson, Elizabeth Sayer, and Shirley Turner.

Thank you to Mitch Pomerantz, California Council of the Blind, and John Arce, Greater Los Angeles Council on Deafness. Herbert N. Hultgren, M.D., Phyllis Cangemi of Whole Access, and landscape architect Carlton Dodge, of FASLA, provided appreciated advice.

Disabled Recreation and Environmental Access Movement (DREAM); President's Committee on Employment for Persons with Disabilities; Todd Lowther and Christine Clopper of the Easter Seal Camp, Empire, CO; Don Bader of Porterville, CA, Developmental Center; Alpha 1, Bangor, ME; Disabled Student Services, Florida International University; Florida Division of Blind Services; Kiwanis Club of International Falls, MN; Craig Hospital Rehabilitation Center, Denver, CO; Physical Access to the Wilderness (PAW), Empire,

CO; and Roger West, Wilderness on Wheels, Grant, CO, were enormously helpful.

Thanks to Scott Deacon, Advanced Mobility, North Hollywood, CA, for the fine work and prompt delivery of our modified van, in which we journeyed across the United States. Ricon Corporation, Sun Valley; Sport Chalet, Marina del Rey; Ralph Appoldt, Invacare; Glen Wells, Wheelchair House, Northridge; and Sue Roth, California Department of Rehabilitation, were also very helpful.

On a personal note, we would like to express our deepest appreciation to friends and family who gave their support, helped with sundry tasks, and assisted with challenges, expertise, and love throughout the years of this project: Phyllis Roth-Feigenbaum, Mollie Himmelfarbe, John and Chris, Donald, Richard and Tracy Tompane, Rebecca Rainey, Jack Misraje, Richard Newman, Claire Berger, Ann Czarkowski, Kathleen Pringle, Mark and Sue Warner, Edward Warschilka, Jr., Michael Harshberger, Richard and Meg Leib, Joseph and Deidre Sitko, Lee and Dawn Finch, Kim Rawdin, Jane Kaplan Goldin, Gloria Petersen Schwartz, and John Amicarello.

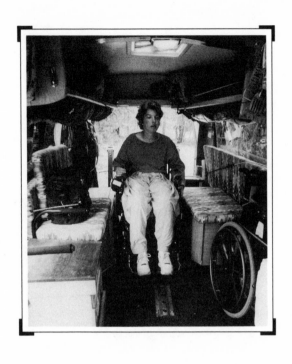

I · EASY
ACCESS
ESSENTIALS

1·WILDERNESS
AND ITS CHALLENGE

"**B**ug Bomb Levels Apartment!" led the news the week before we left our home in Los Angeles for an extended
journey through the national parks in the United
States. A young woman had set out flea bombs in her home,
closed up the place, and left for the day. The pilot light on
her heater combined with the antiflea canisters to cause an
explosion. It seemed as if the complications of city life were
giving us a sign. The national parks beckoned.

This country's crown jewels are the national parks, far
more opulent than any monarch's diamonds. They boast
some of the world's most precious wilderness settings and
opportunities for exploring beyond civilization's reach. The
parks are held in trust for everyone, preserving our wilderness: the uninhabited, uncultivated, and unspoiled reaches
of nature.

In the wilderness, we are all physically challenged. Whether
setting off on a high-mountain backcountry trek or a leisurely
valley stroll, a hiker must always consider physical abilities
and limitations as well as preparations necessary for a rewarding wilderness experience. How far to go, what trail to
take, and what gear to carry are questions for everyone—
including those with physical disabilities. While challenges
may be different depending on one's physical ability, they
are also remarkably equalizing, especially in a wilderness
setting. In these astounding locales, everyone explores his
or her abilities.

Eager to see the country's jewels firsthand, we set out to
visit a selection of wilderness treasures. One of us, Michael,
has long been a backpacker, hiking primitive wilderness

trails, camera in tow. A native of Arizona, he began hiking at age eight with his father. Since then, his admiration for nature has grown as he has backpacked and traveled extensively throughout wildlands. He is today a strong, athletic individual, and these treks are rejuvenating for him.

The other of us, Wendy, more a casual hiker, had walked many of this country's natural trails until hiking took on a new meaning for her some eight years ago. Gradually deprived of her walking ability by a severe case of multiple sclerosis, bit by bit Wendy lost voluntary movement in her legs, and she now has weakness in her hands and upper body. She first encountered these problems in her early twenties but, as with many cases of multiple sclerosis, was not definitely diagnosed until after the disease had progressed. Her physical challenges caused her to make changes in career and life-style. Yet she wanted windswept trees and wildflowers to remain a part of her life. Park journeys presented new questions, including, "Could they be made at all?"

Wendy does not fit the typical image of a camper. She uses an electric wheelchair or a three-wheel battery-powered scooter and requires assistance when traveling. Michael, using his ingenuity and resourcefulness, has adapted camping gear for their specialized needs. The parks became places to enjoy our common interests in exploration and we found a bond that transcends physical abilities. This was an exhilarating discovery.

We did not want to limit our journeys solely to automobile drives through our parklands; we think wilderness is best enjoyed in undeveloped surroundings. Despite Wendy's extensive physical limitations, we believed that we should be able to explore remote natural spots together. And explore we did.

This country's national park system encompasses natural sites that are some of the world's most inspiring and, as our visits revealed, many that are surprisingly accessible. *Easy Access to National Parks* grew out of our experiences as we set out finding ways to comfortably continue our trips through this country's natural areas. It shares the information we have learned about accessibility for everyone on park journeys.

Forty-four million people in this country have some type of disability—and this does not include the many with temporary disabilities, broken bones, or sprained joints. Our travels reveal that people with disabilities have needs similar to those of families with young children (strollers and wheelchairs need similar access accommodations), seniors, and of others who want gentle, low-effort hiking outdoors. Says one friend, a self-described member of the lazy and timid, "I love to hike, but only when I can wear sandals and not sweat very much."

We first found the joys of a moderately accessible hike at the Gateway to the Narrows Trail of Zion National Park in southwestern Utah. The river was running moderately high that summer morning. After the first mile, the hike would be through chilly, waist-deep waters, but the beginning of the trail was paved and had a gentle slope. We followed a ranger carrying poles for distribution to a hiking group she would lead up the rushing Virgin River. Groups of twos and threes were already meandering through the cliffs. We passed a couple with a toddler in a stroller and an infant nestled in a baby backpack. An elderly couple with walking sticks in hand charged ahead of us. We played leapfrog with them all along the trail: First they moved ahead and then we forged the way.

The path wove between towering rocks, which wept water and provided shelter for a lush growth of mosses and ferns. As the river's sound grew, the cliffs' faces reached toward each other closing the sky from view. The concrete path ended at the river, where adventurous hikers wade between ever-narrowing canyon walls and portage around waterfalls. Michael sloshed on.

Wendy stayed at the river's edge, watching and listening to the water run. There, too, sat the elderly couple we had met earlier in the morning. The rest of their group gradually joined them—an assortment of sisters and brothers, all over age sixty-five, who had gathered from around the country for a reunion trip through several national parks. One brother walked with a cane. The couple we had encountered along the trail were in their eighties. Another married couple were the younger brother and sister of the former who had been introduced to each other by their siblings some thirty years earlier. We chatted about their journey and ours as we marveled at the beauty and accessibility of the canyon, both to their senior group at different levels of walking ability and to Wendy, hiking with her scooter.

This was a unique trail and one we almost did not take. From afar, it had looked a bit hilly — and where would Wendy stay as Michael photographed the river? Would she be more comfortable waiting at the tame picnic site near the trailhead? Instead, she parked in the cool green enclave where young children splashed in the water, older acquaintances safely rested, and she could revel in the closeness of the enormous cliffs. No one with a spirit enticed by beauty and a body — able or not to hike in traditional ways — need forego a spot like this.

The first few national parks we visited together served to whet our appetites. We were so impressed with how much of the parks was accessible to varying levels of abilities that we wanted to see how facilities, overlooks, and trails fared all across the national park system.

We began our odyssey by seeking support for our Easy Access journey, during which we would investigate the accessibility of this country's natural treasures. We embarked on two years of fund-raising from insightful and generous foundations, corporations, and individuals dedicated to helping people with disabilities and to providing increased accessibility in the natural environment around the United States.

The congressionally chartered National Park Foundation embraced Easy Access as an important project. With support for our research in place, we went all out. Our goal was to have the same four eyes, as it were, to experience, evaluate, and report to the general public on the opportunities for accessible visits to our national parks. We set off to drive more than 32,000 miles, stay in more than one hundred campgrounds, and personally visit forty-five of the national parks.

We were concerned that some parks would not have adequate opportunities for visitations by people with disabilities. Chaco Culture National Historical Park in northwestern New Mexico was one. In fact, we did not plan to go there at all. Having visited Chaco Canyon several years earlier, Michael did not think the prehistoric pueblo dwellings would offer many opportunities for Wendy with her wheelchair to gain access to the Anasazi ruins.

The access coordinator at Aztec Ruins National Monument, New Mexico, however, encouraged us to visit Chaco. She believed it offered more access opportunities than we thought. In fact, she had heard that a woman using an electric wheelchair had volunteered there one summer and regularly visited many of the ruins.

The dirt road to Chaco is rough and goes through the Navajo reservation. It took us about an hour and a half of rocky driving even to enter the park boundary. Once we arrived, we learned that the temperature had dropped to 6°F the night before, but the afternoon sun was warm and inviting. We began to explore some of the ruins.

Pueblo Bonito was the most extensive. What a marvel! And what access! The central plaza was flat and surrounded by multistory living quarters and storage rooms. Wendy was able to maneuver around the plaza from kiva to kiva and from room to room. Thus we stepped into a place that had been mysteriously abandoned seven hundred years earlier. We could almost see the Anasazi people moving through the village, grinding corn, carrying water, entering the T-shaped doorways of their rooms. We had entered another civilization, another time.

We had another memorable experience in accessibility at Big Bend National Park in Texas. While driving through the park we saw many wonderful formations, but we found few chair-accessible hiking trails to the Rio Grande River, one of the park's highlights. Unexpectedly, we found out about a river trip from Lajitas through Santa Elena Canyon, a full eight-hour journey along lush banks of desert life, extraordinary cliffs, and a few sets of rapids. Michael was enchanted with the opportunity to photograph along the river. Blue heron and snapping turtles did not escape his camera. Wendy sat in her wheelchair with the wheels popped off and the frame securely strapped to the wooden seat of the rubber raft for the entire river trip. She felt like Cleopatra floating down the river on her barge. This was not the Nile, however, but the border between Mexico and the United States, the Rio Grande.

We met with yet another surprise at Hawaii Volcanoes National Park. Amid the volcanic craters and rainforest, the boardwalk Devastation Trail has been built to protect the forest from human foot traffic while the vegetation struggles to rejuvenate following an eruption of cinders in 1959. It has no safety guardrails but is moderately accessible nevertheless. The boardwalk serves as a dynamic classroom on the resurgent rainforest.

The national parks truly are for everyone. These unique national treasures afford each of us opportunities to remain in touch with our natural heritage. Families with young children, seniors, people with disabilities, and anyone else seeking easy-access hiking all deserve to experience wilderness streams and inspiring rock cliffs. We met physical challenges in the parks and left feeling more daringly able. Recreation and the solace of nature can be a great healer and should be available to all.

2 · GETTING
OUT THERE

We returned home for several months after traveling our first 12,000 miles visiting the national parks of the western United States. One night, enjoying civilization before setting out for our next 20,000 miles through the Rocky Mountains, the midwest, and the East, we went to a local Chinese restaurant with friends. As usual, fortune cookies came at the meal's end. Wendy's bore a timely message: "Visit a park. Behold nature." We needed no further encouragement. Four weeks later, we were off again.

Before we took to the road, we had many looming considerations: How to travel with wheelchairs, where to sleep and eat, and what kind of accommodations to make for inaccessible restrooms and showers were just a few. We attacked these challenges with zest, learning what we could acquire and what Michael could provide by applying his building ingenuity and talents. All park travelers and campers have different requirements and tastes. Options range from tents to lodges, campfires to coffee shops.

Previously, Wendy had used her three-wheel battery-powered scooter, made by Motovator of Torrance, California, to visit natural settings. That was great for city and rural touring, but we found that the scooter, which some of Wendy's work associates had nicknamed "the turbo-gerbil," was not practical for long trail hikes. Steep climbs were difficult, and Wendy no longer had the strength in her hands to guide the scooter over long distances. So we looked into other alternatives.

While manual wheelchairs are sufficient for many people with mobility problems, Wendy's upper body had become too weak for her to propel herself in one of these chairs along the trails we took. Even the lightweight sports models were beyond her physical abilities. We found a high-tech Invacare battery-powered electric chair, the Arrow XpR, that could trek up hills and trails having a 1:4 grade. In its standard configuration, it traveled over dirt and grass as well; for the most part the XpR served both as an excellent trail chair and as the indoor and regular-use wheelchair it was designed to be. Rocks and roots, however, posed a challenge for it, and assistance was sometimes necessary. Another outdoor adventurer might prefer the Invacare Arrow XT power base, an all-terrain wheelchair easily adaptable for outdoor use.

We also took the Invacare Action Series 5000, a folding, lightweight manual chair with quick-release wheels. We knew we could rely on the manual chair in the event that the powered chair broke down. (To our delight, it never did.) Wendy used the 5000 in places where the powered chair could not go, usually because of the XpR's weight. On our river-raft trip down the Rio Grande, the 5000 without its wheels was secured to the raft frame so that Wendy could sit in the chair and support herself as we enjoyed the river journey.

Sports and Spokes magazine publishes an annual review of manual wheelchairs and features lightweight sport chairs. The Iron Horse, a wheelchair with full suspension, is designed for rugged outdoor uses like hiking and camping.

The electric wheelchair's batteries need to be charged every two days. Park rangers were helpful in arranging for us to plug our battery charger into a safe 110-volt outlet. We learned to make these arrangements in advance so we could leave the batteries charging overnight in a secure park-service building. In the meantime, Wendy used her manual chair.

Having determined the wheelchairs we would be using for exploring trails, we looked into how and where we would camp, sleep, and eat on our anticipated visits to the parks.

In the course of our research, we visited thirty-seven national parks, four national monuments, two national historical parks, and two national parkways, camping where possible in most of them. We also stayed at dozens of state parks and national forest campgrounds. We hope that the information we have gathered from our trips will help many, though others may have more leisurely agendas.

We began our national park visits car camping with a tent. We chose a tall tent in which Wendy could transfer more easily from her wheelchair to the sleeping bag. Before purchasing or renting a tent, we suggest finding out how much skill and effort and how many people are needed for setup and takedown.

Much as we enjoyed our earthbound sleeping quarters, we soon realized that a van would make a long journey more viable for us, especially since it permitted us to take the powered wheelchair. Vans can be modified to accommodate many different kinds of disabilities. Roofs can be raised. Floors can be lowered. Different kinds of chairs and driving apparatus can be installed. Advanced Mobility of North Hollywood, California, modified our van for wheelchair use, raising the roof 8 inches and lowering the floor 5½ inches. This increased the headroom to ease Wendy's transfer with assistance from the wheelchair to the passenger seat, when preferred. For Wendy to access the van with her wheelchair, we needed a lift; we decided on the Ricon S1000 hydraulic lift.

Michael built and installed various camping conveniences in the van for our comfort. He constructed an ingenious bed system that allowed for the central aisle of the van to be converted into a bed at night but remain accessible for a wheelchair from the rear door lift by day. He built shelves, overhead racks, storage areas, and a small counter for food preparation.

We never pictured our van as a fully tricked-out recreational vehicle (RV) like the many we saw in national park campgrounds. Rather, we were trying to create an environment that would be comfortable and accessible for us as we traveled around the various parks. We had no built-in refrigerator, no stove, no running water. Ours was a hybrid wheelchair-accessible camping van.

One of our natural inclinations while touring the national parks was to find accessible bathroom facilities. We often used park facilities but soon learned that these were not always readily available or locatable even where they did exist. Not wanting to become preoccupied with toileting, we decided that a commode would be a welcome convenience, especially when our bed was set up and blocked the wheelchair access for Wendy to reach the lift and exit the van.

We purchased an off-the-shelf commode for camping vehicles. It was small and basic and could be emptied into campground dump stations. Michael construced a wooden box to raise the commode off the floor of the van, attached a real toilet seat for easier transferring, and used the detachable arms from the Invacare 5000 as armrests. These adaptations were a saving grace on our trip.

Many who prefer not to drive long distances choose to take airplanes, buses, and trains, renting automobiles at park gateway cities. Some rental-care agencies have automobiles with hand controls, which can be reserved upon request. Increasing numbers of buses and trains have lifts and other provisions for persons with disabilities. Airlines are also improving access for people with disabilities, but advanced planning for flying, as for bus or train travel, is recommended. To our knowledge, the only train with wheelchair accessibility into a national park is from the Amtrak station in Williams, Arizona, to Grand Canyon National Park's south rim train station less than 100 yards from a view of the canyon.

Using public transportation does not preclude camping. Backpacking camping equipment can be lightweight and relatively manageable.

One of the most beautiful campgrounds we encountered on our journeys was at Arches National Park, Utah, where we stayed several nights. Throughout the campground, the

La Sal Mountains were visible in the distance. The camp-sites were sprinkled between "fins," high, thin sandstone walls. The arches, formed by a unique erosion process, did not have any wheelchair-accessible trails, but the auto tour winding through the impressive park provided views of sandstone monuments and arches.

Though we usually stayed at national park campgrounds in our van, we stayed in park lodges or local motels during inclement weather—or when we just needed a hot shower and could not find one in a campground.

One night at Arches, for example, it grew very chilly. Not only was our bottled water frozen in the morning, so was the liquid in our commode. At the visitor center the next morning, we learned that the temperature had dipped to 17°F the previous night. We had unexpectedly encountered a cold snap that lasted a week throughout the Colorado Plateau on which Arches is located, and we agreed thereafter that 20°F would be the lower limit for our camping out. That week we spent our nights in lodges and motels.

Many of the national parks have lodge and restaurant facilities within their boundaries, some of which are accessible for people with physical disabilities. Throughout our accounts of the parks in our Best Visits chapters and our At a Glance directory, we will try to describe access to these accommodations. Some parks have nearby lodge and restaurant facilities outside their boundaries, which we do not review in this guide. For more information on these, see *The Complete Guide to America's National Parks* by the National Park Foundation.

When camping, we always have the choice whether to eat by campfire, cookstove, or coffee shop. For information about cooking outdoors, try *Simple Foods for the Pack,* by Vikki Kinmont and Claudia Axcell; *Cooking for Camp and Trail* by Hasse Bunnelle; *The 2 oz. Backpacker,* by Robert S. Wood; *Camp Cooking,* by Bill and Joe McMorris; or *The Well-fed Backpacker,* by June Fleming.

In the parks, sometimes wood gathering for campfires,

and occasionally fires themselves, are prohibited. We will try to give a sense of where those restrictions exist. We could usually get firewood either by gathering it or by purchasing it and, weather permitting, we would sit cooking happily by our campfires. We also had our trusty cookstove for inclement weather and when we were just too tired to go the whole 9 yards.

At one private campground outside Carlsbad Caverns National Park, New Mexico, we found campers enjoying large fires. We had purchased a few logs at the local store but wondered about the origins of all that wood. The next morning, we discovered huge bins of scrap wood left for campers like ourselves by the thoughtful campground concessionaires. That night we too enjoyed a friendly fire, thanks to the free wood.

We learned the value of checking ahead on park policy the hard way. Ater loading up on firewood and fresh food to cook over the coals, we arrived at Guadalupe Mountains National Park, Texas. We pulled into the campground only to find a sign, NO FIRES. The wind, which often gusts to more than 100 m.p.h., put a damper to our dinner plans. Cookstoves are allowed, but try pan-frying a meal in gale force winds! We ate salad and canned tuna.

Of course, sometimes the option to eat in a restaurant is very tantalizing. For instance, the Volcano House at Kilauea Caldera at Hawaii Volcanoes National Park affords a view of the caldera. Even a small drink allows the visitor to get a great look from this fully accessible restaurant and bar.

Often it seemed that we were too busy collecting facts to have funny things happen. Fat chance! Funny and fun went hand in hand. One morning we awoke in a Yellowstone National Park camground in Wyoming to the sound of buzzing like a dive-bombing airplane. Michael quickly got out of his sleeping bag. Outside, a friendly park ranger confronted him. "What's going on?" Michael asked. Answered the ranger, "We have to chop some of these lodgepole pine trees down. They're suffering from root rot, and we're afraid they might fall on unwitting park visitors." What a way to wake up — with trees chopped down around us early in the morning at what we had expected would be a peaceful national park campground! Though abruptly awakened and still sleepy, we left for the day as instructed. The good news was that we found fresh-cut wood for our fire when we returned that evening.

In planning our trip, we decided early on that it would be very important for Wendy to continue the exercise program she practiced at home as much as she could while we were on the road. Michael constructed a portable standing table that could be attached to picnic tables nationwide to help achieve that goal. A standing table is a device by which an individual with paralyzed legs can stand, supported by knee pads and a padded belt, for a length of time usually from thirty minutes to an hour. This helps maintain circulation in the legs and strengthen the muscles as well as encourage good kidney function. The human animal needs to move and be vertical, and the standing table helped Wendy do that.

We left our standing table on the picnic table at our campsite in Yosemite National Park, California, while we went to check some of the trails. When we returned, to our astonishment and consternation, the standing table was gone. Luckily, we had taken the pads and belt with us, leaving only the steel tubing clamped to the picnic table. Not even a physical rehabilitation specialist could have guessed the purpose of the contraption attached to our picnic table. Nevertheless, someone had stolen our exercise system.

We were advised by a ranger that anything could look interesting to anyone. Our beach chair, which had been sitting next to the table, was also missing. We were quite surprised: People often leave such articles at their campsites to alert others that the site remains occupied. From then on, we dismantled our replacement table whenever we left the campsite, a time-consuming nuisance. Evidently, even in national parks—just as in cities and towns—it is prudent to protect property.

We met many interesting people on our travels, people with and without apparent disabilities. Parents often pushed young children in strollers behind us, assuming that baby strollers could wheel anyplace that Wendy's chair could wheel. We met a wide variety of chair users, including some who had wheeled themselves to the tops of very difficult trails. We shared paths with people who had vision and hearing impairments and went canoeing with a triple-amputee expert canoeist.

Most important is to enjoy the parks, which sometimes means taking along aids such as wheelchairs. Park trails can be long and strenuous, or the weather can be enervating. Even if people having temporary injuries or respiratory or cardiac problems or lacking in stamina do not use wheelchairs at home, borrowing or renting a wheelchair can make park exploration easier. Some parks have loaner wheelchairs at the visitor center for use in the park. Wheelchairs can also be rented from local pharmacies, health-supply stores, or rehabilitation-equipment houses. Social service organizations often loan wheelchairs, walkers, crutches, and canes. Don't be too proud. The key is to be safe, comfortable, relaxed, and to have a good time.

Unfortunately, Wendy's multiple sclerosis has worsened over the years; increased weakness can be a normal part of this disease's progression. She often wondered if she would be better off not traveling, but that would not have stopped the disease either. Remaining inside and sitting around hardly seemed the way to live. Going into wilderness areas was a marvelous alternative. We believe that no one should miss these kinds of adventures.

Friends and people we met on the road often asked, "Isn't all this *schlepping* too much for you folks?" In fact, Wendy was often concerned about exactly the same thing, even with Michael doing most of the physical work. At first she complained about the inconveniences of camping. She was always a sucker for a comfortable bed, an accessible shower, and the other amenities of civilization. After a while, though, we both realized that Michael was happier seeing the wonders of our country's natural treasures, the national parks, than doing anything else, and so was Wendy. For both of us, these journeys proved to be irreplaceable, rejuvenating experiences of a lifetime. In fact, our national parks can provide uniquely joyous opportunities for anyone.

3·CHOOSING PARKS TO VISIT

Our explorations of the parks went beyond "windshield experiences," a description of national park visits in which the visitor sees almost all of the sights exclusively from inside an automobile. We first heard this phrase used by a superintendent describing his park. Visitors driving through that wild and scenic western park stop at interpretive placards to view the vast panoramas and colorful rock formations through their windshields but rarely stay more than a few hours. This can be a valid park journey. However, getting out of the car and taking advantage of the opportunities national parks have to offer can often be more rewarding.

Finding out ahead of time how accessible a park is and what it has to offer helps maximize enjoyment of a park. Choosing parks to visit that fulfill your needs and desires is not difficult. We suggest that you consider the attractions and activities you want, the climate and elevations that suit you best, and the accommodations you prefer.

The National Park Service (NPS) has earnestly sought to provide all visitors with opportunities to enjoy and benefit from the parks. Information centers, museums, ranger-led programs, interpretive exhibits, trails, and campgrounds are available and accessible in many parks. Where present, lodging, eating facilities, stores, and services are privately run by concessionaires and are frequently accessible. A few parks remain primitive wilderness untouched by roads, trails, or facilities.

The NPS participates with the U.S. Forest Service in the

Federal Recreation Passport Program. The Golden Access Passport is for people who are medically determined to be blind or have permanent disabilities. The Golden Age Passport is for people sixty-two years and older with proof of age. Both passports, which are complimentary, require citizenship or permanent residence in the United States and provide free admittance to federally operated parks, monuments, historic sites, recreation areas, and wildlife refuges, which usually charge entrance fees. They also provide a 50 percent discount on federal usage fees charged for facilities such as campsites, boat launches, parking lots, and so on. Passports may be obtained only in person at most federal park facilities and need not be acquired before beginning a trip.

The Golden Eagle Passport costs $25 for one calendar year and is for nondisabled persons between the ages of seventeen and sixty-one. It does not cover usage fees; it is valid for entrance fees only and can be obtained in person or by mail from federal parks and offices. All passports cover the occupants of the holder's vehicle.

We found that facilities and trails were sometimes not as accessible as we would have liked them to be. Historic structures are particularly problematic because their access often cannot be modified to accommodate persons with disabilities while preserving the structures' historic integrity. The national parks are, however, sensitive to the requirements of persons with disabilities and at the forefront of this country's growing awareness of the need to have opportunities accessible to everyone.

The National Park Service has a stated policy to comply with federal accessibility standards and urges visitors to write with feedback about the parks' accessibility. Write to the superintendents of the parks you visit with complaints, suggestions, and comments. Park staffs can better make changes when visitors let them know what facilities and trails need to be changed. Written complaints are the best way to spark improvements.

After familiarizing ourselves with the Uniform Federal Accessibility Standards (UFAS) and several recent studies concerning accessibility in outdoor recreation areas, we set out to research and view firsthand forty-five national parks. We met with NPS officials in each park, particularly with persons responsible for coordinating improved access. Rangers filled out our questionnaire about accessible trails and facilities in their parks. Many times we surveyed various trails and facilities with rangers. Most of the time, however, the two of us visited sights and took part in activities on our own after park staff suggested what might be accessible for persons with disabilities.

We arranged regularly to meet other people with disabilities — including individuals with mobility, hearing, vision, and developmental impairments — at the parks. These people, who became our friends, helped us to assess trails and facilities. Their experiences broadened and deepened our own understanding of what accessibility and barriers to accessibility mean to everyone. On a casual basis we met families with young children and seniors who also shared with us what made their park journeys difficult or enjoyable.

When planning a park visit, anyone with a disability or an injury — and even those who are nondisabled — should consult a doctor. Explain the elevation, climate, exertion level, travel style, and living conditions of the trip.

Throughout this book, we recommend assistance at various trails and facilities. Assistance to persons with disabilities comes in many forms. Seeing-eye and hearing-ear dogs, canine companions, and certain adaptive devices can help. Friends, family members, and attendants can also assist persons with disabilities in exploring and enjoying the national parks freely. When we describe assistance, we specifically refer to the human variety.

Usually, the most accessible portions of the national parks are the "frontcountry" developed areas. These range from simple parking pullouts, overlooks, established trails, and campgrounds to built-up areas containing visitor centers, stores, lodging, restaurants, and services.

Frontcountry trails present a broad spectrum of accessibility. They may be hard surfaced and fully compliant with UFAS; they may have some minor barriers such as soft surfaces, small rocks and/or roots, or moderately steep slopes, or they may have severe obstacles like large rocks, stairs, and unprotected drop-offs. All persons with disabilities should thoughtfully gauge their abilities and assistance requirements to match the accessibility and difficulty of the trail.

Hoh Mini-trail in the Hoh Rain Forest of Olympic National Park, Washington, is a fully accessible, level, paved trail and an excellent example of a trail for everyone to enjoy. During our visit we met a family pushing a young son who had cerebral palsy in a wheelchair around the trail. Urging his dad on with enthusiastic gestures, the eight-year-old's only apparent disappointment was that the trail was too short.

We found a further enhancement of full accessibility at the Anhinga Trail in Everglades National Park, Florida. This wide, level, asphalt and boardwalk half-mile trail borders a hammock (a minijungle of hardwood and palm trees) with bridges over large ponds in which alligators live. The trail provides persons with vision impairments an opportunity to experience the wonders of the Everglades. An audiotape describing the trail and its natural inhabitants is keyed to textured cue pads built into the trail. Visitors with vision impairments can sense the cue pads and stop to hear the appropriate audio description on the tape.

Not all frontcountry trails are as fully developed as these. Nevertheless, wheelchair users with athletic and/or skillful abilities and persons with disabilities who may need assistance can enjoy trails with moderate slopes and rough surfaces.

Yellowstone National Park in Wyoming has several trails with boardwalks to protect the environment and to keep

visitors from stepping into the superheated water of geysers and hot springs. These frontcountry trails, although not originally constructed for access by persons with disabilities and thus probably not up to UFAS, are often accessible for skillful wheelchair users or for individuals with assistance. Fountain Paint Pots Trail in Yellowstone is an example of a frontcountry trail that Wendy could visit with Michael's assistance even though the Park Service had not modified the trail specifically for use by persons with disabilities. A portion of the boardwalk was steep, and in one section, a staircase obstructed our wheelchair from completing the loop. To circumvent the stairs, we were able to backtrack and complete our tour, enjoying the colors, bubbling mud, and spouting geysers.

Sometimes the frontcountry can provide unexpected and surprisingly delightful opportunities for visitors who are prepared to encounter steep slopes or rough terrain or who are willing to circumvent possible barriers. Less developed trails, such as those made of dirt, grass, or old road beds, may have barriers, but visitors with disabilities can easily travel others.

Alternative modes of travel are available in many parks. Persons with mobility, vision, or hearing impairments can participate in horseback tours operated by many concessionaires, although assistance is usually required. Snowmobiling is permitted in some parks; it is a favorite winter activity for one Yellowstone National Park ranger who uses a wheelchair as a result of a spinal cord injury.

Park exploration is not limited to ground trails. In some parks visitors can enter remote, roadless areas by taking rafts, canoes, or other boats along the waterways. In fact, most travel is on the water in Biscayne (Florida) and Voyagers (Minnesota) national parks.

The primary feature of Biscayne is the underwater habitat of the Florida Keys. Boarding the glass-bottom boat required descending two steps, but the crew was extremely helpful in assisting Wendy. On our tour, we saw brain coral, sea anemones, parrot fish, stingrays, and a humongous sea turtle. The boat operator told us that people with disabilities are welcome on scuba diving excursions providing they are certified divers.

A very few parks can be toured by helicopter. Michael, having backpacked more than 200 miles of the inner Grand Canyon, feels strongly against these noisy contraptions interrupting the peace that backpackers relish in parks. After hiking for at least a full day to get away from developed civilization, Michael does not appreciate loud reverberations off the canyons's walls in his favorite spots next to the Colorado River. The one helicopter he would appreciate but still does not ever wish to hear would be a rescue chopper.

Yet both of us went on a 30-minute helicopter tour over the Grand Canyon with Kenai Helicopters from Tusayan, Arizona. For individuals who are unable to travel inside the canyon, this may be a way to experience the Grand Canyon's expansiveness.

The backcountry is usually not accessible to persons with disabilities, but there are exceptions. Backcountry in the parks refers to undeveloped areas with large sections of untouched beauty. Park rangers can provide visitors with information on trails and access to the backcountry. Permits are usually required for overnight trips.

For example, in Everglades National Park, the flat Long Pine Key Trail in the Pinelands area offers a good backpacking experience. The trail has undeveloped campsites, and a skillful and/or athletic wheelchair user or a person needing assistance could camp overnight. The park also has a backcountry canoe trail with a moderately accessible camping platform on the water.

We heard (third hand) about an enterprising wheelchair user from New Zealand who took the Lake Chelan ferry from Chelan, Washington, to Stehekin in the Lake Chelan National Recreation Area. He set out on a solo wheelchair backpacking trip, taking an NPS bus 20 miles into North Cascades National Park. He wheeled to Cottonwood Campground and camped several days on the Stehekin River. For adventures like this, carefully inquire with the park in advance to assure proper planning and preparation.

Ranger Steve Eide at Yellowstone National Park, Wyoming, led us to Cascade Lake Trail, a rugged trail he uses when he goes camping at Cascade Lake in Yellowstone. Steve, a strong manual chair user, negotiated logs and gentle hills to a meadow where bison grazed. The trail has significant barriers but can lead to a backcountry experience for athletic and/or skillful wheelchair users.

Park campgrounds are of two types: developed or primitive. Some campgrounds are open during only part of the year, so check before you visit.

Developed campgrounds have individual sites with picnic tables and fire grills, usually with an adjacent parking space. Walk-in sites are by definition some distance from camper parking spaces, but are sometimes in developed campgrounds. Most large developed campgrounds have drinking water, comfort stations or vault toilets, campfire or ampitheater programs, trash receptacles, dump stations, and some active ranger supervision. Some popular national park campgrounds require reservations through MISTIX (P.O. Box 85705, San Diego, CA 92138-5705; 800-365-2267). The remainder offer sites on a first-come first-served basis. Group camping usually requires reservations.

Few national parks have showers, and even fewer have shower facilities accessible to persons with mobility problems. We took a plastic folding beach chair for Wendy to use in showers that were not fully accessible. In lodges and motels, Wendy took showers using the folding chair in bathtubs to ease the transfer from wheelchair to the shower.

Primitive campgrounds are as they sound, most of them far from automobile access and other amenities of civilization. Water may or may not be available or drinkable. Toilets, if existent, would be outhouse-variety pit toilets. Some primitive campgrounds are accessible for people with disabilities, but assistance is often necessary.

No matter what kind of trekking you do, frontcountry or backcountry, it is important to find out what is available in a park you intend to visit and to plan accordingly. *Easy Access to National Parks* has information on fifty parks regarding attractions, activities, elevation, and climate.

Each park's attractions are unique: geological features like volcanoes, mountains, and seashores; biological resources like rainforests, subalpine tundra, and deserts; wildlife habitats for fish, birds, and animals; and cultural heritage sites like Native American ruins and early pioneer homesteads. Activities can include hiking, swimming, powerboating, rafting, canoeing, wildlife watching, fishing, horseback riding, camping, backpacking, skiing, snowmobiling, mountaineering, and touring by boat, bus, or tram. And photography is popular everywhere.

Choose the attractions and activities you want to experience and consider climate and elevation as you plan when and where to visit. Park climates vary seasonally; you'll want to be sure your chosen activities are practical during your visit. Skiing and snowmobiling obviously need snow, but few trails are shoveled in winter for wheelchair users or anyone else who wants to hike. Hot weather can be debilitating when visitors are not properly prepared.

Elevation plays a key role in relative temperature, and caution is advised to prevent hypothermia (lowering of the body temperature). Persons with respiratory and/or cardiovascular problems should consult a physician before going to elevations above 4,000 feet. At a Glance, the directory section of *Easy Access to National Parks,* denotes elevations above 4,000 feet in each park.

Use *Easy Access to National Parks* to help select the park you wish to visit. Contact the park by phone or mail to request information and ask questions about the types of activities that interest you most. Not all park facilities, programs, and activities are available year-round. Some programs and activities, usually noted in park information literature, require reservations or advance notice. Ranger-led programs can usually be adjusted to better accommodate visitors with disabilities when the park is notified in advance.

Once at the park, visitors usually receive an official map/brochure upon entry. Many parks publish a newspaper two to four times a year with current information about camping, road closures, ranger-guided programs, concessionaire operations, accessibility listings, wildlife, natural history, and emergency telephone numbers. The ranger at the entrance station should know whether and where park accessibility guides, which detail information on accessible venues in the park, are available.

No matter what park you decide to visit, advance preparation can help toward a safe, comfortable, and satisfying national park experience.

II · BEST
VISITS

4·BEST VISITS AND ACCESSIBILITY

O ut of the forty-five national parks we visited, fifteen met criteria we felt would merit full-length descriptions. The *Easy Access to National Parks* Best Visits are parks chosen by the two of us for their accessibility, regional significance, and natural scenic beauty. The parks with good accessibility afforded better opportunities for people with disabilities to experience safe and rewarding visits. Parks with regional significance have important biological, geological, cultural, and historic resources for their area of the country. The natural scenic beauty and aesthetic appeal of all national parks we visited were outstanding.

We include in these chapters specific information for persons with mobility problems, deafness and hearing impairments, blindness and vision impairments. Visitors with developmental disabilities can often take advantage of touch exhibits and touch programs; if arranged in advance of a visit, the park may also have interpretive programs suited to an individual's needs. Seniors, families with young children, and individuals not wanting to exert themselves too much (including "lazy and timid" visitors) will also find useful information in Best Visits.

We consider a place fully accessible for persons with mobility problems if individuals with wheelchairs can approach, enter, and use it. For mobility and stability, a wheelchair user optimally requires a level surface without obstructions. Persons with mobility problems who do not use wheelchairs can benefit from the same. So can parents who push young children in strollers. Later in this chapter we will discuss different levels of accessibility.

An equally important issue is programmatic accessibility. Once a person enters a facility, for instance, can he or she participate? Can a person who is blind appreciate a film or a slide prersentation? Can a person who is deaf understand a ranger lecture? Can a child easily view mounted exhibits and display cases? Where a park has programs for persons who are blind or visually impaired, deaf or hearing impaired, or developmentally disabled, we note it. When we do not mention such access, either the program was not in place during our visit or it did not exist.

Each Best Visit details a park's attractions and suggests the easiest ways to enjoy them. We will describe accessibility to trails, visitor information services, facilities, recreational activities, and tours at each Best Visit park. We take into account whether a trail or viewpoint is paved or dirt, steep or gentle in slope, long or short. The park's visitor information services — including visitor centers, ranger-conducted programs, museums, maps, and park guides — are detailed and we note efforts toward increased accessibility, such as captioning, accompanying scripts and sign language, large-print and/or Braille text, audiotapes, and touch exhibits. In our survey we note possible accessibility to restrooms, campgrounds, lodges, restaurants, food and supply stores, bookstores and gift shops, showers, laundries, picnic areas, benches, telephones, and water fountains.

Each Best Visit has introductory descriptions of the park's attractions, location, natural and human history, and plant and animal life. Presented in order of a reasonable tour, each chapter concentrates mostly on the frontcountry areas and has an accompanying map. Each Best Visit concludes with a brief comment, sometimes noting nearby national parks with accessible opportunities.

We have divided physical accessibility into three categories: fully accessible, moderately accessible, and significant barriers. In brief, *fully accessible* means that provisions have been made for people with disabilities, particularly those with mobility impairments. *Moderately accessible* is used for trails and/or facilities that do not meet full accessibility standards and present possible barriers to wheelchair users and persons with differing mobility impairments. Assistance is usually necessary. Trails and facilities with *significant barriers* have no provisions for people with mobility, vision, hearing, and/or developmental impairments. More complete descriptions of these three categories follow:

FULLY ACCESSIBLE: Provisions have been made for people with disabilities, particularly those with mobility impairments.

Trails and facilities exceed, comply with, or nearly comply with the Uniform Federal Accessibility Standards (UFAS) and recent professional studies concerning accessibility to outdoor recreation facilities for persons with disabilities. If the primary feature of a facility or trail is in minimum compliance with UFAS but other features are not in compliance, we consider the facility or trail fully accessible. For example, a restroom with a fully accessible toilet stall but with a wash basin that is not in full compliance with UFAS would be considered fully accessible.

Fully accessible trail surfaces are graded and firm; trail edges offer protection but may not be wide enough for two wheelchairs. Facilities have level entry and 32-inch minimum door width. Comfort stations have grab bars in wide toilet stalls. Trail and ramp slopes are minimal (lineal rise not greater than 1:20). Short sections may be slightly steeper (no greater than 1:12). Slopes are sometimes described by ratios of lineal rise over a given length of level distance. For instance, a ratio of 1:12 means a 1-foot rise over a level distance of 12 feet.

 1:20 slope

Cross slope (across the direction of travel) should be less than 1:50. Level resting spaces with benches should be available at 200-foot intervals.

We have also noted increased accessibility for persons who are blind or visually impaired, are deaf or hearing impaired, or have developmental disabilities, and we have included information about programmatic materials if available.

MODERATELY ACCESSIBLE: Trails and/or facilities that do not meet full accessibility standards and present possible barriers to wheelchair users and persons with other mobility impairments are considered moderately accessible. Assistance is usually necessary.

Individuals with exceptional wheelchair skills, adaptive equipment, slight mobility impairments, or able assistance from other people could use these trails and facilities, but caution is advised. Some trails and facilities have portions that are fully accessible, while other parts may have barriers. Some effort may have been made for improved accessibility. Trail surfaces are maintained and range from smooth to rough with some rocks and roots. Trail edges offer protection only at extreme hazards. Facilities are enterable for persons with a wide range of mobility impairments but can have up to a 1.5-inch step. Doors have a minimum 30-inch width. Comfort stations do not meet full accessibility requirements because of possible problems regarding entryway slope, narrow aisles, and/or stalls without grab bars.

Trail and ramp slopes are moderate (from level to 1:12, portions not greater than 1:8).

 1:8 slope

Moderate cross slope is not greater than 1:25. Trails have occasional level resting spaces with benches.

If available, increased accessibility for persons with vision, hearing, and/or developmental impairment, including programmatic materials, are noted.

SIGNIFICANT BARRIERS: The trail or facility has no provisions for people with mobility, vision, hearing, and/or developmental impairments except for persons with extraordinary abilities or assistance.

Barriers may be one or more steps greater than 1.5 inches in height; an uneven, very steep, and/or slick surface; trails that are dangerous for wheelchair and unsure-foot traffic; comfort stations that have not been modified for accessibility.

Trails and ramps have slopes that are very steep (greater than 1:8) and extreme cross slope (greater than 1:25).

 1:6 slope

Undeveloped areas, boats, and historic structures are examples of park features that usually have significant barriers. Persons with disabilities could use these trails and facilities with assistance. Programmatic materials available may or may not be suitable for persons with hearing, vision, developmental, and/or mobility impairments.

We do not use accessible as a legal term. The NPS is required to bring park access up to the legal definition of accessible.

KEY TO MAP SYMBOLS

 NATIONAL PARK AREA

 OTHER PARK AREAS

 North

			━━━	━━ ━━	········
Interstate highways	U.S. routes	State and county roads	Other roads	Unpaved roads	Hiking trails

 Rivers and Streams

 Small Lakes, Ponds, BAYS, LARGE LAKES, OCEANS, GULFS

 STATE BOUNDARIES

◉ Cities

◉ Towns

♦ Park Office, Visitor Center, Ranger Station, or Information

▲ Campground

✛ Medical clinic

♠ Grove or tree of note

⚓ Marina or boat launch

⛴ Ferry terminal or route

🐎 Riding stable

△ Mountain summit

5,286' Elevation in feet

→ One-way travel

🗼 Fire or lookout tower

✛ Airport

🐟 Fish hatchery

⛷ Ski area

🏕 Picnic area

The following variations are used on the regional maps:

 Interstate highways

☐ State boundaries

1 NP=National Park
NHP=National Historical Park

5·FIFTEEN
GREAT PARKS

ACADIA
NATIONAL PARK
P.O. Box 177
Bar Harbor, ME 04609
Information and TDD: 207-288-3338

When the summer sun rises over the United States, it falls first across Cadillac Mountain in Acadia National Park on Mount Desert, a beautiful island off the coast of Maine. The last ice age gouged and polished the eastern seaboard some twelve thousand to eighteen thousand years ago, leaving Cadillac Mountain as its highest point. Acadia National Park encompasses much of Mount Desert, Isle au Haut, several other small islands, and the mainland's Schoodic Peninsula.

Pronounced like the final course of a meal, Mount Desert is the third-largest island along the east coast of the United States. Acadia National Park, with its deep valleys, lakes, forests, and jagged coastlines pounded by the Atlantic Ocean, spans more than 41,000 acres. Acadia was the first national park established east of the Mississippi River and is today the second most visited in the national park system. Reached by Maine Highway 3, it is 47 miles southeast of Bangor and 164 miles northeast of Portland, both in Maine.

The east side of Mount Desert has a unique system of "carriage roads," the building of which John D. Rockefeller, Jr., sponsored from 1917 to 1933. No automobiles are allowed on the 51 miles of one-lane gravel roads and stone bridges, which loop over mountains and through the valleys of Mount Desert. We found 8 miles of these roads relatively level, providing remarkable access to woodlands and lakes for everyone, including wheelchair users, bicyclists, hikers, and families with youngsters in strollers.

Acadia still shows the effects of glaciers, the last set of which reached what is now the park about eighteen thousand years ago. The ice sheets rounded the mountains and carved the U-shaped valleys before beginning to recede twelve thousand years ago. Somes Sound, the only fjord in the conterminous United States, was cut by a finger-shaped glacier.

Today, ocean waves violently thrash at the park's granite headlands and rocky beaches. Marine life flourishes from the intertidal zone at the shoreline to the deep waters below Acadia's sheer cliffs. Sea stars, urchins, and crabs live in the more shallow tide pools. Lobsters, the crustaceans for which Maine is most famous, live offshore. In deeper waters, four types of whales can be spotted.

On land, the park counts fifty-five mammal species. With more than three hundred kinds of birds, Acadia is considered one of the East Coast's premier places for bird-watching.

Human habitation of the park goes back approximately six thousand years to the Abnaki Indians, who lived on Mount Desert part of the year and left behind huge shell heaps and tree-bark shelters. Norse explorers probably saw the island five hundred years before Giovanni da Verrazzano, an Italian explorer for France, called it *Acadia* during his visit in A.D. 1500. On his mapping survey of "New France" in 1604, Samuel de Champlain was forced to repair his ship on the island. He renamed it *l'Isle des Monts-deserts,* island of barren mountains.

Acadia's colonial history is rich. In 1613, Jesuits established the first French mission in the United States near Somes Sound. Soon after, the British destroyed the mission. This ignited 150 years of war between the French and the British, during which Acadia was a no-man's-land. Louis XIV granted a portion of New France, including Mount Desert, to an ambitious young man self-entitled Sieur Antoine de la Mothe Cadillac. Cadillac stayed on Mount Desert briefly and then went on to found the city of Detroit, Michigan. At the end of the war, New France became New England.

In the nineteenth century, prominent painters of the Hudson River School discovered the charms of Mount Desert, and their works brought attention to the island. Tourism began, and Acadia became a well-known resort for wealthy Americans. Families including the Astors, Carnegies, Fords, Morgans, Vanderbilts, and Rockefellers built summer estates here. Through the energetic stewardship of George Dorr, who later became the park's first superintendent, patrons donated land in an effort to protect Mount Desert from over-development. Acadia became the first park to be formed by private donations. Named Sieur de Monts National Monument in 1916 and designated Lafayette National Park in 1919, the park readopted its original name of Acadia in 1926.

Thompson Island

We entered the park on Maine Highway 3 at Thompson Island over the Trenton Bridge. The Thompson Island Information Center, vault toilet, and telephones are fully accessible. There are International Symbol of Access (ISA)-designated spaces in the parking lot. The park has "Wheelchair Accessibility Guide, Acadia National Park" and "Wheelchair Access Guide, Restaurants, Motels and Campgrounds" available at Thompson Island, the Hulls Cove Visitor Center, and park headquarters. Thompson Island also has a picnic area with a fully accessible site.

Hulls Cove Visitor Center

Continuing on Maine Highway 3, we headed toward Bar Harbor. The visitor center, open May through October, is 8 miles

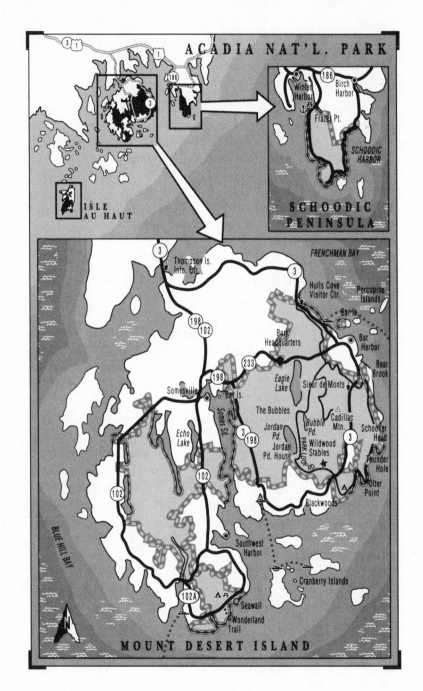

ACADIA NAT'L. PARK

SCHOODIC PENINSULA

ISLE AU HAUT

Winter Harbor   Birch Harbor   186

Frazer Pt.

SCHOODIC HARBOR

FRENCHMAN BAY

Thompson Is. Info. Ctr.

Hulls Cove Visitor Ctr.

Percupine Islands

Bar Is.

Park Headquarters

Bar Harbor

Bear Brook

Somesville

Eagle Lake

Sieur de Monts

Bar Is.

Somes Sd.

The Bubbles

Bubble Pd.

Cadillac Mtn.

Schooner Head

Echo Lake

Jordan Pd.

Jordan Pd. House

Wildwood Stables

PARK LOOP RD.

Thunder Hole

Blackwoods

Otter Point

BLUE HILL BAY

Southwest Harbor

Cranberry Islands

Seawall

Wonderland Trail

MOUNT DESERT ISLAND

from Thompson Island and 2 miles from Bar Harbor. ISA-designated parking is in the upper-level lot. Follow the sidewalk bordering a grassy slope to a walkway into the upper level of the center. The visitor center has an information desk, exhibits, book and map sales, and an orientation film in the theater. The film has an accompanying printed script. An excellent automobile tour of the park on audiocassette, starting at the visitor center, can be rented or purchased here. Restrooms, though moderately accessible inside, are down a steep slope and may require assistance.

Sieur de Monts

From the visitor center, Park Loop Road circles the east side of Mount Desert. Six miles south is Sieur de Monts Spring. Lushly wooded, this area has the Sieur de Monts Spring Nature Center, Abbe Museum, and The Wild Gardens of Acadia nature trail. The parking lot, common to the gardens, nature center, and museum, has ISA-designated spaces and fully accessible toilets.

The gardens feature trees, shrubs, wildflowers, and ferns native to the park. The trail is self-guided with a handout describing the twelve ecosystems represented. Both the handout and labels identifying plant growth are in small print. We found maneuvering on the trail difficult because of the narrow paths and uneven paving stones.

The Sieur de Monts Spring Nature Center has exhibits and a bookstore concentrating on the natural and cultural history of Mount Desert. The exhibits are low contrast and may be difficult to see for individuals with poor eyesight. The rear door has a ramped entrance.

The Abbe Museum exhibits describe Native American history on Mount Desert. The trail from the parking lot to the museum is steep with cross slope and may require considerable assistance. The Hemlock Trail from Sieur de Monts Fire Road is a half-mile moderately accessible old dirt road through spruce trees and is good for bird-watching.

In a wooded area approximately one-quarter mile south of Sieur de Monts, the Bear Brook Picnic Area has some level sites with extended tabletops, raised fire grills, and ISA-designated parking spaces.

Schooner Head Scenic Overlook, off a spur road 2.5 miles south of the picnic area on the Park Loop Road, is down a steep, short trail. Assistance may be needed. Sand Beach, 1 mile further south on the Park Loop Road, has a lowered telephone but a beach trail inaccessible due to significant barriers.

Thunder Hole

One of the park's most popular attractions, Thunder Hole, lies 1.5 miles south of Schooner Head on the Park Loop Road. The ocean has eroded a tunnel-like crack into a basalt seam that is softer than the surrounding granite. Waves surge into the crack and shoot out an opening with a thundering roar. Thunder Hole has a steep path with steps. Surf crashing through the blowhole is thrilling whether seen from the bottom of the path or from high above at the roadside.

Otter Point

At Otter Point, 1 mile south of Thunder Hole, life in the intertidal zone created by the large difference between high and low tides is richly diverse. Since the path to the tidepools is rocky and slippery, strong assistance may be necessary for wheelchair users and for those unsure of foot. Binoculars or telescopes can be helpful for watching marine life from near the beginning of the trail. Check at the visitor center for low-tide times, when viewing is best.

One-quarter mile further, Fabbri Picnic Area has fully accessible tables, grills, and restrooms.

Jordan Pond

A historic tradition of Mount Desert Island continues at Jordan Pond House, 6 miles further from Thunder Hole on the Park Loop Road. In the nineteenth century, many teahouses such as the one at Jordan Pond existed on Mount Desert. Tea is served in the house and on the lawn between 2:30 and 5:30 P.M. late spring to early fall. The lawn looks toward The Bubbles, twin mountains across Jordan Pond.

Jordan Pond House, a gift shop, and restrooms in the house dining room are fully accessible and open late spring to early fall. The parking lot has ISA-designated spaces. Two rocky and narrow trails begin at the parking lot and present significant barriers for wheelchair users.

Carriages and hayrides leave mid-June to Labor Day from Wildwood Stables south of Jordan Pond on the Park Loop Road. The concessionaire will help people with disabilities board the rides. Carriage-seat height is 54 inches above ground, and the seats are narrow and uncomfortable. The hayride wagon is 36 inches above ground, and hay bales can be used to help a rider maintain stability. Call Wildwood Stables for information (207-276-3622).

Bubble Pond

Glacial action formed the valleys that Jordan and Bubble ponds now fill. The 2.5 miles between the two on the Park Loop Road are particularly scenic.

We approached Bubble Pond on a cool June day, accompanied by Ranger Shirley Beccue, who uses a wheelchair as the result of a sledding accident. Shirley was instrumental in developing accessibility in Everglades National Park, Florida, where she worked for more than ten years before coming to Acadia.

A relatively flat carriage road with a bridge follows the west bank of Bubble Pond. Shirley led us to an asphalt pad overlooking the serene pond and then south along the

wooded, gravel road. This and the 5.5.-mile road along Eagle Lake and north to Witch Hole Pond are the most level and accessible to wheelchairs of the carriage-road network.

Cadillac Mountain

Acadia's first superintendent named the park's highest mountain for Sieur Antoine de la Mothe Cadillac, a seventeenth-century resident of Mount Desert and later the founder of Detroit, Michigan. Cadillac Mountain, 2.3 miles from Bubble Pond and the highest point on the Atlantic coast north of Rio de Janeiro, Brazil, has been an important landmark to seafarers for centuries. Cadillac Mountain's pink granite with moire patterns of folded black basalt was carved during the last ice age.

Cadillac Mountain Summit Trail has multiple sets of steps on this short and otherwise easy path to the 1,530-foot mountaintop. The panorama sweeps Mount Desert, Cranberry and

Porcupine islands, Schoodic Peninsula, Penobscot, and Blue Hill and Frenchman bays. Though the trail to the summit may not be accessible for persons with mobility problems, Porcupine Island and Bar Harbor can be seen from the parking lot.

Bar Harbor

The Park Loop Road rejoins itself a half-mile north of Cadillac Mountain Summit Road. To reach Bar Harbor, follow the road signs. From Maine Route 233, Bar Harbor is toward the east.

Bar Harbor is a vacation resort and the largest town on Mount Desert. The "Wheelchair Access Guide, Restaurants, Motels and Campgrounds" features accessible restaurants, lodging, private campgrounds, and services but does not list every facility.

Tour boat and windjammer cruises depart from the harbor. Call Frenchman Bay Co. for information (207-288-3322). Weather on the Maine coast can change quickly, so dress warmly. Boarding the boats is easiest during high tide, when the ramp to the floating dock is most level.

The *Acadian* tour boat has a flat main deck with stairs to the top and bow areas. A small restroom has a 4-inch lip at the door and grab bars inside. We took the *Bay Lady* windjammer trip and, even with the crew's assistance, Wendy found boarding difficult. The crew, overeager to help, grabbed her arms and legs in a hammock carry and inadvertently almost disrobed her in the process! Access was down a steep gangway (because of the low tide) and over a conventional set of steps into the boat's cockpit seating. This sailing tour on Frenchman Bay between the Porcupine Islands and Bar Island can be relaxing on a sunny, calm day, or more than a little exciting in windy conditions.

We took the windammer cruise, accompanied by an energetic supporter of our project, Enid, who surveyed Acadia with us. That afternoon the winds unexpectedly picked up.

The captain headed the ship back toward harbor, but not before all passengers were thoroughly drenched by swells washing over the deck. Those who live along the Maine coast have a saying: "If you don't like the weather, wait fifteen minutes." Back on the dock, the air became still and warm again.

On the bay, we saw brightly painted small buoys marking traps set by fisherpersons to catch lobsters, a specialty of Maine. Many Bay Harbor restaurants and "lobster pounds" serve these crustacean delicacies.

From the water's edge is a closer, wilder view of marine life when low tide exposes the bar connecting Bar Island and Bar Harbor. The lowest tidal levels occur at the first and last quarters of the moon. This sandy bar provides the easiest way for anyone to view an intertidal zone on Mount Desert. Bridge Street in Bar Harbor leads to the bar; visitors can drive, walk, or wheelchair there at low tide. Assistance for persons with physical disabilities may be necessary.

Blackwoods Campground

The east side of Mount Desert has fully accessible camping at Blackwoods Campground 4 miles south of Bar Harbor on Maine Route 3. Blackwoods is open year-round, with running water mid-May through mid-October. In season, June 15 to September 15, camping is reserved through MISTIX (P.O. Box 85705, San Diego, CA 92138-5705; 800-365-2267; TDD 800-274-7275) eight weeks prior to the first night's stay and as late as the day before.

Loops A and B have designated sites with asphalt paths, raised fire grills, extended tabletops, and fully accessible comfort stations. The sites are pleasantly situated in a forest of balsam fir, spruces, and pine. The ampitheater at Blackwoods and the pay telephones between Loops A and B are fully accessible.

Depending on rainfall, blackflies are common in June,

and aggressive mosquitoes pester visitors spring through early fall throughout the park. Campers should be prepared. We combatted the pests with incense coils, citronella candles, nylon-mesh bug-net hoods, and insect repellent.

A private campground, Mount Desert Narrows Camping Resort, has moderately accessible showers for public use. Call ahead for information because the office is up a flight of steps (207-288-4782).

Eagle Lake

The largest body of fresh water on Mount Desert is Eagle Lake, 1.5 miles west of Bar Harbor on Maine Route 233. The parking area has ISA-designated spaces.

A married couple, Richard and Priscilla of Bangor, Maine, explored the carriage road around Eagle Lake with us. Both use electric wheelchairs, she due to spina bifida and he because of a past bout of polio. We went under a stone bridge and took the trail that led to a boat dock and carriage road circling the lake. Richard and Priscilla found the solitude of this remote gravel path a chance to get out of the city and enjoy the wilds of Mount Desert. For a more downhill route, we all took the path clockwise around the lake. Luckily we had no rain, which makes portions of the carriage roads muddy.

Park Headquarters

Park headquarters is open five days a week during winter and seven days a week during summer. One-quarter mile west of the Eagle Lake parking area, headquarters serves as the park visitor center during winter. A ramp on the side of the building affords entry, and the restrooms are moderately accessible.

We toured the west side of Acadia's Mount Desert taking Maine Route 233 west from park headquarters to Route 198, then north around Somes Harbor at the head of Somes Sound. Large lobsters inhabit this 168-foot-deep inlet, the only fjord in the continental United States.

After turning south at the junction on Route 102 toward Somesville, we veered left where Route 102 divides south of Somesville and continued south toward Southwest Harbor. One mile south of Somesville, glacier-carved Echo Lake had a ramp to a sand beach on the lake. Assistance may be required on the beach.

Seawall

At Seawall, rocks thrown by ocean waves formed a natural dam, creating a saltwater pond. South of Southwest Harbor the road separates into Routes 102 and 102A. Veering left, we stayed on Route 102 and continued 3 miles south of the junction to Seawall Pond Campground and Picnic Area.

Seawall Campground has an ISA-designated campsite with a nearby moderately accessible restroom. Access to the ampitheater is level.

Seawall Picnic Area, across from the campground on the ocean side of the road, has some sites level enough for use by people with mobility problems. The rocky beach at Seawall Picnic Area looks out on the Atlantic Ocean and the Cranberry Islands. We watched a lobsterperson navigate a small boat among high swells to retrieve the day's catch in the traps.

The Wonderland Trail begins 1 mile from Seawall Campground. An old road with flat and some moderately steep sections winds through a maple, pine, and fir forest before looping over granite cliffs high above the shore. This trail will challenge everyone, and wheelchair users can benefit from assistance.

From Wonderland, Route 102 circles around Mount Desert's southwest shore and rejoins Route 198. Somesville, Seal, Bass, Southwest, and Northwest harbors cluster around their town wharves where the day's catch is unloaded. These towns, with their crisp architecture of simple lines and steep roofs, retain a nineteenth-century charm found only where modern life has not fully encroached.

Schoodic Peninsula

Schoodic Peninsula, on the mainland across Frenchman Bay from Mount Desert, delivers expansive views of the Maine coast from granite and basalt headlands, Acadia's primary rock formation. From the park's main entrance at Thompson Island, Maine Route 3 goes north near Ellsworth to U.S. Highway 1 north. One mile after Winter Harbor, Maine Route 186 begins a scenic one-way loop around the Schoodic Peninsula, entering the park near Frazier Point.

The picnic area at Frazier Point has fully accessible extended tabletops and raised fire grills; however, the restrooms are not accessible. At the end of a 1-mile dirt road, Schoodic Head Overlook requires a short walk to the top, which may be accessible with assistance.

In 1947, fire raged for two weeks during the late Indian summer. The flames burned 17,000 acres on the northeast side of Mount Desert, including 10,000 of parkland. Few animals or humans were hurt, but the loss of buildings to fire contributed to the end of Acadia's grand "cottage era" of large summer home estates, a decline that had begun with the Great Depression.

Much of the 1947 fire burned in an older coniferous (conebearing) forest of spruce, fir, pine, and hemlock trees. These trees had created a high, dense canopy that deeply shaded the forest floor, limiting the diversity of plant growth. Initially after the fire, pioneering species such as birch and aspen reclaimed the forest. These deciduous trees sprout in full sun where conifers cannot. Conifers will eventually replace the fast-growing but short-lived birch and aspen by plant succession. These deciduous trees contribute to a greater plant diversity by blocking less sunlight than do conifers. In autumn, the deciduous trees flare into a spectacular array of color. Today everyone can enjoy the verdant forests in addition to the round-topped mountains, sculpted valleys, and Atlantic coastline of Acadia National Park.

(See *At a Glance: East and Midwest Region*.)

BRYCE CANYON NATIONAL PARK

Bryce Canyon, UT 84717

Information and TDD: 801-834-5322

Fantastic odd-shaped forms eroded out of ancient lake deposits display brilliant mauve, red, orange, and white colors in Utah's sun. The Paiute Native Americans hunted in this region during summer. A Paiute myth tells how the legendary Coyote turned the bad people who lived here into rocks, as recalled by Indian Dick in 1936. Dick said the Paiutes called Bryce Canyon "Angka-ku-wass-a-witts," which his nephew, Indian Johnnie, translated as "red painted faces."

In 1875, Ebenezer and Mary Bryce homesteaded in the valley beneath the rock cliffs for five years until they abandoned their settlement near present-day Tropic, Utah, after acknowledging that it was a "a hell of a place to lose a cow." The Bryces' mark was left. The canyon still bears their name.

Bryce Canyon National Park is in southwestern Utah, 220 miles northeast of Las Vegas, Nevada, and 253 miles south of Salt Lake City. The park can be entered only from the north via Utah Route 12. Nearby, Zion National Park is 84 miles southwest of Bryce and 136 miles northeast of Las Vegas. Both parks are about 2.5 hours from the Grand Canyon's North Rim.

The Paunsaugunt Plateau at Bryce Canyon National Park looks out on 200-mile vistas, remarkable scenes easily enjoyed from many of the accessible rim viewpoints along the 35 miles of paved road. The park has a fully accessible trail along the rim, a moderately accessible Bristlecone Pine Loop Trail at Rainbow Point, and many accessible facilities. Especially notable are some of the canyon horse trails accessible to people with disabilities, provided the individual has enough balance, and upper-leg and body strength to stay astride. These trails wind down into the cliff formations so that the rider may experience the wildlife and Bryce's colored rocks close up. There may be some limitations for persons with respiratory and cardiovascular conditions since the park's elevations are between 7,835 feet near the entrance and 9,105 feet at Rainbow Point.

Water over time creates the variety of colors, pinnacles, and towers of the hoodoo-studded geological formations. Hoodoos are the vertical rocks rising from the canyon floor for which Bryce has become famous. Milky beiges, pinks, grays, creamy whites, mauves, and corals frame the spires, walls, and arches of Bryce Canyon. These ever-changing rocks, including formations called Wall Street, Fairyland, and Silent City, are constantly reformed by time and water.

Bryce is not a canyon in the classic sense but a natural ampitheater hollowed out of the Pink Cliffs of the Paunsaugunt Plateau, 9,100 feet above sea level. The Pink Cliffs are at the top of the Grand Staircase, a stepped progression of rock layers carved by erosion and extending south from Bryce down to the Kaibab Plateau at the Grand Canyon. The hoodoos at Bryce are eroded 50-million- to 70-million-year-old lake deposits. Ancient lakes covered what is now the Grand Canyon to southern Idaho between the Rocky Mountains and Nevada. Water continues to reshape the hoodoos. The result is an ever-changing, not-to-be-missed myriad of limestone layers creating wondrous and colorful shapes that reach skyward.

Eighteen miles long and at times 5 miles wide, Bryce Canyon is home to more than 50 species of mammals and around 450 plant types. The bristlecone pine tree, one of the longest-living organisms on the planet, is found here. Golden eagles, red-tailed hawks, owls, Stellar's jays, ravens, blue grouse, and nutcrackers live in Bryce year-round, while more than 150 bird species migrate through the park during the year.

Maj. John Wesley Powell and Capt. Clarence E. Dutton,

both explorers of the Grand Canyon, much of the Rockies, and the Southwestern United States, visited the area in 1872 before Ebenezer and Mary Bryce arrived. Dutton's journal noted the exquisite sights of the area. A forester from the old Sevier National Forest, J. W. Humphrey, visited the area in 1915 and began writing about the wonders of Bryce. The interest generated led to the establishment of Bryce Canyon as a national monument in 1923 and its redesignation as a national park in 1924.

Fairyland Point

We turned south off Utah State Route 12 and entered Bryce Canyon National Park after climbing for many miles from the hot Virgin River Basin onto the welcome cool high plateau. Less than a half-mile inside the park boundary, we turned toward Fairyland Point, 1 mile from the Park Road. This short, flat trail afforded us our first view of Bryce's spires looking like row upon row of striped rocky rainbows forming a jagged, pointy, irregular series of columns. The trail from the ISA-designated site to the overlook has some slope and cross-slope problem areas for wheelchair users.

Visitor Center

The entrance station and visitor center are .8 mile south of the Fairyland Point turnoff on the Park Road. The visitor center has ISA-designated parking spaces in its lot and is enterable by a slightly steep ramp. The center's information and book-, map-, and poster-sales area has a lowered desk. "Bryce Canyon Access Guide," foreign-language versions of the park brochure, exhibits, and lowered telephones are at the visitor center. A slide presentation with captioning available on request shows in a fully accessible auditorium. Inquire at the center about available scripts for persons with hearing impairments, which accompany some interpretive programs. The moderately accessible restrooms have narrow

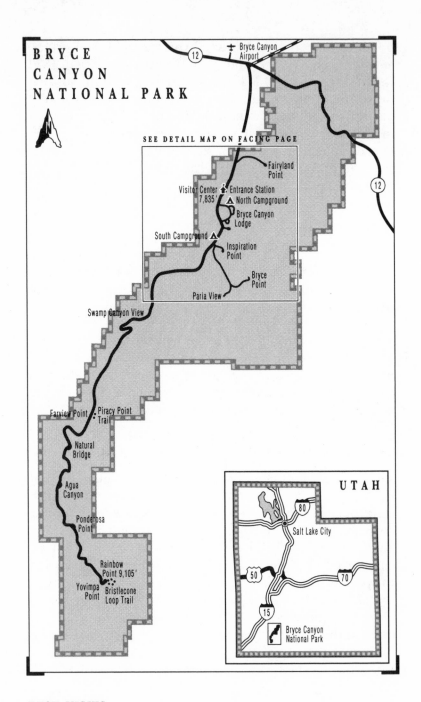

BRYCE CANYON NATIONAL PARK

SEE DETAIL MAP ON FACING PAGE

Bryce Canyon Airport

Fairyland Point

Visitor Center 7,835'

Entrance Station

North Campground

Bryce Canyon Lodge

South Campground

Inspiration Point

Bryce Point

Paria View

Swamp Canyon View

Farview Point

Piracy Point Trail

Natural Bridge

Agua Canyon

Ponderosa Point

Rainbow Point 9,105'

Yovimpa Point

Bristlecone Loop Trail

UTAH

Salt Lake City

Bryce Canyon National Park

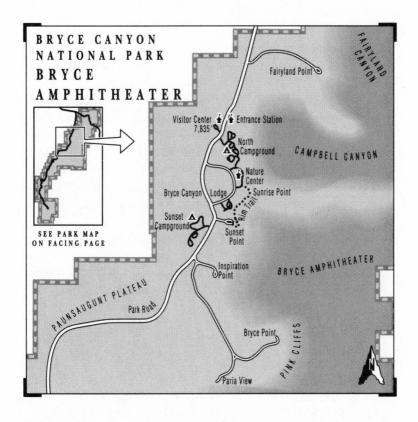

BRYCE CANYON
NATIONAL PARK
BRYCE
AMPHITHEATER

SEE PARK MAP
ON FACING PAGE

Fairland Point

Visitor Center
7,835'

Entrance Station

North
Campground

CAMPBELL CANYON

Nature
Center

Bryce Canyon Lodge

Sunrise Point

Rim Trail

Sunset
Campground

Sunset
Point

Inspiration
Point

BRYCE AMPHITHEATER

PAUNSAUGUNT PLATEAU

Park Road

Bryce Point

PINK CLIFFS

Paria View

FAIRLAND CANYON

toilet stalls with grab bars. Touch exhibits include a piñon pine tree and a wooden horse, saddled and bridled as if ready for a trip into the canyon. This area is extremely busy in summer when the park receives most of its 1.2 million annual visitors.

North Campground

Approximately 1,000 feet south of the visitor center, North Campground has two ISA-designated sites in Loop D. These are for tent camping. Neither site #94 nor site #95 is adequate for full accessibility. Surfaces are not paved, access from the parking spaces is difficult, the sites lack privacy, and only site #95 has an extended picnic-table top. Both are near the only moderately accessible restrooms in North Campground, which have narrow toilet stalls with grab bars. The ampitheater is not accessible for persons with mobility problems.

A store, a laundromat, and showers are near North Campground toward Sunrise Point. The store, where groceries, wood, and fast food are available, is moderately accessible with assistance. The laundromat is enterable to wheelchair users. Attempts to make the coin-operated showers accessible are valiant, but the facilities still fall short of full accessibility. Assistance would be needed for all but the most agile wheelchair user.

Sunrise Nature Center is a historic log building that is enterable except for a small step from the path to the stone plaza in front of the entrance. The nature center, open during the summer, displays exhibits, provides backcountry information, and has book, map, and poster sales.

Rim Trail

We found the most accessible trail in Bryce to be the breathtaking halfmile paved Rim Trail between Sunrise and Sunset points embracing the canyon's rim. Sunrise Point, at the north end of the trail, is perched atop a steep although paved slope that some might choose to forego in favor of the vistas afforded from the flatter areas equipped with benches.

From Sunrise Point we gazed at the sheer cliffs of Boat Mesa and at the enchanting hoodoos in Queens Garden. The path from the ISA-designated parking space near the store to Sunrise Point is rough in places and has sections with gentle slopes. The level walk along the astounding canyon offers unobstructed views of purple-, yellow-, and pink-colored hoodoos. Silent City, another collection of colorful hoodoos, can be seen from Sunset Point. Nearby restroom facilities are spacious and fully accessible to wheels. The path from the ISA-designated site to the overlook is easily negotiated. Our visit here included a thunderstorm visibly moving

BRYCE CANYON NATIONAL PARK.
Photo by Michael Tompane.

in its gray and flashing fury across the horizon; the weather can change quickly at this canyon. For watching sunsets, we recommend Inspiration Point, a higher vantage point overlooking Bryce Canyon and a greater portion of the Paunsaugunt Plateau.

Bryce Canyon Lodge

Bryce Canyon Lodge has a wheelchair-accessible dining hall, gift shop, and restrooms. Two guest rooms in the motel unit are moderately accessible and may require assistance. These are spacious and picturesque, as are the rest of the lodge's accommodations nestled in ponderosa pines. Reservations for this lodge, run by TW Recreational Services, can be made by phoning 801-586-7686. The lodge receives guests mid-May through September.

Horseback Rides

Bryce Canyon Trail Rides staff will assist persons with hearing, vision, developmental, and mobility problems to explore the hoodoos in the canyon on horseback. Corrals are located just east of the lodge. For further information, contact the lodge horseback ride desk, or call 801-834-5228 or 801-679-8665.

Sunset Campground

While there are no provisions for people with disabilities to camp at Sunset Campground, the campfire presentations here are wheelchair accessible and easier to attend than those at North Campground amphitheater.

Inspiration Point, Bryce Point, and Paria View

Bryce Canyon National Park offers many other lookout points to which one can drive and then easily walk or wheel for impressive vistas. A road to Inspiration, Bryce, and Paria viewpoints leaves the Park Road .3 mile south of Sunset Campground. We found Inspiration Point to be the best place from which to view sunsets. The point's lower section of trail from the parking lot is short, moderately sloped, and paved. The upper lookout's trail has a very steep slope and is difficult even for some nondisabled persons to climb, although it is paved to its peak. Inspiration Point offers excellent views of the Silent City, Cathedral, and Fairy Castle formations.

Bryce Point is 2.1 miles further down the road and has ISA-designated parking spaces and a paved, relatively steep trail. The trail is moderately accessible to the first viewpoint but has a steep downhill slope thereafter and no edge or end-of-trail protection. This trail has views of featured formations along the way. Alligator, Wall of Windows, Cathedral, and Hat Shop are visible from Bryce Point.

Paria View, the last lookout point on this spur road, looks south into Indian Canyon and the Paria River Valley. Parked automobiles may block the trailhead to the overview. The trail to the first viewpoint is flat and paved. A further viewpoint requires assistance on account of steep slopes. The drive back to Park Road is 1.8 miles.

Swamp Canyon

South on Park Road is the Swamp Canyon Viewpoint and trailhead. The view is astounding and well worth the roadside stop. A gentle dirt-dovered trail winds through the woods and is an easy jaunt for walkers and wheelers. This site also offers a comfortable waiting place for companions who want to stay behind as fellow hikers take the loop between Sheep Creek Trail, the Under the Rim Trail, and Swamp Trial, about a one- to two-hour jaunt by foot.

Farview Point

Farview Point, 5 miles south of Swamp Canyon Viewpoint and trailhead on Park Road, has a short, flat, paved path to a level overlook. The view is toward the east toward the Paria River Valley and reveals a natural bridge. A natural bridge results from the erosive forces of streams or rivers. The parking area has no ISA-designated spaces. Piracy Point Trail, a short path to an overlook, is accessible with assistance.

Natural Bridge

The next pullout 2 miles south of Farview offers a view of Natural Bridge, actually a natural arch. In contrast to a bridge, an arch is an opening in a rock formation caused by wind, water, and/or cold. Natural Bridge Viewpoint may require assistance from the parking lot, which has no ISA-designated spaces.

Agua Canyon and Ponderosa Canyon Viewpoint

Agua Canyon, 1.5 miles south of Bryce Natural Bridge, and Ponderosa Canyon Viewpoint, another 1.5 miles from Agua Canyon, are flat asphalt viewpoints with moderate access adjacent to the parking lots. Neither has ISA-designated parking spaces.

Rainbow Overlook and Yovimpa Point

The Park Road ends 2.5 miles from Ponderosa Canyon Viewpoint and 18 miles south of the visitor center. The parking lot there does not have ISA-designated spaces, nor are the comfort stations accessible without assistance. The picnic tables are not extended and are on soft dirt. An outdoor shelter has steps leading to and from the exhibit area.

An alternate rough paved path leads to Rainbow Overlook, the highest point in Bryce Canyon National Park at 9,105 feet, accessible for wheelchair users with assistance. Yovimpa Point is a short, flat paved trail looking 100 miles south down the Grand Staircase to the Kaibab Plateau at the North Rim of the Grand Canyon in northern Arizona.

One of the high points of our Bryce Canyon visit was the 1-mile-loop Bristlecone Pine Trail, beginning from Rainbow Point parking lot. The trail surface was dirt and loose sandstone with rock border on both sides. We went over some moderate and steep slopes with a few rocks in the path as we wound through woods of Douglas and white fir, occasionally exiting the woods to discover colorful vistas. The oldest tree in the park, a bristlecone pine more than seventeen hundred years old, endures at this southernmost accessible point of the park. The trail is a bit tricky, but panoramic views of southern Utah and northern Arizona made the journey well worth taking.

Bryce Canyon National Park affords ample access to a visual spectacle. Its places for quiet observation of rock spires, pinnacles, crags, and arches invite any visitor to contemplate the forces of water and time that have shaped and carved Bryce's colorful layers. More than touring, more than walking, take advantage of the canyon's grandeur and the opportunity to remain still and observe intricate natural features, an activity within anyone's reach.

Worth a Visit

Also a part of southern Utah's Grand Staircase and not far from Bryce, Zion National Park has accessible opportunities. A noted park feature is the Zion–Mt. Carmel Tunnel drilled and blasted 1.1 miles through solid rock. The Gateway to the Narrows Trail, the most accessible in the park, is a paved 1-mile path on which, with assistance, wheels can wind along the Virgin River. A fully accessible unisex restroom is at the trailhead. Lower Emerald Pools is a moderately accessible trail that traverses a wooden bridge across the Virgin River and goes along a paved and dirt path through the woods to the pools. Since the trail has some steep drop-offs, assistance may be necessary.

Watchman and South campgrounds have campsites reserved for persons with disabilities. The Zion Lodge, operated by TW Recreational Services (as is Bryce Lodge), has fully accessible rooms (801-586-7686).

A half-hour drive east from Bryce is Kodachrome Basin State Park. Sunrise and sunset yield intense warm hues on the smooth rust-colored sandstone mounds unique to this area. The campsites are flat and wheelchair accessible. New facilities, accessible and with showers, are being constructed in the campground. Restrooms at the nearby group campsite are fully accessible.

(See *At a Glance: Desert Southwest Region.*)

CARLSBAD CAVERNS NATIONAL PARK

3225 National Parks Highway
Carlsbad, NM 88220
Information: 505-785-2232
Recorded Information: 505-785-2107

I magine being lowered 170 feet into the earth in an iron bucket attached to a single cable. Early in the century, adventurous spelunkers braved this journey into the darkness of Carlsbad Cavern two at a time. The bucket went down a shaft originally dug to mine bat guano for agricultural fertilizer before Carlsbad Cave National Monument was created in 1923. Accounts in *National Geographic* incited readers to risk the descent into a wondrous large cave with awesome natural decorations. We entered the same cave, only our iron bucket was a modern elevator descending 750 feet into an underground world with a trail possible for most anyone to explore.

Both a cave and a desert mountain park in southeast New Mexico, Carlsbad Caverns National Park lies in the foothills of the Guadalupe Mountains 27 miles southwest of Carlsbad, New Mexico, and 165 miles east of El Paso, Texas. Two caves are open to public tours: the earlier-discovered Carlsbad Cavern and New Cave.

The 46,775 acres of scenic Chihuahuan Desert above the caves are habitats for cacti, trees, and shrubs well adapted to hot summers and cool winters. Visitors are most curious about the bats and rattlesnakes, but the park has other significant mammal, bird, reptile, and insect populations.

Underground caves are typically difficult to explore, but in this most accessible cave park in the United States, the NPS has achieved a significant accomplishment. The access in the Big Room of Carlsbad Cavern is remarkable for people with disabilities.

On the surface, Carlsbad's desert is revealed on a self-guided auto tour through a mountain canyon 250 million years old. At the edge of an ancient inland sea, skeletal structures of tiny marine creatures cemented with lime (calcium precipitated from salt water) to form a massive limestone reef. The ocean receded, leaving a basin of gypsum and salts. Sediments from nearby hills covered the reef for millions of years. The buried reef was slowly uplifted, and groundwater collected along fractures in the limestone. The water absorbed carbon dioxide and formed carbonic acid, dissolving pockets of rock. Over a few million years, the weak acid ate away at the limestone to form the large caverns. Essentially, the size and contours of the caves were defined at this point. Acidic water drained from the underground chambers when the old reef uplifted again, exposing the reef above the surface, the present Guadalupe Mountains.

Pictographs at the caverns' natural entrance indicate that Native Americans knew of this cave. Evidence inside the cavern shows that they visited no later than A.D. 900 and probably did not range deep into the caves.

Exploration beyond the entrance reportedly began in 1883 when a father lowered his twelve-year-old son, Rolth Sublett, past the first hazardous ledge into Carlsbad Cavern. When cowboys witnessed millions of bats exiting the Cave at sundown, two decades of guano (bat dung) mining began in 1888. The guano, abundant in nitrates, fertilized southern California citrus groves. Reports of the wondrous cavern traveled far, and visitors entered the cave via the same bucket used for raising guano to the surface. Carlsbad Caverns was proclaimed a national monument in 1923 and was upgraded to national park status in 1930.

Visitor Center

We entered the park from the U.S. Highway 62-180 turnoff at White's City, 20 miles south of Carlsbad. The visitor center is 7 miles west of White's City in the Guadalupe Mountains.

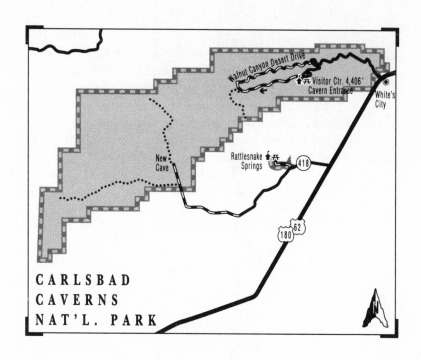

**CARLSBAD
CAVERNS
NAT'L. PARK**

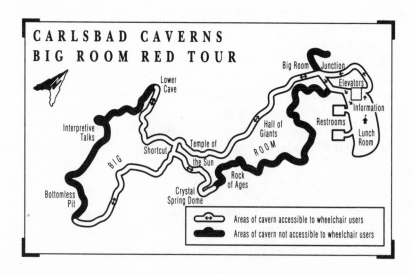

**CARLSBAD CAVERNS
BIG ROOM RED TOUR**

Areas of cavern accessible to wheelchair users

Areas of cavern not accessible to wheelchair users

The parking area has ISA-designated spaces in front of the visitor center's main entrance.

Gentle ramps lead to the double-door entrance of the visitor center. An information desk, cave-tour tickets, exhibits, and restrooms and a theater, gift shop, bookstore, and coffee shop are fully accessible on the same level. The park has an "Access Guide."

At a reasonable rate, a government-approved children's nursery at the visitor center cares for small children of visitors making the cavern trip. Parents can check children in and out of the nursery only with proper identification, usually a driver's license. Pets are not permitted in the caves, and leaving pets in cars may be fatal for them. Air-conditioned kennels are available. Check at the gift shop in the visitor center for child nursery and pet kennel services.

Visitors use hand-held radios on the self-guided tours in the cavern to receive interpretive information. A small rental fee is charged for these receivers at the visitor center. Information about the cave is broadcast in English, Spanish, and children's English. Receivers amplified for those with hearing impairments and receivers designed for wheelchair and crutch users are available. Check at the information desk.

A film about the caverns, with hearing-aid amplification and captioning, plays in the theater, which has wheelchair seating. The exhibit room has displays about the process of cave formation, the history of exploring the caves, recent explorations of Lechuguilla Cave, archeological finds, and bats.

The caves are open for touring on a regular basis, generally from 8:30 A.M. to 5 P.M. The last entry during winter is 3:30 P.M. The cave temperature is a steady 56°F. Wear a sweater or light jacket. The main Carlsbad Cavern has two self-guided tours, the Blue and the Red, but in winter rangers sometimes lead the first half of the Blue Tour.

The longer Blue Tour enters the cave through the natural entrance, reached by a 300-yard outdoor trail from the visitor center. Blue Tours take about three hours, cover 3 miles, are strenuous, and are not recommended for anyone with health problems. The Blue Tour is long and tiring for young children, and strollers are not allowed in the cave for safety reasons.

From the natural entrance, the trail descends 830 vertical feet and ascends 80 feet in 1.75 miles to the underground lunchroom. The Blue Tour passes through the Main Corridor, Green Lake Room, and Papoose Room before joining the Red Tour near the entrance to the Big Room.

Park rangers, upon request, will assist people with physical disabilities on the Red Tour of the Big Room. The Red Tour begins with a 750-foot elevator descent from the visitor center to the underground lunchroom. This rapid descent is an engineering marvel. A moderately sloped, asphalt, paved, 1.25-mile trail forms a large H pattern in the awe-inspiring Big Room. Some areas at each end of the H are not wheelchair accessible and are so marked with barriers. When using a wheelchair on this trail, use caution, because the traffic flow often moves in the opposite direction. The trail is damp in some places. Both the Blue and Red tours return to the surface by elevator. The underground lunchroom has cold and hot drinks, box lunches, a limited assortment of gift items, photography supplies, and fully accessible restrooms.

We toured the cave with Ranger Danny Cantu, who has a serious vision impairment. He guided us on a tour through the Big Room, the largest underground chamber in the Western Hemisphere. After passing the Big Room junction where the Blue and Red tours combine, Danny pointed out various cave decorations, or speleothems. In the Hall of Giants, Giant Dome and Twin Domes loom over the trail. Domes are large-sized stalagmites, limestone formations that rise from the cave floor. Lime-rich drops fall on the cave floor, slowly building deposits upward. Giant Dome is more than 60 feet high.

BIG ROOM,
CARLSBAD CAVERNS NATIONAL PARK.
Photo by Michael Tompane.

Ranger Cantu showed us delicate soda straws and stalactites hanging above Temple of the Sun's intricate calcium patterns. Soda straws grow as thin straws from the ceiling and allow water to drop through their hollow tubes. Ranger Cantu pointed out other decorations, like draperies, cave bacon, cave popcorn, and cave pearls. Water percolating through the limestone is the predominant process forming these decorations. Underground pools are visible along the path.

The NPS hired a professional lighting consultant to design the tastefully dramatic lighting. Interpretation through the cavern is excellent, both on trailside exhibits and in areas where radio messages about cave features are transmitted to hand-held receivers.

After taking the elevator to the surface, we encountered daylight once again. Desert Trail near the visitor center may require assistance on steep slopes.

Bat Flight

Visitors can observe the bat flight in summer from the amphitheater where park rangers lead nightly programs. The amphitheater is located near the cavern's natural entrance; the trail from ISA-designated parking in the lower lot is level and paved with asphalt and flagstone. A fully accessible unisex vault toilet is near the amphitheater.

At sundown, hundreds of thousands of bats swarm quickly out of their daytime roost to the Pecos and Black River valleys, where they devour insects. For locating food and navigating in the dark, bats use echolocation, a unique kind of sonar also used by mammals like whales and dolphins. The bats return at dawn with a distinctive buzzing sound.

Carlsbad Caverns hosts seven kinds of bats, but mostly Mexican free-tails. Mother bats give birth in June. The baby bats hang with mothers from the ceiling, developing for four to five weeks until they are mature enough to swarm out with the adults to feed at nightfall. The bats migrate to Mexico for warmer weather in late October or early November.

Walnut Canyon

Carlsbad Caverns National Park is situated in the Chihuahuan Desert, one of the four major deserts in North America. The self-guided Walnut Canyon Desert Drive begins a half-mile from the visitor center and leads the visitor on a 9.5-mile one-way dirt road through the desert scenery of the Guadalupe Mountains. This is an auto tour, and there are no accessible trails in the canyon.

While Michael spent his childhood in desert areas of Arizona, Wendy grew up in the lushness of New York's eastern seaboard. It is not surprising, then, that Wendy expected the desert to be arid and almost lifeless. She soon learned differently as Michael shared his love and knowledge of the hardy desert. Extreme heat and cold, as well as brief torrential rainfalls between long arid periods, characterize American

Southwest deserts. A complex array of plants and animals thrive surprisingly well in the Chihuahuan Desert.

We saw mule deer pick their way along rocky limestone ledges and heard coyotes howling nightly. Mountain lions, badgers, fox, rabbits, and squirrels live in the mountain desert park, along with rattlesnakes, scorpions, and tarantula spiders. Golden eagles, turkey vultures, and hawks ply the wind currents, while ground-hugging quail nestle in the sotol and soaptree, both of the yucca family. Unique to the desert are ocotillo, agave, prickly pear, and hedgehog cacti.

The "Walnut Canyon Desert Drive" brochure identifies the sharp-pointed leaves of the lechuguilla, saw-toothed edges of the sotol, and canelike cholla as well as other flora of the Chihuahuan Desert. During our visit in autumn, we saw cottonwood, western soapberry, and maple leaves turn color.

Rattlesnake Springs

Rattlesnake Springs Picnic Area is in a shaded drainage 14 miles from the visitor center. Return to White's City and turn south on U.S. Highway 62-180. After 5 miles, turn onto County Route 418. Three miles from the turn off the main highway, the road reaches Rattlesnake Springs. Route 418 continues 9 miles further to the parking lot for New Cave and Slaughter Canyon.

The picnic area has level, grassy sites (some paved), picnic tables with extended tops, and a fully accessible comfort station. One picnic table for visitors in wheelchairs has a packed trail to the parking lot.

New Cave

Carlsbad Caverns National Park has more than seventy-five known caves. The famous main cavern and New Cave, two of the largest caves in Carlsbad, are the only ones in the park open for visitation without special permit. New Cave was discovered by a goat herder in 1937.

New Cave tours are by advance reservation. Call 505-785-2232, or inquire at the visitor center. New Cave is undeveloped. To take the rugged flashlight tour led by rangers, bring a flashlight, sturdy walking shoes, and drinking water.

Overnight Accommodations

Since there are no campgrounds or lodging in the park, we stayed at Park Entrance RV Park and Campground located in White's City. The RV Park has electric, water, and sewer hookups and showers, difficult to enter for wheelchair users. The campground, in a grassy area with a few trees, has neither designated sites nor facilities for persons with physical disabilities. The grounds are flat, and firewood is provided free of charge. White's City also has gas stations and a motel, restaurant, store, and gift shop. Many services and accommodations are available in Carlsbad, 20 miles northeast of the park entrance.

Recent explorations of Lechuguilla Cave in Carlsbad Caverns National Park have attracted worldwide scientific attention. At 1,565 feet, Lechuguilla is the deepest cave in the United States and the fourth longest. Ambient temperature is a high 68°F, and humidity is 95 to 100 percent. Rare cave decorations found include 20-foot-long gypsum chandeliers, 12-foot soda straws, and "balloons" of hydro magnesite formed by a thin layer of the mineral and gradually pumped by water to very slowly expand like a balloon. Subaqueous helictites, found only in Lechuguilla, are the oddest speleothems. Helictites apparently defy gravity by capillary and hydrostatic flow, creating crazy shapes that resemble irregular spirals. Exploration by speleologists, geologists, and other scientists is continuing in this wilderness cave. Since there has been little damage by humans to Lechuguilla, it remains in pristine condition and is of great value to cave science worldwide.

Worth a Visit

Living Desert Zoological and Botanical State Park, on the north side of Carlsbad, is just off U.S. Highway 285. The park, on a ridge top overlooking the city, exhibits animals indigenous to the Chihuahuan Desert and more than one hundred native and exotic desert plants. A level, paved, 1.5-mile path allows visitors to view species in large enclosed areas that would be very difficult to observe in the wild. Restrooms are moderately accessible.

Guadalupe National Park, 40 miles south of White's City on U.S. Highway 62-180, is a rugged mountain park with few access opportunities for visitors with disabilities. A new visitor center, however, is fully accessible.

(See *At a Glance: Desert Southwest Region.*)

CHACO CULTURE NATIONAL HISTORICAL PARK
Star Route 4, Box 6500
Bloomfield, NM 87413
Information: 505-988-6727

At its high point, Chaco Canyon was an Anasazi cultural center where thirteen large "towns" and hundreds of smaller villages developed at an accelerated pace known by few other peoples in the prehistoric Southwest. The Chacoan Anasazi's freestanding multistory masonry and extensive road system were centered in the wide level valley of Chaco Canyon between A.D. 900 and A.D. 1200. Chaco probably played a central role in the economic and ceremonial life of the Anasazi in the San Juan Basin area. For a fuller discussion on the development of the Anasazi culture, see Mesa Verde National Park Best Visit.

Chaco Culture National Historical Park, in the Four Corners region (the area of the Colorado Plateau common to Arizona, Colorado, New Mexico, and Utah), is located in a remote section of northwestern New Mexico 138 miles south of Mesa Verde National Park, 62 miles from Bloomfield, New Mexico, and 174 miles northwest of Albuquerque, New Mexico. The last miles leading to the park by either of its two entrances are over rough dirt roads, not passable in wet weather without four-wheel drive. The park's elevation is approximately 6,200 feet. There is no gasoline, food, or lodging within the park, but a campground and limited water are available.

We were surprised at the accessibility of some of the prehistoric ruins in Chaco Canyon. We never expected to take a wheelchair along old stone walls, through plazas, and around kiva rims in a pueblo built one thousand years ago. Significant barriers block many of the ruins, but portions of five great houses are moderately accessible with assistance and provided us with insights into the Chaco phenomena.

Chaco Culture National Historical Park preserves this canyon unique to the Anasazi culture. During certain seasons, the population of the canyon may have swelled to thousands, while year-round inhabitants probably numbered in the hundreds. Archeologists speculate that many of the rooms in the large pueblos were not living quarters but were used for special purposes, perhaps storage, and much of the population visited Chaco from outlier villages for important occasions. Outliers varied in size from small wayside communities to complex towns like those excavated at Aztec Ruins National Monument in Aztec, New Mexico, 70 miles north of Chaco. (Aztec Ruins are very accessible during dry weather.)

An abundance of turquoise, pottery, seashells, and other artifacts originating from other regions have been found in Chaco Canyon, suggesting that Chaco was a major trade center. The Anasazi traded as far east as Kansas, west to the Pacific coast, and south into modern-day Mexico. Only about 50 percent of the pottery found in and around the ruins is indigenous to Chaco.

Many of the pueblos were built over a period of 250 years from A.D. 900 to A.D. 1150, and the progression in masonry techniques can be seen in the walls still standing. Three different types of architecture exist from this period at Chaco: Bonito, McElmo, and Hosta Butte. Four of the very large pueblos, such as Pueblo Bonito and Chetro Ketl, were built as D-shaped multistory dwellings oriented along solar and lunar alignments. McElmo-type villages, laid out in compact units, had enclosed kivas, which reflected strong influence from the San Juan River region north of Chaco. Smaller, mostly single-story villages of the Hosta Butte style were inhabited concurrently with the Bonito and McElmo structures and are thought by archeologists to have been year-round residences.

Roads, portions of which are faintly visible today, radiated from Chaco Canyon to outlier villages. Approximately 30 feet wide, the Chacoan roads were mostly straight lines of hard-packed surfaces, often accentuated by earthen mounds. Where the roads encountered canyon walls, steps were cut into the cliffs. The existence and use of these roads provoke much modern speculation.

The Great Pueblo culture in Chaco Canyon probably ended about A.D. 1150 when the inhabitants began abandoning the area. Nobody knows why the Chacoans left. A variety of factors, such as droughts, depletion of natural resources, and changes in networks concerning social, economic, and ceremonial ties, may have led to the abandonment.

We turned southwest off New Mexico Highway 44 at Nageezi Trading Post onto a 26-mile washboard-rough dirt road through the "checkerboard" reservation, the eastern part of the Navajo Reservation where sections of land belong alternatively to the Navajo Tribal Nation, the U.S. Government, and private owners. By following signs at main junctions and keeping to the most traveled portions of the road, we arrived at Chaco Culture National Historical Park Visitor Center in about ninety minutes. Via an alternate route from the south, Chaco is 61 miles north of U.S. Interstate 40 at Thoreau, New Mexico. Follow State Route 371 north 24 miles to Crownpoint. A few miles north of Crownpoint, turn east on State Route 57, which turns north and becomes a dirt and gravel road for the final 21 miles to the visitor center. Though shorter in "dirt miles" than the northern route, this road is rougher and more dangerous when wet.

Visitor Center

The visitor center has a paved parking lot with ISA-designated spaces, curb cuts, and level entry to the building. The interior is fully accessible, with an information and sales desk, books and gift items, exhibits, and three movies available

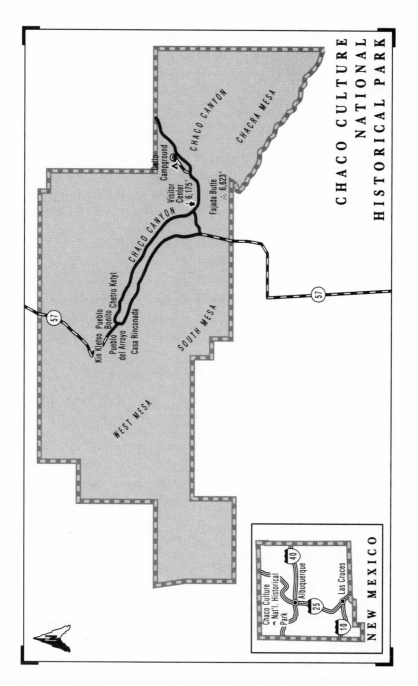

with captioning and printed transcriptions available on request. Plaster-cast models of several ruins can be handled and observed on request. The restrooms are not easily accessible since they have heavy entrance doors and narrow stalls without grab bars, both significant barriers. A small picnic area in front of the visitor center has several tables, including one with an extended top, which we found too high for comfortable use.

The center's museum, with exhibits that are easily viewable from wheelchair and child level, helped us gain insights into the Chaco experience. Here is a brief history of Chaco Canyon, and sections of reconstructed walls using authentic masonry techniques assist the visitor in distinguishing between various periods of Chacoan building. An impressive array of pottery, baskets, jewelry, tools, and objects believed by experts to have had ceremonial significance are on display.

Chetro Ketl

Chaco Canyon has a Park Loop Road for touring the ruins open for visitation. The trails through Chetro Ketl and Pueblo Bonito both begin at the second parking lot on the road 4 miles from the visitor center. The parking lot has ISA-designated spaces and fully accessible vault-type toilets using a Swedish-designed waste recycling principle.

Chetro Ketl is one of the more accessible ruins in Chaco Canyon and one of thirteen great pueblos found along 20 miles of Chaco Wash. Characteristic of all Bonito-type pueblos, it was constructed according to a preconceived plan. The pueblo has more than five hundred rooms and sixteen kivas built between A.D. 900 and A.D. 1120.

The half-mile self-guided trail with accompanying brochure is gravel and packed dirt. Assistance is necessary in places. From the trailhead, Pueblo Bonito is visible to the west. A 60-foot-diameter great kiva is viewable from the path in the large plaza of Chetro Ketl.

Kivas are subterranean chambers believed to have been used for family or clan gatherings and rituals. Great kivas, larger in size and with more features than common kivas, were used for ceremonies and were a constant architectural feature through Chaco Anasazi history.

The trail leads north from the plaza via a steep slope through a lower level of rooms in the back-wall section of the ruin where assistance for wheelchairs is necessary. The trail along Chetro Ketl's north wall can have sandy areas where persons using wheelchairs will need assistance.

Pueblo Bonito

Pueblo Bonito is the largest structure in Chaco Canyon. Covering more than 3 acres, it had as many as five stories and eight hundred rooms during its greatest period from A.D. 1000 to A.D. 1120.

Wheelchair users will find parts of the self-guided trail moderately accessible, while other portions have significant barriers. The first part of the trail up to an overlook above where Threatening Rock fell on Pueblo Bonito in 1941 is moderately accessible, and assistance up the steep incline may be necessary. The trail has an accompanying brochure.

We visited Chaco twice during our surveys of the parks. During our first visit, the trail along Bonito's south wall was hard-packed dirt and an easy path for Wendy's wheelchair. On our second visit, the same path had become very loose with sand and difficult for wheelchairs to travel.

We entered the ruin's plaza to find distinctive Bonito-style stone walls and T-shaped doorways, two great kivas, and several smaller kivas. Forty kivas have been found at Pueblo Bonito.

Pueblo Del Arroyo

Pueblo Del Arroyo, a quarter-mile from Pueblo Bonito and northwest of the Park Loop Road, is another great pueblo.

With about 280 rooms and more than 20 kivas, the ruin is named for its proximity to the main channel of Chaco Wash, which altered course about 60 feet south in the mid-1800s. The path through the ruin is gravel and packed dirt. The north side is fairly level, but around the south side are steps and steep inclines, significant barriers for wheelchair users. There is a bench along the trail.

The masonry at Pueblo Del Arroyo uses a wider variety of stones than at Chetro Ketl and Pueblo Bonito. Erected more quickly than most other great houses, Del Arroyo was built primarily between A.D. 1075 and A.D. 1110. Most unique to Del Arroyo is the round tri-wall structure just west of the central plaza. This circular room is similar to structures built north of the San Juan; the purposes of these rooms are still unknown.

Kin Kletso

A quarter-mile northwest of Pueblo Del Arroyo, Kin Kletso is an example of McElmo-type architecture. It was built in the late 1000s, and the masonry style and compact floor plan suggest influence from the San Juan River region. The town design is without a central plaza, and the five kivas are encompassed within the room blocks. The pueblo may have been three stories high with as many as one hundred rooms.

We left the parking lot and followed a level dirt path circling the ruin. The ruin trail descends a short, steep incline, so assistance is necessary. It led us to viewing points on a flat trail behind the ruin where we could see various rooms and the more-concentrated town plan of Kin Kletso. Down another very steep path is a vault toilet.

For persons who can climb a steep incline over rocks, a backcountry trail from behind Kin Kletso goes up the cliffs. The trail offers an overview of Kin Kletso and proceeds to the mesa top for views of Pueblo Bonito with its distinctive D shape and the many features of Chaco Wash. A registration box is situated at the trailhead behind Kin Kletso.

Casa Rinconada

Returning to the Park Loop Road, Casa Rinconada is three-quarters of a mile from Kin Kletso. The vault toilet is fully accessible and near the parking lot.

Casa Rinconada (Spanish for house in a box canyon), on the south side of the canyon, is a great kiva at the highest point of a dirt trail that passes three small excavated house sites. Hosta Butte–type structures, numbered but not named by the Park Service, were built on top of earlier dwellings. Some speculate that these sites, inhabited contemporaneously with the great pueblos, were the main living dwellings in Chaco Canyon. The great pueblos were primarily for large ceremonies, food storage, and other public use, although a few of the rooms appear to have been residential.

A portion of the trail to the great kiva of Casa Rinconada is steep and can be slippery when wet. Although down several high steps, this is the only kiva open to public entry in Chaco Canyon. The best view from a wheelchair is at the south portal, and we found it to be a great view. Wendy was able to see many of the details of the great kiva from above while Michael climbed down and inspected the niches in the wall, the bench surrounding the central floor (which is common to great kivas), the four roof-support foundations, a firebox, and two square stone boxes thought to have been foot drums. On the north section of the kiva floor, a spiral set of stones encircles a *sipapu*, the symbolic hole in the Earth from which humans emerged into this world. There are two entrances in the kiva's north wall, one from an antechamber adjacent to the kiva and the other from underneath the antechamber, the latter a unique feature to Casa Rinconada. Before descending the steep trail back to the parking lot, we looked across the canyon to Pueblo Bonito.

Gallo Campground

About 1 mile from the visitor center, Gallo Campground has many flat, unpaved, moderately accessible sites. Two campsites are designated for people with disabilities, and a fully accessible unisex comfort station is in the middle of the campground. Camping is on a first-come first-served basis. The group campsite is available for reservation by mail or telephone. For information, call the park. Potable water is only available from a spigot outside the visitor center. Tucked under the cliff wall in the campground are a few small ruins, built by people from the San Juan River region who moved to Chaco in the mid to late 1200s.

Traditional agricultural and ritual practices of Zuni, Hopi, Acoma, and Pueblo tribes who today live in northern New Mexico and Arizona carefully follow the cycles of Earth's movement around the sun. Proper planting preparations depend on anticipating the vernal and autumnal equinoxes. Sun priests observe the sun's position in the sky and announce seasonal progressions to the tribe.

Archeological studies suggest that the Chacoan culture was likewise concerned with the sun's cycle throughout the year. Three archeoastronomical sites in Chaco Canyon are of particular note. Prior to winter solstice, the setting sun casts a narrow beam of light through a second-story corner door along the south wall of Pueblo Bonito. Chacoan sun priests could have monitored this beam, watching for its position to fall precisely in a corner at sunrise on the winter solstice. At the great kiva of Casa Rinconada, the summer solstice sunrise casts light through the kiva's northeast portal into a niche in the wall. Fajada Butte, Chaco Canyon's dominant promontory at the east end of the wash, has spiral petroglyphs where on the summer solstice a sliver of sunlight passes between two of three standing slabs of rock to bisect the spiral at noon. These features contribute to the challenge of understanding the Chaco culture, a highpoint of Anasazi civilization in the Southwest.

(See *At a Glance: Desert Southwest Region.*)

EVERGLADES NATIONAL PARK

P.O. Box 279
Homestead, FL 33030
Information and TTY/TDD: 305-247-6211
Shark Valley Information: 305-221-8776
Everglades City Information: 813-695-3311

E verglades National Park occupies a portion of the tip of the southern Florida peninsula, which separates the Atlantic Ocean and Gulf of Mexico. Here, tropical- and temperate-zone environments intermingle as nowhere else in North America. The largest mahogany tree in the United States shares a landscape with dwarf cypress hundreds of years old. Four types of mangrove provide a breeding ground for the Gulf's many crustaceans. Everglades has the greatest concentration of sawgrass in the world.

The term *Everglades* derives from *glade,* an opening in a forest. The Everglades are seemingly unending glades of sawgrass prairies in southern Florida. Sawgrass, a grassy tall sedge with saw-like edges, abounds in marshes.

Everglades National Park is the second largest national park outside of Alaska in the United States. It may well be the most accessible large wilderness-area national park in the country.

The park, established in 1947, encompasses some 1.4 million acres on the southwest corner of the Florida mainland, 45 miles southwest of Miami. It protects many rare endangered and threatened life-forms such as crocodiles, Florida panthers, manatees, and loggerhead turtles. Alligators commonly cross the tropical trails where visitors wander. An ever-changing bird show features great white heron, roseate spoonbills, and white ibis.

Everglades occupies a flat, almost-level limestone plateau with the park's high point culminating about 8 feet above sea level. Another example of the park's gentle elevation is at Shark Valley Slough, hidden beneath sawgrass. A slough is a shallow, slow-moving waterway. Shark Valley Slough starts at Lake Okeechobee and extends 120 miles. It drops only 15 feet over its entire course to the ocean.

A variance of only a few inches in elevation here radically affects the plant growth. Sawgrass gives way to stands of trees such as hardwood hammocks; pinelands; bay, cypress, and willow heads; and mangrove swamps. We explored accessible trails as they wove through each of these.

The park is enterable in three areas: Shark Valley, Everglades City, and the main park entrance in the southern section. An access guide booklet, *Accessibility Everglades National Park,* is available at each information station and visitor center.

Shark Valley

In the heart of the Everglades, which extends from Lake Okeechobee to the Florida Keys, is Shark Valley, located on Highway 41, 50 miles from the Main Visitor Center, 40 miles west of Miami, and 42 miles east of Everglades City. The parking lot has ISA-designated parking spaces and fully accessible comfort stations. Shark Valley Information Center (305-221-8776) has a bookstore and vending machines.

The principle activity at Shark Valley is to tour the 15-mile loop road south into a portion of the Shark River Slough. The Bobcat Trail at Shark Valley is a fully accessible half-mile boardwalk near the start of the tram-tour station with interpretive placards. An audiotape that corresponds with cue pads on the trail is available at the information center.

The Shark Valley Road is usable only by foot, wheelchair, bicycle, or tram tour. The tram tour is an ideal option for families, seniors, and those who want to take a ride through the park. Call ahead to the concessionaire, Shark Valley Tram Tours, for reservations (305-221-8455).

A tram car has provisions for wheelchairs, a very steep (1:6) ramp, and wheelchair lock-downs. Wheelchair users, when making reservations for a tram tour, ask for the tram with the ramp and lock-downs.

The guided tour on the covered, open-air tram cars was our first introduction to the wildlife of the Everglades. Alligators and blue herons populate the slough. Midway in the tour we stopped and climbed off the tram to visit the Shark Valley observation tower. The tower has a circular winding ramp with an approximately 1,200-foot-long moderately steep (1:8) slope. The tower looks upon lush vegetation around a small pond in which alligators live. A moderately accessible restroom is at the base of the tower.

Everglades City

Everglades City, entryway to the Ten Thousand Islands, section of the park, is 92 miles from the Main Visitor Center and 80 miles west of Miami. Take Highway 41 to Route 29 south to the Gulf Coast Ranger Station. The parking lot has ISA-designated spaces.

One can expect to find shorebirds and an occasional manatee near the Gulf Coast Ranger Station. This ranger station has a visitor center (813-695-3311) with fully accessible restrooms, a gift and book shop, telephones, and boat-tour tickets for sale on the first floor. Stairs lead to the second floor, which has no wheelchair access. Persons with mobility impairments can ask in the gift shop for assistance from the ranger.

Canoes are available for rental at the visitor center gift shop. There are no particular provisions for canoeists with disabilities. Canoe trail information is available at the second-floor desk, Everglades City is at the north end of the 99-mile Wilderness Waterway canoe trail. Backcountry permits are required for overnight canoe trips.

An approximately 1 ¾-hour boat cruise leaves from Everglades City into the heart of the Ten Thousand Islands area.

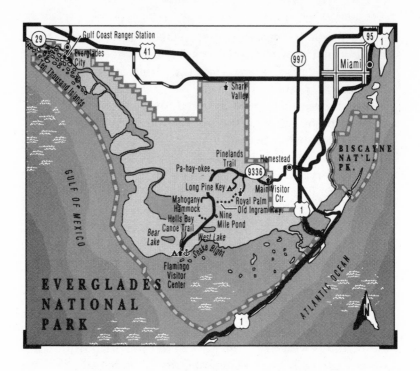

The *Manatee II,* a newer boat, has a moderately accessible head with grab bars. Sunset cruises on the *Manatee II* leave at 6 P.M. January through March. Call ahead for more information (Everglades National Park Boat Tours, 813-695-2591). The concessionaire will assist persons with disabilities onto the boat.

Main Entrance and Southern Section

The Main Visitor Center is just inside the park boundary 12 miles southwest of Homestead, Florida, on State Route 9336. The parking lot has ISA-designated spaces, a fully ramped walkway, and fully accessible restrooms, always open, across the breezeway from the visitor center. Telephones and a water fountain next to the restrooms are at a wheelchair-accessible height. The park has installed TTY/ TDD on the main park number.

The center is fully accessible. A multilingual phone in front of a mural features an audio message about the park linked to the mural. Children will especially like making these phone calls. Visitors with vision impairments can ask for assistance with the phone mural. There are also scripts of the mural message for persons with hearing impairments. A captioned orientation film is available on request and has accompanying scripts. A photographic exhibit and displays about each section of the park are in the main room of the center. Books are sold here. The information-sales counter has a lowered section, and the park access guide, maps, and brochures are available at the desk.

Royal Palm

From the Main Visitor Center, we passed through the entrance station and drove 2.5 miles to the turnoff for Royal Palm Visitor Center, which is next to the fully accessible Anhinga and Gumbo-Limbo trails. This area of the park is one of the premier places in which to view the diverse teeming wildlife of the Everglades. The Taylor Slough flows through here.

Royal Palm has ISA-designated parking and a ramp to a small information station and bookstore. The information station also has a loaner wheelchair, and fully accessible restrooms are across the breezeway.

The Anhinga and Gumbo-Limbo trails are designed for all visitors. Everyone, including families with young children, seniors, and those with physical disabilities, will delight at the close views of the Everglades' wildlife. The Gumbo-Limbo is paved and the Anhinga is boardwalk and asphalt. Both are very level.

Gumbo-Limbo is a thickly forested half-mile trail through a lush tropical hardwood hammock of royal palm, strangler ficus, and gumbo-limbo trees. In southern U.S. jargon, a *hammock,* from the American Indian word *hamaca,* is a dense mini jungle of hardwood and palm-tree species on a few inches of soil above the limestone.

These hammocks are protected by a ring of limestone outcroppings and shrubbery, which helps the hammock to resist fire. The hammock is host to birds as well as vines, orchids, ferns, and bromeliads hanging from trees, creating aerial gardens. The path is narrow and uneven at some points because of tree roots.

Anhinga Trail, a half-mile in length, skirts the hammock. Built around several ponds in the slough, it is named for the anhinga, a bird that dives and swims underwater for fish. We visited during the end of the dry season when alligators crowded toward the few remaining ponds. One 'gator crossed the trail in front of shocked visitors.

Diana, Peter, Lari, and Alan wheeled with us on the Anhinga Trail. Our visitors were of varying wheelchair abilities and Alan, who is nondisabled, assisted his wife Lari. The group appreciated the level boardwalk, which bridged the ponds and went through dense shrub growth.

As well as being wide and level, both these trails offer a unique feature for visitors with vision impairments. The Anhinga and Gumbo-Limbo trails have textured cue pads along their left sides. A free audiocassette player and tape designed for visitors with vision impairments are available from the information station-bookstore for use on the trails. Call ahead to assure that the tape-player batteries are charged.

Dannie and Doreen, a married couple living in Miami and both blind since birth, joined us another day on the Anhinga Trail. Dannie and Doreen had brought their own smaller, lighter-weight cassette machine, but the tape would not play properly on it. They were familiar with the type of cassette player the park provides but were disappointed at the unit's weight since they had to carry it on the half-mile trail.

Dannie and Doreen could tell by cane use and foot touch on the cue pads where to stop and play the tape about a pertinent area. They were pleased and impressed by the instructive interpretation the tape provided. Often they were able to identify plant and animal life along the trail even without the tape. They knew that a nearby tree was a palmetto by the sound the wind made blowing through its fan-shaped leaves and that a fish was in front of them when it broke the water's surface. As they approached a boardwalk, Danny and Doreen anticipated a swampy area by its smell. They had no difficulty finding the cues for the tape. They were, however, briefly confused at a junction on the trail where a trash can partially blocked the turn. Danny had reviewed the Gumbo-Limbo Trail tape previously and liked it as well.

For those who would like a more isolated, moderately accessible experience, try the old roads in the Royal Palm area, most notably the Long Pine Key Nature Trail in the Pinelands area. This trail is also a possibility for backpacking since the flat trail has two primitive campsites. Long Pine Key Nature Trail is most easily accessed from Long Pine Key Campground. Arrange with the park for barriers across the roads to be removed. A permit is required for overnight backcountry camping. For more information about these less-frequented areas, pick up the free map, "Hiking and Biking Trails of the Pinelands," at the visitor center.

Long Pine Key Campground

The Everglades' flatness is an advantage for accessible camping. There are designated sites in Loop A at both Long Pine Key and Flamingo campgrounds. Almost all campsites at both campgrounds in the park are flat and grassy. No reservations are taken, but ISA-designated sites are held until the end of the day before being filled by other campers.

Long Pine Key is 6 miles from the Main Visitor Center. The designated site is near the fully accessible comfort station in Loop A. Each site is surrounded by low-growing saw palmetto, giving some privacy from other sites.

Except from December to March, camping in the Everglades means camping with mosquitoes. Besides using insect repellent, try bedecking a campsite with incense coils and citronella candles, available at most Florida hardware stores. Wearing light-colored, long-sleeved clothes also helps ward off the buggers. Nylon mesh nets over the head protect the face. An additional strategy is to soak a netted jacket, called a Shoo Bug jacket, with repellent before wearing it. Shoo Bug jackets are available from Cole Outdoor products of America, 801 P Street, Lincoln, NB 68508. Pretest insect repellent for personal sensitivities. Better yet, visit the Everglades only during the months of December to March, when cooler temperatures usually ground the winged warriors.

Pinelands Trail

The half-mile Pinelands Trail, 7 miles from the Main Visitor Center, winds through a portion of Long Pine Key pinelands, the largest remaining stand of Dade County pines. These pines, which have fire-resistant bark, occupy an elevated limestone outcropping. They root in the peat of decomposed plant matter, which collects in solution holes, small shallow pits eaten into the limestone by water and weak acids.

The asphalt trail is a gentle hike. It is bumpy because of roots, which can make wheeling difficult. This moderately accessible trail has no edge protection.

Pa-hay-okee

Pa-hay-okee, from the Seminole tribe name for grassy waters, is a .3-mile boardwalk trail 13 miles from the Main Visitor Center. The trail negotiates a transition zone between the sawgrass prairie and a hammock and has an unusual interpretive approach. Placards quote master poets such as Thoreau, Blake, and Whitman and give information about the sawgrass.

The level trail is fully accessible until midway when a flight of steps leads to an observation tower. Diana, Peter, Lari, and Alan were chagrined when they reached this point. They had to turn back the way they had come on the path, circle around, and wheel on the other half of the trail until stopped again by the observation tower. Thus they missed an opportunity to see the grasslands extending for miles from this high point in the interior of the park.

Mahogany Hammock

Mahogany Hammock is a tropical hardwood hammock featuring the largest mahogany tree in the United States. It is almost midway between the Main Visitor Center and Flamingo Visitor Center on the main park road.

The damp, dark jungle hosts rare paurotis palms and small multicolored Lignus tree snails. The loop trail, less than a half-mile, is boardwalk with railings and benches along the way. It has two moderately steep inclines. To take these inclines downhill, tour the hammock counterclockwise.

Nine Mile Pond

Nine Mile Pond is 27 miles from the Main Visitor Center and 7 miles from Mahogany Hammock. This is the beginning of the mangrove region. Mangroves, noted for growing with aboveground roots in low-oxygen soil with high salinity, create a band of dense growth along the park's coast.

This pond is a trailhead for the Nine Mile Pond Canoe Trail, just part of the 131 miles of established canoe trails in the park. The visitor centers offer complete information about canoeing in the park. Backcountry permits are required for overnight canoe trips. Canoe rentals are available at the Gulf Coast Ranger Station gift shop and at the marina store in Flamingo. A canoe outing could be fun for the family in Florida Bay or the Ten Thousand Islands area.

We were fortunate to have expert canoeist Ted Brodis take us on the pond. Ted is a triple amputee as a result of a Vietnam War injury. Married and the father of two, he enjoys canoeing as a recreational pastime. His skill inspired us.

Ted unlashes his solo canoe from his cartop carrier, lifts the canoe down to a wheeled portage cart, and wheels himself and his canoe down to the water's edge completely unassisted. His wheelchair is adapted for one-armed use. He boards the canoe by transferring from the beach using his upper-body and arm strength. Ted told us that, without legs, his lower center of gravy helps him to balance in the canoe. The only adaptive aid he uses is rubber protection to prevent him from harming the wooden oar handle with his right arm prosthesis. Ted paddles and steers from one side of the canoe, using a C-stroke technique. Ted's canoe skills were impressive, and he shared with us the feelings of independence and self-confidence that canoeing affords him. His disability became superfluous in a canoe.

Ted's wife, Sallie, and author Michael followed Ted as he skillfully led them through the pond populated by fourteen alligators. The amphibians had sought out water during a recent drought and the latter part of the dry season. As the two canoes reached the far end of the pond, an oar slap on the water caused a massive assembly of roseate spoonbills, little blue heron, great white heron, snowy egrets, and white ibis to take flight.

No provisions have been made for accessibility at Nine Mile Pond. The beach-landing area with hard rock shore is below a gentle grassy slope to the pond. Ted notes that this is the only pond shoreline in the Everglades without mud. Many bird-watchers visit the pond at dusk with their binoculars and cameras.

Hells Bay Canoe Trail

Hells Bay Canoe Trail is marked about every 100 yards, but it is muddy and shallow in the first section before it widens out for the rest of its 5.5 miles. Pearl Bay Chickee is little more than halfway along the water trail after Lard Can Chickee. While there are many chickees with wilderness campsites for canoeists, Pearl Bay is the only one that has moderately accessible facilities for people with disabilities. A *chickee* is an open-sided raised platform with a thatched palmetto roof. In the park, chickees are built over water to help campers keep away from bugs. There is a 1-foot-high boat slip built above the water, while other chickee slips are 4-feet above the water. The platform at Pearl Bay is about 25 percent larger than the other campsites on chickees in the park. Stairs lead to the railed platform, and the chemical toilet is in a moderately accessible wooden shed. Assistance is necessary, and permits are required for overnight excursions.

West Lake

West Lake is another canoe trailhead 31 miles from the Main Visitor Center. It also has a .4-mile boardwalk trail over the brackish lake through mangrove trees. The mangroves nurture many crustaceans and fish such as blue crab, stone crab, spiny lobster, shrimp, snapper, and mullet. The parking lot has ISA-designated spaces; fully accessible restrooms are next to the boat launch ramp. Biting insects will be plentiful except in the coolest months of December through March.

Snake Bight

The old road to Snake Bight goes through a tropical hardwood hammock culminating at a boardwalk excellent for bird-watching. This moderately accessible 1.6-mile trail may require thick wheelchair tires and/or assistance. The surface will be soft in the rain, and mosquitoes abound April through November.

Bear Lake

The turnoff to Bear Lake is less than a mile from Flamingo Visitor Center and approximately 37 miles from the Main

Visitor Center. The day we arrived in Everglades National Park, rangers discovered a crocodile nest in the middle of the old roadbed to Bear Lake. They closed the road and trail to protect this rare and endangered reptile. Reports are that, when not a crocodile nursery, this 1.6-mile trail (one way) is a fully accessible route to fish or bird-watch at Bear Lake. The road and trail parallel a wilderness canoe trail.

Flamingo

The Flamingo section of the Everglades is at the end of the main park road, 38 miles from the Main Visitor Center. Flamingo is the most developed area in the park, with lodging and a marina, store, gas station, visitor center, restaurant, and campground, all accessible.

Unfortunately, we made the mistake of visiting Flamingo at the end of April when the mosquitoes were busy attacking any warm-blooded being. Mosquitoes can be intolerable during the warm, wet summer season (April through November). Call ahead since conditions vary with rainfall, temperature, and other environmental factors.

Flamingo Visitor Center is on the moderately accessible second level of a building complex shared with a gift shop, lounge, restaurant, and grill. Visitors with mobility impairments may require assistance up a ramp with a 10 percent grade (1:8 slope) to the visitor center and restaurant. The visitor center has a ranger information desk, a small museum with exhibits, and an audio diorama. The audio diorama helps anyone to learn more about the park. Scripts to the audio diorama are available for visitors with hearing impairments. All other facilities on the second level are fully accessible. Restrooms are located near the restaurant. There is a lowered telescope in the breezeway.

The Guy Bradley Trail is a fully accessible 1-mile shortcut from the visitor center to the amphitheater. Wildlife on this trail, which traces Florida Bay, include rabbits, pelicans, and ibises.

For those who are able to climb steps to board a tram, the Wilderness Tour tram leaves from the visitor center. There is no room on board to sit in a wheelchair. Tours are available in winter months (December to March) only.

The Florida Bay boat tours leave from the marina (weather permitting) and are excellent for everyone, including children and seniors, wanting to experience marine life. The boat is moderately accessible, depending on tide height, and has a fully accessible head. The 1½-hour cruise takes passengers out on Florida Bay for a perspective of the Everglades' open-bay regions. We saw bottlenose dolphins, brown pelicans, and cormorants.

The tour is operated by TW Recreational Services; we recommend calling ahead for reservations and assistance (305-253-2241). TW Recreational Services will assist persons with disabilities in boarding. The same company also operates the Whitewater Bay cruise on a different boat, not accessible to everyone who uses a wheelchair.

The marina area has a gas station and moderately accessible store for food, convenience items, canoe rentals, boat tickets, and a telephone.

TW Recreational Services provides lodging in the area, including a motel with a swimming pool and cottages, two of them — O and P — fully accessible. O and P sleep four persons each and can be rented together or separately. They have kitchenettes, wide doors, and air-conditioning, and wide doors connecting them can be opened if desired. O has a tub with grab bars, and P has a shower stall with a seat, grab bars, and a 4-inch step.

When we arrived at our cottage each evening, we gathered everything we needed for the night from our van and made a mad dash to the door, trying to shut out the bloodthirsty pests. In spite of our speed and repellents, we always received some bites.

Between the cottages and the campground is Eco Pond, a former waste-water treatment pool that now offers the best bird show in town, according to park naturalists. An observation deck up a flight of stairs completely blocks the view of the bird show for anyone unable to gain access to the deck. There is a moderately accessible quarter-mile grassy trail around the pond, which is good for bird-watching in the surrounding vegetation December through March. Thick wheelchair tires and/or assistance are strongly recommended.

Flamingo Campground, about a mile past the visitor center, is flat, grassy, and open throughout. Loop A has a designated site near a fully accessible unisex comfort station complete with cold-water shower. No reservations are taken, but the ISA-designated site is held until the end of the day, when other campers may occupy it.

Flamingo Amphitheater, between the cottages and the campground, is fully accessible. It is situated on a picturesque spot on Florida Bay. The amphitheater is on the Guy Bradley Trail from the visitor center.

The Coastal Prairie Trail begins at Loop C of the campground. This is a moderately accessible 7.5-mile one-way trail. Thick wheelchair tires and/or assistance are recommended on this old road. Be on guard; this is another habitat where mosquitoes are plentiful.

Everglades National Park is today an extremely fragile environment. Although the 1.4 million acres of the Everglades are surrounded by water, fresh water is at a premium, and human activity threatens the precarious balance of life that the park now nurtures. The amount of water taken from Lake Okeechobee by the cities and farms to the north and east of the park lower freshwater resources for the Everglades.

In one step to further protect the Everglades, Congress has appropriated monies to expand the eastern boundaries of the park. The addition of 110,000 acres will protect a vital wetland habitat crucial to wading bird life. If fresh water becomes too scarce, the sawgrass marshes will dry up and be less resistant to fire. Humans may forever alter the ecological balance achieved over the last ten thousand years.

Worth a Visit

Biscayne National Park is an underwater park 26 miles east of the Everglades' Main Visitor Center. A glass-bottom boat tour (Biscayne Aqua-Center, 305-247-2400) leads visitors on a discovery of brain coral, sponges, rays, parrot fish, turtles, and other underwater wildlife in the Florida Keys. The boat has two steps. There is also a dive boat tour. Tour personnel will assist persons with physical impairments to board, but there is no wheelchair lock-down.

(See *At a Glance: East and Midwest Region.*)

GRAND TETON
NATIONAL PARK

P.O. Drawer 170
Moose, WY 83012
Information: 307-733-2880
Recorded Information: 307-733-2220
TDD: 307-733-2053

When glaciers receded from northwest Wyoming about ten thousand to fifteen thousand years ago, the chiseled, scenic Teton Range remained. Today, this is one of the most awesome ranges of mountains in North America and the youngest of the Rockies. Formed by a sharp, tilting uplift along a geologic fault, these steep, jagged pinnacles rise more than an exalted mile above the valley floor of Jackson Hole.

The glaciers dumped mixed assortments of rock on the valley's floor, forming morainal dams that created the park's piedmont lakes: Jackson, Leigh, Jenny, Taggart, Bradley, and Phelps. The Snake River feeds Jackson Lake with melted snowpack accumulated from the Teton Range. These lakes sometimes act like mirrors, reflecting snow-capped mountains that border them.

Grand Teton's beauty attracts mountain climbers, photographers, hikers, boaters, and visitors interested in sport fishing. Many scenic spots, sports, and activities are accessible to persons with disabilities. Elevations on park roads range from 6,354 feet near the south entrance to 7,593 feet on Signal Mountain Road. Persons with respiratory and/or cardiovascular problems should consult with a physician before visiting areas at these altitudes. The top of Grand Teton Peak, at 13,770 feet, is the park's highest point.

Grand Teton National Park is in northwestern Wyoming, 7 miles south of Yellowstone National Park's south entrance and 5 miles from Jackson, Wyoming, on the John D. Rockefeller, Jr. Memorial Parkway. The parkway runs north-south from West Thumb in Yellowstone to the south entrance of Grand Teton National Park. The Teton Park Road is a loop through the central part of the Jackson Hole valley along the base of the Teton Range extending from Moran Junction to Moose Junction.

Moose, pronghorn, bighorn sheep, bison, black bears, mule deer, and coyotes are among the species of large mammals in the park. Many elk can also be spotted in Grand Teton. Bald eagles and ospreys glide above the rivers and creeks in search of fish and small rodents.

Pioneering French trappers called these imposing, pointy peaks "les Trois Tetons" (the three breasts). Trappers and explorers, however, were not the first visitors. Evidence of Native American presence in the shadow of the Tetons reveals an 8,000-year history of human activity in the area.

Mountain men called isolated high-mountain valleys "holes." The valley along the eastern base of the Teton Range is named Jackson Hole, after David Jackson, one of the foremost American trappers of the late 1820s and early 1830s.

Establishment of the park was fraught with controversy. Early proposals to add the Tetons to Yellowstone National Park failed. The main portion of the Teton Range and the glacial lakes at the base of the mountains became Grand Teton National Park in 1929. The valley, however, was not included.

Horace Albright, superintendent of Yellowstone, encouraged John D. Rockefeller, Jr. to purchase land in Jackson Hole for later inclusion in Grand Teton National Park. Local cattle and dude ranchers opposed the addition, however, until a compromise was reached after World War II. Rockefeller's gift was accepted and Jackson Hole added to the park in 1950. One of the results of that compromise provided Grand Teton with the only airport in a U.S. National Park.

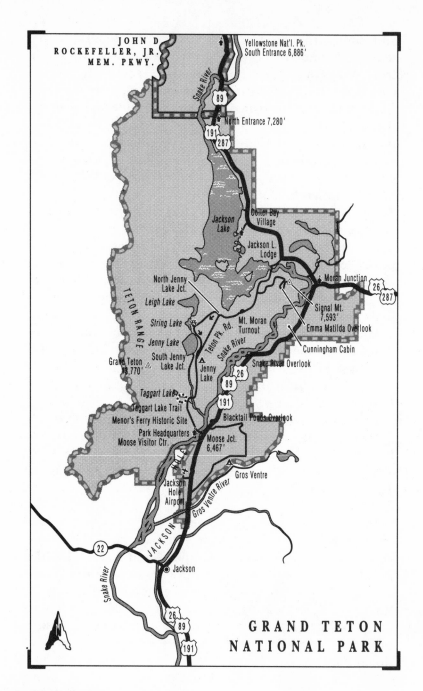

JOHN D
ROCKEFELLER, JR.
MEM. PKWY.

Yellowstone Nat'l. Pk.
South Entrance 6,886'

Snake River

89

North Entrance 7,280'

191
287

Jackson
Lake

Colter Bay
Village

Jackson L.
Lodge

North Jenny
Lake Jct.

Moran Junction

26
287

Leigh Lake

Signal Mt.
7,593'

TETON RANGE

String Lake

Mt. Moran
Turnout

Emma Matilda Overlook

Teton Pk. Rd.

Snake River

Cunningham Cabin

Jenny Lake

Grand Teton
13,770'

South Jenny
Lake Jct.

Jenny
Lake

Snake River Overlook

26
89
191

Taggart Lake

Taggart Lake Trail

Menor's Ferry Historic Site

Blacktail Ponds Overlook

Park Headquarters
Moose Visitor Ctr.

Moose Jct.
6,467'

Jackson
Hole
Airport

Gros Ventre

Gros Ventre River

JACKSON

22

Snake River

Jackson

26
89
191

N

GRAND TETON
NATIONAL PARK

Colter Bay

We entered Grand Teton from Yellowstone on a brisk autumn day. The brilliant oranges and yellows of aspen and willow satisfied our desire to see fall colors.

At our first stop at Colter Bay Village on Jackson Lake (6,772 feet), 16 miles from the north entrance, we found restaurants, lodging, stores, showers, trails and a marina, laundromat, service station, post office, picnic area, horse rental, and visitor center. The visitor center and services are open generally from mid-May to late September. Unfortunately, access was minimal, but a trail by the lake and parts of the Colter Bay Visitor Center were accessible and worthwhile.

The Colter Bay Visitor Center has a concrete ramp at the south end of the building near the moderately accessible restrooms. The visitor center is moderately accessible, but assistance is recommended to enter both the top main floor and the Native American Museum interpretive level enterable from the outside. Those with mobility problems may need assistance at the bookstore and information desk, both high. A park orientation presentation is fully accessible to persons with mobility problems. A large-print script accompanies the presentation for those with hearing and moderate vision impairments. An audiotape with narrative description for persons with vision impairments is available. Park information in Braille can be found at the information desk. The park newspaper, the *Teewinot,* gives current information about accessible ranger-led activities.

The Lakeshore Foot Trail begins north of the visitor center just off a concrete path leading toward the lake. Follow signs to the amphitheater and continue down the moderately steep asphalt path to the lake. Lakeshore Foot Trail begins near the marina and becomes a dirt path around a peninsula. The trail has roots and cross slope, but we spent a few hours enjoying the lake scenery on this 1.5-mile round-trip. Assistance is recommended.

Colter Bay Amphitheater, just north of the visitor center,

is fully accessible for those with mobility problems. Colter Bay Campground currently has no designated accessible sites, and the comfort stations have steps. Finding no other facilities without significant barriers at Colter Bay, we headed to Jackson Lake Lodge area.

Jackson Lake Lodge

Jackson Lake Lodge (6,838 feet), 5 miles south on the John D. Rockefeller, Jr. Memorial Parkway, is a full-service resort with horses, float trips, and gift and apparel shops and a restaurant, grill, lounge, beauty shop, swimming pool, and gas station. There are some fully accessible rooms. The Mural Room restaurant is accessible by elevator. The public restrooms are moderately accessible. Jackson Lake Lodge is memorable for spectacular views across the lake to the Teton Range.

Signal Mountain

Signal Mountain Road turnoff is 4 miles south of Jackson Lake Lodge and 3 miles from Jackson Lake Junction on the Teton Park Road. The road took us up through aspen and pine forest. We parked our van and took a paved, short but steep, moderately accessible trail to Jackson Point. We were rewarded with a grand view of the Teton Range. Emma Matilda Overlook (7,593 feet) is at the end of the 5-mile Signal Mountain Road. The trail is very steep and unprotected. Wendy did not take this one. The view is a 360-degree panorama of Jackson Hole.

The Signal Mountain area has a hilly campground near the lake with no accesible comfort stations. The last of three loops has camping possibilities for people with mobility problems, although assistance may be required. The lodge has a ramped entrance and a guest room that is moderately accessible. Signal Mountain Restaurant is fully accessible and offers windowed views of the Tetons across Jackson Lake.

The gift shop and restrooms are also fully accessible. Mt. Moran Turnout, between Signal Mountain Road and Jenny Lake, is a splendid place from which to view the Tetons at sunset or observe elk.

Jenny Lake

Four miles south of Signal Mountain at North Jenny Lake Junction we chose the one-way road to Jenny Lake (6,783 feet). We first came to Cathedral Group Scenic Turnout for a look into a few canyons that penetrate the Tetons. We turned right to the String Lake picnic area. We were told that String Lake Trail may be too sandy for wheelchair users to enjoy. We understand a fully accessible trail will be built here in the future.

Jenny Lake Campground, a half-mile south of String Lake, has flat sites (none ISA designated), and the female's comfort station in a renovated historic log cabin is moderately accessible. The male's comfort station is scheduled to be modified soon. The campground closes for the winter in late September. Snowmobiles and snow coaches are allowed on park roads, and Jenny Lake is a park-authorized winter visitor destination. The nationally known landscape painter Harrison Crandall homesteaded at Jenny Lake. His log cabin studio still stands near the campground.

Jenny Lake has a fully accessible store, but the ranger station and lodge have no provisions for wheelchair use. The restaurant at Jenny Lake is fully accessible. The sandy social trails near the lake's edge are being paved, with completion scheduled in 1993. Boat service is available for tours on the lake. The concessionaire will assist persons boarding the boat. For information, call 307-733-2703.

Taggart Lake Trail

At South Jenny Lake Junction, we rejoined the Teton Park Road and headed for Taggart Lake. We were told the trail here is accessible, but construction kept Wendy from exploring it. Michael found Taggart Lake Trail a level path through open meadow to a moraine where a fire had burned in 1985. An interpretive brochure describes the forest-fire regrowth area. Wheelchair users will find it next to impossible to reach the lake, but the first half-mile of the trail is fully accessible.

Menor's Ferry

Menor's Ferry Historic District on the Snake River has a current-operated river ferry, a natural history museum, historic vehicles, and Menor's and Noble cabins. These turn-of-the-century buildings were restored in 1949, and a replica of the ferry was constructed in 1990. The trail to Menor's Ferry begins 3.5 miles south of Taggart Lake parking area at the Chapel of the Transfiguration parking lot. The path is asphalt and dirt with some steep sections. Assistance may be needed. All cabins have steps to the porches, thresholds, and narrow doors.

Moose Village

The Moose Visitor Center and park headquarters are near the southern junction of Teton Park Road and the John D. Rockefeller, Jr. Memorial Parkway. The Moose Visitor Center has ISA-designated spaces, ramped curb cuts, and flat entry. The center has a fully accessible unisex restroom with twenty-four-hour access from outside. The exhibits and most of the bookstore are fully accessible. Park personnel will assist with books and information. The information desk, however, is too high for wheelchair users and children. Park brochures and maps are available at the desk. A park orientation presentation is fully accessible to those with mobility problems. There is a large-print script to accompany the presentation for those with hearing impairments. Park information in Braille and an audiotape with narrative description for persons with vision impairments is available at the information desk. Across the road from the visitor center is a store, gasoline station, and post office.

Dornan's is a half-mile east of the visitor center across the Snake River. The area has canoe rentals and a well-stocked grocery and deli, bar that serves hot lunches during off-season, liquor store, and gift shop, all moderately or fully accessible. In fact, if you have a yen for cornish game hen, fresh cheeses, and health-food items we recommend this as an oasis. A mountaineering shop and a bicycle rental and repair shop are also there, but persons with mobility problems may require assistance up a couple of high steps to the level boardwalk in front of them.

Blacktail Ponds

From Moose Village Junction, we turned north on the John D. Rockefeller, Jr. Memorial Parkway (also known locally as the Outer Highway) to explore the east side of Grand Teton. After 2 miles, we stopped at Blacktail Ponds Overlook for a fully accessible view looking over a marsh. A placard here describes the local history.

Snake River Overlook

Six miles further north is another fully accessible overlook, Snake River. This is one of the views for which Grand Teton National Park is best known: the spectacular range of peaks, Jackson Hole, and the Snake River. Ansel Adams photographed from near this point, and a placard here is etched from one of his works.

Cunningham Cabin

A vivid reminder of early homesteading in this region is found at Cunningham Cabin, 4 miles from Snake River Overlook and 7 miles south of Moran Junction. Pierce and

Margaret Cunningham, one of the first families to settle in the northern part of the valley, established this homestead in 1890.

This well-preserved cabin is a realistic example of nineteenth-century frontier life, once the access-conscious visitor gets past the challenging buck and rail fence at the entrance to the former ranch. The entry is a historically authentic trap to deter cattle from exiting. It can also trap wheelchair users. Wendy was able to power around the extremely tight turn with minimal assistance. On the other side of the fence, we went back in time.

The cabin has flat access to the low windows of the two rooms joined by a covered veranda in this traditional "dog-trot" construction of the early homesteading days. We could almost see the Cunninghams preparing food on one side of the cabin and retiring to the other for bedroom and living quarters. Narrow doors and raised thresholds prevent wheelchairs from getting into the rooms. A narrow, three-quarter-mile trail with rocks and cross slope circles the cabin. In 1895, this cabin became a barn and blacksmith shop.

To help them grow crops in the poor, dry, rocky soil, the Cunninghams built irrigation ditches. These remain today. Narrow bridges, possibly hazardous to wheelchair users or those with vision impairments, cross the irrigation ditches. Assistance may be useful in this area.

Severe winters contributed to the difficulty of maintaining a profitable ranch here, and the Cunninghams sold their property in 1928. Other ranchers in Jackson Hole began promoting the recreation and scenery of the area and developed a popular dude-ranch industry. Many of the dude ranchers proved to be strong supporters for the initial establishment of Grand Teton National Park in 1929. Later, some opposed the addition of Jackson Hole.

Less well preserved than Cunningham Cabin and not as accessible, Pfeiffer Homestead is another historic building located 5 miles north of Kelly, a small town near the eastern boundary of the park.

Gros Ventre Campground

The most accessible campground at Grand Teton National Park is Gros Ventre (pronounced grow-vont), named after the Native American tribe. Located 10 miles from Moose Village off the John D. Rockefeller, Jr. Memorial Parkway, Gros Ventre is a wooded campground with large flat sites and a fully accessible comfort station in Loop D.

We were there in late autumn when the changing leaves of the black cottonwood cast an orange tint throughout the area. As campfires reached toward the fall moon, we smelled the strong perfume of sage. This most accommodating campground in the southern section of Grand Teton can serve as a base from which to tour the entire park. The amphitheater is fully accessible.

Jackson Hole Airport, the only commercial airport in a national park, is between the southern park boundary and Moose Village. Visitors are invited during two weekends in April to witness the Grouse Strut. This fully accessible event is held on the airport runway where, snow permitting, the grouse engage in their annual mating ritual. Check with park rangers for dates.

Everywhere in the park, the Tetons are an awesome presence. Mountaineers relish the challenge of using rope, piton, and carabiner to ascend these peaks. Luckily, there are also many ways for those wanting easily accessible visits to enjoy the Tetons. This park offers opportunities for visitors of all abilities to enjoy nature. The clouds, glaciers, and light always change as they play among the peaks, the dynamic Teton Mountains.

(See *At a Glance: Rocky Mountains and Great Plains Region.*)

HAWAII VOLCANOES NATIONAL PARK

Hawaii Volcanoes National Park, HI 96718
Information: 808-967-7311
Eruption Information: 808-967-7977

Ancient Hawaiian myth recounts how Pele, the goddess of volcanoes and fire, built the chain of Pacific volcanic islands known as Hawaii. The story describes Pele's older sister, Na Maka o Kaha'i, the goddess of the sea, chasing Pele from volcano to volcano. Continuously in search of refuge, Pele created sixteen fiery volcanoes forming the eight Hawaiian islands, with the ninth one in process.

Hawaii Volcanoes National Park preserves Pele's present refuge on the big island of Hawaii, including Mauna Loa summit and its northeast slope, the Kilauea Caldera, the Southwest and East rift zones, and some of the recent lava flows to the ocean. The volcanoes are active yet surprisingly accessible to everyone for observation. The park's entrance is off Hawaii Route 11, 29 miles from Hilo.

Modern scientific explanation of the islands' formation parallels the myth of Pele. Hawaii sits in the middle of the Pacific plate, one of the tectonic plates into which geologists divide Earth's crust. The islands of Hawaii formed over a relatively stationary hot spot under the middle of the plate. This hot spot sends a plume of molten rock, the source of Hawaii's volcanoes, welling up through Earth's thin crust.

The Pacific plate moves north 2 to 4 inches per year. Plate movement alters the magma flow from the stationary hot spot to a volcano. As the plate moves over millions of years, molten lava continues to pour, but at a new point on the ocean floor. This causes the old volcano to die and a new island to form south of the previous volcano. Kauai, Pele's legendary first home, has rocks 5 million to 6 million years old. The oldest rocks on the big island, Hawaii, are less than a million years old.

The five great volcanoes of Pele's big island sanctuary on Hawaii probably began forming under the sea 6 million years ago. Mauna Kea, Mauna Loa, Kilauea, Hualalai, and Kohala are shield volcanoes. Mauna Loa and Kilauea have rolling plateaus bordering cliff-bounded calderas. A caldera is formed by violent collapses of earth a few hundred feet at a time within the crater. Geologists believe this occurs when flows of molten rock leave a void under the volcano so that the summit is unable to support its own weight. Kilauea Caldera is 2 to 3 miles wide and about 400 feet deep.

We set out for our volcano journey not expecting to see much of the volcano nor its geologic activity. Instead, we met with a series of delightful surprises. Our expedition to Hawaii Volcanoes National Park, including volcanic and rainforest terrain, turned out to be an inspiring sojourn. Hiking active volcanic areas could seem foreboding to even the most adventurous. Hawaii Volcanoes, however, welcomes visitors even as its volcanoes spew molten lava from the Earth at the various rift zones. Remarkably, individuals with disabilities, families with young children, seniors, or those who don't want to hike too hard can enjoy such fascinating and potentially dangerous terrain. For us, being able to get close to an active volcano by wheelchair was a welcome surprise. For that matter, having access to a volcano and even hiking across the crater, as many do, is a gift for everyone.

Kilauea Visitor Center and Volcano House

Kilauea Visitor Center is wheelchair accessible and houses exhibits about the volcanoes, a film on the volcanoes' geology, updates on current volcanic activity, and fully accessible bathrooms. The park plans to remodel the visitor center, changing it into a nature center and improving access to the facility. The information/sales desk is currently too high

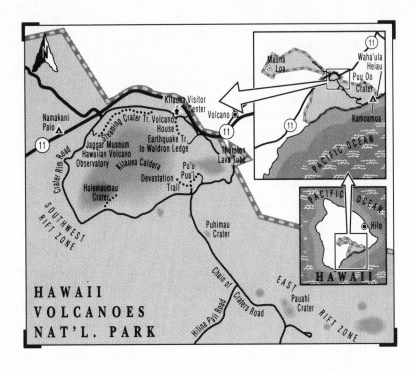

for wheelchair users, and there are no provisions for visitors with vision or hearing impairments.

Across from Kilauea Visitor Center along a short trail is the Volcano House with a wheelchair-accessible dining hall offering breakfast, lunch, and dinner and with a fully accessible snack bar, gift shop, and lowered telephone. The restrooms are fully accessible. The dining hall's top floor is wheelchair accessible and features a floor-to-ceiling glass wall running the room's length and facing breathtaking Kilauea Crater. A fully accessible bar/lounge also has a magnificent crater view from a half-wall picture window.

The Volcano House has one specially designed guest room for individuals with disabilities. Reservations for the lodge can be made by writing P.O. Box 53, Hawaii Volcanoes National Park, HI 96718, or phoning 808-967-7321.

A ranger told us that too many people visit the park only briefly, stopping for the buffet lunch at the Volcano House and a quick peek at the crater. Think of this as only the beginning. Hawaii Volcanoes National Park offers many lookout points; drive to them and then easily walk or wheel to vistas along Crater Rim Drive and Chain of Craters Road. And while accessibility seems on first look to be limited at this park, the concentration on environmental preservation has resulted in some excellent access benefits like boardwalks and trails for experiencing this active volcanic wonder up close.

Waldron Ledge

A violent earthquake, with its epicenter where Kilauea and Mauna Loa abut, shook all the islands in 1983. Portions of the caldera's rim toppled into the Kilauea Caldera, destroying parts of Crater Rim Drive. Today the fully accessible Earthquake Trail to Waldron Ledge, starting near the Volcano House, is a .6-mile one-way excursion. It follows the remaining blacktopped portions of the road, complete with yellow dividing lines uplifted and shifted by the quake, offering views over the jagged edge where the road fell into the caldera. Molasses grass, imported by big-island ranchers for cattle grazing, is encroaching on the asphalt and creating a fire hazard to the park. Waldron Ledge, once a popular lookout, now feels ghostly with its abandoned speed limit signs and empty parking spaces. The view of the crater from the overlook is breathtaking and all the more powerful amidst this quiet desolation.

Jaggar Museum

Thomas A. Jaggar Memorial Museum has the park's finest exhibits on volcanology, natural history, the mythology of Pele, and paintings by noted Hawaiian artist Herb Kane.

Perched at the edge of Kilauea Crater 2.5 miles from Kilauea Visitor Center, Jaggar Museum is adjacent to the Hawaiian Volcano Observatory.

The museum has a level entrance through double doors and is fully accessible throughout. There are fully accessible restrooms and a lowered telephone. The bookstore sales desk is too high for adequate wheelchair use. A roving ranger answers visitors' questions and offers interpretive information. A guide to museum exhibits is available.

A 9½-minute captioned video with large–print script chronicles the history of the park's volcanic eruptions. From behind a glass wall, the museum's instrument room displays seven of the Hawaiian Volcano Observatory's seismographs measuring earthquakes, including a long period tiltmeter, able to record Earth activity worldwide.

Portions of the Steaming Crater Trail are moderately accessible. Steaming Bluff Overlook, a quarter mile from the parking lot, is paved and fully accessible. The next 2 miles along the edge of Kilauea Caldera to the Jaggar Museum are over gravel and may require some assistance.

Halemaumau Crater

We arrived at Halemaumau Crater, a center of Kilauea's volcanic activity, 2.5. miles from Jaggar Museum counterclockwise around the Crater Rim Drive. Tall curls of steam reach high into the air, seeming to suggest that another eruption is imminent. But Halemaumau has been boasting Pele's presence in this way for years.

The moderately accessible trail to a thrilling viewpoint over the steaming crater is rocky but not very steep. It can be negotiated by wheels with some difficulty, but wheelchair users may need assistance. Anyone with respiratory and/or cardiovascular problems needs to avoid this area because of the sulfur dioxide gases emitted in the area and when driving by this area should close car windows and vents until past the parking lot.

Devastation Trail and Pu'u Pua'i

Devastation Trail and Pu'u Pua'i Overlook parking lots are 2 miles further along Crater Rim Drive. Chief Park Ranger Jim Martin suggested we survey this trail, although it is not regarded as fully accessible for visitors with disabilities. We found it a remarkable experience. A parking lot at either end of the trail allows for a round-trip excursion or for a driver to pick up visitors after a one-way hike.

Kilauea Iki crater spattered lava throughout this area in 1959, forming Pu'u Pua'i. Cinder and pumice blanketed the lush rainforest.

Two kinds of lava are found in the park: *pahoehoe* and *a'a.* At Pu'u Pua'i Overlook, the lava is pahoehoe, which solidifies into a black, shiny, smooth surface often interrupted by billowy, wrinkled, coiled shapes. A'a, which pahoehoe can become during a flow, solidifies as small, rough chunks of black rock.

The Devastation Trail is a well-kept boardwalk built to allow the destroyed area to regenerate undisturbed while conservation experts study it. Along the trail, piles of black rock and burned stumps of ohia trees suddenly replace trees and greenery. Many airborne roots are now visible as uplifted trees struggle for renewed life. This devastated area experiencing regrowth will fascinate anyone.

The boardwalk has some modest inclines, and wheelchair users should note that the trail slants more downhill in the direction from the Pu'u Pua'i Overlook parking lot to the Devastation Trail parking area. A companion to a wheelchair user could be of assistance since there are guardrails only at the interpretive placards.

Thurston Lava Tube

Prior to the Kilauea Caldera collapse in 1790, lava flowed from the crater toward Hilo Bay. Thurston Tube formed five hundred years ago when lava cooled and hardened around the edges of the molten flow, creating a tunnel beneath the solidified top. As the eruption subsided, the hot center drained from the tunnel, forming what is known as a lava tube.

Thurston Lava Tube is 1.25 miles from Pu'u Pua'i Overlook. Three sets of stairs lead down into a small crater filled with a dense fern forest inhabited by native Hawaiian birds. After the stairs, the trail is a short level asphalt paved path to the lava tube entrance. Inside the tube the path is damp and rough in places. Ohia tree roots descend to the tunnel, and in some spots the ceiling is low. The ascent from the lava tube is up two flights of stairs. A fairly level trail through the rainforest returns to the parking lot.

We learned of several wheelchair users who had entered the tube at the exit's stairs. They had either taken the steps on their derrières or had nondisabled assistance. Once in the tube, they were able to wheel through the tunnel to the crater fern forest and return the same way they came.

Namakani Paio Campground

Near the Kilauea Caldera area is Namakani Paio Campground, just off Hawaii Route 11, 3 miles from Kilauea Entrance Station. The campground is flat and has a lowered telephone, but the toilets have narrow doorways with a step. Inexpensive primitive cabins are also available. They have a step at the entrances, sleep four, and come with bed linens, towels, soap, blankets, and an outdoor barbecue. Bring an extra blanket or sleeping bag. Inquire about cabins at Volcano House.

Chain of Craters Road

Chain of Craters Road starts at Crater Rim Drive across from the Devastation Trail parking lot. Neither water nor gasoline is available on this road to Hawaii's south coast. We highly recommend *Road Guide to Hawaii Volcanoes National Park,* by Barbara and Robert Decker, available at park booksales areas.

Chain of Craters Road is a 21-mile drive with overlooks and flat pullouts along a series of craters. One mile from its beginning, Puhimau Crater on the left side of the road has a moderately accessible overlook via a short, asphalt trail.

The Hilina Pali Road turns off at the 2.25-mile point on the Chain of Craters Road. Hilina Pali (*pali* are cliffs) looks over the big island's south coast from 2,000 feet above the water. The 9-mile side road ends at a moderately accessible picnic shelter with a table. Assistance may be needed on a steep ramp to the shelter.

A mile further on the Chain of Craters Road from the Hilina Pali Road turnoff, Pauahi Crater affords an opportunity to view the long, deep crater caused by collapse after magma drained from beneath the cooled lava surface. The rim is accessible by an asphalt trail, but a moderately steep ramp may require assistance.

The scenery on Chain of Craters Road alternates between

rainforest and barren lava flows. Before reaching the coast, the road traverses several recent lava flows dating from 1969 to 1974. The Pu'u Loa Petroglyphs, carved in the pahoehoe lava by early Hawaiians, are associated with an old custom. Scoops were cut in the rock, and a newborn's *piko,* or umbilical cord portion, would be placed in the hole and covered by a rock. The .7-mile trail, too narrow for wheelchairs, is over pahoehoe lava to a short circular boardwalk protecting the brittle carvings.

Kamoamoa Campground

Kamoamoa Campground, on the Chain of Craters Road between Pu'u Loa Petroglyphs and the road's end, has become more popular since the 1986 eruptions because it is now closer to the recent lava flows than any other campground. No special provisions for people with disabilities have been made. The picnic area in the coconut grove at the edge of the beach may be accessible to wheelchair users with assistance. Pit toilets are not modified.

Puu Oo Crater

New volcanic fountain activity began in the Kilauea East Rift Zone in January 1983. That same year, in June, Puu Oo started cone building with 800- to 1,500-foot spouts of white hot lava shooting upward. In November 1986, rivers of yellow, orange, and red lava from Kupaianaha lava lake flowed to the coast, covering the road between Waha'ula and Kalapana.

Hawaii Volcanoes National Park has one of the oldest and most significant *heiaus* (temples) on the Hawaiian Islands. Waha'ula Heiau (pronounced "hay ou") stands 7.5 miles from Pu'u Loa Petroglyphs on the Chain of Craters Road. Constructed in the thirteenth century, Waha'ula Heiau, the temple of the red-mouth, was the site for the ritual of human sacrifice.

When we visited Hawaii Volcanoes, the Waha'ula Visitor

Center stood between the Chain of Craters Road and the Waha'ula Heiau. On June 22, 1989, lava flows from Kupaianaha lava lake consumed the visitor center. Recent lava flows buried ten thousand to thirteen thousand archeological sites, including the village of Ka'ili'ili and the stone walls of Pou Pou. But Pele, in her mysterious way, spared Waha'ula Heiau. Today the visitor center and access to the temple exist no more.

A mobile home at the end of the road temporarily serves as a visitor center. The mobile home is up a few steps, but the rangers will come outside to assist with information if needed. Nearby vault toilets may be difficult for those with mobility problems. A rugged, marked 1.0- to 1.5-mile trail over new pahoehoe goes to the edge of molten lava. The trail markers are moved as the lava flow changes. Uneven surfaces may be traversed with assistance.

Flowing molten lava may also be seen on the other side of the flow from Waha'ula at Highway 130's end in Kalapana. By day, steam rises from the ocean where the molten rock meets the water. By night, the lava glows red as it moves into the ocean, extending Pele's island home.

While driving along the island's south shore, visitors can see steam rising southeast of the beaches. This is the site of what in ten thousand years or so may be Hawaii's newest island, Loihi, now 3,000 feet underwater and about 20 miles offshore. Pele, the goddess of fire, is evidently preparing her next refuge.

Worth a Visit

Haleakala National Park is a short flight away on the island of Maui. Haleakala is a dormant volcano that last had volcanic activity in 1790. The park has a fully accessible visitor center with observation windows overlooking the crater, a large relief map, which is wheelchair accessible, and interpretive boards mounted overhead detailing Haleakala's geologic story. The park has one moderately accessible trail, the quarter-mile Hosmer Grove Nature Trail. It is rocky, slippery, and rooty, and wheelchair users should be athletic or have assistance on it. Horseback rides into the crater are available.

For more information, see *Hawaii (Big Island) Travelers Guide for Handicapped Persons,* available from Commission on the Handicapped, Old Federal Building, 355 Merchant Street, No. 215, Honolulu, HI 96813; 808-548-7606.

(See *At a Glance: Alaska and Hawaii.*)

MESA VERDE
NATIONAL PARK
Mesa Verde National Park, CO 81330
Information: 303-529-4465

W hen the Anasazi abandoned their cliff dwellings in southwestern Colorado, they left remnants of a culture fascinating to casual visitors and archeologists alike. At Mesa Verde, thousands of ruins and artifacts of the Anasazi (a Navajo expression for "the ancient ones" or "my ancient enemies") are found. This pre-Columbian Stone Age culture inhabited a large area in the southwest United States extending from the Rio Grande River Valley in northern New Mexico and southern Colorado to the Colorado River in Arizona and Utah. A culturally distinct group of these innovative builders, farmers, and pottery makers lived in what is now Mesa Verde National Park from approximately A.D. 550 to A.D. 1300.

While many cliff houses required ladders for entry and took advantage of the rough terrain for protection, today accessible opportunities are available for visitors of all abilities. Wheelchair users, families with young children, and seniors will find many excavated, preserved, and restored ruins accessible for exploration. Binoculars or telephoto lenses can help visitors view ruins from overlooks. The park's "A Guide to Accessibility at Mesa Verde National Park" brochure is available at Far View Visitor Center and Chapin Mesa Museum.

Virginia McClurg, a founder of the Colorado Cliff Dwellers Association, first rented rights from the Native American Weminuche Ute tribe to protect the Anasazi ruins from pot hunters. Mesa Verde National Park was established by Congress in 1906 to preserve the dense concentration of ruins from destruction by pot hunters and collectors of highly prized Anasazi artifacts.

In 1915, Mesa Verde became the first park to introduce evening campfires with interpretive programs. This led to the first National Park Service museum and ranger-guided tours focusing on the cultural and historical significance of a national park.

The first Anasazi in the Southwest were of the Early Basketmaker Period, which began around A.D. 1 and lasted until about A.D. 450. These people began about A.D. 55 to build small groups of pithouse dwellings, semisubterranean homes, in what is now Mesa Verde National Park. The pithouses were typical of structures built during the Modified Basketmaker period, which continued until approximately A.D. 750. In addition to hunting and gathering food, the Anasazi of this period grew agricultural crops of corn, beans, and squash. Pottery was introduced, altering food preparation and dietary habits.

The Developmental Pueblo Period between A.D. 750 and A.D. 1100 marked a time of significant advances in building techniques and farming methods. Pottery was refined. From the pithouse evolved both new multistory stonework structures above ground for living, working, and food storage, and the kiva, an underground chamber believed to be used for clan and tribal rituals. During this time, dwellings were built on top of the mesas or in wide valleys. Reservoirs and farming terraces were built, possibly to control water availability for both villages and crops.

The Great (or Classic) Pueblo Period flourished between A.D. 1100 and A.D. 1300. In the latter portion of this period, the Anasazi constructed the huge stone cliff dwellings of up to two hundred rooms for which Mesa Verde is well known. Archeologists have found tools, weavings, jewelry, and advanced black-on-white pottery dating from this time.

At its peak, Mesa Verde probably supported a population of five thousand people. Dendrochronology (tree-ring dating) reveals a record of droughts beginning in A.D. 1276. The Anasazi abandoned the magnificent cliff towns by A.D. 1300 because of a variety of conditions: droughts, depleted and eroding soil, diminished game, exhausted timber supply, and a growing season shortened by cool weather.

Experts have found evidence that the Anasazi used much of the native flora on Mesa Verde: yucca for basket making and cordage, piñon pine for firewood, Utah juniper bark and branches for building. They ate the edible fruit of the prickly pear and nuts from the piñon pine. The Anasazi domesticated turkeys for food and made blankets from turkey feathers.

Today, mule deer are plentiful, especially in the Gambel oak, piñon pine, and juniper communities. Coyotes, black bears, cougars, bobcats, desert cottontail rabblits, chipmunks, and squirrels are found throughout the park. Birds include the turkey vulture, great horned owl, marsh hawk, golden eagle, raven, canyon wren, and Stellar's jay.

Mesa Verde National Park is situated on a high network of mesas above the Montezuma and Mancos valleys. Elevations in the park range from 6,000 feet to 8,500 feet. Persons with respiratory and/or cardiac conditions should limit activities accordingly.

The park entrance, off U.S. Highway 160, is 10 miles east of Cortez, Colorado, and 36 miles west of Durango, Colorado. The Park Road, steep and with sharp curves, winds 21 miles from the entrance station to park headquarters. Visitors pulling trailers and visiting the park for day use only can leave trailers in a parking lot less than a mile from U.S. Highway 160 and near the entrance station.

Morefield Village

We first stopped at Morefield Campground (6,890 feet) in a hollow dotted with Gambel oaks behind a prominent cliff in the area, Knife Edge. The campground, open mid-April through September, has four sites in Navajo Loop designated for persons with disabilities. The sites are on dirt surfaces with some raised fire grills and picnic tables with extended tops. Wheelchair users can enter the nearby moderately

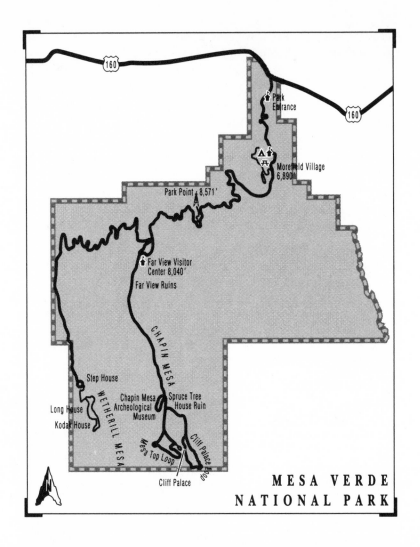

Map labels:
160
160
Park Entrance
Morefield Village 6,890'
Park Point 8,571'
Far View Visitor Center 8,040'
Far View Ruins
CHAPIN MESA
Step House
WETHERILL MESA
Long House
Kodak House
Chapin Mesa Archeological Museum
Spruce Tree House Ruin
Mesa Top Loop
Cliff Palace Loop
Cliff Palace
N

**MESA VERDE
NATIONAL PARK**

accessible comfort stations. The toilet stalls have grab bars but are narrow. A lowered telephone is by the comfort station nearest the camp entrance. An asphalt path leads to the fully accessible amphitheater. Scripts are available for people with hearing impairments. Camping is on a first-come first-served basis. For campground information, call 303-529-4474.

Near the campground, Morefield Village has a store, gift

shop, snack bar, laundromat, lowered telephone, and gas station, all fully accessible. Some of the narrow, coin-operated shower stalls are being modified for use by persons with mobility problems. We brought a folding plastic chair, which barely fit into a narrow stall.

Visitors can leave cars at Morefield and take bus tours to the ruins. The buses have no accommodations for wheelchair users. Finding a parking space near the ruins can be difficult during the busy summer season, so taking the bus can save aggravation.

Park Point

The Park Road runs generally north-south between the park entrance to the southern end of Chapin Mesa. Park Point turnoff (8,571 feet) is a .6-mile spur off Park Road, 6.2 miles south of Morefield. The short trail to the point is a moderately accessible narrow asphalt path to a panoramic view over 12,000 square miles of the Four Corner states: Colorado, Utah, Arizona, and New Mexico.

Far View

Further down Park Road, at the north end of Chapin Mesa, Far View (8,040 feet) is 5 miles from Park Point, 15 miles from the park entrance, and at the junction with the 13-mile road to Wetherill Mesa. Far View has a visitor center, motor lodge, restaurant, cafeteria, gift shop, and gas station.

On the east side of the road, the visitor center looks over Soda Canyon; it is open during summer months. The parking lot across the road is connected by a tunnel to the steep ramped entrance at the visitor center. An ISA-designated space is in a small lot next to the base of the visitor center, reachable via the service road. Restrooms located near the beginning of the ramp are moderately accessible with wide stalls and grab bars. The long steep incline of the ramp makes the approach to the visitor center moderately accessible;

the interior of the center is fully accessible. The park brochure is available in Braille. Exhibits are generally easy to view; however, a few exhibit cases are small, and the print is difficult to read. The exhibits feature artifacts recovered from ruins in the Mesa Verde area and exquisite examples of crafts and jewelry by modern-day Native American artisans.

Far View Motor Lodge offers fully accessible accommodations in two rooms with well-designed shower stalls modified for persons with disabilities, and another four rooms with grab-bar–equipped bathtubs. The lodge restaurant is fully accessible and has an amplified telephone. The gift shop and cafeteria at Far View Terrace are fully accessible.

Far View Ruins, 1.1 miles south of the visitor center, is the first site along the Park Road where the impressive Anasazi ruins of Mesa Verde may be viewed. Built between 1100 and 1300, this may have been one of the most densely inhabited portions of Mesa Verde; it received more rainfall than other areas of Chapin Mesa.

At Far View, the Anasazi constructed Far View House and an area that could have been a gathering place, ball court, or water reservoir. Only five of the estimated fifty units in the immediate vicinity are excavated. Visitors can wander through them, including the impressive Far View Tower and Pipe Shrine House. Only the plaza at Far View House is moderately accessible to people using wheelchairs. A self-guiding brochure is available.

Chapin Mesa Archeological Museum and Spruce Tree House Ruin

At the southern end of Chapin Mesa, 4.5 miles south of Far View Ruins, are the archeological museum and a number of cliff dwellings. Chapin Mesa Archeological Museum (6,969 feet) has exhibits, a slide presentation given October to May, Braille transcription of the park brochure, a wheelchair for loan, and a bookstore where visitors can view a video of the park's highlights. Across from the museum are a gift shop, food service, picnic area, and restroom, all fully accessible.

The archeological museum is an information center with extensive exhibits of Native American artifacts. Much of the informative exhibit text may be difficult for people with vision impairments to read without assistance. The museum has several steps at different levels between exhibit areas. Rangers and staff will assist by placing a steep ramp for visitors with mobility problems.

We especially enjoyed the examples of pottery and intricate basketry excavated from ruins by professional archeologists. Small-scale dioramas depicting the various phases of inhabitation at Mesa Verde were particularly instructive and helped us better relate to the ruins we were soon to visit.

Spruce Tree House Ruin is open all year with ranger-guided tours departing from in front of the museum in winter. The ruin is self-guided in summer, and a brochure is available. The paved trail is a half-mile round-trip and has gravel in front of the ruin. It is strenuous and uneven. Assistance is strongly recommended for persons with mobility and sight impairments.

Spruce Tree House Ruin is built under an overhang in a large alcove, well protected from the elements. Ninety percent of the approximately 114 rooms and 8 kivas constructed between 1200 and 1276 are still intact and unrestored. One hundred people are believed to have lived in the three-story Spruce Tree House, a modern-day name given for a large Douglas spruce (fir) that grew in front of the ruin. Local cowboys Richard Wetherill and Charles Mason had stumbled upon Spruce Tree House while looking for lost cattle and shimmied down the tree to gain entrance to the dwelling. The tree was cut down before the park was established.

Typical of Southwest Pueblo structures, Spruce Tree House has small plaza areas, partly over kiva roofs. Experts believe the plaza served as a work and social area for the inhabitants. Women prepared food and made pottery and baskets while men fashioned tools, dressed game, and organized for farming. The rooms were used for living in, for storage, and, during inclement weather, for work.

In her chair, Wendy was able to maneuver in front of the ruin, including around a kiva. Throughout the ruins in the Four Corners area, kivas are found in many shapes, sizes, and configurations. Most Mesa Verde kivas are circular with a bench around the outer perimeter interrupted by vertical pilasters. A ventilator shaft provides fresh air. The floor has a deflector between the shaft and fire pit. A *sipapu* (see-PAH-poo), symbolizing the place of the people's emergence into this world, is usually found north of the fire pit. The entrance was by ladder through an opening in the roof, which also served to vent smoke.

Another kiva in the plaza has been restored, and Michael was able to climb down a ladder to experience the underground chamber as it might once have existed. Modern-day Pueblo cultures use kivas as part of their social and ceremonial practices.

Mesa-Top Loop

From the museum area, Ruins Road, which has two loops, leads to dozens of ruins. We first took the one-way Mesa-Top Loop 6 miles through a series of Anasazi dwellings dating from A.D. 575 to A.D. 1300. A self-guiding pamphlet accompanies the tour of Anasazi development on Chapin Mesa. All sites on the Mesa-Top Loop are accessible for people with disabilities (except the last, Sun Temple), and each parking area has an ISA-designated space.

The first site on the loop is an early pithouse from the Modified Basketmaker Period (A.D. 500–750). A short paved path around the shallow two-chamber pithouse allows for full accessibility. After passing the spectacular Navajo Canyon Overlook, we took the 500-foot easy trail to a view of Square Tower House. Occupied between 1200 and 1300, it originally had more than eighty rooms. The four-story-high tower was part of a larger many-storied structure.

The next ruins were a series of pithouses and early pueblo villages ranging from A.D. 674 through A.D. 950, when the

Anasazi gradually moved their dwellings above ground. These aboveground structures are called pueblos. They are indicative of the Developmental Pueblo Period, which evolved during this time. The Anasazi continued to farm beans, corn, and squash and adopted the bow and arrow to replace the atlatl, an earlier spear-throwing weapon. All these sights have level and paved trails around the ruins.

We found the next stop especially fascinating because this site had hosted three successive pueblo villages built one on top of the other, the last about 1075. Kivas from each of the three villages can be seen from the asphalt paths that surround the sites. The toilet at this stop is fully accessible.

Sun Point Pueblo, Sun Point, Oak Tree House, Fire Temple, and New Fire House overlooks all have moderately accessible points from which to see ruins built about 1200. Sun Point Pueblo is from the period just prior to Anasazi movement from the mesa tops into the cliffs. Sun Point Overlook affords the visitor views of a large number of dwellings across two canyons. All these overlooks allow views of cliff dwellings built in the last stages of habitation on Mesa Verde.

The Mesa-Top Loop continues to Sun Temple. The Anasazi did not complete Sun Temple before abandoning the area around 1300. The best accessible view of Cliff Palace is from the parking lot at Sun Temple. The largest cliff house in North America built during the Great (or Classic) Pueblo Period, Cliff Palace had 217 rooms and 23 kivas and housed more than 200 people.

Nondisabled people reach Cliff Palace via extensive stairways and ladders from the mesa top opposite Sun Temple. The only accessible overlook on Cliff Palace Loop, about half way around the loop, is of Hemenway House (bring binoculars).

Wetherill Mesa

Wetherill Mesa has several accessible excavated ruins on the mesa top and several cliff-house overlooks. The path to one cliff dwelling, Step House, can be accessible for wheelchair users if assistance is strong and extremely adept. The mesa, named for the Wetherill family, is 13 miles from Far View and open only during summer months. Visitors can take the bus tours from Morefield or Far View or drive their own vehicles less than 25 feet in length and under 8,000 pounds.

A minitram tour is one means of visiting all but one ruin on Wetherill Mesa. Minitrams depart the parking lot area every half-hour from 8:55 A.M. to 4:55 P.M. A very steep (1:4+) movable ramp is put in place by the driver for wheelchair users to embark and debark the tram. Assistance is necessary.

We were fortunate to join Ranger Bob Erner's tour with Youth Conservation Corps members. Our first stop was the Badger House Community Trail, a chronological sequence of mesa-top habitation at Wetherill Mesa, from Modified Basketmaker pithouses to Great Pueblo dwellings. An easily accessible, level, paved trail with self-guiding brochure and interpretive wayside exhibits connects the four excavated sites.

The first site is a pithouse from A.D. 650, when Anasazi lived in small villages. The pithouse has two sections, the larger used for living and sleeping. To construct the walls, the Anasazi used a technique called *jacal*, smoothing mud over wood poles. The sipapu, similar to those found in kivas built during later periods, is clearly evident on the floor. The second section, an antechamber, was used for storage.

The next site, from the Developmental Pueblo Period, consists of blocks of adjacent rooms reflecting a rapid change in building styles. Most walls are built with rocks and mud mortar. Nearby is a great kiva where the Anasazi later built houses atop the dirt and debris that had gradually filled the chamber.

Badger House is further along the path; there we were fascinated by a tunnel connecting the kiva with a tower. The kiva and tower were built in the 1200s as an addition to the living rooms, which date from the 900s. The walls are of stones set in mortar, a refinement over jacal.

The last site on the trail, Two Raven House, was occupied in the 900s and into the 1000s. It includes an oven, a turkey fence, a small pueblo, and a small kiva.

A few feet from Two Raven House, we caught the next tram to Kodak House Overlook. The short paved trail to the viewing platform is moderately accessible and affords a good look at a ruin protected by a cliff overhang. The next passing tram took us to Long House Overlook. The viewing-area trail has some moderately steep slopes where wheelchairs may need assistance. Long House, the second largest cliff house in Mesa Verde, has ranger-guided tours through the dwelling. The trail down to the ruin is a strenuous quarter-mile hike with about fifty stair steps.

The trail to Step House begins a few yards south of the snack bar near the Wetherill Mesa parking lot. We visited Step House on a hot summer day, and Wendy welcomed the extremely adept assistance. More than a half-mile long, this strenuous trail begins with a dirt portion. To avoid steps, Wendy used the exit trail to the ruins. She was assisted in her descent down the cliffside; anyone using a wheelchair will require assistance since the trail's switchbacks, though paved, are steep and rough.

At Step House, ruins from two different time periods exist side by side: Modified Basketmaker pithouses and a Great (Classic) Pueblo cliff dwelling. One of the pithouses, built around A.D. 626, has been partially reconstructed by the NPS to show the building technique and design typical of the time. Thirty to forty Anasazi occupied the large pueblo during the 1200s. Plaster with painted designs remains on the interior walls of one kiva. Petroglyphs and toeholds are also carved into the rock cave walls.

The Anasazi of Mesa Verde departed from the mesas and cliff houses by 1300. What happened to these industrious farmers, potters, and town builders is an oft-pondered question. They probably migrated to other areas in the Southwest, where effects of the thirteenth- and fourteenth-century droughts were less severe. Archeological evidence suggests that some Mesa Verdeans may have briefly resettled in Chaco Canyon, northern New Mexico. The descendants of the Anasazi make up the modern-day Pueblo tribes, including the Hopi, Zuni, and Acoma. These Native Americans are today well-known for their exquisite jewelry and pottery.

The existence of kivas in both present-day Pueblo villages and prehistoric Anasazi dwellings suggests a compelling cultural link between the two. Perhaps the rituals practiced today in Acoma, Zuni, and Hopi kivas are similar to those of the Anasazi who lived long ago on the mesas and in the cliffs of Mesa Verde.

(See *At a Glance: Desert Southwest Region.*)

OLYMPIC
NATIONAL PARK
600 East Park Avenue
Port Angeles, WA 98362
Information: 206-452-4501

Olympic National Park, Washington, is the largest road-less wilderness in the continental United States. On a peninsula surrounded by the Pacific Ocean, the Strait of Juan de Fuca, and Puget Sound, it contains the prime remnant of virgin rainforest in the world's temperate regions. Olympic's variety of geographical features within one park is unmatched.

Offshore islands dot 57 miles of rugged, unspoiled coast stretching up to coniferous forest, subalpine meadows, and glaciated peaks. Olympic's abundant wildlife includes bald eagles, Roosevelt elk, and Columbian black-tailed deer. Salmon jump up river cascades to spawn.

Founded in 1909 as a national monument and designated a national park in 1938, Olympic is a World Heritage Park (recognized internationally for its scenic beauty) and a World Biosphere Reserve (to protect natural resources).

Even with few roads, five main approaches reach into the park: Hurricane Ridge, Elwha Valley, Soleduck, Hoh Rain Forest, and Quinault. These afford easy-access travel to paths through rainforests, a wilderness beach walk, trails among fragile subalpine meadows with high-ridge views, and a valley path leading to a waterfall.

We approached Olympic from the south on a rainy night in August. The northeast side of the park averages 17 inches of moisture per year, while 40 miles directly west, Hoh Rain Forest receives 145 inches. Be prepared for wet weather any-time on the peninsula. Water-repellent protective gear and warm clothing for the higher elevations and cool evenings may be needed any day of the year. The climate is that of a West Coast marine zone heavily influenced by the ocean. From early November to late June, mountain areas are snow covered. August and September are usually best for clear views and minimal rain. Park road elevations range from sea level to 6,007 feet. Persons with cardiovascular and/or respiratory problems should take precautions at the higher altitudes.

Part of the delight of visiting Olympic is in getting there. Highway 101, renowned for its scenic stretches, encircles the park. To explore the Olympic peninsula from the south or coastal routes, U.S. 101 leads into the park through either Aberdeen or Olympia, both in Washington. To approach from the east, the ferry service from Seattle crosses Puget Sound, landing in Bremerton or Winslow. There is also regular service most of the year from Victoria, British Columbia, to Port Angeles, Washington. For schedules, write to Washington State Ferries (Seattle Ferry Terminal, Pier 52, Seattle, WA 98104) and/or Blackball Transport (Foot of Laurel Street, Port Angeles, WA 98362). Port Angeles has lodging, restaurants, and a wide variety of stores. Many have accessible facilities.

We began our visit to Olympic National Park at the Pioneer Visitor Center south of Port Angeles on the north side of the park. The visitor center, including restrooms, is entirely accessible and has an open information desk, an orientation slide presentation, various interpretive information, exhibits about the park (some for touching), and a bookstore. Park maps are available here as well as at the entrance stations to the park. A large-print booklet for visitors with vision impairments, "Ever Changing, Ever Green," is available at the information desk.

Michael Smithson, assistant chief naturalist and athletic wheelchair user, met with us and detailed the accessible features of the park. He says of Olympic's accessibility, "If you know where to go, you can have a good time."

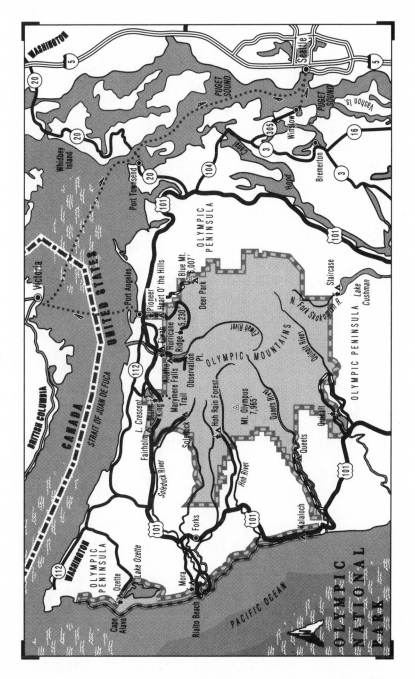

Hurricane Ridge

Hurricane Ridge, 17 miles south of the Pioneer Visitor Center, is the most popular point from which to see the park's highest mountain, Mt. Olympus (7,965 feet). The first time we visited, the weather was foggy and the visibility poor. On a clear day, Hurricane Ridge could satisfy anyone interested in expansive mountain views and subalpine meadows. Looking up the Elwha Valley, we saw heavily forested mountains capped by active glaciers around peaks crowned by clouds: the Olympic Mountain Range.

The Hurricane Ridge Visitor Center (5,230 feet) is fully accessible and for day use only. To enter the center from the parking lot, there is a gradual ramp from the west side, an easier entrance than the steep front doorway. The upper level has an information desk, exhibits, a small enclosed viewing porch, and a unisex fully accessible restroom. The lower level is accessible by an elevator available upon request at the information desk. This level offers a cafeteria, a gift/book shop, and another unisex fully accessible restroom; it exits to a popular viewpoint adjacent to the visitor center. A placard designates the prominent mountain and valley features. A paved trail with a moderately steep grade leads from the viewing area up to the parking lot.

The three Hurricane Ridge Nature Trails, north of the visitor center, are asphalt pathways winding through subalpine meadows. Although originally constructed to preserve the fragile meadowland around Hurricane Ridge, the trails are excellent for visitors who want to stroll or wheel through this high open country. Summertime brings wildflowers throughout this spectacular natural resource, peaking in mid to late July.

The Big Meadow Loop is the easiest and shortest. Cirque Ridge Trail is slightly more challenging. High Ridge Trail is longer and steeper with much dirt and gravel. Regardless, the views from all three are stupendous. In early summer, portions of the trails may be snow blocked.

Not as well known but with uniquely grand views of the mountains is the nearby moderately accessible Picnic Unit A located halfway between Hurricane Hill and the center. Unit B, sharing the same parking lot, has trees that provide accessible protection from sun and wind. The units share moderately accessible comfort stations (barrier-free entry without wide stalls or grab bars).

Skilled wheelchair users have taken the trail to the summit of Hurricane Hill. Only the first portion is moderately accessible, having steep grades with cross slope, and even there, assistance might be necessary. The remainder of the trail has significant barriers.

To complete an exploration of the Hurricane Ridge area frontcountry trails and to get a great look at Mt. Olympus, take the 7.8-mile single-lane dirt road to Obstruction Point. Be sure to check weather and road conditions at the visitor center information desk.

In search of a place to camp, try Heart of the Hills Campground 12 miles down the hill from Hurricane Ridge Lodge. Heart of the Hills campsites are surrounded by an old-growth mixed-conifer forest including an ISA-designated site with a moderately accessible comfort station (without grab bars). If the designated site is occupied, many others are suitable. Raccoons also like this campground, so be prepared to stow food in critter-proof places like automobiles. The amphitheater is accessible, but persons with mobility impairments may require assistance.

Elwha Valley

The Elwha Valley region lies west of Heart of the Hills and the Hurricane Ridge Road. There, we delightedly found a marvelous attraction for easy access just inside the park boundary and entrance station. The Madison Falls Trail is a 200-yard-long macadam path designed for easy access. The trail takes off from the parking lot, which has ISA-designated spaces. Russ Dalton, a Park Service trail maintenance crew member, convinced planners that Madison Falls Trail could be built for accessibility by visitors with mobility problems, like his ten-year-old daughter Carrie, who has severe cerebral palsy. Carrie took us on the trail her father had built.

We climbed a gentle slope winding along the edge of a woods. A resting bench sits at a curve halfway up the trail. When we rounded the last twist in the trail, our quiet was interrupted by the rush of cascading water. Madison Falls tumbles 100 feet down a basalt cliff. The trail ended with an observation platform, giving us full view of the falls and a taste of the mist from Madison Creek. Carrie excitedly told us, "I like the sun on my face; I like the wind and I like the leaves."

Two other attractions in the Elwha Valley are Observation Point at the end of the Elwha Valley Road and Olympic Hot Springs. A 2.5-mile hike along a closed road leads from Observation Point to Olympic Hot Springs, undeveloped natural pools on a hillside.

There are two campgrounds in the Elwha Valley, Elwha and Altaire, with moderately accessible sites, fully accessible unisex pit toilets with grab bars, and moderately accessible comfort stations without wide stalls or grab bars. We stayed at Altair, near the Elwha River, where the sites are wooded and spacious. Many are level with well-packed earth, yet none are ISA designated.

Lake Crescent

Lake Crescent, a long body of water bordered by spruce-forested hills, is 16 miles east of Elwha on Highway 101. The west side of Spruce Railroad Trail along the lake edge is a bicycle path usable by wheelchairs for the first 1.5 to 2 miles.

Marymere Falls Trail begins near the fully accessible Storm King Ranger Station. After going under the highway via a tunnel, the 1.2-mile trail wanders through old-growth forest. The going is moderately easy, except for a steep hill in the first half-mile and the last 50 yards, where assistance may be necessary. Reaching the river and falls would be very difficult in a wheelchair.

Lake Crescent Lodge is at a picturesque location on the lake's south shore. The restaurant entrance is barrier free, and two rooms at the Storm King Motel are enterable but without fully accessible bathrooms. Their doors are narrow, and no modifications have been made for accessibility. The new West Lodge will have two fully accessible units with bathtubs.

Olympic Park Institute, at Rosemary Inn near Storm King, is a private non-profit organization that conducts environmental education courses. It is the location of the only Elder Hostel in a national park. It has fully accessible rooms, restrooms, and wheel-in showers. The Elder Hostel program is for people over the age of fifty-five focusing on natural and human resources in the park. Write Olympic Park Institute (HC 62 Box 9T, Port Angeles, WA 98362).

On the north shore of Lake Crescent, Fairholm Campground has some moderately accessible facilities.

Soleduck

We continued our journey at Soleduck River Valley, 16 miles from Lake Crescent. At Highway 101's junction with Soleduck River Valley Road are fully accessible pit toilets near an interpretive exhibit. A few miles along the Soleduck River we came upon the Salmon Cascades, where we looked down to the Soleduck River from a fully accessible viewing platform. The salmon jump from pool to pool during their annual September–October upstream run to their spawning grounds. The interpretive exhibit is mounted low and in large print.

Sol Duc Hot Springs Resort offers a restaurant, hot springs, a lodge, and cabins, all fully accessible (206-928-3211). The resort's lodge has two fully accessible rooms. The hot springs have a ramp for accessing the springs, and the resort will supply a wheelchair for use in the water. Soleduck Campground has a reserved ISA–designated site and a fully accessible amphitheater. The Park Service told us that a fully accessible Ancient Groves Trail may be built in the next few years in this area.

Ozette

To reach the Lake Ozette-Cape Alava area, take Route 112 from Port Angeles, or Burnt Mountain Road from Sappho, Washington, on Highway 101, to Clallam Bay. Continue west on Route 112 for 2 miles and turn left on the road along the Hoko River, following the signs to Ozette, 26 miles from the turnoff.

One of our crew members, Char, spent several days with Katy Jo, a nondisabled friend, in the Lake Ozette area. Char has excellent upper-body strength and is a talented sports-chair user. She reports that the 3.3-mile trail from Ozette to Cape Alava is a narrow boardwalk with occasional steps for the first portion. While thrilled with the scenery, she encountered extreme difficulty. Even with assistance, Char does not recommend it to chair users at this time.

The campground has no sites designated as accessible, but portions are fairly level around the fully accessible comfort station. The ranger station has a fully accessible comfort station that is closed in winter. Swan Bay, 4 miles south of the ranger station, has fully accessible pit toilets open year-round.

Mora and Rialto Beach

We were pleased to find the Rialto Beach boardwalk picking up from a paved trail through the woods and leading to the beach. This synthetic-material boardwalk takes the visitor 150 feet to the sands' edge. The day we visited, Rialto was foggy with a misting rain and a dreamlike quality. Driftwood lined the gray-pebbled beach. Along this shore is the Pacific Coast Trail. A picnic area with moderately acces-

RIALTO BEACH,
OLYMPIC NATIONAL PARK.
Photo by Michael Tompane.

sible tables in the woods is adjacent to the Rialto boardwalk trail.

Mora Campground with level sites in an old-growth forest is one of Ranger Michael Smithson's favorite campgrounds in the park. Loop B has an ISA-designated site reserved for use by persons with disabilities, and nearby is a fully accessible comfort station with wide stalls and grab bars.

Mora is off a road that branches west from Highway 101, approximately 2.5 miles south of the town of Sol Duc and 1 mile north of the town of Forks. Look carefully for the sign pointing to Mora. There are many stores in Forks for resupplying.

Hoh Rain Forest

Nine miles south of Forks is the turnoff to the Hoh Rain Forest, the largest temperate-zone rainforest in the Northern Hemisphere. We were struck with the ensemble of abundant flora and fauna in the forest areas we visited. On the

road to Hoh we spotted a bald eagle fishing in the river, diving to the water, then flying upstream for more than a mile.

We took the Hoh Mini-trail with Ranger Michael Smithson, Wendy's brother Dick and his wife Char, who had met
us in the park to help with our book research and video
production. The Mini-trail is a fully accessible quarter-mile
asphalt loop behind the visitor center. The center, with an
information desk, a bookstore, exhibits, and restrooms, is
fully accessible.

In this most uniquely preserved mixed-conifer rainforest,
we observed rare ferns, mosses, fungi, lichens, and mushrooms. A wooden bridge crosses a stream brimming with
salmon fry. The trail has placards interpreting the most significant natural resources.

The Hoh Rain Forest is a world-renowned natural wonder,
and this minitrail, though short, is a must-see during a visit
to the Pacific Northwest. Take some time, for here is an opportunity to become engulfed in verdant dense forest filled
with an aura of silence.

Several other trails branch from the minitrail, none of
which are very wheelchair accessible. Nevertheless, we ven-
tured forth to the Hall of Mosses. Michael Smithson and
Char, both superb wheelchair athletes, wheeled up the steep
and root-laden incline without assistance. Wendy, with her
powerful electric wheelchair, needed the help of two strong
men, Dick and Michael, to traverse the bumpy and cross-
sloped trail. Michael Smithson later said that had been the
first ascent for a powered chair.

Beyond the treacherous 200-foot approach, the Hall of
Mosses Trail is flat, inviting, and a pleasure for all. The easiest route is to take a left at the top of the initial incline and
return the same way. Welcome to fairyland! Western red cedar are draped with delicate webs of moss. Curtains of
greenery stretch from sky to the forest floor. Each layer of
the canopy filters the sun's golden highlights into this wilderness of wonder. The soil is softly covered with conifer needles and leaves, supporting sorrel and mushrooms. Ferns

grow out of mosses rooted in the bowls of trees. Reaching the Hall of Mosses may be a lot of effort for some visitors, yet this is a memorable, almost magical place. Wheelchair users may need assistance along the entire trail because the latter section is rocky, rooty, and steep over a ridge.

The Hoh Rain Forest Campground is moderately accessible, including the comfort stations, which have standard-width doorways and stalls. By publication of this guide, a fully accessible unisex toilet may have been installed.

Visitors should come prepared with rain gear when visiting rainforest areas on the west side of Olympic, but don't be scared away. Sunshine and pleasant days occur throughout the year and are especially common from June through October. Inclement weather, however, is frequent and can be intense during winter.

Kalaloch

Kalaloch, on the ocean near the southwest corner of Olympic National Park, is 5 miles north of Queets, Washington, on Highway 101. It boasts the only accessible campground in the park that has sites on the beach. There are three fully accessible designated campsites: two nestled in protecting woods and one in the open near views of the Pacific. The comfort stations are fully accessible, and the amphitheater is moderately accessible.

There is a path to the beach with steps. On the beach, the sand is packed hard enough for wheelchairing at low tide. Nearby and just outside the park is Kalaloch Lodge with cabins and rooms that are not wheelchair accessible. The dining room is fully accessible, but the restrooms are up a flight of stairs.

Staircase and Deer Park

On the east side of the peninsula are two more opportunities to experience Olympic: at Staircase in the southeast corner and Deer Park to the northeast. Staircase is 15 miles from Hoodsport, Washington. Follow the signs to Lake Cushman State Park and continue past the state park to Big Creek; then turn left onto National Forest Route 24.

At Staircase, a trail along the Skokomish River leads to Staircase Rapids and is reliably reported to be fully accessible. The picnic area, campground, comfort stations, and amphitheater are reported to be moderately accessible.

Deer Park Road is a spectacular 17-mile, narrow, steep, winding dirt drive that climbs to 6,007 feet in elevation on Blue Mountain. The road, closed by snow in winter, begins 3 miles east of Port Angeles on Highway 101. The Blue Mountain Trail is reported to be accessible with assistance. The pit toilets are not accessible. Camping is primitive and allowed only in the summer.

Olympic National Park has a broad spectrum of both ecological diversity and access opportunities. As a World Heritage Park and Biosphere Reserve, it is recognized internationally for its scenic beauty and for the protection of valuable natural resources in it. The park has the largest and best of the world's temperate-zone virgin rainforest and the largest stand of old-growth mixed-conifer forest in the conterminous United States. It hosts the largest living specimens of Alaska cedar, subalpine and Douglas firs, and western hemlock; many diverse aquatic species; and one of the vaster areas of subalpine meadows in North America.

Today, less than 20 percent of old-growth forest in the Pacific Northwest remains, threatening increasing numbers of wildlife. Olympic National Park is the largest sanctuary for the maintenance of many of these diverse ecosystems and may be the only protected area large enough to preserve them.

Worth a Visit

North Cascades and Mount Rainer national parks are both less than 200 miles from Olympic. We found accessibility at Mount Rainer, other than the visitor centers and two trails, to be less inviting than at Olympic and North Cascades.

North Cascades, though a rugged, mountainous park on the Canadian border, has exceptional opportunities for visitors with disabilities. One of our favorites is Happy Creek Forest Walk. The .3-mile loop trail is a fully accessible, wide boardwalk with handrails winding through lush forest along Happy Creek. A novel feature of Happy Creek Forest Walk is that the trail is elevated in places, giving all hikers a closer view of the forest's canopy layers and wildlife than ground-level trails afford.

Kevin Kennedy, National Forest Service ranger and wheel-chair user, guided us to Rainy Lake Trail in the Okanogan National Forest with his daughter Shannon. The trail is a fully accessible 1-mile asphalt path through a hemlock and fir forest to Rainy Lake at the base of a glacial cirque, a large circular gouge carved by a glacier in the granite.

Newhalem Campground, near the west entrance of the park, has level sites and excellent fully accessible comfort stations (with heat!). In this beautiful campground, the sites are ensconced in an old-growth forest of western cedar.

North Cascades provides unique accessible wilderness opportunities through the richly forested and mountainous Pacific Northwest.

(See *At a Glance: Pacific States Region*.)

REDWOOD
NATIONAL PARK
1111 Second Street
Crescent City, CA 95531
Information and TDD: 707-464-6101

"Tall trees with red wood," recounted Chinese explorer Hui Shan in A.D. 499 after his travels along the northern Pacific coast. Could this be the first written description of the California coast redwoods? We do know that Fray Juan Crespi, with the 1769 Portola Expedition exploration of the California coast, saw these tallest trees in the world and wrote about *Palo Colorado,* the red tree.

An estimated 2 million acres of this impressive old-growth forest once stood in California. Also known as ancient or virgin, these forests have never been logged. Today, only 96,000 acres still stand. Redwood National Park and thirty-one California state parks preserve 80,000 acres of ancient coast redwoods, with the remainder in private ownership.

Redwood National Park and three California state parks — Prairie Creek Redwoods, Del Norte Coast Redwoods, and Jedediah Smith Redwoods — are contiguous, connected by a 36-mile stretch of U.S. Highway 101 along northern California's Pacific coast. Orick, California, at the south end of the Redwood Parks, is 315 miles north of San Francisco. Crescent City, California, is adjacent to the north end of the parks. We found that the parks have accessible features for everyone, ranging from a wide boardwalk path bordering an estuary to duff-covered trails in deeply shaded redwood groves.

The parks encompass three distinct areas: the coastal redwoods, dominating a diverse forest; 40 miles of rocky seashore pocketing sandy beaches; and broad rivers bordering open prairies. The grassy prairies are the only flat, treeless portions of an otherwise mountainous and hilly terrain. The parks' three rivers — Redwood Creek, Klamath, and Smith — can roar or gently loll through the landscape depending on rainfall. The rugged seacoast dotted by sea stacks, rock pinnacles just offshore, can be stormy, fogbound, or mellow with summer sun. And then there is the forest.

The ancient coast redwood forest is a biological powerhouse. The ground is a carpet of entangled sword, maidenhair, and five-finger ferns; salmonberries; and rhododendrons — damp and green spiked with flecks of color. This verdant forest thrives in the moist climate created by the ocean and contained by the coast redwoods.

The vitality of the coast redwoods depends on this moderate climate. Winter rain, summer fog, and the redwood's leaf design are crucial elements in maintaining the tall trees. The pattern of the needlelike redwood leaves helps the forest retain moisture from fog in the air. By condensing on the redwood's foliage and dripping to the ground, fog helps replace water lost through evaporation and transpiration during hot, dry summers. Transpiration is a process by which water is exchanged with air through the trees' leaves. The summer fog also has a cooling influence on the redwood belt, giving coastal areas a fairly constant temperature with average highs and lows varying approximately 10°F between winter and summer.

The coast redwoods are the tallest living trees in the world. In 1963, the National Geographic Society found the tallest tree measuring 367.6 feet near Redwood Creek in the Tall Trees Grove. These trees live an average of five hundred to seven hundred years, with some as old as two thousand years. The coast redwoods have no known susceptibility to disease or insect damage. The thick bark of the adult trees makes them extremely fire resistant.

Three varieties of redwoods live on Earth: the coast redwoods (*Sequoia sempervirens*), the giant sequoia (*Sequoiadendron giganteum*), and the small dawn redwood (*Metasequoia glyptostroboides*). The last, thought to be extinct, was discovered in China in 1944. Giant sequoias thrive only on the western slope of the Sierra Nevada in California and are the world's largest living organisms. The name, *sequoia*, honors the Cherokee Chief Sequoyah, who devised an alphabet of his people's language.

Redwoods have existed on Earth for 160 million years; according to fossil records, the coast redwoods in their present form have grown on the California coast for at least 20 million years. During the dinosaur era, redwoods ranged across North America, Europe, and Asia. When the last great ice age retreated ten thousand years ago, the changed climate left northern California as the only native region for coast redwoods. The redwood belt extends 450 miles from Salmon Creek near Big Sur, California, north to the Chetco River in southern Oregon. The belt covers from the ocean inland an average of 30 miles. The Redwood Parks preserve groves of tall trees in Humboldt and Del Norte counties, California.

As on most of California's coast, the geology of the Redwood Parks is complex. The coastal ranges are made up of distorted sedimentary rocks pushed up along geologic faults between the colliding Pacific Ocean floor and the North American continent. Rivers have carved steep canyons from the softer rock while erosion has rounded the mountaintops.

The rivers are spawning grounds for salmon and for steelhead and cutthroat trout. The lagoons at the ocean's edge support smelt, perch, and herring. Clams, starfish, sea urchins, and mussels live in the intertidal pool communities. Off the park's coast, the endangered California gray whale migrates between the Arctic and Mexico. Seals, porpoises, and sea lions are commonly sighted from shore. More than 350 bird species either pass through or live in the parks. On land, black bears, mountain lions, bobcats, beavers, otters, and the stately Roosevelt elk inhabit the park's forests and grassy prairies.

Native American Indians — the Yurok, Tolowa, and Chilula — lived in what are now the Redwood Parks along Redwood Creek basin and the Klamath and Smith rivers. Beginning in the mid-1500s and into the late 1700s, Spanish and English explorers sailed along the coast but made no note of landing in the parks' area. Russian and English trappers and traders infrequently visited, as did groups on Spanish land expeditions. Jedediah Strong Smith, leading the first overland expedition from the East to the Pacific, entered what are now Redwood National Park lands in 1828. The Smith River is named for the famous mountain man.

The area experienced its first economic boom in 1850 with both the discovery of gold at Gold Bluff and the beginning of logging. Soon after, efforts began for protection of the coast redwoods. Conservationists won a small victory in 1902 when the California legislature established the first coast redwood preserve, Big Basin Redwood State Park in Santa Cruz County.

Many people called for a Redwood National Park, and in 1918 the Save-the-Redwoods League was organized. Finally, after fifty years of debate and controversy, Redwood National Park was founded in 1968 with a mandate to preserve old-growth redwood forest. The League, the Sierra Club, and the National Geographic Society were pivotal in the park's establishment. The park was expanded by 48,000 acres to 78,000 acres in 1978. The adjacent Prairie Creek Redwoods, Del Norte Coast Redwoods, and Jedediah Smith Redwoods state parks total 26,000 acres. The Save-the-Redwoods League has been responsible for the purchase and donations of lands and instrumental in creating thirty-one state parks protecting precious ancient redwood groves in northern California.

During the dedication of Redwood National Park in 1968, a young park ranger from Yellowstone stood in Lady Bird Johnson Grove and promised himself that someday he would become superintendent of this park. More than twenty years later, now as park superintendent, William Ehorn bills Redwood "the greatest park in the world." We found this to be one of our favorite national parks, too.

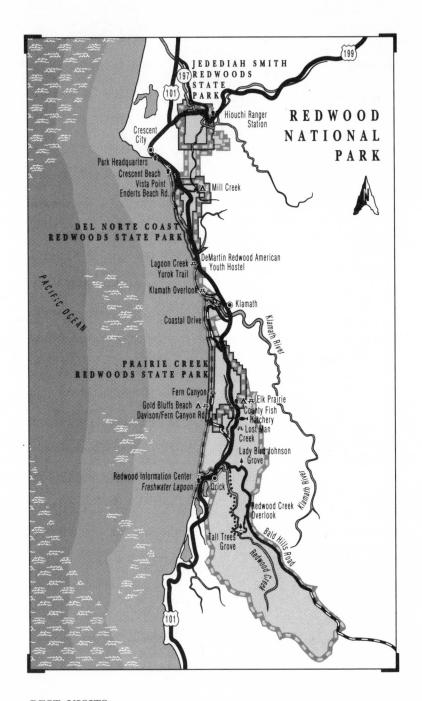

Redwood Information Center

As we entered the Parks from the south we drove by Freshwater Lagoon, a spit of land along U.S. Highway 101 with a nondeveloped campground by the beach. The information center, a quarter-mile further north, has ISA-designated spaces in the parking lot.

Redwood Information Center is a tastefully constructed building of—you guessed it—redwood. Wide wooden ramps with handrails lead into it. The information and book-sales desk, touch table, three-dimensional tactile map, and ocean-viewing telescope are lowered for children and wheelchair users. A nineteen-minute film is available on request in a fully accessible theater room and has an accompanying script for persons with hearing impairments. Restrooms and lowered telephones are fully accessible. The park's "Access Redwood National Park" brochure is available at the information counter. Tickets for the Tall Trees Shuttle Bus can be purchased here, but the buses are not wheelchair accessible.

Views of the beach from the information center are superb, and in the fall, winter, and spring whale-watching is a favorite activity. We took the Redwood Creek Estuary Nature Trail north of the information center. The neat and aesthetically designed wide quarter-mile boardwalk trail has several benches along the way. It goes along the estuary to a small lagoon where Heermann's gulls, killdeer, and migrating birds stop to feed. Another path from the information center, wheelchair usable for part of the way, leads toward the beach and a picnic area on sandy terrain.

Lady Bird Johnson Grove

From Redwood Information Center, we took U.S. Highway 101 north 3 miles through Orick to the Bald Hills Road turnoff. Lady Bird Johnson Grove parking lot is 2 miles from Highway 101. A large-print interpretive brochure is available at Redwood and Crescent City information centers.

One of the best opportunities to enjoy a virgin-growth redwood grove is at Lady Bird Johnson Grove, named for the former first lady. From the parking lot, we began the 1-mile trail; immediately we encountered its most difficult portion. A steep incline approaches the bridge that crosses Bald Hills Road. The incline almost demands assistance for wheelchair users. The other side of the bridge has a similar steep incline. A gravel path, less than a quarter-mile long, leads to the duff-covered trail through the grove. Past the plaque commemorating the 1968 dedication of Redwood National Park, tree roots make the trail bumpy.

When we entered the stillness of the ancient redwood grove, a Stellar's jay occasionally shattered the quiet as the sounds of civilization fell away under 300-foot-tall trees. Strokes of sunlight penetrated the dark shadows of the deep evergreen forest. Unfortunately, we had to leave the spell cast by this old-growth forest too soon.

Redwood Creek Overlook

From the Redwood Creek drainage, the narrow and steep Bald Hills Road ascends to near a crest above the redwood groves. Redwood Creek Overlook, 3.5 miles from Lady Bird Johnson Grove, has an outstanding view over Redwood Creek. An asphalt path from the parking lot with ISA-designated spaces leads to a fully accessible picnic area with extended tabletops at the rim of the overlook. Vault toilets are fully accessible.

The 1978 congressional mandate for expansion of the park included the entire Redwood Creek watershed and had provisions for rehabilitating the Redwood Creek area. Previously, clearcutting had caused severe erosion and landslides and destroyed salmon-spawning grounds; hundreds of miles of tractor roads had scarred the hillsides. Thirty thousand acres of the Redwood Creek expansion are part of the rehabilitation program to both protect existing old-growth areas and attempt to reestablish the forest. Both old-growth stands and areas in the rehabilitation program can easily be seen from the overlook.

Tall Trees Grove

The turnoff to the Tall Trees Grove is 1 mile south of Redwood Creek Overlook on Bald Hills Road. The trailhead to the grove is reached by a 5-mile dirt road. A free permit, available at Redwood Information Center, is required. A shuttle bus also transports visitors from mid-June through mid-September and leaves from the information center for the 17-mile ride. Tickets for the Tall Trees shuttle bus can be purchased at Redwood Information Center, but the buses are not wheelchair accessible. The 1.3-mile loop trail has significant barriers, and hikers with mobility problems will require a tremendous amount of assistance on steep slopes, eroded areas, and gravel surfaces; however, athletic wheelchair users have traversed it. The path near the world's tallest tree is flat for two-thirds mile.

Redwood Creek Trail

Returning on Bald Hills Road toward U.S. Highway 101, Redwood Creek Trail begins from a parking lot on the left a quarter-mile before U.S. 101. A picnic area and vault toilets (not wheelchair accessible) are at the trailhead. There are no ISA-designated parking spaces or curb cuts from the parking lot to the trail. Redwood Creek Trail is an 8.2-mile old roadway with bridges at stream crossings, which are removed in winter when the water is high. The trail's bridges are too narrow and have approaches too steep for wheelchairs. Its first 1.5 miles are fairly level but have ruts and eroded areas.

Davison/Fern Canyon Road

Davison/Fern Canyon Road turns off U.S. 101, .8 mile north of Bald Hills Road. This narrow, unpaved, 6-mile road to Gold Bluffs Beach and Fern Canyon affords views of the coast for whale-watching and of a large Roosevelt elk herd on the prairie between Gold Bluffs Beach and the cliffs. Fern Canyon trail is an easy .7-mile walk in summer but is in a creekbed and not accessible for wheelchair users. Sword, five-finger, and maidenhair ferns cover the 50-foot-high canyon walls carved by Home Creek.

Lost Man Creek

The road to Lost Man Creek, off U.S. Highway 101, begins across from the Caltrans field office, a half-mile north of Davison/Fern Canyon Road. This inspiring drive through redwood forest is unpaved and leads to the place where Redwood National Park was dedicated as a World Heritage Site.

Off the parking lot are fully accessible vault toilets. Lost Man Creek Trail begins at a gate. The trail has picnic sites with extended tabletops along the first quarter mile. The 11-mile unpaved old roadbed for hiking, bicycling, or wheelchairing (automobiles and motorbikes are prohibited) joins Bald Hills Road near Redwood Creek Overlook. The solitude of this road is comforting as it borders Lost Man Creek and an old-growth redwood forest. The first mile is level and suitable for wheelchair use; thereafter the road is steep in places.

Fish Hatchery

The Humboldt County Fish Hatchery is less than a half-mile from Lost Man Creek. A wheelchair-accessible bridge over Lost Man Creek allows for observation of salmon and steelhead spawning. The hatchery nurses Chinook salmon, trout, and steelhead in long outdoor ponds open for public viewing and offers an exciting experience for children. Decks border some of the ponds, but these have steps, obstructing wheelchair use. Others are without decks and accessible to everyone.

Elk Prairie

Elk Prairie, 2 miles north of the county fish hatchery, is part of Prairie Creek Redwoods State Park. Park headquarters has a small, enterable visitor center with information, book sales, and exhibits. The wall presentation about Roosevelt elk and their mating habits is at an acceptable height for children and wheelchair users. It details how the male elk congregate peacefully most of the year until the fall rutting season when competition for females becomes intense. The successful bulls establish harems of several cows, and calves are born in late spring.

On request, the visitor center loans audiocassettes and a Braille handbook for the Revelation Trail to persons with vision impairment. This half-mile self-guided trail for everyone begins behind the center on a flat asphalt path among old-growth redwoods of Elk Grove. A specially designed portion of the trail with rope and wood handrails gives people with vision impairments an opportunity to touch, feel, and smell forest vegetation. This part of the trail has steep and narrow sections off the asphalt where a wheelchair user may need assistance. Though we had difficulty with Wendy's powered wheelchair on this latter section, we found it an experience for all the senses as we touched the myriad native plants and trees on the trail.

Elk Prairie Campground, a half-mile past the entrance station, has an ISA-designated campsite on an asphalt pad. The pad was too short and narrow for Wendy to exit the van with our rear door wheelchair lift. Fortunately, we found campsites at Mill Creek in Del Norte Redwoods State Park more suitable.

The comfort station toilet stalls were fully accessible, but the moderately accessible shower stalls were narrow.

Elk often graze in the prairie bordering the campground, which makes this a prime area to view these magnificent animals with their broad racks of antlers. If these "megamammals" are not enough, try watching the Prairie Creek Redwoods State Park's renowned Banana Slug Derby. Check with the park for derby dates.

The California State Parks accept reservations for all campgrounds in the system. For reservation information, call MISTIX at 800-444-PARK (7275). Persons with hearing impairments can call MISTIX TDD number 800-272-PARK (7275).

Coastal Drive

The southern terminus of the narrow Coastal Drive is 5.7 miles north of Elk Prairie. This 8-mile scenic drive was a portion of the old U.S. Highway 101 prior to the 1964 washout of Douglas Memorial Bridge crossing the Klamath River. Coastal Drive is not recommended for trailers and RVs between Alder Camp Road and Flint Ridge.

The drive passes many overlooks with interpretive placards designed for windshield viewing, except at Gold Bluffs Beach Overlook, where a stone wall blocks the view. October through June, whales can be seen from most viewpoints. This portion of unspoiled coast is one of the more beautiful parts of northern California.

Near the junction with Alder Camp Road, High Bluffs Overlook has a picnic area with extended tabletops and one fully accessible vault toilet. We followed a paved path in an old gravel quarry to the overlook, from which we saw waves thrashing against Split Rock to the south and White Rock, a large sea stack, just to the north.

The Coast Road continues north past Flint Ridge, ending

at the northern juncture with Alder Camp Road and the Douglas Memorial Bridge wayside exhibit. The return to U.S. Highway 101 is 1 mile further.

Klamath Overlook

After crossing over the Klamath River and through the town of Klamath, the Requa Road returns to the coast high above the north banks of the Klamath River to Klamath Overlook.

As we looked out from the paved picnic area of Klamath Overlook, fog shrouded our view so that we saw only gray instead of clear blue skies and sun-filled reflections on the ocean. We could not see the horizon line where the ocean ended and the sky began. These were the famous coastal fogs, an important aspect of the redwood habitat.

Klamath Overlook has ISA-designated parking spaces, curb cuts, asphalt paths, picnic tables with extended tops, and a moderately accessible vault toilet.

Lagoon Creek and the Yurok Trail

This freshwater refuge for birds is 3 miles north of Requa Road on U.S. Highway 101. Lagoon Creek picnic area has fully accessible picnic tables with extended tops, a fully accessible comfort station, and a wheelchair-accessible fishing platform reaching out into Lagoon Pond.

From the Lagoon Creek picnic area parking lot, the 1-mile Yurok Trail is a moderately accessible dirt path. A self-guiding brochure details the sights and history of the area. The trail is bumpy but fairly level up to a steep slope before the first overlook of False Klamath Cove. Even if the blackberries that grow into the trail are trimmed and if the trail is not wet and slippery from rain, assistance is recommended. The second half of the path is more challenging in steepness and narrowness, particularly where the trail loops back after leaving the coast promontories.

DeMartin Redwood Hostel

One of the nicest and most accessible hostels on the Pacific coast is DeMartin Redwood American Youth Hostel, a half-mile north of Lagoon Creek. Call 707-482-8265 for information. The accommodations are ramped and retrofitted for wheelchair use in this former pioneer's homestead.

Mill Creek Campground

Mill Creek Campground in Del Norte Redwoods State Park, 6 miles north of Lagoon Creek and 5 miles south of Crescent City, has well-developed moderately accessible camping. Our campsite in the forest was on fairly level, hard-packed earth that turns muddy during rain. We especially appreciated the wide, barrier-free, fully accessible showers near our site. The comfort stations have fully accessible toilet stalls. The amphitheater is moderately accessible to persons with mobility problems. For reservation information at California state park campgrounds, call MISTIX at 800-444-PARK (7275). Persons with hearing impairments can call MISTIX TDD number 800-272-PARK (7275).

Vista Point

Vista Point, a turnout on U.S. Highway 101, 2 miles north of the Mill Creek Campground turnoff and 3 miles south of Crescent City, has ISA-designated spaces and interpretive placards. We enjoyed watching the sunlight play against the Pacific Ocean from this viewpoint, which overlooks the coast from the headlands south of Enderts Beach to the harbor at Crescent City, north.

Enderts Beach Road

Leading to Crescent Beach, Crescent Beach Overlook, and Enderts Beach, Enderts Beach Road is less than a mile north of Vista Point and across U.S. Highway 101 from Humboldt Road. We took the 2.3-mile road along the beaches south of Crescent City. We first stopped at Crescent Beach, which has ISA-designated parking and a picnic table with an extended top. If one can negotiate the sand, there are opportunities for bird-watching, fishing, and enjoying the beach. Crescent Beach Overlook is an excellent spot for whale-watching September through May. Wheelchair use is limited to the parking lot. Approximately a quarter-mile from the overlook, Enderts Beach Trail begins at the end of the road; it arrives at a small primitive campground with a composting toilet at Nickels Creek. Enderts Beach's tide pools can be explored at low tide, but they are slippery, uneven, and not accessible to persons with mobility problems. Ranger-led interpretive talks through this fragile intertidal zone are conducted in summer according to low-tide times. From the shore we looked north to see the lighthouse near Crescent City and the many sea stacks surrounding Crescent City Harbor, and south to the massive rock cliffs. Next we left the Parks' seashore to head inland.

Crescent Beach Information Center, overlooking the ocean, the expanse of Crescent Beach, and adjacent wetlands, is located up the first driveway to the left on Enderts Beach Road. The center was the former home of the McNamara family, whose roots run deep in Del Norte County history. It has ISA-designated parking, a ramped walkway to the entrance, and fully accessible restrooms. The center features cultural exhibits of local Native American life and lore, interpretive exhibits of the coastal zone ecosystems, and sells books and posters.

Crescent City: Redwood National Park Headquarters and Information Center

We returned to U.S. Highway 101 and continued north 2 miles into Crescent City to Redwood National Park Headquarters and Information Center at Second and K streets.

An ISA-designated parking space is on the street in front of the building under a bridge connecting the information center with the park's administration building. The information center has curb cuts and level entry. The information and book-sales counter is not lowered, but book and map displays are easily reachable. The restrooms are too narrow for wheelchair users to enter. The park's "Access Redwood National Park" brochure is available upon request at the information counter.

Stout Grove

From the information center in Crescent City, we returned to U.S. Highway 101, traveled south for a half-mile, and made a left onto Elk Valley Road. Just under 1 mile further, we made a right at Howland Hill Road, which turns into a narrow, gravel track through a large preserve of old-growth coast redwoods in Jedediah Smith Redwoods State Park. We wound our way along the thickly wooded road with huge trees almost brushing our vehicle.

The Stout Grove Trail begins 5 miles from Crescent City on the Howland Hills Road, 3 miles south of the Hiouchi Ranger Station. The half-mile duff-covered dirt loop trail is wheelchair accessible, except for a moderately steep short asphalt section from the parking lot down into the grove. Two offshoots of the trail, one down to Mill Creek and the other to the Smith River, are narrow, rooty, and too steep for wheelchairs.

As we hiked through Stout Grove, we were struck by its profound quiet. The ancient grove blocks out unwanted noise, absorbing all sound except for the whispers of a companion, the cawing of ravens, and the rapid tap of woodpeckers.

By shielding the cold, wet storms of winter and containing the moist fog that cools in summer, the coast redwoods' dense canopy creates a sheltered environment. Five-foot-high sword ferns, leathery-leafed salal, delicate maidenhair, and five-finger ferns with slender ebony-toned stems thrive in sphagnum moss mats in open areas between the trees. Mushrooms, fungi, and redwood sorrel, a small green cloverlike growth, lie in the duff at the foot of the magnificent redwoods. This living plant mass subdues the roaring distractions of modern life, allowing us, as we lingered in the grove, a quiet chance to listen to nature's soft movement.

Hiouchi

From Stout Grove, Howland Hill Road becomes Douglas Park Road. Two miles from the grove, we turned left onto South Fork Road and in a half-mile crossed both the South Fork of the Smith River and the Smith River proper. We then made a left turn onto U.S. Highway 199 toward Hiouchi Information Center and Ranger Station.

The center has a ramped entrance to the building, interpretive displays, and an information and book-sales counter that is not lowered. A picnic table with extended top is around the parking lot from the center on the grass lawn. A telephone and fully accessible restrooms are adjacent to the parking lot, which has ISA-designated parking.

From Hiouchi, NPS rangers guide kayak trips down the Smith River between early June and mid-July. Accessing the river is steep and rough, but people with disabilities can go kayaking if they give advance notice. Kayakers must be more than ten years of age and able to swim. Call Redwood National Park for information (707-464-6101).

Jedediah Smith Redwoods State Park Campground and Visitor Center

Jedediah Smith Redwoods State Park, a half-mile west of Hiouchi on U.S. 199, has trails and a campground, visitor center, and amphitheater. Surrounded by the campground, the visitor center has a narrow entrance for wheelchairs and an information and book-sales counter. The fully accessible amphitheater is outside the visitor center. There is an ISA-designated parking space for this complex.

The campground has an ISA-designated campsite with a nearby fully accessible comfort station complete with showers accessible by wheelchairs. These are similar to the facilities at Mill Creek Campground in Del Norte Redwoods State Park. Jedediah Smith Redwoods State Park receives on the average a few inches of snow twice each winter. For reservation information, call MISTIX at 800-444-PARK (7275). Persons with hearing impairments can call MISTIX TDD number 800-272-PARK (7275).

The state park and river are named for Jedediah Strong Smith, the first American of European descent to explore what are now the Redwood Parks. Smith's party journeyed from California's Central Valley to the northern coast in 1828. The Smith River is the last great wild river in northern California. Its entire watershed was recently made into the Smith River National Recreation Area.

The forests of the Redwood Parks are preserved remnants of an ecosystem that is quickly disappearing from northern California. The coast redwood, as well as all its surrounding forest life, make up what is known as a climax community, a complex ecosystem that will perpetually sustain its stable state. It will maintain itself for centuries unless natural catastrophe or humans upset its equilibrium.

John B. Dewitt, executive director of the Save-the-Redwoods League, told us that of 96,000 acres of old-growth coast redwoods presently remaining in California, 80,000 acres are preserved in Parks. Of these, 20,000 acres are in Redwood National Park and 60,000 in 31 California state parks. Mr. Dewitt estimates that at the current rate of logging, none of the old-growth forests outside the parks will remain by the year 2006. Our visit revealed to us the beauty we will lose if the ancient groves are destroyed.

(See *At a Glance: Pacific States Region.*)

ROCKY MOUNTAIN NATIONAL PARK

Estes Park, CO 80517
Headquarters: 303-586-2371
TDD: 303-586-8506
West Unit: 303-627-3471

Among the imposing mountains of Rocky Mountain National Park, tiny wildflowers of singular beauty bloom in the subalpine tundra. These fragile blossoms blanket the highlands for only six to eight weeks after the snow melts in late June. During the remainder of the year, these amazing plants survive despite the harsh winds, blowing snow, and extreme cold of arctic conditions common to this stark, treeless region.

The Rocky Mountains are the dominant range of North America. They rise from the south in New Mexico and extend north far into Canada. Rocky Mountain National Park occupies a portion of the central southern Rockies including the Front and Mummy ranges. It encompasses 414 square miles 70 miles northwest of Denver via Highway 36.

Rocky Mountain National Park preserves a pristine spectrum of diverse high-mountain life zones and scenery: snow-capped peaks, subalpine tundra, glacier-carved valleys, forests, lakes, waterfalls, and meadows. Elk, bighorn sheep, mule deer, and beavers are some of the wildlife living in the Rocky Mountains.

During the summers, early Native Americans hunted in what has become the park. Evidence of game drives and of sites used for the quest of personal visionary experiences have been found. French and American trappers most likely frequented the area, but the first written record is from 1820 when the expedition led by Maj. Stephen H. Long to the Rockies explored parts of the Front Range. Members of the survey party exulted in the high peaks they spotted, and the tallest peak (14,255 feet) would later be named for Major Long.

Homesteaders and ranchers settled the area around Estes during the late 1800s. Concerned about the growing development in the area, writer and conservationist Enos Mills spearheaded efforts to protect Colorado's high-mountain wilderness. The park was established in 1915. Today it is recognized as a World Biosphere Reserve.

Rocky Mountain National Park combines access opportunities with unique natural resources. Visitors can meander along easy trails circling unspoiled lakes, browse over beaver-dammed ponds, and explore the subalpine tundra with its intricate wildflowers.

Three distinct life zones exist in the park. In the lowest, the montane zone (below 9,000 feet), Douglas fir, ponderosa pine, lodgepole pine, and aspen grow. Grassy meadows thrive in the zone's lower valleys. Engelmann spruce, alpine fir, and limber pine loom above mosses, orchids, and heath in the subalpine zone (9,000 feet to 10,500 feet). The highest zone, the subalpine tundra (10,500 feet and above) is windswept, rocky, and almost barren. Wildflowers and cushion plants must endure low temperatures, winds that reach about 100 miles per hour, deep snowbanks, and the potent ultraviolet radiation of the thin atmosphere. This area above the tree line covers one-third of the park.

Rocky Mountain National Park has two east-side entrances at Estes Park. One is via Highway 34 to Fall River Entrance Station. The other leaves Estes Park on Highway 36 to Beaver Meadows Entrance Station. Another entrance is through Grand Lake, Colorado, near the southwest part of the park. Trail Ridge Road, the highest paved thoroughfare in the United States, stretches 50 miles through the park, connecting the eastern and western sides. Near the headwaters of the Colorado River, the road crosses the Continental Divide. There are no food stores or gas stations in the park, but Alpine Visitor Center has a snack bar and gift shop with supplies. Estes Park and Grand Lake are the nearest sources of full supplies and services. Before starting on the 50-mile Trail

Ridge Road, have a full tank of gas and check the radiator.

Estes Park is at an elevation of 7,522 feet. Frontcountry trails in the subalpine tundra are more than 12,000 feet high. These elevations can cause shortness of breath and possible dizziness; people with respiratory and/or cardiovascular problems should be especially careful. Park rangers strongly recommend that visitors check with a physician before ascending to 12,000 feet. Everyone should have sun protection and light jackets for high-elevation travel.

Visitor Center

We drove on Highway 36 through Douglas fir and ponderosa pine and came to the main visitor center (7,840 feet). Designed by Taliesen Associates, an organization founded by Frank Lloyd Wright, the upper (main) floor of this two-story building is easily accessible from the parking lot. There is ISA-designated parking.

The visitor center has an information desk where park brochures, an accessibility guide, maps, and a Braille description of the park are available. A film about the park (without captioning) is wheelchair accessible from the upper (main) floor. A captioned slide show is available with advance notice. The bookstore is on this level; its aisles might be too narrow for wheelchair maneuverability. There are lowered public telephones. Moderately accessible restrooms are behind double doors next to the information desk in the park headquarters administration area.

To explore the park itself, we went from the visitor center through the Beaver Meadows Entrance Station. We continued from the entrance station and turned left on Bear Lake Road toward Moraine Park.

Moraine Park

Moraine Park Museum (8,160 feet) is about a mile south of the turnoff from Highway 36. In a historic structure built

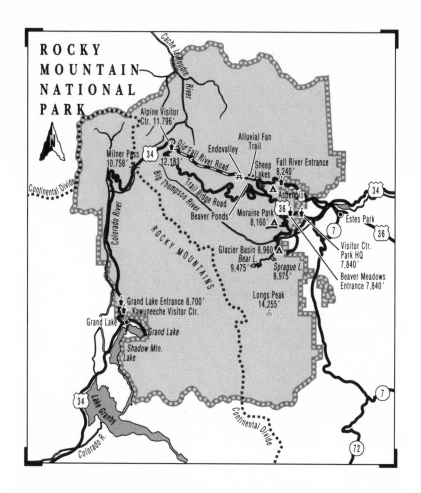

ROCKY
MOUNTAIN
NATIONAL
PARK

N

Cache la Poudre River

Alpine Visitor
Ctr. 11,796'

Milner Pass
10,758'   34   12,183'   Old Fall River Road

Continental Divide

Endovalley

Alluvial Fan
Trail

Sheep
Lakes

Fall River Entrance
8,240'

Trail Ridge Road

Big Thompson River

Colorado River

ROCKY MOUNTAINS

Beaver Ponds

Aspenglen

Moraine Park
8,160'   36

Estes Park

34

US
34

7

36

Glacier Basin 8,960'
Bear L.
9,475'

Sprague L.
8,975'

Visitor Ctr.
Park HQ
7,840'

Beaver Meadows
Entrance 7,840'

Longs Peak
14,255'

Grand Lake Entrance 8,700'
Kawuneeche Visitor Ctr.

Grand Lake

Grand Lake

Shadow Mtn.
Lake

34

Lake Granby

Continental Divide

7

Colorado R.

72

of natural stone, the museum houses an impressive collection of wildlife indigenous to the Rocky Mountains. A video
about the park begins with the push of a button. This is a
fun place to visit for anyone interested in natural history
as well as for children.

There is ISA-designated parking and a curb cut in front
of the museum leading to a moderately accessible asphalt
ramp to the ground-floor level. There are moderately accessible restrooms behind the information/sales desk. Up a steep

ramp and several steps are exhibits of Rocky Mountain national Park history and a slide presentation. Plans are under way to remodel the Moraine Park Museum to create more exhibit space, better access, and fully accessible restrooms.

The turn to Moraine Park Campground is across the road from the museum. The campground has trees and open spaces in hilly terrain. Sites are developed for tents or RVs. Moraine Park is open year-round. From June through September, reservations must be made through MISTIX (P.O. Box 85705, San Diego, CA 92138-5705; 800-365-2267; TDD 800-274-7275) eight weeks prior to the first night's stay and as late as the day before.

An ISA-designated site is across from a fully accessible comfort station in Loop A. The site has extended picnic tables, and the fireplace grill is on the ground. Every site in this campground is slightly hilly. A few other comfort stations might be enterable for some wheelchair users but are not modified for full accessibility. Wood gathering is prohibited, but firewood is sold in the campground. The amphitheater is moderately accessible along a dirt trail off Loop C. Wheelchair users may need assistance.

There are no shower or laundry facilities in Rocky Mountain National Park. Dad's Maytag Laundry in Estes Park, however, has public showers that are moderately accessible.

Wendy's brother Dick and his wife Char decided to see Moraine Park on horseback. Visitors may arrange for guided rides at stables near Moraine Park Campground. Char, who has a spinal cord injury, and Dick, who is nondisabled, report that the wranglers were extremely cooperative and say that arrangements could be made to assist persons with a variety of disabilities. In fact, the stable allowed Dick and Char to ride the horses back to their automobile so they would not have to climb a steep incline from the corral to the parking lot.

After their ride, Dick and Char met us at a moderately accessible picnic area in Moraine Park by the roadside about halfway between the campground and the road to Glacier Basin. Hot and hungry, they told us about their adventures over lunch.

Glacier Basin

The wooded and very level Glacier Basin Campground (8,960 feet) is 4 miles south of Moraine Park. There are no designated sites or facilities for people with disabilities at Glacier Basin. Most sites would be suitable for anyone; however, each comfort station has a step at the entrance. The amphitheater is accessible once a 2-inch step is crossed.

The Bear Lake Shuttle Bus departs from the parking lot across the road from the campground. The buses do not accommodate wheelchairs. If possible, use the bus on busy days to avoid parking congestion at Bear Lake.

Sprague Lake

One mile south of Glacier Basin, Sprague Lake (8,975 feet) is a fine example of a place for everyone. The Sprague family built this man-made fishing lake for their resort guests before Rocky Mountain National Park was established.

Set in a forest of Douglas fir, lodgepole pine, and Englemann spruce, the clear blue lake rarely exceeds 60°F. Reflections of Notchtop Mountain and Hallets and Taylor peaks float on the mirrorlike surface.

The trail is an asphalt, gravel, and boardwalk 1-mile loop. For the easiest visit, take the trail clockwise since the first half is fully accessible. The second half of the trail has rocks, roots, and narrow and steep portions. This section is moderately accessible, and assistance is needed.

Halfway around the lake is a sign pointing to Handicamp, which Rocky Mountain National Park created to give people with disabilities a backcountry-type experience. It has group camping for up to ten people, two large picnic tables, a fully accessible vault toilet, a fire ring, and a grill.

Only the provided firewood can be burned. The site can be reserved for up to three days; write to the park or call 303-586-2371.

We were fortunate to visit Handicamp with a group of eager teenagers who have muscular dystrophy and were spending a week at the Easter Seal Camp in Empire, Colorado. They adeptly used their powered wheelchairs along the trail to Handicamp.

A park naturalist guided them and us on an informative tour. He pointed out aspen branches that had been eaten and discarded by beavers that had earlier occupied the stream below the lake. Our group spotted a brood of ducklings clumsily following their mother out of the lake and up the bank. Mallard ducks make Sprague Lake their summer home, using the reeds along the side of the lake as nesting grounds. At Sprague Lake our group enjoyed an accessible trail through a remarkable section of Rocky Mountain National Park.

The parking lot has ISA-designated spaces and moderately accessible comfort stations. New fully accessible facilities are under construction.

Bear Lake

Continuing south from Sprague Lake 5.5 miles, the road ends at Bear Lake (9,475 feet). This popular attraction is a 30-foot-deep alpine lake formed by a now-defunct glacier.

Shuttle bus service to Bear Lake leaves from a parking lot across the road from Glacier Basin Campground. There is ISA-designated parking and a curb cut to a steep approach from the parking lot that leads to the lake. The restrooms are moderately accessible up another steep slope with no modifications inside. New fully accessible facilities are planned, but until they are built, wheelchair users may need assistance.

Char, with her wheelchair, and Dick took the moderately accessible paved half-mile trail that circles the lake. Winding among alder, juniper, limber pine, quaking aspen, Douglas fir, and Engelmann spruce, the trail has a self-guiding brochure. The first half of it, counterclockwise around the lake, is fairly level and paved. The most reachable view of Long's Peak in the park is on the northwest portion of this path. Char and Dick found that the remainder of the trail has short steep sections, rocks and roots, and a few narrow places. Assistance may be needed.

Several other trails also start at Bear Lake. Alberta Falls and Nymph Lake are short hiking possibilities for family outings. Check at the ranger information booth about suitable trails.

Fall River

The Fall River Entrance Station (8,240 feet) is an alternate point of entry from Estes Park on Highway 34. The turn for Aspenglen Campground is one-fifth of a mile inside the park boundary.

Most of the tent pads at Aspenglen are elevated. There are no level sites except #5, which is ISA designated and across the road from two pit toilets, each with a step for entry. At the other end of the campground, the amphitheater is fully accessible and has an ISA-designated parking space and a fully accessible flush-toilet restroom.

Rocky Mountain's famous bighorn sheep can be spotted 2 miles west of Fall River Entrance Station at Sheep Lakes. Many days in June and July, generally between 11 A.M. and 2 P.M., sheep come down the mountains to chew on the salty mud in the marshes around Sheep Lakes. Park only in turnouts and drive slowly (5 mph). The sheep have right-of-way.

To reach Alluvial Fan Trail, take Highway 34 one-quarter past the Sheep Lakes turnout to Endovalley Road. Three-quarters of a mile west on Endovalley Road is the first (east) parking lot for Alluvial Fan Trail.

The Lawn Lake Dam burst in 1982, creating an alluvial fan (rock moved in a spreading fashion by water). The flood pushed tons of debris down Roaring River canyon, depositing huge boulders in the fan. The half-mile moderately accessible trail with interpretive wayside exhibits is an asphalt path that traverses the fan. Viewable from the trail, Roaring River Fall rushes down, then flows under a wooden footbridge before joining Fall River.

A second (west) parking lot is at the end of the trail. For a downhill jaunt through the alluvial fan, start from the first (east) parking lot. Since this is not a loop trail, return uphill or meet transportation at the second lot.

Endovalley Picnic Area, a picturesque forested spot on the Fall River, is a mile west of Alluvial Fan Trail. There are no fully accessible ISA-designated sites. Some of the pit toilets may be enterable, at best.

The Old Fall River Road, a 9.5-mile one-way dirt road open only in summer months, takes off near the Endovalley picnic area. This route was primarily used before Trail Ridge Road was built. It is an alternate route to the Alpine Visitor Center and offers access to views of Chasm Falls. According to a ranger, visitors will get spectacular views of the mountain system from the road. If the road is uncrowded, take the one-way Old Fall River Road to Alpine Visitor Center and return via the Trail Ridge Road. Otherwise, return on the Endovalley Road to Highway 34.

Trail Ridge Road

Stupendous views, wildlife, subalpine tundra, the Continental Divide, and alpenglow sunsets enchanted us as we traveled the Trail Ridge Road (8,930 feet to 12,310 feet) over the "roof of the Rockies." This was not only a highlight of our visit to Rocky Mountain National Park, but ranked among the best of our experiences in national parks across the United States.

The Trail Ridge Road begins at Deer Ridge Junction, 6 miles from Fall River Entrance Station and 5 miles from the main visitor center. We stopped first at Beaver Ponds, a mostly boardwalk three-quarter-mile trail over ponds created and inhabited by beavers. Except for a moderately steep ramp from the parking pullout to the ponds, this trail is fully accessible. Strolling the boardwalk across the chain of ponds, we saw beaver lodges in the distance. Interpretive wayside exhibits along the trail tell the story of the beaver. The back half of the trail is a pleasant asphalt and dirt path through shady forest.

Many Parks Curve Overlook (9,600 feet), 4.5 miles west of Deer Ridge Junction, provides an incredible view of many "parks." In an older sense of the word, *park* means a flat open grassy area. Among the parks seen from this point are Moraine, Estes, and Horseshoe.

The parking lot has a hazardous slope near the road crossing for the wooden path to the overlook. The wooden path and overlook are fully accessible.

Up the road is Rainbow Curve Overlook (10,080 feet), 10 miles from Deer Ridge Junction. The overlook offers vistas of the Hidden Valley Ski Area and beaver ponds. The pullout has a moderately accessible vault toilet, ISA-designated parking, and a curb cut.

Forest Canyon Overlook (11,600 feet) is 14 miles from Deer Ridge Junction. A moderately accessible, paved, one-quarter-mile trail leads to an awesome view of snow-capped peaks 3,200 feet above Forest Canyon. We were now in the subalpine tundra.

Along the path we went by patches of snow in lawnlike meadows. The asphalt path intrudes on purple, yellow, and white alpine wildflowers. Stay on the path. Subalpine tundra is extremely fragile, and some species grow only one-quarter inch per year. Trampled areas may take hundreds of years to grow back.

The day we trekked into the subalpine tundra was the hottest day of several decades in the western United States. Denver hit 102°F and Los Angeles 108°F; Phoenix airport closed because the tarmac was too soft in the 122° heat. We were happily cool and even needed light sweaters at 12,000 feet

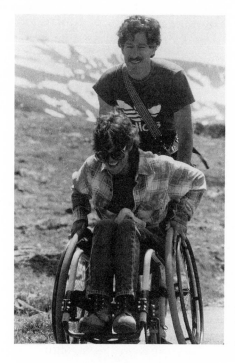

ROCK CUT TRAIL,
ROCKY MOUNTAIN
NATIONAL PARK.
Photo by Michael Tompane.

on the windy ridge tops. Snow can fall here on any day of the year.

Rock Cut (12,310 feet), 16 miles from Deer Ridge Junction, is the highest front-country trail in Rocky Mountain National Park. The parking lot has ISA-designated parking, fully accessible vault toilets, and curb cuts to the trail. Rock Cut Trail is paved but steep in sections and features a spur path into gneiss rock formations geologically older than most of the Rocky Mountains.

Ascending further into the subalpine tundra toward large mushroom-shaped rock outcroppings, we met with shortness of breath. Interpretive signs approximately every 100 feet encourage visitors not acclimatized to high altitude to rest often. Even though we had spent a week in the park above 9,000 feet, we found ourselves working to breathe on the trail.

Early spring begins in late June or early July with a fantastic mixture of flowers. Rock Cut Trail enters a fellfield, a ridge rendered dry by wind exposure. The plants of fellfields grow low to the ground in cushions and carpets. The low, tiny vegetation survives by reducing evaporation to conserve moisture.

Between Rock Cut and the Alpine Visitor Center are Iceberg Pass, Tundra Curves, Lava Cliffs, and Gore Range overlooks, all automobile pullouts for additional views of Rocky Mountain's splendid high country.

The Alpine Visitor Center at Alpine Pass (11,796 feet), open early summer to early fall depending on snow level, is 22 miles from Deer Ridge Junction and 27 miles from Kawuneeche Visitor Center at the southwest entrance to the park. There are ISA-designated parking spaces, curb cuts, and fully accessible restrooms. Pit toilets in the parking lot are open when the visitor center is closed. The center has exhibits, books and maps for sale, an information desk, and large-print copies of the park brochure. A snack bar is adjacent to the visitor center. Alpine Pass is the terminus of Old Fall River Road, which starts at Endovalley.

Trail Ridge Road crosses Milner Pass (10,758 feet) and the Continental Divide 4.5 miles west of Alpine Visitor Center. The parking lot has ISA-designated parking and fully accessible pit toilets.

The Continental Divide separates the North American drainages. From the west side, waters empty into the Pacific Ocean; from the east, they flow toward the Atlantic. Here the Colorado River headwaters on one side of the Divide begin their 1,400-mile passage to the Gulf of California. The Cache La Poudre River headwaters flow from the other side eventually to join the Mississippi River. Wendy was thrilled to know that at the interpretive wayside exhibit she was straddling the Continental Divide.

The Timber Lake Trailhead pullout, 10 miles south of Alpine Pass, has fully accessible pit toilets. Timber Creek Campground (8,950 feet), 2.5 miles further south, is open all year and has a few sites that may be accessible but are not ISA designated. The comfort stations have significant barriers, and water is not available in winter.

Kawuneeche and Grand Lake

Grand Lake Entrance Station and the Kawuneeche Visitor Center (8,700 feet) are 8 miles south of Timber Creek Campground near the southwest corner of Rocky Mountain National Park. The visitor center has ISA-designated parking, an orientation film with captions, and exhibits that are easily seen. A large relief map of the park is difficult to see from a wheelchair and too large for children or persons with vision impairments to easily access features through touch. The bookstore sells an audiotape auto tour describing Trail Ridge Road from Kawuneeche to the east side of the park. Restrooms, located outside the visitor center, are moderately accessible and always open. The nearby town of Grand Lake offers many services.

The first documented party to successfully climb Long's Peak left from Grand Lake in 1868 when William N. Byers, editor of *The Rocky Mountain News,* joined an expedition led by Maj. John Wesley Powell, geologist, professor, and explorer. Major Powell's right arm had been amputated during the Civil War. The group rode horseback southeast for two days and hiked above the timberline for two more days before Powell, Byers, and five other men arrived at the summit of Long's Peak.

More than a century later, in 1987, another explorer with a disability gained the top of Long's Peak. Michael T. Smithson, park ranger and naturalist, became the first climber with paraplegia to ascend the mountain. Accompanied by two partners, Smithson used his upper-body strength and technical climbing skills to negotiate the peak's north-face boulder and ice fields to reach the top.

Few consider the summit of Long's Peak a place where

people with disabilities would go. Major Powell and Smithson prove otherwise. The desire and ability to meet challenges is for everyone, and Rocky Mountain National Park presents a range of experiences from the very accessible to the exceedingly difficult.

Worth a Visit

Wilderness on Wheels is a .7-mile boardwalk trail through aspen, spruce, and pine forest up a mountainside near Grant, Colorado, 60 miles from Denver. The trail, which continues to grow as volunteers build it board by board, has nine campsites with raised platforms for tents, raised fire grills, and picnic tables with raised, extended tops. Fully accessible restrooms and a battery-charging station for electric wheelchairs are also available. The trail, open mid-April to mid-October, is free, but donations are accepted. Call Wilderness on Wheels for information and reservations (303-988-2212).

(See *At a Glance: Rocky Mountains and Great Plains Region.*)

SEQUOIA AND KINGS CANYON NATIONAL PARKS

Three Rivers, CA 93271
Information: 209-565-3341

H ale D. Tharp, the first Caucasian to see the sequoias of Giant Forest in what is now Sequoia National Park, was led to the grove in 1858 by Potwisha Native Americans. Drawn to the area in search of a summer grazing range for his cattle, he later made a seasonal home beside a meadow inside a giant sequoia log hollowed out by fire.

While exploring the giant sequoia belt in 1875, preservationist John Muir met up with Hale Tharp, who invited Muir back to his log home for a few days. Thus the man who claimed to be the first non-Native American visitor in the region met the naturalist key to the giant sequoias' protection from human destruction.

In fall of 1890, Congress enacted legislation designating what are now Sequoia and Yosemite national parks and the Grant Grove portion of Kings Canyon National Park to preserve the giant sequoia trees. Sequoia is the nation's second national park and California's first. Originally set aside as General Grant National Park, in 1940 it became a larger park, Kings Canyon. Jointly managed since 1943, Sequoia and Kings Canyon national parks are in the southern Sierra Nevada of eastern California, 180 miles northeast of Los Angeles and 265 miles southeast of San Francisco.

Although these are rugged mountain parks, they have some excellent, accessible trails through the relatively level groves of giant sequoias. Auto touring along Kings Canyon Highway reveals unparalleled views into one of the deepest gorges in North America, Kings Canyon. The canyon walls open out at Cedar Grove, sometimes called "the other Yosemite Valley."

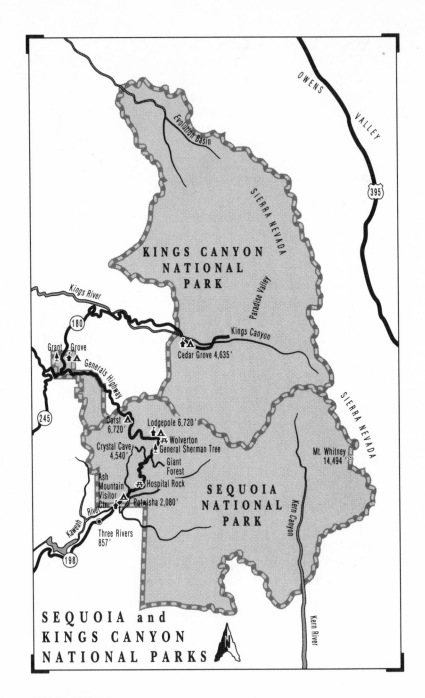

OWENS VALLEY

395

Evolution Basin

SIERRA NEVADA

KINGS CANYON
NATIONAL
PARK

Paradise Valley

Kings River

180

Grant Grove

Generals Highway

Kings Canyon

Cedar Grove 4,635'

245

Dorst
6,720'

Lodgepole 6,720'

Wolverton

Crystal Cave
4,540'

General Sherman Tree

Giant
Forest

SIERRA NEVADA

Mt. Whitney
14,494'

Ash
Mountain
Visitor
Ctr.

Hospital Rock

Potwisha 2,080'

Kaweah River

SEQUOIA
NATIONAL
PARK

Kern Canyon

Three Rivers
857'

198

SEQUOIA and
KINGS CANYON
NATIONAL PARKS

N

Kern River

Giant sequoias (*Sequoiadendron giganteum*), the largest living organisms on Earth, grow only on the west slope of the Sierra Nevada. Mostly found between 5,000 feet and 7,000 feet in elevation, seventy-five natural groves remain. The coast redwoods (*Sequoia sempervirens*), the world's tallest trees, and the small dawn redwood (*Metasequoia glyptostroboides*) are other members of the redwood family.

The trunk of the largest tree in the world, the General Sherman at the northwest portion of Giant Forest, weighs about 1,385 tons, has a maximum diameter of 36.5 feet, and stands 275 feet high; its largest branch is 6.5 feet in diameter. The tree's estimated age is 2,300 to 2,700 years. The oldest sequoia known is determined to have lived about 3,200 years in Sequoia National Park.

Giant sequoias are disease, insect, and fire resistant. Sequoia reproduction is actually closely tied to the fire cycle. Fires burning downed branches and undergrowth around the base of the big trees enrich the soil, where seeds released from the trees' cones sprout. Neighboring trees killed by the fire allow life-giving light to reach the seedlings.

Native populations of rainbow and Little Kern golden trout are being reintroduced to streams draining the western Sierran slope. The Sierra Nevadan parks are also a natural habitat for gray fox, bobcats, coyotes, mule deer, and black bears. Unfortunately, careless human visitors either leave food temptingly available or hand-feed these wild animals, upsetting their natural relationship with the environment, endangering both humans and animals.

The Sierra Nevada was formed from molten magma deep in Earth's mantle between 200 million and 60 million years ago. The magma cooled over millions of years beneath Earth's surface into crystalline granite formations of igneous rock. Pockets of marble, gneiss, and schist, found in Sequoia and Kings Canyon national parks at places like Crystal Cave (Sequoia) and at Boyden Caves in Sequoia National Forest, are remnants of an older formation that eroded and washed down into the Central Valley of California.

The new Sierran block of granite, 400 miles long and 60 to 80 miles wide, was uplifted over the last 60 million years. The eastern escarpment of the Sierra Nevada has been gradually tilted upward, creating six peaks over 14,000 feet in Sequoia National Park. Crowning these is Mt. Whitney, which, at 14,495 feet, is the tallest mountain in the contiguous United States.

Several large canyons carved by rivers and glaciers punctuate the Sierran peaks. The lower section of Kings Canyon, cut in a V shape by the Kings River, is one of the deepest gorges in North America, deeper than both the Grand Canyon in Arizona and Hell's Canyon of the Snake River in Idaho. A glacier scoured the upper part of Kings Canyon into a U-shaped valley similar to Yosemite Valley.

SEQUOIA NATIONAL PARK

Ash Mountain Visitor Center, Park Headquarters

We entered Sequoia National Park from Three Rivers, CA on California Highway 198. Our first stop was Ash Mountain Visitor Center. It has fully accessible restrooms open twenty-four hours seven days a week. The fully accessible center has an information desk, exhibits, and book sales.

Driving northeast on Generals Highway from Ash Mountain toward the sequoia groves is a remarkable experience. The Sierra Nevada looms imposingly overhead, its granite heights contrasting with the Kaweah River below. Park roads are between 1,700 feet and 8,000 feet in elevation.

Potwisha Campground and Hospital Rock

Situated in an oak woodland, Potwisha Campground is 3 miles northeast of Ash Mountain Visitor Center on Generals

Highway. The campground, near the junction of the Marble and Middle forks of the Kaweah River, has a fully accessible comfort station, water fountain, lowered telephone, and ISA-designated site with raised food storage bin (bear box) and picnic table with an extended top.

Hospital Rock, 1.6 miles from Potwisha Campground, was a key Potwisha tribal village in the area. Pictographs cover the side of a rock but have not been deciphered by contemporary scientists. Across Generals Highway from the placards describing Hospital Rock is a picnic area with ISA-designated parking, fully accessible comfort stations, lowered telephone, and picnic tables with extended tops.

Crystal Cave

The turnoff to Crystal Cave (4,540 feet) is 8.4 miles further along Generals Highway. A narrow dirt road limited to vehicles under 6,000 pounds leads 6 miles from the turnoff to the cave parking lot. The cave is open summer months only.

Heat and pressure under Earth's surface compressed limestone deposits in this region into marble 250 million years ago. Water seeping from the surface became a weak acid that dissolved pockets in the rock. Over millions of years the acid ate away at the marble, forming Crystal Cave with its cave decorations of draperies, stalactites, and stalagmites. The cave entrance is down a half-mile steep trail with steps. It is not wheelchair or walker accessible, and no strollers or backpacks are permitted. Cave temperature is a cool 48°F. Check at the visitor center for tour schedule.

Giant Forest

In 1875, John Muir walked through these enormous sequoias and called them "the Giant Forest." Four of the five largest living giant sequoias grow here. Accessible trails, notably the Trail for All People (Round Meadow), the Crescent Meadow

Trail to Tharp's Log, and the Congress Trail (with the General Sherman Tree at its beginning), highlighted our visit to Giant Forest (6,410 feet to 6,870 feet).

Crescent Meadow

From the Generals Highway turnoff to Crystal Cave, the hard right turn to Crescent Meadow Road is 2 miles further along the highway, leaving from the right (south) side of the Giant Forest Village parking lot. Crescent Meadow Road circuits the southern portion of the Giant Forest for 9.4 miles. Auto Log, 2.3 miles from Giant Forest Village, reminded us of old hand-painted postcards depicting unique features in national parks. Visitors can park their cars on top of a fallen giant sequoia for a family photo (or VCR) op.

The turn to Moro Rock is 1.5 miles further along Crescent Meadow Road. Moro Rock provides views over the Middle Fork of the Kaweah River toward the Great Western Divide. The path to the viewpoint has significant barriers (including a stairway) for persons with mobility problems.

Crescent Meadow Road ends at the trailhead for Crescent Meadow Trail. The comfort station is adjacent to the parking lot, has a step to enter the men's side, and has narrow, unmodified stalls in both women's and men's facilities. A nearby picnic area on the forest floor has moderately accessible sites with no provisions for people with disabilities.

The Crescent Meadow loop trail is a packed-dirt 1.8-mile path around Crescent Meadow to Log Meadow and Tharp's Log, returning to Crescent Meadow. This large Sierran meadow is plentiful with wildflowers in midsummer and aptly named for its shape. John Muir dubbed Crescent Meadow "the Gem of the Sierra." We hiked the first .8-mile easy, moderately accessible part to Tharp's Log and back with friends who live in New York City. Ginny, Wendy's college roommate, shared how touring the parks with us surveying accessible opportunities opened her eyes to the possibilities and difficulties of "chairing" through nature. (This was her second outing with us.)

The sometimes bumpy trail skirts the south tip of Crescent Meadow before entering a mixed-conifer forest dominated by giant sequoias. We reached Log Meadow and Tharp's Log, Hale Tharp's summer cabin inside a log. After we ate lunch looking across the meadow of dense sedges, we realized that continuing on the trail would involve slopes too steep for Wendy and her powered wheelchair. We retraced our tracks.

Giant Forest Village

This village has a moderately accessible cafeteria and a gift shop, store, and gas station. Open in July and August, an information booth up a set of outdoor stairs is not accessible to wheelchair users. There are two restrooms, one next to the cafeteria with doorways too narrow for wheelchairs and another with stairs near the information booth. A fully accessible restroom is at Giant Forest Lodge behind the lodge office.

The lodge has five large rooms, well designed to be fully accessible for wheelchair users. The shower has a tub with grab bars and a high-quality bath bench supplied by the lodge. The path from an ISA-designated parking space is rough and steep. A wheelchair user may need to park next to the laundry room and enter the guest rooms via the ramp. The lodge's restaurant is up three steps but level inside. Near the restaurant is the Giant Forest amphitheater, moderately accessible across a bumpy and sandy area from the asphalt walk behind the lodge office.

Trail for All People and Round Meadow

We visited the Trail for All People with Elizabeth, Jim, and Shirley of the Porterville, California, Developmental Center. The fully accessible .6-mile asphalt trail circling Round Meadow is bordered by giant sequoias. Having the oppor-

TRAIL FOR ALL PEOPLE,
SEQUOIA NATIONAL PARK.
Photo by Michael Tompane.

tunity to hear white-headed woodpeckers and Brewer's black-birds in an accessible grove of ancient big trees made this a memorable day. From their wheelchairs, Elizabeth delighted in pointing up to the tops of the sequoias while Shirley appreciated the wayside exhibits. Jim, on his wheeled gurney, observed Douglas squirrels scampering across the path to the meadow.

The Trail for All People, built with the help of volunteers and donations, is just south of the lodge restaurant and a quarter-mile north of Giant Forest Village. The parking lot has ISA-designated spaces and a fully accessible vault toilet.

A 1.2-mile trail to Sunset Rock also leaves from this parking lot. The hard-packed dirt trail is moderately accessible with a few short sections of narrow passage and steep inclines. Assistance may be necessary, particularly for wheelchair users attending a ranger-conducted activity on the rock.

General Sherman Tree and Congress Trail

The General Sherman Tree is the most popular spot in Sequoia National Park — and no wonder. This tree is Earth's largest living organism. The short asphalt trail around the tree has fully accessible areas, but there are moderately steep slopes from the parking lot. Restrooms below the General Sherman Tree near the turn from the highway are moderately accessible. They have narrow doorways and narrow toilet stalls without grab bars but with no significant barriers. There is one ISA-designated parking space in front of the restrooms.

The 2-mile Congress Trail begins at the General Sherman Tree and loops past some of the largest trees in the world. Visitors can use a self-guiding brochure on this trail and see trees named for Chief Sequoyah, the United States Senate, the House of Representatives, General Lee, and President McKinley, among others.

This moderately accessible trail is paved but has stretches of broken asphalt. It is steep, rooty, and with cross slopes in some places. Persons unsure of foot, wheelchair users, or young children may need assistance. The marked cutoff near stop 7, which shortens the trail, is very steep with cross slope.

Wolverton

Wolverton, a half-mile north of the General Sherman Tree, offers horseback riding and a picnic area during summer.

Lodgepole

The Lodgepole area (6,720 feet), 1.5 miles north of Wolverton on Generals Highway, has a visitor center, a large developed campground, and services. Across from the visitor center and open during summer months only are coin-operated public showers with a separate wheel-in stall, a deli/snack bar, and a gift shop, all with unobstructed entrances. The store stocks food, wood, and camping supplies. A laundromat and a full-service gas station with a lowered telephone are open year-round.

The visitor center has a fully accessible entry and an information and book-sales counter, exhibits, hands-on exhibits, a theater, and a lowered telephone. The moderately accessible restrooms at the north side of the building have short ramps to the door thresholds, wide stalls with grab bars, and lowered sinks.

In season (late May through early September), camping is reserved after April 1 and not more than fifty-six days in advance through MISTIX (P.O. Box 85705, San Diego, CA 92138-5705; 800-365-2267; TDD 800-274-7275) eight weeks prior to the first night's stay and as late as the day before. Sites are assigned at the campground, not by MISTIX. During winter months, only the parking lot is plowed for the campground.

Lodgepole Campground has two moderately accessible sites for use by persons with disabilities. The dirt sites are on a slight slope near the comfort station. They have raised bear boxes, picnic tables without extended tops, and no raised fire grills.

Dorst Campground

We were pleased to stay at Dorst Campground (6,720 feet) 8.5 miles northwest of Lodgepole on Generals Highway. Less developed than Lodgepole, Dorst is a newer campground in a mixed-conifer forest with white fir and sugar and Jeffrey pines. Sites are available on a first-come first-served basis. When we stayed at Dorst there were two ISA-designated sites with extended picnic-table tops near fully accessible comfort stations with electric outlets but without electric lights. The group campsite is available by mail reservation. For information, call the park at 209-565-3341. The amphitheater is accessible to wheelchairs but only by a back road; check with a ranger for information.

As Generals Highway continues north toward Kings Canyon National Park, it enters Sequoia National Forest. A concession-run chalet at Stony Creek has lodging: 209-561-3314.

KINGS CANYON
NATIONAL PARK

Grant Grove

Congress first set aside Grant Grove as General Grant National Park in 1890; the grove and the Kings River watersheds to the Sierran crest were incorporated in 1940 as Kings Canyon National Park. The General Grant Tree, the world's third largest living organism, is on a trail accessible to everyone.

Grant Grove is 17 miles northwest of Dorst Campground on Generals Highway, about 1.5 miles north of the junction with California Highway 180. Facilities in Grant Grove Village include a visitor center, three campgrounds, cabins, public showers, and a restaurant, gift shop, market, and gas station. The horse stables are open during summer months only. The visitor center has ISA-designated parking, a flat entrance, an information desk, a book- and map-sales area, exhibits, and a touch table. The restrooms are fully accessible with wide (though shallow) stalls and grab bars.

The restaurant, gift shop, lowered telephone, and lodge office for the cabins are fully accessible. Cabins have steps and narrow doorways presenting significant barriers. The public showers have steps and narrow stalls. From the ISA-designated parking space, the market is up a steep asphalt slope and a ramp.

The .3-mile round-trip General Grant Grove Trail loops

through an impressive stand of giant sequoias, incense-cedar, and pine. The fully accessible paved trail has an excellent accompanying self-guiding brochure. Standing next to the tall trees on the trail, we could not see their tops. When we were at a distance from them we could better appreciate their enormous size. Although its trunk quickly narrows, the General Grant Tree's base is even wider than the General Sherman Tree in Giant Forest. We found a number of interesting sites on the trail, such as double-trunk sequoias and the Fallen Monarch, a huge fallen sequoia that served as a cabin and, at another time, before the park was founded as a hotel/saloon. The U.S. Cavalry used the Fallen Monarch as a temporary horse stable when it first administered the park.

Beginning a few yards to the west of the parking lot, North Grove Loop is a 1.5-mile path with a few steep sections. Non-disabled hikers and athletic wheelchair users will find more solitude on this trail.

Grant Grove has three campgrounds: Azalea, Sunset, and Crystal Springs. Azalea is open all year, the others late May to mid-September. All are available on a first-come first-served basis. No sites have raised fire grills.

Sunset Campground, about 1.3 miles north of the junction with California Highway 180, is relatively flat in an incense-cedar and pine forest. It does not have a designated site for persons with disabilities, but many sites could be used. Near site #5 is the most enterable comfort station of Sunset. The men's side is flat and the women's is up two steps. Neither is modified with wide stalls or grab bars.

Crystal Springs Campground is .4 mile north of the visitor center on the road toward Panoramic Point. The ISA-designated site (#6) has a level parking pad and a picnic table with an extended top. Although the comfort station has a sloped entrance that may be difficult for wheelchair users, the interiors are fully accessible. Crystal Springs is the smallest campground in the Grant Grove area, and we found it to be the quietest.

Azalea Campground, the largest in the area, is on the road to General Grant Tree Trail. The ISA-designated site is #51, a very flat and sunny space adjacent to a fully accessible comfort station.

Panoramic Point offers an opportunity to look out over Kings Canyon toward the Monarch Divide. The point, 2 miles northeast of Grant Grove Village, is up a steep slope, but it is moderately wheelchair accessible. The road is open during summer months only.

Kings Canyon and Cedar Grove

For us, part of the allure of Kings Canyon National Park was the giant sequoia groves; another part was the spectacular canyon carved by the Kings River. The deepest canyon in North America, Kings Canyon, enthralled us with its shaggy granite walls dotted by pockets of oak and pine. The automobile drive from Grant Grove to Cedar Grove twists, turns, and delights. The canyon's hues of orange, red, beige, and black become especially brilliant at sunset. Cedar Grove facilities and the road are closed November through April.

On its 32-mile zigzagging journey to Cedar Grove, Kings Canyon Highway leaves the park north of Grant Grove to traverse Sequoia National Forest, passing Kings Canyon Lodge and Boyden Cave before re-entering the park. Neither the lodge nor cave has provisions for accessibility.

Cedar Grove has a ranger station, three campgrounds, public showers, and horseriding stables, and a lodge, snack bar, store, laundromat, and gas station. The ranger station has a small ramp over its threshold and provides information about Cedar Grove. Books and maps are sold there, and it has a lowered telephone. Nearby is a fully accessible amphitheater for ranger-led programs.

Sentinel Campground is the only one of the three with an ISA-designated site, #10. The site is reserved for persons with disabilities; others may use it with the understanding that they will vacate it if someone with a disability arrives.

Site #10 is level, has a picnic table with an extended top, and is near a fully accessible comfort station.

The Cedar Grove Lodge has five fully accessible rooms and a short-order snack bar, store with food and camping supplies, laundromat, lowered telephone, and gas station. The public showers have a wheel-in stall designed for wheelchair users.

Roaring River Falls, 3 miles east of the ranger station toward Roads End, was a highlight of our Kings Canyon visit. We took a short, moderately accessible paved trail with two short, steep grades to a scenic spot overlooking Roaring River Falls; from there we watched the Roaring River plunge over a smooth granite chute as the sun dipped behind Sentinel Ridge.

In the past, John Muir gave talks at Roads End Rock and Zumwalt Meadow. Park rangers today continue the tradition by leading nature walks through the area. Wheelchair users are welcome but may need assistance.

The accessible parts of Sequoia and Kings Canyon national parks are all on the western slope of the Sierra. More than 90 percent of these parks is roadless wilderness. For those who can venture into the backcountry, the Kern River basins, Mt. Whitney, Paradise Valley, and Evolution Basin tantalizingly await. But everyone can visit the giant sequoias and the spectacular Kings Canyon, and these are just some of the park's valuable assets.

(See *At a Glance: Pacific States Region.*)

YELLOWSTONE
NATIONAL PARK
P.O. Box 168
Yellowstone National Park, WY 82190
Information: 307-344-7381
Emergencies: 911

F ew believed early trappers and explorers when they described a "Yellowstone Wonderland" in northwest Wyoming Territory filled with spouting geysers, bubbling mud pots, and intensely colored steaming hot springs. The first official expeditions in the early 1870s confirmed that these were not exaggerated yarns. Not only did these thermal spectacles exist, the expeditions also reported large freshwater lakes drained by waterfalls plunging into deep canyons.

Testimony from members of these respected expeditions (the Folsom-Cook-Peterson, the Washburn-Doane, and the Hayden) ignited some conservation-minded individuals to advocate preserving this diverse wilderness area forever. Railroad and tourist interests backed the movement, resulting in the world's first national park, Yellowstone, established in 1872.

Yellowstone National Park is mostly in northwest Wyoming, with portions in Idaho and Montana. It is a short drive north of one of the great mountain parks, Grand Teton National Park, and 64 miles from Jackson, Wyoming. Elevations on park roads are between 5,314 feet at Yellowstone's north entrance and 8,530 feet in Sylvan Pass near the east entrance. Persons with respiratory and/or cardiovascular problems should be careful not to overexert themselves at these altitudes.

Yellowstone's Grand Loop Road, built in a figure eight, leads visitors through the park's five regions: Mammoth (northwest), Geyser (southwest), Roosevelt (northeast), Canyon (central-east), and Lake (southeast).

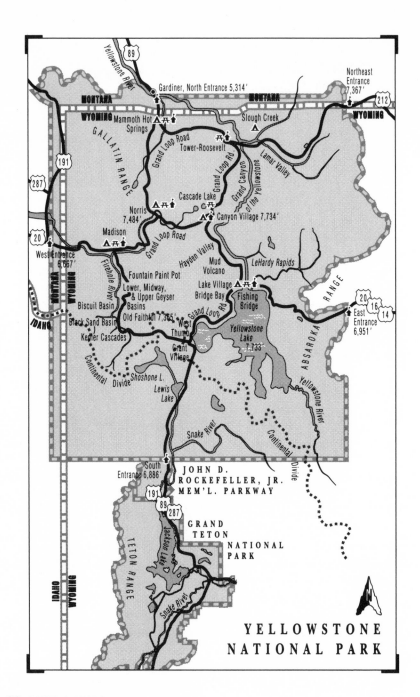

YELLOWSTONE NATIONAL PARK

We entered Yellowstone National Park from Gardiner, Montana, at the original entrance near Mammoth Hot Springs through an archway inscribed "for the benefit and enjoyment of the people." We were profoundly impressed the entire week we spent in Yellowstone. The 2.2 million acres of mostly pristine wilderness are unbelievably diverse. Many of the famous geysers, hot springs, mud pots, and fumaroles are located on the Yellowstone caldera where 2 to 3 million years ago huge sections of rock collapsed several thousand feet, forming a crater.

In addition to the geothermal features, Yellowstone Lake, and the falls of the Yellowstone River, the entire area encompasses a vibrant complex of animals, plants, and active geology. Microorganisms unique to warm, fresh water thrive beside violent eruptions of superheated steam. Free-wandering herds of bison, elk, and moose ford rivers teeming with native fish and waterfowl.

Furthermore, this is a very accessible park. Many of the popular features—geyser basins, waterfalls, rapids, lakes, campgrounds, and historic lodging—are enjoyable for visitors of all abilities. Since crossing the geothermal features could damage the fragile environment and be dangerous for anyone, the NPS has constructed boardwalks and asphalt paths throughout the various thermal areas. So anyone— including wheelchair users, those with other physical disabilities, families with young children, seniors, and people who do not wish to overly exert themselves—can visit most of these fascinating regions with relative ease.

During Yellowstone's 1988 fire, approximately 743,880 acres of parkland experienced some degree of burning. Our visit occurred on the first anniversary of the fire being extinguished. The NPS has determined that 15 percent of the park received *canopy burn,* meaning trees in the forest will probably die. Mixed degree of burn and nonforested (meadow and grassland) burn accounted for an additional 15 percent.

The aftereffects of the fire are evident throughout the park and viewable from many points along the road. In the sunny areas with canopy burn, grass and flowers sprout at the foot of blackened stumps. We saw a bison cow grazing in what had been a dense lodgepole pine forest, a place that previously would have been too shady to support grasses. Here is a natural ecosystem in transition using fire in a process to promote vigorous regeneration.

Mammoth

Our first encounter with accessibility at Mammoth Hot Springs (6,239 feet) in the park's northwest corner, south of Gardiner, was disappointing. Many of the historic structures, now park headquarters, were part of the original Fort Yellowstone, built for the army a century ago. We would hope that access modifications to the historic buildings could be made while their historic value is maintained. We were able, however, to drive through Officer's Row and get a sense of the early days. As we proceeded through the park, we found other access opportunities more fulfilling.

Mammoth Hot Springs has park headquarters, various facilities, and services. Albright Visitor Center, located in Mammoth, is moderately accessible with assistance. The park has a "Guide to Accessibility for the Handicapped Visitor," which can be obtained here. Moderately accessible restrooms are found at the visitor center's third floor and at the Terrace Grill across from Mammoth Hot Spring Hotel. There is accessible lodging in Mammoth at the Aspen dormitory during the winter only. Mammoth Campground has no accessible facilities because of the rocky and hilly terrain.

The aptly named Mammoth Hot Springs are huge circular terraces of travertine limestone formations. South of the public and government buildings in Mammoth are parking areas for the Lower Terraces trails. While there is no curb cut or designated parking, once over the curb the short stroll to Liberty Cap, a 37-foot-high cone, is fully accessible. Across the road is Opal Terrace with a moderately accessible trail leading to an opal-colored spring, which has been intermittently active since 1978. Other trails around the terraces have steps or steep grades. Further south, we took the one-way Terrace Loop Drive off the Grand Loop Road around to Lower Terrace Overlook (no curb cut) and several spectacular features in the Upper Terrace area.

The Bunsen Peak Road is a dirt, one-way drive (no trailers or RVs; subject to closure at any time based on weather conditions) around the 8,564-foot-high mountain. The turnoff is a few miles south of the Terrace Loop Drive, and the road returns near Mammoth.

On the way from Mammoth Hot Springs to Norris, we spotted moose grazing near Beaver Lake. The picnic area has fully accessible tables and a vault toilet with handrails.

Norris Geyser Basin

The hottest geyser basin in Yellowstone is Norris (7,484 feet), 21 miles south of Mammoth. There are ISA-designated parking spaces and fully accessible restrooms in the parking lot.

We toured the basin with park rangers Sonya Capek and Janet Ellis. While at that time the Porcelain Basin area was not wheelchair accessible, some improvements have been completed so that it now has a fully accessible path to below the museum. After the bottom of the steps leading from the museum, the rest of the trail still has a few very steep and cross-sloped grades. Assistance may be necessary.

The basin is stark and barren, colored by mineral oxides and devoid of plant life because of the water's acid level. Ledge Geyser in full eruption is particularly impressive.

The Back Basin at Norris boasts the world's largest geyser, Steamboat. When it erupts, which is seldom, Steamboat spews water up to 380 feet in the air. The trail is moderately accessible, and users with mobility impairments may require assistance to the geyser crater before encountering a set of stairs. To continue, retrace the route and follow the signs to Echinus and the Back Basin.

Echinus Geyser erupts more regularly than Steamboat, every thirty to seventy-five minutes. We watched as water slowly filled the sinter-lined (geyserite) crater and began to boil, leading to the eruption. A boardwalk trail without steps but with steep slopes leads to Echinus. Assistance is recommended.

We followed the longer trail, more than a mile one way, through the Back Basin along hot springs and warm pools displaying colors caused by minerals and algae. A few of the memorable geysers there include Vixen, Pearl, and Pork Chop, the latter of which exploded, probably for the last time, in September 1989. Now all that remains of Pork Chop is a pile of rocks. Much of the trail is boardwalk. Some sections are very rough. Assistance is strongly recommended in the gravelly and cross-sloped areas past Pork Chop. Either route to Echinus requires backtracking if one needs to avoid stairs.

Madison

We stopped at dusk to watch elk in Gibbon Meadow as we drove south on the Grand Loop Road toward Madison Junction (6,858 feet). Further down the road from the Meadow is the turnout for Gibbon Falls, a tumbling cascade of the Gibbon River at the edge of Yellowstone's caldera. The Gibbon Falls picnic area has a fully accessible vault toilet.

Madison Junction is 14 miles southwest of Norris and 14 miles east of West Yellowstone, Montana, a town with restaurants, lodging, gas, groceries, laundry, and wilderness suppliers.

The Madison Explorers' Museum near Madison Junction has exhibits about the early visitors to Yellowstone. From the parking lot is a steep slope, a step at the museum entrance, and toilets inaccessible for wheelchair users.

Firehole Canyon Drive is just south of the museum. The Firehole River joins the Madison River just below Firehole

Falls, visible from this one-way drive. There is a swimming hole where hot spring water mixes with the cool river. Anyone wanting to swim must first negotiate a flight of stairs.

Madison Campground has a fully accessible flush-toilet comfort facility in Loop A. Sites are available on a first-come first-served basis, though none has been ISA designated or is fully accessible. Most sites in Loop A are level with hard-packed dirt. We stayed in the lodgepole-pine forest at Madison four nights during an unseasonably warm spell in late September. We were not alone. As usual, Yellowstone National Park campgrounds were crowded.

Madison Campground was populated by all types of campers from all parts of the world. We parked our trusty van between a senior couple in a recreation vehicle and a young Swiss couple with a tiny, modern backpacking tent. As we sat by our fire one evening, we were astonished when two 35-foot Class A motor homes drove into the campground, each towing a personal helicopter. (Such helicopters cannot be used in the park.) Ah, America!

Lower Geyser Basin

Fountain Paint Pot (7,020 feet), 7 miles south of Madison, is a unique boardwalk nature trail. The walk is fully accessible except for one brief section with a moderately steep slope. In this single area we saw a selection of Yellowstone's geothermal features: hot springs and geysers, which have ample water; mud pots and mud volcanoes, which have limited water; and fumaroles and steam vents, which have no liquid water, only steam.

Steve Eide, a summer ranger at the park and a strong manual wheelchair user, took us through the Lower Geyser Basin. Steve is majoring in environmental studies, is twenty-five years old, and has a spinal-cord injury. He guided us up a short boardwalk past Silex Spring to Fountain Paint Pot, a circular basin of clay and silica mud that bubbles and spouts.

Close by are Leather Pool and Red Spouter, the latter formed by a 1959 earthquake. Red Spouter, a fumarole in summer and a hot spring from late fall to early summer, reacts to the changing water table. Further along the board-walk, we observed the Fountain group of geysers from a viewing platform above a flight of stairs. So that we could be closer to the geysers and avoid the stairs, Steve suggested we circle around and take the other end of the boardwalk.

The parking lot has ISA-designated spaces and moderately accessible vault toilets.

Across Grand Loop Road from the Fountain Paint Pot parking lot is Firehole Lake Drive. It leads to Great Fountain Geyser, which erupts every eight to twelve hours. We waited several hours on two separate afternoons for the geyser to shoot its 75- to 150-foot-high spray. No eruption. All we had to show for waiting were sunburns. The terraces of sinter around Great Fountain fill with water and are by themselves quite a display. The viewing area has steps, but the geyser is visible from the parking lot. The White Dome, Pink Cone, and Firehole Lake groups of springs and geysers are also visible along the way back to the Grand Loop Road.

Nearly a mile south of the Firehole Lake Drive turnoff on the east side of the Grand Loop Road we had lunch at the Whiskey Flat picnic area, where a coyote and a large raven tried to share our food. Fully accessible vault toilets are in this area.

Two miles further south on the Grand Loop Road, Midway Geyser Basin (7,168 feet) contains two of the largest hot springs in the world: Excelsior Geyser and Grand Prismatic Spring. As a geyser, Excelsior had been dormant since 1890, but it erupted again in 1985. There have been no other eruptions, and it now releases more than 4,050 gallons of hot water per minute. We crossed a bridge and watched, intrigued, as Excelsior's steaming water rushed down a hill into the Firehole River. The path is asphalt with a steep cross-sloped section leading to an easily negotiated circular boardwalk.

Grand Prismatic Spring, along the boardwalk, is considered

to be the largest hot spring in Yellowstone. The prism effect of colors radiates from blue near the center to green, yellow, orange, and finally red at the fringe.

Upper Geyser Basin

Nine miles south, Biscuit Basin (7,245 feet) holds several geothermal delights. The 1959 earthquake changed the character of Sapphire Pool and Rusty Geyser, increasing her activity. There is no curb cut from the parking lot, and the paved approach to Sapphire Pool has a short, steep portion. We became enamored with Shell Geyser, a regularly active, churning pool spouting every several hours. We looked down into the geyser from the boardwalk, which circles Biscuit.

Black Sand Basin (7,297 feet), 3 miles south along Grand Loop Road, is Michael's favorite group of geysers and hot springs. The dramatic thrusts of Cliff Geyser and the calmly reflective Emerald Pool complement each other. After the steep downhill slope from the parking lot with no curb cut, we took the easy boardwalk throughout Black Sand.

Nearby is the world's most well-known geyser, Old Faithful (7,365 feet), only one of the marvels in this park full of wonders. The area within 2 square miles of Old Faithful holds nearly a quarter of the geysers in the world, and we found this to be a haven for wheels, be they on wheelchairs, baby strollers, or even bicycles.

We first saw Old Faithful erupt at night after dinner. Each time we saw it blow, the interval, light, and steam were strikingly different. The park's world-famous feature is surrounded by a level, circular disconcertingly bumpy boardwalk (women using wheelchairs, wear your cross-my-hearts) with benches for resting and viewing.

Times for expected eruptions are posted in Old Faithful Inn and Lodge as well as at the visitor center. The center is moderately accessible and has an information desk, a bookstore, and exhibits. The center presents an audiovisual program about the park in its theater, which is enterable but has no other provisions for people with disabilities. A pamphlet on the show is available. The public restrooms outside the center are moderately accessible. The most accessible restrooms in the vicinity are at Old Faithful Inn and Old Faithful Lodge. Each has unisex fully accessible facilities.

The boardwalks and paths through the basin allow easy access to most of the geothermal features. Morning Glory Pool, 1.4 miles from Old Faithful, is at the far end of the pathways.

We toured Geyser Hill first. The boardwalk has very short sections with moderately steep grades. Continuing past Beehive Geyser, Lion Group, the spectacular Grand Geyser, Beauty Pool, and Riverside Geyser, the boardwalk ends at Morning Glory Geyser. Some portions of the trail have steep slopes. Later, we took the fully accessible bike path trail up to Castle Geyser, a busy and noisy geyser spewing aurally as well as visually. There are steps between Castle Geyser and the bridge over the Firehole River.

Old Faithful Inn, a national historic landmark, has a dining room (for dinner, make reservations), bar, and gift shop, all fully accessible, around the huge fireplace in the picturesque main lobby. Fully accessible rooms are at the Old Faithful Snow Lodge, which we found to be modern and spacious. The bathrooms are accessible with a grab-bar–equipped tub. Make reservations well in advance with TW Recreational Services (307-344-7311).

Old Faithful Lodge, on the other side of the geyser from the Inn, has a cafeteria, snack bar, and gift shop, all fully accessible. Hamilton General Store is moderately accessible.

Kepler Cascade

Back on the Grand Loop Road, we went 2 miles east to Kepler Cascades (7,530 feet) on the Firehole River upstream from the Old Faithful area. The fully accessible viewing platform offers a dazzling overhead look of the cascades.

We headed back to our campsite at Madison and readied ourselves to begin exploring the east side of the park.

Tower-Roosevelt

In north-central Yellowstone we left the thermal areas for the Tower-Roosevelt region (6,270 feet) approximately 45 miles from Madison Junction. At Roosevelt, we found meadows, gorges, and forest much burned by the 1988 fire. Here are a view of a petrified redwood tree, the Roosevelt Village area, and a moderately accessible overlook of Tower Falls. Roosevelt Lodge, which has a dining room, a gift shop, and restrooms, is moderately accessible. The rustic cabins have no provisions for persons with disabilities. Horseback and stagecoach rides are available. Call the concessionaire, TW Recreational Services, for information (307-344-7901).

After viewing Tower Falls, 2 miles southeast of Roosevelt Village, we headed northeast into the Lamar Valley, where wildflowers bloom prolifically in the springtime. We returned to Tower Junction and continued south on the Grand Loop Road. We went over Dunraven Pass and saw the expanse of the Yellowstone caldera.

Cascade Lake

Ranger Steve Eide led us to the Cascade Lake Trail picnic area (7,850 feet), 17.5 miles south of Tower Falls or 1.5 miles north of Canyon Junction on the Canyon/Tower Road. After lunch he showed us a rugged trail he uses to go backpacking at Cascade Lake.

Cascade Lake Trail is a backcountry path with logs laid across to control water from washout. Steve negotiated the logs and gentle hills of this trail in his manual chair, but Wendy's electric wheelchair was unable to jump the logs. Steve took Michael to a meadow where bison grazed. This outing has significant barriers but is doable for athletic wheelchair users.

CASCADE LAKE TRAIL,
YELLOWSTONE
NATIONAL PARK.
Photo by Michael Tompane.

Canyon

The Grand Canyon of the Yellowstone River begins where the Upper and Lower falls enter a crescent-shaped gorge. The canyon then curves north to Tower Falls. Canyon (7,734 feet) is 19 miles south of Tower-Roosevelt and 12 miles east of Norris Geyser Basin.

There are north and south rims, both near Canyon Junction. On the south rim, Steve Eide guided us to Artist Point, where Thomas Moran had executed his famous painting of the Lower Fall. While the overlook is level and offers views of the falls from several points, the moderately accessible trail has a steep portion with cross slope. Assistance may be necessary.

The Uncle Tom's Trail Lookout toward the Upper Fall is fully accessible. The trail to a viewing terrace above the Lower Fall is a tough, moderately accessible route. Entry to the comfort station is moderately accessible, but no provisions have been made in the interior for persons with disabilities.

The north rim area has a visitor center, dining room, cafeteria, snack shop, gift shop, and restrooms, all only moderately accessible. Canyon Lodge and entry to the stage-coach and horseback rides have stairs. A shower and laundry are also moderately accessible. Check with TW Recreational Services for information (307-344-7901).

Hayden Valley

The environs of Yellowstone support the park's well-known large herds of magazine-cover mammals: bison, elk, bears, deer, and moose. While driving the 16 miles between Canyon and Lake Yellowstone, we saw great numbers of these animals grazing in the wide, rolling expanses of Hayden Valley. We watched bison crossing the road, regularly holding up traffic and entertaining human visitors. The wild animals can be dangerous. Never approach or feed any animal in the park.

Mud Volcano, about 10 miles south of Canyon, marked our reentry into the thermally active areas. Hot springs, fumaroles, and mud pots seethe and boil. The region underwent changes after a series of earthquakes in 1978–1979. Many trees were killed, old features increased in activity, and new ones formed on the surface. It was raining when we went to Mud Volcano, emphasizing the dense steam rising from the hot spots.

We followed the boardwalk to Mud Volcano and continued to Dragon's Mouth. The walk has short sections of moderately steep slopes and loops around back to the parking lot, where there is a fully accessible vault toilet.

We took an asphalt trail, with a very steep grade in the first portion to Black Dragon's Caldron. The dramatic, evil-looking spring heaves black mud up from the bottom of an acidic pool. It first appeared in 1948 and continues to grow.

One of the most pleasant afternoons we spent at Yellowstone was at LeHardy Rapids on the Yellowstone River, 1.5 miles south of Mud Volcano. The trail along the river connects two parking areas off the Grand Loop Road inter-rupted by stairs one-third of the way from the south end. We started at the north end on a dirt path that becomes a boardwalk. Here we enjoyed several highlights of our wild-life experiences at Yellowstone. Cutthroat trout leapt through the whitewater, possible prey for the blue heron perched on the far bank. Later, we came across a small group of bison fording the river.

Yellowstone Lake

Yellowstone Lake has five areas developed for lake recrea-tion. Fishing Bridge, Lake Village, Bridge Bay, West Thumb, and Grant Village. Bridge Bay has the only moderately ac-cessible boat-docking and tour facilities. Boat tour conces-sionaire employees will assist persons with disabilities. They will carry a person who uses a wheelchair from the dock onto the boat, but will not allow the wheelchair on the boat. Call ahead to TW Recreational Services (307-344-7901).

Fishing Bridge, operated by TW Recreational Services, is by reservation and for hard-sided vehicle and RV camp-ing only. It is the sole campground in Yellowstone with full hookups.

West Thumb Geyser Basin is a moderately accessible geo-thermal area. It is a dynamic spot for watching geysers spout just off the lake's shore.

There are two lodges with accessible accommodations at Yellowstone Lake. The Lake Yellowstone Hotel, a national historic landmark, has five moderately accessible units in the Sandpiper Annex. Grant Village Lodge has twelve mod-erately accessible rooms. At both, some rooms are more ac-cessible than others. Check with TW Recreational Services.

Campgrounds at Bridge Bay and Grant Village have no ISA-designated sites or modified facilities. Both areas are moderately accessible and not difficult to negotiate. Sites at Bridge Bay can be reserved through MISTIX (P.O. Box 85705, San Diego, CA 92138-5705; 800-365-2267). Grant Village has the advantage of showers located close by. The concessionaire will make arrangements for people with disabilities. Check in several hours ahead. There are no widened shower stalls or grab bars, but plastic chairs for sitting in the stalls are available. The restrooms near the showers and laundry are fully accessible.

Lewis Lake

Lewis Lake is between Yellowstone Lake and the south entrance to the park, approximately 10 miles north of the latter. There is a campground on relatively level land, and parts of it are moderately accessible. Not all the toilets have accessible entryways. The lake boat dock is not accessible.

Yellowstone has thermal features found nowhere else in the world. Only if it were possible to visit New Zealand, Iceland, and Africa simultaneously could the Yellowstone experience be duplicated. To further have waterfalls, wildlife, and an unusually accessible wilderness area makes Yellowstone one of this country's premier national parks.

(See *At a Glance: Rocky Mountains and Great Plains Region.*)

YOSEMITE
NATIONAL PARK
Yosemite Park, CA 95389
Information: 209-372-0265
Recorded Information: 209-372-0264
TTY: 209-372-4726

A world of surpassing beauty, so perfect and
intense that we cannot imagine . . .
— Ansel Adams, 1931

Yosemite has all the characteristics of a fine masterpiece: a balance of form, composition, texture, and color. Like a great work of art, Yosemite's beauty is unquestionable. Waterfalls cascade over sheer cliffs into the valley below while high above smooth domes and spires of granite create the almost-formal look of this natural setting.

Featuring 8 miles of paved trail through the Yosemite Valley, parts of Yosemite National Park's scenic frontcountry are accessible to everyone. Most developed facilities and trails in the valley, including the trail to the base of the famous Yosemite Falls, are at least moderately accessible. Forests, huge granite formations, meadows dotted with wildflowers, groves of giant sequoias, and a winter ski program for people with disabilities are some of the park's pleasurable opportunities for the access-conscious visitor.

Situated in the central Sierra Nevada of eastern California, Yosemite is 193 miles southeast of San Francisco and 315 miles northeast of Los Angeles. Elevations on the park's roads range from 2,127-feet to 9,945 feet. Visitors with respiratory and/or cardiovascular problems may wish to consult a physician before venturing above 4,000 feet.

The first people to live in this area called it *Ahwahnee,* meaning "deep grassy valley," and themselves the *Ahwahneechee.* These Native Americans migrated from the Great Basin more than four thousand years ago. They were threatened when thousands of miners moved into Indian country after gold was discovered in the Sierra foothills (1849–1850). The Mariposa Battalion entered Yosemite Valley in 1851 and moved a group of the Ahwahneechee to a reservation near Fresno, California. Later, the relocated Native Americans returned to live for a while in the valley.

Yosemite's popularity spread quickly as it attracted tourists, jeopardizing the valley's virgin condition. President Abraham Lincoln signed a bill passed by Congress in 1864 mandating that the state of California protect and preserve Yosemite Valley and the Mariposa Grove of giant sequoias. John Muir, the famous conservationist, spent his first summer at Yosemite in 1868. Largely as a result of his energies, Yosemite was established as a national park in 1890. Yosemite National Park and the original mandated lands were combined in 1906.

The Sierra Nevada, from the Spanish words for "snowy mountains," were formed between 200 million and 60 million years ago from molten lava deep in the Earth's mantle. Over millions of years, the magma cooled very slowly beneath the Earth's surface into crystalline formations of igneous rock. This granite was uplifted and became exposed over the last 60 million years. The sculpted surfaces of granite—like Half Dome and Sentinel Dome—were rounded and smoothed when erosive glaciers moved down the Tuolumne and Merced river canyons. Sheer cliffs like El Capitan resulted from bedrock joints being split by uplift. Rocks continue to flake off (exfoliate) even today as water freezes and expands in the cracks of the huge granite forms.

Yosemite has three groves of giant sequoias: Mariposa, Tuolumne, and Merced. These big trees, the largest living organisms on Earth, grow only in the Sierra Nevada. Some are 250 feet in height, 15 to 20 feet in diameter, and possibly two thousand to three thousand years old.

We entered Yosemite late at night via Highway 140. We awoke the next morning beside the Merced River surrounded by the splendors of Yosemite Valley.

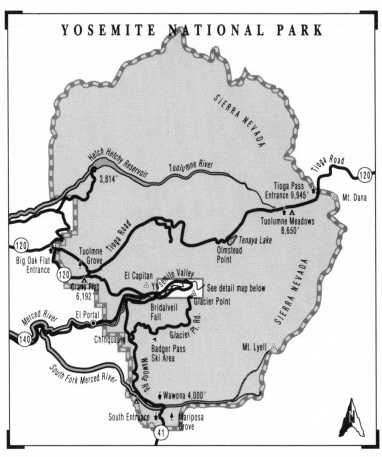

YOSEMITE NATIONAL PARK

SIERRA NEVADA

Hetch Hetchy Reservoir
3,814'

Tuolumne River

Tioga Road

120

Tioga Pass
Entrance 9,945'

△ Mt. Dana

Tuolumne Meadows
8,650'

Tenaya Lake

Olmstead
Point

120

Tuolmne Grove

Big Oak Flat
Entrance

120

Crane Flat
6,192'

El Capitan

△ Yosemite Valley

See detail map below

El Portal

Glacier Point

Merced River

Bridalveil
Fall

Glacier Pt. Rd.

SIERRA NEVADA

140

Chinquapin

Glacier
Point

Mt. Lyell △

South Fork Merced River

Badger Pass
Ski Area

Wawona Rd.

Wawona 4,000'

South Entrance

Mariposa
Grove

41

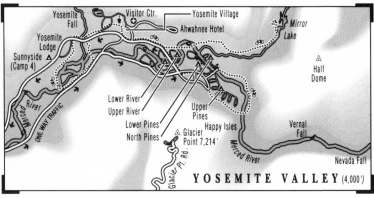

Yosemite
Fall

Visitor Ctr.

Yosemite Village

Ahwahnee Hotel

Mirror
Lake

Yosemite
Lodge

Sunnyside △
(Camp 4)

△ Half
Dome

Merced River

ONE WAY TRAFFIC

Lower River
Upper River

Upper
Pines

Lower Pines
North Pines

Happy Isles

Glacier
Point 7,214'

Vernal
Fall

Glacier Pt. Rd.

Merced River

Nevada Fall

YOSEMITE VALLEY (4,000')

Yosemite Valley

The Yosemite Valley (4,000 feet) is a bustling town with ten thousand to twelve thousand people recreating or working in it each day. Its services include visitor centers, an Indian Museum, campgrounds, restaurants, gift stores, sports shops, ice cream shops, and lodging and a medical clinic, gas station, post office, gallery, Ansel Adams Photography Studio, food market (Yosemite Valley Store), laundromat, delicatessen, pizza parlor, courthouse, fire department, dog kennel, and recycling center, all fully accessible.

Restrooms, also fully accessible, are located at the visitor center and in restaurants. Volume-control telephones are located at the parking lot on the east side of Yosemite Valley Store.

Cars are permitted to drive most of the road system that goes through the valley, and free shuttle buses operate throughout the village, lodging, and campground areas in the eastern end of the valley. Three of the ten buses are equipped with wheelchair lifts and two have tie-downs. The buses run on a regular schedule. Call the Yosemite Transportation System (209-372-1241) for the schedule. Traffic and parking are often congested, so we recommend using the shuttle whenever possible.

The village campgrounds, restaurants, lodging, and trails are connected by 8 miles of paved bicycle paths, which are excellent thoroughfares for wheelchair users. Pedestrian paths are also suitable for everyone: families with young children and strollers, seniors, and those looking for an easy walk.

On one part of the bike path on the edge of Ahwahnee Meadow, Mark Wellman passed us in an arm-driven tricycle as he conducted part of his daily workout routine. Mark is a park ranger and Yosemite's access coordinator. He uses a wheelchair as a result of a backcountry climbing accident. In June 1989, he and his climbing partner, Mike Corbett, completed a historic eight-day ascent up the face of El Capitan.

The two had developed an apparatus that allowed Mark to use his upper-body strength to climb "El Cap." Mark executed eight thousand pull-ups while Mike set and removed protective devices along the vertical route.

Valley Visitor Center

Valley Visitor Center, in the heart of Yosemite Village, has an information desk, book and map sales, and an orientation slide show and short videodisc program, both with captioning available. Ask for an access guide for people with disabilities. Large-print versions of trail guides for the Village of Ahwahnee self-guided trail and A Changing Yosemite nature trail are available. A park road guide and auto tour audiotape are available from the visitor center and from information stations. Sign-language interpretation is available during summer months. Some ranger-led programs listed in the *Yosemite Guide* newspaper are also signed.

ISA-designated parking for the visitor center is behind the nearby post office. Fully accessible restrooms are adjacent to the visitor center. The Indian Museum and Art Museum Gallery are in the building next to the visitor center, and both are wheelchair accessible.

The Village of Ahwahnee trail begins directly behind the visitor center and can be an enlightening experience for all ages. The self-guided trail is fully accessible. We toured the Ahwahneechee village, reconstructed by the NPS as it might have been circa 1872, with Jeff Samco, an interpretation ranger for the park. Jeff has a vision impairment, wears thick glasses, and, to read, holds large-print documents literally up to his nose.

Jeff took us first to a *chuckah,* an acorn storage structure made with branches and pine boughs, and to an *umacha,* a winter shelter of poles and cedar bark. Jeff pointed out the village *hangi,* or roundhouse used for ceremonies, and the sweat lodge next to it. Village life centered around the granite pounding rock where women ground acorns into a fine flour used for acorn cakes and mush, the preferred dietary staples of the Ahwahneechee.

Another self-guided nature trail, A Changing Yosemite, begins in front of the visitor center. The trail follows the bike path west and has numbered posts corresponding to information in the trail booklet, available in large print at the visitor center. This is a 1-mile loop of Cook's Meadow skirting black oak and incense cedar groves.

Yosemite Falls

At the road near the end of the Changing Yosemite trail, the moderately accessible Lower Yosemite Fall trail begins. Visitors can also drive and park in the fall trail's lot with ISA-designated spaces. A unisex restroom adjacent to the parking lot is fully accessible.

Before taking the trail, look up to see Yosemite Falls' entire 2,425-foot drop into the valley. This is the highest waterfall in North America and the second highest in the world. Yosemite Falls is actually a series of two falls divided by a cascade. Rapidly melting snow in the spring creates heavy runoff so that the falls gush over the cliffs. At the end of summer the water can become a trickle or, in drought years, completely dry.

The trail is a paved and level quarter-mile round-trip with some potholes and small rocks. The last 50 feet have steep sections. This moderately accessible trail ends at the boulder-strewn base of the Lower Fall. When we were there on a warm early-autumn day, the falls were running low; the spray off the boulders felt refreshing, and we found the view awe-inspiring.

Valley View

When the photographer Ansel Adams first visited Yosemite National Park in 1916, he wrote, "We finally emerged at

Valley View—the splendor of Yosemite burst upon us and it *was* glorious." At Yosemite, Adams would make some of his most renowned photographs.

Valley View Overlook (3,990 feet) is near the intersection of the outward-bound valley road from Yosemite Village and Highway 120, known as the Big Oak flat road. The view is from the parking area.

Bridalveil Fall

From Valley View we turned left, crossed Pohono Bridge, and followed the signs to return to the village. Bridalveil Fall parking lot is approximately 1 mile further on the right.

Wendy's brother Dick and his wife Char had joined us at Yosemite for a few days. With Mark Wellman, we trooped off to Bridalveil Fall in the western end of the valley, Mark in his sport wheelchair, Char in her sport wheelchair, Wendy in her electric "tractor" chair, and Dick and Michael on foot.

The moderately accessible trail to Bridalveil Fall is paved but steep in sections. Even though Char and Mark each have excellent upper-body strength, they had to push hard to gain the top of this quarter-mile trail. Winter visitors can expect snow and icy patches, which create bumps in the asphalt.

Bridalveil Creek plunges 620 feet to the valley floor in a long, thin, wispy train of water, usually blown delicately in the breeze—hence the name Bridalveil. The five of us crowded into the observation area at the trail's end to watch the fall.

Happy Isles

Any automobile displaying a placard for persons with disabilities (obtainable from state governments or the visitor center) is permitted on the road to Happy Isles and Mirror Lake. Other visitors can reach these areas on the free shuttle bus, by bicycle, or on foot. By car, continue eastward 5 miles from Bridalveil Fall past Housekeeping Camp and take

TENAYA LAKE,
YOSEMITE NATIONAL PARK,
CALIFORNIA.
Photograph by John Livzey.

RAFT TOUR, SANTA ELENA CANYON,
BIG BEND NATIONAL PARK, TEXAS.
Photograph by Michael Tompane.

RAPIDS, SANTA ELENA CANYON,
BIG BEND NATIONAL PARK, TEXAS.
Photograph by Big Bend River Tours.

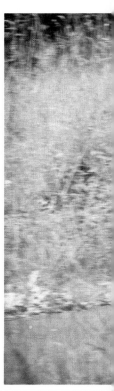

MADISON CREEK TRAIL,
OLYMPIC NATIONAL PARK, WASHINGTON.
Photograph by Richard A. Roth.

HOH RAIN FOREST,
OLYMPIC NATIONAL PARK,
WASHINGTON.
Photograph by Michael Tompane.

ELWHA VALLEY,
OLYMPIC NATIONAL PARK,
WASHINGTON.
Photograph by Richard A. Roth.

**BELOW, TOP: ROARING RIVER FALLS,
KINGS CANYON NATIONAL PARK, CALIFORNIA.**
Photograph by Michael Tompane.

**BELOW, BOTTOM: BIG MEADOWS CAMPGROUND,
SHENANDOAH NATIONAL PARK, VIRGINIA.**
Photograph by P. D. Fyke.

MOUNT OLYMPUS FROM HURRICANE RIDGE,
OLYMPIC NATIONAL PARK, WASHINGTON.
Photograph by Michael Tompane.

SPRUCE TREE HOUSE,
MESA VERDE NATIONAL PARK, COLORADO.
Photograph by Michael Tompane.

**CASA RINCONADA,
CHACO CULTURE NATIONAL
HISTORICAL PARK, NEW MEXICO.**
Photograph by Michael Tompane.

YAKI POINT, SOUTH RIM,
GRAND CANYON NATIONAL PARK, ARIZONA.
Photograph by Michael Tompane.

RAINY LAKE,
OKANOGAN
NATIONAL FOREST,
NEAR NORTH CASCADES
NATIONAL PARK,
WASHINGTON.
*Photograph by
Michael Tompane.*

OCONALUFTEE
PIONEER FARMSTEAD,
GREAT SMOKY MOUNTAINS
NATIONAL PARK,
TENNESSEE.
*Photograph by
Michael Tompane.*

FOREST CANYON
OVERLOOK,
ROCKY MOUNTAIN
NATIONAL PARK,
COLORADO.
*Photograph by
Richard A. Roth.*

RANGER SIGNING FOR THE DEAF,
MALTESE CROSS CABIN,
THEODORE ROOSEVELT
NATIONAL PARK, NORTH DAKOTA.
Photograph by Michael Tompane.

OPPOSITE: SCOUT GROVE,
JEDEDIAH SMITH REDWOODS
STATE PARK, NEAR REDWOOD
NATIONAL PARK, CALIFORNIA.
Photograph by Michael Tompane.

BELOW: PAHAYOKEE TRAIL,
EVERGLADES NATIONAL PARK,
FLORIDA.
Photograph by Michael Tompane.

Photograph by John Livzey.

the turnoff toward Curry Village and the day-use parking area. After .3 mile, make a right turn on the road marked with ISA signs and Do Not Enter; the road leads .7 mile further to Happy Isles.

The Merced River separates into channels at Happy Isles after descending from the high Sierra in a series of waterfalls, the last being 317-foot-high Vernal Fall. Microecosystems flourish on the isles in this deltalike watercourse. Bridges connect trails meandering through the islands. One bridge to an island is now fully accessible, and a project is under way to make the whole Happy Isles area accessible to all.

The 212-mile John Muir Trail to Mt. Whitney begins at the bridge without steps. Moderately accessible and difficult trails lead to islands in the channeled river. A .9-mile trail to Vernal Fall bridge is very steep. The Happy Isles Nature Center is enterable from the rear (river side) for those who want to avoid steps. The center has ecological exhibits, especially directed toward children, concerning the habitats around Happy Isles. The center is open during summer months and on spring and fall weekends.

An accessible telephone is located between the bridge and an ice cream stand, which operates during summer months.

Mirror Lake

During times when water is plentiful, Half Dome and Mt. Watkins reflect on the surface of Mirror Lake, 1.6 miles from Happy Isles on the restricted road. Sediments are slowly filling in the lake, and Mirror Lake will eventually become a meadow, much the way other lakes have become meadows over time at Yosemite.

A viewing area on the west side of the lake overlooks this scene of sculptured granite formations and their reflections. A moderately accessible 3-mile dirt trail circles the lake, but use it cautiously; horses frequently lay road apples on this passage.

The lake is accessible to an automobile with an ISA placard.

Others must hike from the shuttle bus stop at the foot of the small hill. To return to the village and campgrounds, turn right at the first junction from Mirror Lake.

Campgrounds

Upon entering Yosemite Valley via Highway 120 or 41, follow the signs 5.5 miles to Upper and Lower Pines campgrounds. These have the only fully accessible campsites in the valley. Like all valley campgrounds, they require reservations year-round through MISTIX (800-365-2257). The campground reservation office in the day-use parking lot is moderately accessible, and campsites may be available on a day-to-day basis.

Loop A of Lower Pines has asphalt paths to a fully accessible comfort station. Most sites are flat, the dirt surface is hard packed, and one site has a picnic table with an extended top. Fully accessible public showers are available at nearby Curry Village.

We stayed in both Upper and Lower Pines campgrounds and enjoyed the ponderosa pines surrounding our sites. Unfortunately, we learned that people bring their problems with them to the national parks. Upon returning from a day of touring the valley, we discovered that someone had made off with Wendy's standing table, which had been securely fastened to the picnic table in our site, along with a folding chair. Do not leave irreplaceable items at your campsite.

Sunnyside Campground, 1 mile west of the Valley Visitor Center, is open on a first-come first-served basis. It has moderately accessible, level, walk-in campsites with a nearby fully accessible comfort station.

Lodging

Curry Village accommodates visitors in tent cabins, cabins, and hotel rooms. For people using wheelchairs, there are ten moderately accessible or fully accessible cabins; they do not have bathrooms, but accessible toilets and showers are nearby. Curry Village (open spring to fall and weekends and holidays during the winter) has gift and mountain shops and bike rentals and a cafeteria, snack bar, bar, and tour desk, all fully accessible. Winter snow may inhibit access to cabins.

Yosemite Lodge, west of Yosemite Village, is open year-round. It has an amphitheater, restaurants, and bike rentals and a cafeteria, lounge, ministore, gift shop, and tour desk, all fully accessible. There is also a swimming pool, which may require assistance. Near the registration desk is a fully accessible restroom. The gas station is across the road.

Accommodations in the lodge run the gamut from deluxe rooms to rustic cabins without baths. The hotel building has one fully accessible room. We stayed in one of the accessible cabins with fully accessible bathrooms. Deer grazed just off our front porch in the early mornings and late evenings.

We were elated to find a large wheel-in shower complete with a padded fold-down bathing bench and both wall-mounted and hand-held shower heads. Since the cabins are situated in a clearing, reaching them during winter snows can be difficult. We found these facilities to be the most accessible in any national park we visited.

The Ahwahnee, a National Historic Landmark and a renowned hotel, is open year-round. A restaurant, gift shop, lounge, and unisex restroom are fully accessible. Two cottage units are easily enterable and have fully accessible bathroom and shower stalls.

Another activity at Yosemite is rock climbing. Between the Ahwahnee and Yosemite Village, Mark Wellman gave us a real treat. Along with Dick and Char, we met this innovative rock climber at Church Bowl, a popular short-pitch climbing area. We scrambled up a casual trail to watch Mark and his partner Mike Corbett climb. Mike helped Mark secure his climbing harness and protective gear.

Mike then led a route up the rock to a tree and tied off

a rope while Mark finished testing his gear. Tying the end of the rope to his wheelchair, Mark attached a ratcheted pull-up bar to the rope. With a few strong pulls, Mark began to scale the rock, leaving his chair at the base attached to the rope like an anchor. His strength, conditioning, and dedication impressed us.

The evening before this climb, we had sat in the presence of three unforgettable climbers of El Capitan: Warren Harding, who scaled it first (in 1958); Mike Corbett, who has climbed it the most (more than forty times); and Mark Wellman, who accomplished the first ascent by a person with a spinal cord injury (1989). Mark and Mike successfully climbed Half Dome in 1991. Yosemite Valley had engaged and inspired us with its beauty and the memorable accomplishments of spirited people.

Glacier Point

To visit Glacier Point, take the exit road west from Yosemite Valley Village. Follow the signs toward Glacier Point and/or Wawona. An overlook immediately before the Wawona Tunnel, Tunnel View, offers an impressive vista of the valley and its most notable features. The Wawona Road (Highway 41) climbs 7.5 miles from the valley to Chinquapin, with Wawona straight ahead another 13 miles or Glacier Point 16 miles to the left.

Glacier Point (7,214 feet), on top of a sheer cliff, delivers a panorama of the valley and its glacier-carved formations. To the southeast, the Merced River flows over Nevada and Vernal falls into the valley. Eastward, the face of Half Dome is seen practically edge on. Mt. Watkins, North Dome, and Yosemite point stand shoulder to shoulder in the north. The entire drop of Yosemite Falls and El Capitan complete the sweep.

The .6-mile trail from the parking lot to Glacier Point is fully accessible, although some sections are moderately steep and assistance may be required. The parking lot has ISA-designated parking spaces. Restrooms, a snack bar, and a gift shop are moderately accessible. The open-air geologic exhibit is up a flight of stairs.

The road to Glacier Point is closed in winter at Badger Pass Ski Area, the oldest ski operation in California. Badger Pass has a "sit-ski" program, which allows an adult or child with paralysis of the lower body to ski in a kayaklike device. The skier controls the sit ski with upper-body movement and short poles while tethered to a trained, nondisabled companion. Instructions and sit-ski rentals (to pupils only) are by advance reservation. The program is conducted by the Yosemite Ski School. Call 209-372-1330 for information and to sign up for lessons.

Wawona

Wawona (4,000 feet) is 13 miles south of Chinquapin and 5 miles north of the South Park Entrance Station on Highway 41. Located on the South Fork of the Merced River, the area has riding stables and a hotel with restaurant, golf course, gas station, and grocery store.

The Pioneer History Center consists of a stagecoach office, a jail, cabins, homes, barns, other historic buildings, and wagons and carriages gathered from around the park. A historic covered bridge spans the South Fork of the Merced River. Near the parking lot are moderately accessible restrooms.

The Wawona Hotel, an elegant, historic structure, has accommodated guests for more than a hundred years. The California-style Victorian building graces a large lawn where deer sometimes graze. Wheelchair users can enter two rooms, although the rooms are not fully accessible. Communal bathrooms for lodgers are not wheelchair accessible. The restaurant is fully accessible through the rear entrance. Restrooms outside at the rear of the hotel have no modifications and narrow doors. The Wawona Hotel is open Easter week through Thanksgiving Day and for a few weeks around Christmas and New Year's days.

The Wawona area of Yosemite offers a flavor of the Gold Rush and pioneering days in the Sierra. During summer months the park presents living-history activities such as stagecoach rides, campfires, parades, old-fashioned games, and tours.

Mariposa Grove

The park's largest grove of giant sequoia trees, the Mariposa Grove (6,200 feet), is 2 miles from the South Park Entrance Station and 35 miles south of Yosemite valley. Here stands the Grizzly Giant, perhaps the oldest living sequoia.

Fire can be a friend to the giant sequoias, burning other plants on the forest floor, which complete with the sequoia seedlings for sunlight. Burned plant matter provides a mineral-rich soil in which future giants can better grow.

There are ISA-designated spaces and a fully accessible vault toilet in the parking lot. Any automobile displaying a placard for persons with disabilities may drive through the grove but must follow a tram tour. Check with the tram dispatcher for tour times. An audiotape cassette of the interpretive tour is available for persons following the tour in automobiles. The tape is not specifically designed for people with visual impairments.

Hetch Hetchy

Hetch Hetchy Reservoir is north of Yosemite Valley outside the Big Oak Flat Entrance Station. After leaving the park, take Evergreen Road north to Camp Mather and turn right on Hetch Hetchy Road. The road ends at O'Shaughnessy Dam (3,814 feet) 6 miles from the turnoff. The reservoir fills a valley of the Tuolumne River that resembled Yosemite Valley until the Tuolumne was dammed to supply San Francisco with drinking water after the 1906 earthquake.

Tioga Pass Road

Crossing through the high Sierra, Tioga Pass Road (Highway 120) rises from 6,192 feet at Crane Flat to 9,941 feet at Tioga Pass, the park's east entrance. The road, the highest paved through-road in California, is closed in winter. Timberless peaks, domes, and flowering meadows line this road in Yosemite's high-mountain region.

The first time we attempted Tioga Pass Road in mid-October, a threatening winter storm forced the NPS to close the road at Crane Flat. After the heavy winter snows melt, Tioga Pass Road is open for summer visitation from May to October.

From Crane Flat 10 miles north of Yosemite Valley to Tioga Pass is 45 miles. There are no suitable accommodations along Tioga Pass Road for visitors requiring fully accessible facilities. Campgrounds with significant barriers but possibly usable by persons with disabilities exist at White Wolf (7,800 feet) and Porcupine Flat (8,100 feet). White Wolf has a restaurant, cabins with baths, and tent cabins, all with significant barriers.

The view across the high peaks down into Yosemite Valley from Olmsted Point stands as one of the highlights of Tioga Pass Road.

Tenaya Lake

Tenaya Lake Campground, two miles east of Olmsted Point, has several flat sites which may be moderately accessible, although the ground is sandy in places. The comfort stations have a step at the entry and narrow stalls without grab bars.

From the campground, views of the lake are moderately accessible by portions of a trail composed of dirt and rock. Several picnic areas are located by the lake farther east on Tioga Pass Road, but there are no accommodations for people with mobility problems.

Tuolumne Meadows

At Tuolumne Meadows (8,650 feet), summer wildflowers abound over the largest subalpine meadow in the high Sierra. Cathedral Peak casts a jagged shadow across the meadow at sunset.

Tuolumne Meadows Visitor Center has a moderately accessible (with cross slope) ISA-designated parking space at the top of the service road above the main (lower) parking lot. The small visitor center has an information desk and bookstore and is fully accessible via a ramp around the east side of the building to a rear entrance. There are moderately accessible restrooms in the main (lower) parking lot.

A fully accessible unisex restroom is at Tuolumne Meadows Store/Grill, a half-mile east. A gas station is nearby.

Tuolumne Meadows Campground, open only in summer, has informally set aside four flat sites for people with disabilities. The nearby comfort station is enterable on the men's side, but the women's side has a step for entry. The facilities are not improved for accessibility.

Reservations through MISTIX (P.O. Box 85705, San Diego, CA 92138-5705; 800-365-2267; TDD 800-274-7275) are necessary from June 21 to October 15. Several rustic tent cabins around Tuolumne Meadows Lodge are accessible by wheelchair. Four steep steps lead to the toilets and showers in the bathhouse. The office and desk area have a one-step barrier at the door. The ranger station has a telephone fully accessible to wheelchair users. There are no restrooms at the restaurant.

Lembert Dome, a glacially polished granite dome, is visible from a parking lot on the Lembert Dome/Dog Lake Trail Road. Further along, at the end of the road, a half-mile-each-way trail goes from the horse stables to Soda Springs and Parsons Lodge. The trail is moderately accessible and may require assistance. The parking lot has a fully accessible comfort station.

Tioga Pass

Tioga Pass Entrance Station (9,945 feet), where the eastern escarpment of the Sierra Nevada drops off into the Great Basin, marks the boundary of Yosemite National Park.

Since the discovery of Yosemite, conservation of its pristine natural wonders has been a constant concern. The 1864 mandate that set aside Yosemite Valley and Mariposa Grove of giant sequoias proved to be the inspiration for the creation of America's national parks. The park idea did not ensure, however, that the parks' ecology would remain safe from human spoliation.

The National Park Service, by William C. Everhart, mentions an 1891 Department of Interior report noting great destruction evident throughout all parts of the Yosemite Valley. This description came almost thirty years after the congressional mandate aimed at protecting the valley and sequoia groves. Preserving the environment of Yosemite as well as that of all our national parks remains a challenge today.

> Thousands of tired, nerve-shaken, over-civilized people are beginning to find out that going to the mountains is going home; that wilderness is a necessity; and that mountain parks and reservations are useful not only as fountains of timber and irrigating rivers, but as fountains of life. —JOHN MUIR, 1898

(See *At a Glance: Pacific States Region.*)

6 · FOUR MORE VISITS: FIRST THE BAD NEWS, THEN THE GOOD

Whenever we approached a park, we felt a sense of anticipation. We were particularly eager to visit two parks whose highlights had extraordinary reputations in the national park system: Great Smoky Mountains National Park, Tennessee and North Carolina, the most visited national park in the country with 9 million visitors every year; and Grand Canyon National Park, Arizona, the only one of Seven Natural Wonders of the World in the United States. Unfortunately, our great expectations were dashed by the minimal amount of access afforded at both of these parks.

On the other hand, two parks where we anticipated having very little access surprised us. Both Voyageurs National Park, Minnesota, and Big Bend National Park, Texas, had unusual water opportunities, making these parks distinctively accessible.

We would like to share some brief highlights of these four parks without going into the detail of a Best Visit. For these parks, refer to the maps distributed at each entrance station.

GREAT SMOKY MOUNTAINS NATIONAL PARK

Gatlinburg, TN 37738

Information: 615-436-1200

Great Smoky Mountains National Park protects areas of mountain and forest. Forty percent of the park constitutes the largest virgin forest in the eastern United States. Many of the lands were acquired from timber companies, farmers, and local residents prior to establishment of the park in 1934. The park also conserves the cultural heritage of Appalachian Mountain people who farmed and lived a self-reliant life in these rugged mountains from the early nineteenth century until establishment of the park in 1930.

The park provides a "Guide to Accessibility for the Disabled" about park trails and facilities that can be visited by wheelchair users and people with other disabilities. Much of the park can be appreciated by auto tours, a more accessible option than the 900 miles of hiking trails that traverse the mountains. We were disappointed, however, because many of the facilities that could easily be accessible for people with disabilities had obstacles to prevent safe and enjoyable experiences for all visitors.

The towns of Gatlinburg in eastern Tennessee and Cherokee in western North Carolina are near the boundaries of Great Smoky Mountains National Park.

Sugarlands Visitor Center

Entry to the visitor center requires assistance because of a tight space and a heavy door at the head of a ramp. Fortunately, the lobby information desk, exhibit area, book sales, and audiovisual room are on one level and fully accessible.

The slide program and movie have printed scripts available upon request at the information desk. An orientation audiotape for persons with vision impairments is available. The restrooms and water fountain outside the center are fully accessible. The visitor center parking lot has ISA-designated spaces with curb cuts.

Laurel Falls Trail

Between Sugarlands Visitor Center and Elkmont Campground, Laurel Falls Trail is a steep and long paved path to a waterfall. Assistance is strongly recommended on this 2.5-mile round-trip.

Roaring Fork Motor Nature Tour

To reach this self-guided auto tour, leave the park via U.S. Highway 441 into Gatlinburg, Tennessee, turning right at Airport Road. In a few miles, the Roaring Fork Motor Nature Tour begins. With the trees growing close to the road, a profound quiet greets tourists. A brochure accompanies the tour. We stopped at some of the pullouts, but not many were accessible for Wendy's wheelchair because the slopes to them were steep and rooty. Nevertheless, riding through a forest such as this was very rewarding.

Cades Cove Visitor Center

The Cades Cove auto tour takes the visitor on an 11-mile journey through this pioneer area first settled in 1819 after the state of Tennessee acquired the land from Native Americans. At one time, Cades Cove had 137 households; several of the buildings still stand today. Many have steps and/or high porches not accessible to wheelchair users. A brochure describing the remaining structures of Cades Cove is available at the beginning of the tour.

Three steps block access to the visitor center for wheelchair users. A loose-leaf binder has photographs and descriptions of the cove's features. There are ISA-designated spaces in the parking lot and fully accessible restrooms near the building.

Newfound Gap

This overlook, at the top of U.S. Highway 441 near the Tennessee-North Carolina border, is one of the most famous in Great Smoky Mountains National Park. A short, paved trail next to the parking lot provides remarkable views of the Great Smoky Mountains toward the Blue Ridge Mountains. The restrooms are down a moderately steep incline, and while they are fully accessible inside, an 8-inch-high step must be negotiated to gain entrance. We understand that funding often runs short of needs, but we also feel that first things must be done first. We urge that priority be given to getting inside the comfort station, possibly with a ramp, and then to interior revisions.

Clingmans Dome

This half-mile paved trail spirals up to a lookout tower with views of the mountains and ridges for which the Great Smoky Mountains are well known and photographed. The panorama is spectacular from this 6,643-foot elevation. The entire incline is steep and a hard push for a wheelchair user. Assistance is strongly recommended; this can be a breathless walk even for a nondisabled visitor on foot. Often it is windy and cool at the top of the tower. Hold onto hats and camera lenses. Michael lost one of each.

Mingus Mill

The moderately accessible trail leads to the Mingus Mill, where the Mingus family built its first waterwheel in the 1790s, and where demonstrations of grain milling are conducted today. Unfortunately, steps block the access to the mill for visitors using wheelchairs. A printed guide and photographs of inside the mill are available.

Oconaluftee Visitor Center

The visitor center is fully accessible, but uneven flagstones can be bumpy for wheelchair users or difficult for others to walk across without tripping or sliding. The center has exhibits, an information desk, and a book-sales area. The parking lot has ISA-designated spaces with curb ramps. Restrooms are fully accessible with wide stalls and grab bars.

The Pioneer Farm Village is located outside the visitor center. It includes an assortment of old buildings and a stable with horses and is representative of life in the mountains as it may have been more than a hundred years ago. The moderately accessible dirt trail has some rough spots and may require assistance.

Deep Creek

Near the southern border of the park, 15 miles west of Oconaluftee, Deep Creek Trail is an old roadbed with gentle slopes. Ask at the ranger station for the gate to be opened at the trailhead of this half-mile dirt trail to a waterfall on Deep Creek. Assistance may be necessary on this moderately accessible journey. On hot summer days, Deep Creek is a popular spot for inner-tube floating.

Camping

Great Smoky Mountains has six frontcountry campgrounds with fully accessible comfort stations. Smokemont, Elkmont, and Cades Cove each offer fully accessible sites having picnic tables with extended tops, raised fire grills, and paved surfaces. They must be reserved through MISTIX (P.O. Box 85705, San Diego, CA 92138-5705; 800-365-2267) for camping between May 15 and October 31. The remaining three camp-grounds offer sites on a first-come first-served basis. They are not fully accessible, but Abrams Creek and Cataloochee have flat natural terrain.

(See *At a Glance: East and Midwest Region.*)

GRAND CANYON NATIONAL PARK

P.O. Box 129
Grand Canyon, AZ 86023
Information: 602-638-7888
TDD: 602-638-7772

We first visited the Grand Canyon at its North Rim and were markedly disappointed in its lack of access for persons with disabilities. The popularity of the Grand Canyon had led us to assume that it would be more accessible. The Park has embarrassingly poor access at both the North and the South rims. An accessibility guide, "Access for Visitors," is available at the visitor centers.

The rims, 215 miles apart by road, are only 10 miles across the canyon from one another. The South Rim attracts 90 percent of the park's visitors. As it has done over the last 6 million years, the Colorado River flows through and carves the canyon by erosion. The canyon is about 1 mile deep and varies from 600 feet to 18 miles in width. The park road elevations range from approximately 8,000 feet on the North Rim to 7,000 feet on the South Rim. Overexertion at these altitudes can be hazardous for anybody, especially for people with respiratory and/or cardiac problems.

We do not want to dampen anyone's enthusiasm for seeing this spectacular canyon. There is no other like it. But while some trails and overlooks afford visitors with disabilities remarkable views, there are simply not enough. Following is a selection of some of the opportunities available at this thrilling scenic marvel.

The South Rim

The Park Visitor Center has an information desk, a booksales area, exhibits, a fully accessible drinking fountain, and moderately accessible restrooms. The main doors are heavy. The auditorium is wheelchair accessible and has a captioned slide show about the park. The center has ISA-designated parking with curb cuts and a volume-control lowered telephone.

The Mather Amphitheater has evening programs in the summer. Its entrance is via a short asphalt path from the upper parking area east of the visitor center.

The Yavapai Museum, with good views of the canyon, has exhibits, book sales, a silent film about the canyon's formation, and touch exhibits. The parking lot has ISA-designated spaces next to a walk with cross slope. Restrooms near the parking lot are enterable. Stalls are narrow.

The North Rim

The Grand Canyon's North Rim, closed during winter, is sorely lacking in ramps, curb cuts, easily reachable viewpoints, and restrooms. Most North Rim trails are narrow and rough. The self-guided nature trail at Cape Royal leads from the parking lot to near the canyon's edge. The trail is paved and has a portable toilet literally 18 inches up from the ground. Point Imperial has one moderately accessible comfort facility.

The Grand Canyon Lodge has a registration desk, information desk, and cafeteria on the main floor. The restaurant is down a long flight of steps, but a mechanical lift is available for persons with mobility problems. The lodge has no accessible bathroom, and no rooms here have been modified for accessibility. Several cabins are moderately accessible. We stayed in a Frontier Cabin equipped for use by persons with mobility problems. Its small interior made maneuvering awkward for Wendy with her three-wheeled scooter.

A lift similar to the one in the restaurant is installed on the outside veranda and lowers people who are not stair climbers down to an area with spectacular views. From here we sipped drinks and watched the sun set behind the canyon. Unfortunately, this lift was not working properly during our visit, and it took Michael's mechanical expertise to make the lift operate correctly. The employees were compassionate and helpful. The entrance to the indoors from the veranda, however, was up a few steps; a modest ramp would have made the indoor warmth accessible to Wendy.

The North Rim Campground has no sites designated for people with disabilities. The restrooms are up steps and have narrow stalls without grab bars. The laundry and public showers have no provisions for persons with disabilities. The moderately accessible camp store has a small threshold and narrow aisles.

West Rim Drive

West Rim Drive, 13 miles to Hermits Rest from Grand Canyon Village, is normally closed to automobile traffic, but, after applying for a pass at the visitor center, persons with disabilities are allowed to drive the road. Blind visitors with guide dogs may also be driven on West Rim. The free tram along the drive is not wheelchair accessible.

Unfortunately, most of the viewpoints and overlooks along West Rim also have significant barriers for people with mobility problems. Trailview Overlook, the first pullout on the drive, has a ramp to the River to Rim wayside exhibit but no access to the overlook. Maricopa Point and Powell Memorial are also key viewing points with access blocked by steps. Hopi Point, a popular sunset-viewing spot, has a magnificent view from the overlook, which is nine steps down from the parking level. Wendy was able to enjoy the sunset only from the parking lot. However, Hermits Rest has a fully accessible overlook into the canyon with a fully accessible comfort station.

The snack bar, gift shop, and vending machines are obstructed by steps.

East Rim Drive

The 23-mile drive to Desert View from Grand Canyon Village has approximately twenty overlooks, none accessible except Desert View. This area has a moderately accessible snack bar, store, and gift shop and fully accessible comfort stations. A paved path with steep slopes leads to an overlook of the Colorado River near the Desert View Watchtower. The tower ground floor has good views out the windows, but the upper floors can only be reached by steep stairways.

In our view, many of the West and East Rim Drive overlooks could easily be made fully accessible.

Tusayan

The ruins of several prehistoric Native American communities of the Anasazi are found in and around the Grand Canyon. One simple village, the Tusayan pueblo, is a partially excavated ruin on the South Rim. Home to no more than twenty inhabitants for twenty to twenty-five years, Tusayan was built about 1185. The approximately fifteen rooms were used for living and food storage in this farming community. A moderately accessible dirt path loops around the ruin. Tusayan had a distinctive pottery style, examples of which are displayed at the Tusayan Museum.

The entrance to this museum has a 1-inch-high threshold at the doorway but is otherwise accessible for wheelchair users. The exhibits, however, have dim lighting, which may be problematic for persons with vision impairments. The portable toilets are not accessible to wheelchair users.

Alternatives

An alternate way to view the canyon, though expensive, is by helicopter. We took a thirty-minute ride with Kenai Helicopters (606-638-2412), and it was truly an extraordinary experience. (For more details, see Chapter 3.)

River rafting down the Colorado is another option for seeing the canyon up close. Day trips from Page to Lee's Ferry, both in Arizona, as well as trips as long as two weeks through the entire canyon are available.

Grand Canyon Village

The village on the South Rim has six lodges and restaurants, two campgrounds, showers, laundry, clinic, post office, mule-ride trailhead, train station, store, and bank. Several canyon overlooks are accessible. Only Maswik Lodge has fully accessible room accommodations. The restaurants at El Tovar and Maswik Lodge are fully accessible. All other lodges and restaurants have varying degrees of moderate accessibility.

Mather Point has one fully accessible overlook, but steps down to the other viewing areas block wheelchair access. The Rim Trail, from Yavapai Museum to near El Tovar, is moderately accessible with assistance. Near El Tovar are several fully accessible views into the canyon. The viewing tubes, or reticles, are too high for young children or persons using wheelchairs to reach.

Mather Campground has several ISA-designated sites on packed dirt, picnic tables with extended tops, some raised fire grills, and a fully accessible unisex comfort station. Sites must be reserved year-round through MISTIX (P.O. Box 85705, San Diego, CA 92138-5705; 800-365-2267; TDD 800-274-7275). Trailer Village has RV sites with full hookups. Call 602-638-2631 for information.

Camper Services, located near Mather Campground, offers a fully accessible shower next to the enterable laundromat. The shower is stunning in spacious design and functional detail except for a very significant mistake: Water use is regulated by a timer mounted on the wall 8 feet above the floor! The laundry manager assisting Wendy to start the shower had to climb up on an apple crate to reach the illustrious device. The manager then left Wendy to shower herself.

When the water shut off after seven minutes, Wendy, still covered with soap, was left shivering until Michael brought her some towels. He located the attendant and learned how to reset the timer. The ironic incident of finding a timer mounted so far from a wheelchair user's grasp in an otherwise fully accessible shower is still one of our most amazing park adventures with nonaccessibility.

(See *At a Glance: Desert Southwest Region.*)

VOYAGEURS
NATIONAL PARK
P.O. Box 50
International Falls, MN 56649
Information: 218-283-9821

V oyageurs National Park, Minnesota, which spans thirty
glacier-carved lakes, pleasantly surprised us. Voyageurs
is essentially a water park, and we were delighted to
discover that it did offer some accessible opportunities for
touring.

Native Americans first populated this area. The fur trade
of the eighteenth and nineteenth centuries brought Europe-
ans to this wild region. French-Canadian canoeists, *voyageurs,*
paddled through the waterways transporting furs downstream
and supplies upstream. The park waterways link Lake Superior and Lake of the Woods. The park was established in
1975.

Voyageurs' winters are very cold and snowy. Cross-country
ski, snowshoe, and snowmobile travel can be enjoyed, and
when the lakes are frozen solid, cars drive on the 7-mile-long
Rainy Lake Ice Road. Check with park rangers for further
information.

Summers at Voyageurs are short, and most exploration of
the park then must be conducted on water. Boats and canoes
can be rented in Island View, Kabetogama, Ash River, and
Crane Lake. Houseboats, with flat decks and interiors, appear to be good options for wheelchair users, but we were
unable to inspect one. Float planes can also be rented. There
are seven boat launches for private boats, which are welcome.

Fishing for walleye, northern pike, and bass is a favorite
sport in these Minnesota lakes. A Minnesota state fishing
license is required to fish in park waters. Fisherpersons in
the Canadian waters of Rainy, Namakan, and Sand Point lakes

are required to have an Ontario fishing license, which is strictly enforced.

There are four entrances to the park where visitors can leave their cars and begin boating through the lakes: Rainy Lake, near International Falls; Kabetogama, 26 miles southeast of Rainy Lake; Ash River, 11 miles east of Kabetogama; and Crane Lake, 25 miles north of Orr, Minnesota. The park shares its northern boundary with Canada.

Rainy Lake

Rainy Lake Visitor Center, open all year, is fully accessible with an information desk, book- and map-sales area, and fully accessible restrooms. Exhibits feature birchbark canoes, sleds, and skis reminiscent of the early voyageurs. A slide show has an accompanying printed script for people with hearing impairments. An audiotape of bird calls and songs can be played in the bookstore and may be very helpful for everyone, especially people with vision impairments. The center also has a touch exhibit of fur pelts, animal traps, and tools of the lake region.

The Ernst Olzoholser Nature Trail, leaving from outside the visitor center, is a fully accessible quarter-mile paved trail through the north woods around Black Bay Marsh.

The North Canoe Adventure leaves from the Rainy Lake dock and is a ranger-led group trip on a 26-foot replica of the voyageurs' canoe. Other canoes and boats can also be rented and taken on Rainy Lake. Check with local concessionaires for availability and accessibility. These boating opportunities are rewarding ways to see this water park.

The *Pride of Rainy Lake* tour boat also leaves from the dock outside the visitor center on its excursions around this lake, carved from rock as old as 2.7 billion years by glaciers. Cruises are available from May through September, and schedules can be obtained from Voyageurs National Park Boat Tours (Route 8, Box 303, Department F-9, International Falls, MN 56649; 218-286-5470).

We went on the *Pride of Rainy Lake* with a group of seniors, many using wheelchairs, hosted by the International Falls Kiwanis Club. As on many such cruises, a park naturalist narrated our tour along the lake, pointing out remarkable woodlands, loons (the Minnesota state bird), and the rookery where herring gulls and cormorants flourished. Several of our cruise companions had grown up on the shores of Rainy Lake and had many old tales to share with us. The concessionaire is most accommodating to persons with disabilities. Call ahead for information.

Kabetogama Lake

The visitor center at Kabetogama, open seasonally, is small but fully accessible. Exhibits include folk art, photography, and an extensive touch table. The comfort station is fully accessible. Guided canoe trips are also available.

Public tours are offered on the *Betsy Anna* cruise boat, which stops at the historic Kettle Falls Hotel and the Namakan Lake landing. Cruises are available from May through September; obtain schedules from Voyageurs National Park Boat Tour (218-286-5470).

We were fortunate to accompany Ranger Jim Dougan in his boat around Lake Kabetogama. He showed us beaver houses and a wide assortment of birds, including a great blue heron, turkey vultures, and a bald eagle. He took us to the 70-year-old Kettle Falls Hotel with facilities that are not accessible for people with mobility problems. The ramped dock and the path to the hotel are moderately accessible. Steps leading up to the hotel meant that Jim and Michael had to assist Wendy up to the old lumberjack lodge, where we enjoyed lunch. Boat rentals, boat fuel, and a mechanized boat portage between Rainy and Namakan lakes are additional services at Kettle Falls.

Camping on lake islands, reachable only by boats, is possible, although there are no facilities for campers with disabilities. Ranger Dougan believes that the sites at Lost Lake and Williams Island would be the most accessible for people with mobility problems, although campers would need to exit their boats and climb up a dirt embankment on each of these islands.

The only campground accessible by automobile is at Wooden Frog State Park near Kabetogama. There are no sites or comfort stations designated for full accessibility.

(See *At a Glance: East and Midwest Region.*)

BIG BEND
NATIONAL PARK
Big Bend National Park, TX 79834
Information: 915-477-2251

After experiencing weeks of cold temperatures on the Colorado Plateau, we were thrilled to reach Big Bend National Park, Texas, with its warm weather over 70°F in October. Although the terrain is rough and steep, the park is accessible in an unusual way via river rafts on the Rio Grande River.

The elevations of the road in this park range from approximately 1,800 feet to 5,679 feet, and the temperatures extend from 25°F on winter nights to more than 100°F on summer days.

The park, established in 1944, encompasses three main geographic features: the Chisos Mountains, the Chihuahuan Desert, and the Rio Grande River. *Big Bend* refers to a large turn in the river that today marks the park's 107-mile southern boundary. Running through this desert country, the river supports a habitat for beavers, jackrabbits, kangaroo rats, turtles, and a myriad of birds like cardinals, summer tanagers, sandpipers, killdeer, and cliff swallows. The river cuts through limestone mountains, creating three beautiful canyons. The Rio Grande can best be experienced by taking a rafting trip available through local outfitters. People with physical disabilities are welcome.

The Chihuahuan Desert is one of four great deserts in North America, the others being the Mojave, the Sonoran, and the Great Basin. Ninety-seven percent of Big Bend National Park is Chihuahuan Desert, mostly accessible by car. High-clearance vehicles are often recommended for dirt roads. Park road maps and guides are invaluable, and heat, loose rocks, and prickly plants challenge everyone. Though warm and generally dry, the desert with its summer rains is a lush green home for the roadrunner, and colorful flowering cacti. One of the Chihuahuan's indicator plants, the distinctive, sharp-bladed lechuguilla, is used to make cordage and household items.

The golden eagle and the coyote make their homes in the Chisos Mountains. Verdant leafy bushes and tall trees permeate these mountains, where ponderosa pine, Douglas fir, quaking aspen, and Arizona cypress live in their southernmost habitat of the United States. One suggested mode of seeing the Chisos is by horseback. Ridership is limited by the concessionaires for safety reasons, but some persons with disabilities may have the skills required to ride.

Native Americans probably first lived in the Big Bend country ten thousand years ago, maybe more. Spanish explorers crossed the Rio Grande in search of fertile fields, gold, and silver in the sixteenth and seventeenth centuries. Large-scale documented exploration did not occur until 130 years ago.

Chisos Basin

We first entered Big Bend National Park from the north entrance on U.S. Highway 385. We stayed at the Chisos Basin Campground, which has no sites designated for people with disabilities or accessible comfort stations. A moderately accessible bathroom is available at the Chisos Basin Ranger Station. A lodge and restaurant in Chisos Basin are moderately accessible. Most trails are rock and dirt with steep grades. One short self-guided trail, the Window View Trail, is paved with benches. Lost Mine Trail near Panther Pass is moderately accessible for the first mile.

Panther Junction and Dugout Wells

Panther Junction is at the intersection of U.S. 385 and Rio Grande Village Road. It has a moderately accessible visitor center and comfort stations. The auditorium is not accessible to people with mobility problems and has no provisions for people with vision or hearing impairments. The only fully accessible trail in the park is the 100-foot Panther Path, a self-guided nature trail outside the visitor center.

We took Rio Grande Village Road from Panther Junction to Dugout Wells, which, at the turn of the century, had one of the few schoolhouses in the Big Bend country and was hence considered the cultural center of the Chisos Mountains. Dugout Wells has a moderately accessible shaded picnic table and a moderately accessible pit toilet. A dirt but relatively flat paved trail winds through Dugout Wells revealing extraordinary wildflowers, ocotillo, purple prickly pear cactus, and inspiring views of the Chisos Mountains. The trail grows more steep, sometimes with significant barriers. Assistance is often required.

Rio Grande Village

From Dugout Wells, Rio Grande Village is 20 miles from Panther Junction on the Rio Grande Village Road. The visitor center has a paved parking lot and a ramp to its entrance.

Rio Grande has a moderately accessible campground with flat dirt sites and a store. The comfort stations have a step at their entrance. The only showers in the park are at the Rio Grande Village store. These are narrow and only moderately accessible. Assistance may be necessary. The toilets and sink in these bathrooms are moderately accessible.

A self-guided three-quarter-mile nature trail with a brochure leaves from the Rio Grande Village campground. The first portion of the trail is boardwalk over marshy waters. The trail then becomes dirt and steeper with significant barriers. Assistance may be necessary.

Castolon

The Ross Maxwell Scenic Drive on the southwest side of the park leads to historic Castolon on the Rio Grande River.

Here, the U.S. Cavalry began protecting American settle-ments in 1913 from Mexican revolutionary group raids. Castolon still has the remnants of this fort, including bar-racks, officers' quarters, and small homes. All paths through this area are dirt, sometimes rocky and only moderately ac-cessible. None of the buildings has a ramp for entrance. The store at Castolon has steps. The Cottonwood Campground has moderately accessible sites and pit toilets.

Rio Grande River

Traveling through the beautiful park, we never seemed to get up close to the famous Rio Grande River. We then learned of the Big Bend River Tours based in Lajitas (Box 317, Laj-itas, TX 79852; 915-424-3219).

Our tour guide, Ed, met us at the Big Bend River Tours office in Lajitas. After being bussed to the riverbank, we loaded the rafts with our day's supplies. Ed lashed Wendy's manual wheelchair (with the wheels off) to the frame of the raft, where she could comfortably support herself on the eight-hour journey through the Santa Elena Canyon. The canyon is noted for 1,500-foot-high sheer canyon walls. Ed and the two other guides masterfully rowed the entire group down the relatively calm river. The "Rockslide," a rolling rush of water through rocks, reminiscent of a slalom-course se-ries of gates, was our only whitewater rapid.

We had lunch on a sandy area shaded by tamarisks along the banks of the river. The rafters also conduct overnight tours with deluxe gourmet meals cooked over open fires. One was hosted by famous Cajun chef Pierre Prudhomme. Our meal was more of the cold-cut–sandwich variety but was plentiful and welcome. After all, we were there to see the canyon for a day and had little time for extensive culinary delights that could be prepared in the wilderness. This river trip was one of the highlights of our national park journeys.

(See *At a Glance: Desert Southwest Region.*)

The bad news is that some of the parks with the grandest attractions in the national park system lack accessible views, trails, and facilities, and we hope this improves. The good news is that persons with disabilities can use alternative means of travel to make apparently impossible terrain more easily accessible.

III · AT A
GLANCE

7·INTRODUCTION

At *A Glance* provides information helpful for planning visits and for use in fifty national parks. The parks are arranged alphabetically within 5 regions: East and Midwest, Rocky Mountains and Great Plains, Desert Southwest, Pacific States, and Alaska and Hawaii. A description of the park's principle attractions introduces each entry.

"Easy Access Highlights" are prominent park features visitors will particularly want to experience. Most are accessible by trail, automobile, boat, or guided tour.

"Activities" for visitors particular to a specific park are noted. Because most parks afford opportunities for photography and ranger-led programs, including evening presentations, nature walks, and youth-oriented activities, we do not list these on a park-by-park basis.

"Location" is given from the nearest major urban area most easily found on a road map. "Medical Facilities" offering a wide variety of services in proximity to the park are given. Prior to travel, visitors anticipating medical attention during park visits (for instance, dialysis) may want to contact the facility regarding available medical services.

"Terrain" describes elevations above sea level on park roads. Persons with respiratory and/or cardiovascular problems should consult a physician before ascending to elevations above 4,000'. Slow acclimation to higher elevations is less hazardous than rapid ascent.

"Climate" information characterizes seasonal changes and includes a chart of averaged daily high and low temperatures for each month. We wish to express our thanks to the National Park Foundation for use of its Climatables™ and the National Park Service for its climate information. Severe weather may complicate many outdoor activities.

In "Visitor Centers," accessibility to visitor center facilities and information stations is described and rated as fully accessible, moderately accessible, or with significant barriers. We also describe informational and interpretive programs available for visitors with disabilities, including materials for persons with hearing and visual impairments. Visitors with developmental impairments may find touch exhibits and visual presentations helpful. If arranged with the park in advance, interpretive programs suited to the individual's needs may be possible. Where they exist, park museums are also described in this section. If available, "Access Guides" for park visitors with disabilities are listed. Many parks distribute a newspaper several times a year that contains park accessibility information.

"Accessible Trails, Viewpoints, and Sites" are rated as fully accessible, moderately accessible, or with significant barriers.

"Campgrounds" and camping facilities accessible to persons with mobility problems are described and rated as fully accessible, moderately accessible, or with significant barriers. An ISA-designated campsite is fully accessible unless otherwise noted. The few backcountry and primitive campsites listed usually have significant barriers. While planning a park visit, check ahead for campground availability and to find out if reservations are needed.

"Lodging and Services" lists overnight accommodations, restaurants, snack bars, gas stations, post offices, galleries, gift stores, food markets, showers, and laundromats available within park boundaries and in nearby towns. The accessibility for accommodations and services is rated and, if necessary, briefly described. Most park lodging, including accessible facilities, requires reservations and often must be booked months in advance, so call or write ahead to the concessionaire while planning a park trip.

"Tours and Sports" notes availability of tours by bus, tram, boat wagon, carriage, helicopter, and airplane and lists opportunities for river rafting, horseback riding, crosscountry skiing, and snowmobiling. It also gives information about equipment rentals for accessible activities in the park. Many parks have lists of tour guides, outfitters, and equipment providers.

The "Authors' Notes" section shares some of the authors' experiences and impressions of the park. If this section is not included in a park entry, the authors did not personally visit the park. Sometimes additional information is included under "Ranger's Notes."

8·EAST AND MIDWEST REGION

ACADIA NATIONAL PARK
Established 1919   40,771 acres
P.O. Box 177
Bar Harbor, ME 04609
Information and TDD: 207-288-3338

Rocky shorelines along the Atlantic Ocean, rounded mountaintops of glacier-sculpted granite, and lush forests brilliantly colored in autumn grace Acadia National Park. Carriage roads make the woodlands uniquely accessible to hikers and wheelers. Somes Sound, the only fjord in the lower forty-eight states, and Cadillac Mountain, the highest point on the eastern seaboard, distinguish this first national park established east of the Mississippi River. (See *Best Visits*.)

EASY ACCESS HIGHLIGHTS
- Bubble Pond
- Eagle Lake
- Jordan Pond House
- Nature Gardens
- Seawall
- Cadillac Mountain
- Thunder Hole
- Schoodic Peninsula

ACTIVITIES: Hiking, bicycling, carriage and hay-wagon riding, marine-life viewing, auto touring, boat touring, cross-country skiing, snowmobiling.

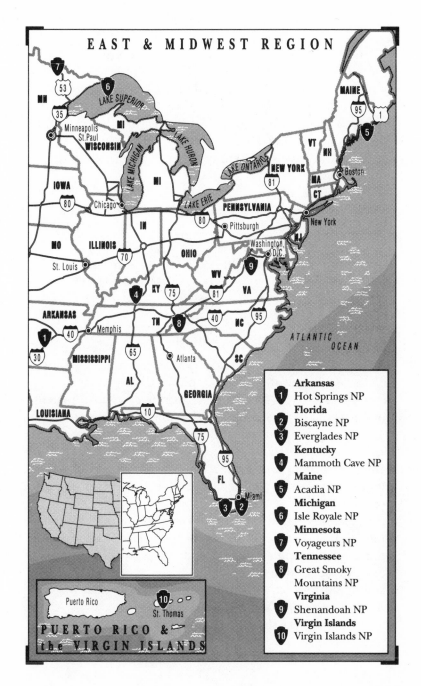

EAST & MIDWEST REGION

MN

Arkansas
1 Hot Springs NP
Florida
2 Biscayne NP
3 Everglades NP
Kentucky
4 Mammoth Cave NP
Maine
5 Acadia NP
Michigan
6 Isle Royale NP
Minnesota
7 Voyageurs NP
Tennessee
8 Great Smoky
  Mountains NP
Virginia
9 Shenandoah NP
Virgin Islands
10 Virgin Islands NP

PUERTO RICO &
the VIRGIN ISLANDS

Puerto Rico

St. Thomas

LOCATION: Mount Desert — 47 miles southeast of Bangor, ME, and 164 miles northeast of Portland, ME, reached by Maine Route 3.

MEDICAL FACILITIES: Mt. Desert Island Hospital, Bar Harbor.

TERRAIN: Elevations from sea level to 1,530′. Highest point is Cadillac Mountain. Most accessible features below 1,500′.

CLIMATE: Changes quickly from sun to rain and/or fog. Warm summer days with some chilly nights; cold with moderate snows in winter.

Averaged Daily Temperatures at Bar Harbor 30′ (F°)

	J	F	M	A	M	J	J	A	S	O	N	D
Highs	31	32	39	50	61	70	76	74	66	57	46	35
Lows	15	16	24	34	42	50	54	54	49	42	33	20

Source: Climatables™, courtesy of the National Park Foundation.

VISITOR CENTERS AND MUSEUMS

All have ISA-designated parking spaces.

THOMPSON ISLAND INFORMATION CENTER: Ramped entrance, fully accessible vault toilet, telephones.

HULLS COVE VISITOR CENTER: Flat entrance from ISA-designated parking in upper lot. Information desk, exhibits, book and map sales, orientation film with accompanying script (no large print). Audiocassette automobile tour for rent or purchase. Restrooms, down a steep slope, may require assistance; interiors moderately accessible. Open May through October.

PARK HEADQUARTERS: Ramp entrance on side of building; moderately accessible restrooms. Serves as park visitor center during winter; open 7 days a week during winter, 5 days a week during summer.

SIEUR DE MONTS SPRING NATURE CENTER. Ramped entrance to rear door. Exhibits and bookstore.

ABBE MUSEUM: Very steep approach path presents significant barrier.

ACCESS GUIDES
"Wheelchair Accessibility Guide, Acadia National Park" and "Wheelchair Access Guide, Restaurants, Motels and Campgrounds" available at visitor centers.

ACCESSIBLE TRAILS, VIEWPOINTS, AND SITES
FULLY: Carriage roads at Bubble Pond, Eagle Lake, and Breakneck Ponds.
MODERATELY: Sieur de Monts Fire Road, Nature Garden, 1st half of Wonderland, most carriage roads.

ACCESSIBLE CAMPGROUNDS
BLACKWOODS: Several ISA-designated sites with extended tabletops, raised grills, fully accessible comfort stations, fully accessible amphitheater. Reserve June 15 through September 15 through MISTIX (P.O. Box 85705, San Diego, CA 92138-5705; 800-365-2267; TDD 800-274-7275).
SEAWALL: 1 ISA-designated campsite with moderately accessible comfort station. Level access to amphitheater. MOUNT DESERT NARROWS CAMPING RESORT: Moderately accessible showers for public use. 207-288-4782.

LODGING AND SERVICES
No lodging in park.

JORDAN POND HOUSE: Fully accessible restaurant.
TOWNS OF BAR HARBOR, SOUTHWEST HARBOR, NORTHWEST HARBOR: Full services.

TOURS AND SPORTS
TOUR BOAT AND WINDJAMMER CRUISES: From Bar Harbor Frenchman Bay Co. (207-288-3322).
CARRIAGE AND HAY-WAGON RIDES: Carriage seat height 54″; haywagon seat height 36″. Mid-June to Labor Day, from Wildwood Stables (207-276-3622).
BICYCLE RENTALS: Many in Bar Harbor.
CANOE RENTALS: Maine Wilderness Paddlers (207-244-5854).

AUTHORS' NOTES
The close proximity of ocean and mountains impressed us. We stayed at Blackwoods Campground and found it comfortable except for the mosquitoes and blackflies in June. The fresh seafood available on Mount Desert is inexpensive and delicious. Highlights for us were Thunder Hole, Seawall, and dramatic views of the islands off the Maine coast from Cadillac Mountain.

BISCAYNE NATIONAL PARK
Established 1980   169,345 acres
P.O. Box 1369
Homestead, FL 33090-1369
Information: 305-247-PARK (7275)

Biscayne National Park is an underwater park of the Florida Keys, an important habitat for marine life around a living coral reef. Visitors tour the park by glass-bottom or private boat and enjoy snorkeling and scuba diving. (See *Best Visits: Everglades National Park.*)

EASY ACCESS HIGHLIGHTS
• Glass-Bottom Boat Tour

ACTIVITIES: Fishing, boating, snorkeling, and scuba diving, bird-watching.
LOCATION: 40 miles south of Miami; 10 miles east of Homestead; 26 miles east of Everglades National Park.
MEDICAL FACILITIES: J. A. Smith Hospital, Homestead.
TERRAIN: Elevations from sea level to 8'. Flat limestone formation covered by shallow marshlands.

CLIMATE: Subtropical. Dry, warm, pleasant winters (December through March); hot, wet season late April until November. Mosquitoes intensely active April through November.

Average Daily Temperature (°F)

	J	F	M	A	M	J	J	A	S	O	N	D
Highs	74	74	77	80	83	86	87	88	86	83	79	75
Lows	63	63	66	71	74	76	78	78	77	74	69	64

Source: Climatables™, courtesy of the National Park Foundation.

VISITOR CENTERS AND MUSEUMS
Both have ISA-designated parking spaces. Assistance may be needed at all docks.

CONVOY POINT VISITOR CENTER: Information desk, exhibits, small aquariums, book- and map-sales area, restrooms, picnic area, all fully accessible. Open year-round.

ELLIOT KEY VISITOR CENTER: Reachable only by water; fully accessible restrooms.

ACCESS GUIDES
None.

ACCESSIBLE TRAILS, VIEWPOINTS, AND SITES
None.

ACCESSIBLE CAMPGROUNDS
None.

LODGING AND SERVICES
No lodging in park. Gasoline dock at Convoy Point.

HOMESTEAD: Lodging and services.

TOURS AND SPORTS
GLASS-BOTTOM BOAT TOUR: Biscayne Aqua-Center. Boat has 2 steps, but crew will assist persons with disabilities in boarding (305-247-2400).

DIVE-BOAT TOUR: Welcomes people with disabilities provided they are certified divers.

AUTHORS' NOTES
On the glass-bottom boat tour we took, brain coral, sponges, sea anemones, parrot fish, sting rays, and a humongous sea turtle were visible under the boat.

EVERGLADES NATIONAL PARK
Established 1947   1,398,694 acres
P.O. Box 279
Homestead, FL 33030
Information and TTY/TTD: 305-247-6211
Shark Valley Information: 305-221-8776
Everglades City Information: 813-695-3311

Everglades National Park may well be the most accessible large wilderness area in the country. Stands of mangrove, cypress, and pine accompany the greatest concentration of sawgrass in the world. Fish, birds, alligators, and crocodiles thrive in this large subtropical park. (See *Best Visits.*)

EASY ACCESS HIGHLIGHTS
• Anhinga Trail
• Gumbo-Limbo Trail
• West Lake
• Bear Lake
• Shark Valley
• Flamingo
• Florida Bay
• Ten Thousand Islands

ACTIVITIES: Hiking, bird-watching, fishing, canoeing, touring by boat or tram.

LOCATION: Main Visitor Center—11 miles west of Homestead; 45 miles southwest of Miami. Flamingo—38 miles south of Main Visitor Center. Shark Valley—40 miles west of Miami. Everglades City—82 miles west of Miami.

MEDICAL FACILITIES: J. A. Smith Hospital, Homestead; Naples Community Hospital.

TERRAIN: Elevations from sea level to 8′. Flat limestone formation covered by shallow marshlands.

CLIMATE: Subtropical. Dry, warm, pleasant winters (December through March); hot, wet season late April until November. Mosquitoes intensely active April through November.

Averaged Daily Temperatures (°F)

	J	F	M	A	M	J	J	A	S	O	N	D
Highs	76	76	80	83	86	88	90	90	89	85	81	77
Lows	56	57	61	65	69	73	75	75	74	70	63	58

Source: Climatables™, courtesy of the National Park Foundation.

VISITOR CENTERS AND MUSEUMS

MAIN VISITOR CENTER: Near south entrance. ISA-designated parking available. Fully accessible information desk, exhibit area, phone message mural, orientation film (captioned upon request), bookstore, restrooms, water fountain, telephone. Scripts for film and phone mural at desk.

ROYAL PALM VISITOR CENTER: 4 miles inside park entrance. Moderately accessible information station, bookstore, and phone; fully accessible restrooms, water fountain, and drink machines.

FLAMINGO: 38 miles inside park entrance. Moderately accessible up a steep ramp. Fully accessible information desk, museum/exhibit area, audio diorama (printed script available at desk), lowered telescope in breezeway; moderately accessible restrooms adjacent to restaurant.

SHARK VALLEY: 50 miles north of Main Visitor Center, with moderately accessible bookstore and vending machines and fully accessible restroom.

EVERGLADES CITY: 92 miles northwest of Main Visitor Center. Up a flight of stairs, but with gift shop, phones, and restrooms on ground floor, all fully accessible.

ACCESS GUIDES
Park booklet *Accessibility Everglades National Park* available at visitor centers and information centers.

ACCESSIBLE TRAILS, VIEWPOINTS, AND SITES
FULLY: Anhinga, Gumbo-Limbo, Guy Bradley, and Bobcat trails; Shark Valley Loop Road.
MODERATELY: Pinelands, Long Pine Key Nature Trail, Old Ingram Highway, Pa-hay-okee, Mahogany Hammock, West Lake, Snake Bight, Bear Lake, Coastal Prairie.
PRINTED DISPLAYS: At Anhinga, Gumbo-Limbo, Pinelands, Pa-hay-okee, Mahogany Hammock, West Lake, Shark Valley Loop Road, and Bobcat Trails.
INCREASED ACCESSIBILITY FEATURES: For visitors with blindness or visual impairments, audio tapes and players for Anhinga and Gumbo-Limbo trails available at Royal Palm bookstore. Bobcat Trail audio tape available at Shark Valley information desk.

ACCESSIBLE CAMPGROUNDS
LONG PINE KEY: ISA-designated site with extended table and raised grill, near fully accessible comfort station. Fully accessible amphitheater.
FLAMINGO: ISA-designated site with extended table and raised grill, near fully accessible unisex comfort station with shower. Fully accessible amphitheater.
PEARL BAY CHICKEE: Primitive backcountry canoe campsite up steps; with chemical toilet. Assistance may be needed.
LONE PINE KEY TRAIL: 2 primitive campgrounds in flat areas.

LODGING AND SERVICES
FLAMINGO LODGE: 2 accessible cottages with equipped kitchens, air-conditioning, pool privileges, and standard phones.

Limited services after May 1 (information and reservations: TW Recreational Services, 305-253-2241). Fully accessible gift shop and the moderately accessible Flamingo Restaurant near visitor center. Hours vary seasonally. Sandwiches and drinks served year-round at the fully accessible Buttonwood Lounge. Marina area has fully accessible telephone and a general store for groceries, convenience items, fishing supplies, boat and canoe rentals, and tickets for boat cruises. Gas station adjacent to store.

EVERGLADES CITY: Gift shop, canoe rentals, boat-cruise tickets.

SHARK VALLEY: Bookshop, bicycle rentals, tram tour.

TOURS AND SPORTS

BOAT TOURS: With assistance. Florida Bay from Flamingo (305-253-2241); Ten Thousand Islands from Everglades City (813-695-2591).

TRAM TOURS: Shark Valley (printed script available; 305-221-8455); Flamingo tram car (305-253-2241) moderately accessible.

CANOE RENTALS: At Gulf Station and Flamingo Marina.

AUTHORS' NOTES

Most facilities offer at least partially accessible opportunities for anyone. In particular, we found the Anhinga Trail to be one of the few universally accessible trails in the entire park system. It is a level boardwalk and asphalt path ideal for everyone: elders, families with children and/or strollers, people with physical disabilities, and those who want an interesting, easy hike. Those with vision impairments can take advantage of an excellent interpretive audiotape correlating with optional cue pads on the trail. As for campgrounds, we preferred Lone Pine Key. It had no showers but was cooler than Flamingo and had fewer biting insects. The cottages at Flamingo are among the best accessible lodging in the national park system.

GREAT SMOKY MOUNTAINS NATIONAL PARK

Establishment completed 1934   520,004 acres
Gatlinburg, TN 37738
Information: 615-436-1200

Great Smoky Mountains National Park preserves rugged for-ested mountains and the heritage of the Appalachian cul-ture that developed here in the early 19th century. Fully accessible trails and facilities are limited in this most-visited park in the national park system. (See *Best Visits: Four More Parks.*)

EASY ACCESS HIGHLIGHTS
- Pioneer Village
- Newfound Gap
- Clingmans Dome
- Roaring Forks
- Cades Cove
- Deep Creek

ACTIVITIES: Hiking, wildflower viewing, fishing, horseback rid-ing, auto touring.
LOCATION: The park, adjacent to Gatlinburg in eastern Ten-nessee and to Cherokee in western North Carolina, is bi-sected by U.S. Highway 441.
MEDICAL FACILITIES: Swain County Hospital, Bryson, NC; Fort Sanders Sevier Medical Center, Sevierville, TN.
TERRAIN: Park road elevations between 1,100' and 6,643' at Clingmans Dome. Persons with respiratory and/or cardiac ailments should consult a physician before ascending to high altitudes.
CLIMATE: Warm, humid summers with frequent showers; warm days with cool nights during late springs and early autumns; winters cool with snow at higher elevations. Tem-peratures on mountain ridge colder than daily averages.

Averaged Daily Temperatures at 2,100′ (°F)

	J	F	M	A	M	J	J	A	S	O	N	D
Highs	48	51	60	70	76	82	84	84	78	70	59	51
Lows	25	26	33	42	48	56	60	59	53	41	32	27

Source: Climatables™, courtesy of the National Park Foundation.

VISITOR CENTERS AND MUSEUMS
All have ISA—designated parking spaces.

SUGARLANDS VISITOR CENTER: Moderately accessible entrance requires assistance. Information desk, exhibits, book and map sales, slide and movie programs with printed scripts, and orientation audiotape upon request for persons with vision impairments. Fully accessible restrooms and water fountain outside the center.

CADES COVE VISITOR CENTER: Significant barriers; steps to historic building with exhibits. Nearby fully accessible comfort station.

OCONALUFTEE VISITOR CENTER: Fully accessible, but uneven flagstones can be a hazard. Exhibits, information desk, book and map sales area. Fully accessible restrooms.

ACCESS GUIDES
A handout, "Guide to Accessibility for the Disabled," available at visitor centers.

ACCESSIBLE TRAILS, VIEWPOINTS, AND SITES
MODERATELY: Laurel Falls Trail, Little River Trail,* Newfound Gap, Clingmans Dome, Mingus Mill, Pioneer Village, Deep Creek.*

ACCESSIBLE CAMPGROUNDS
ELKMONT: Fully accessible sites with picnic tables with extended tops, raised fire grills, paved surfaces, and amphitheater. Reserve through MISTIX (P.O. Box 85705, San Diego, CA 92138-5705; 800-365-2267; TDD 800-274-7275).

*Ask ranger to open gate for wheelchair access.

CADES COVE: Fully accessible sites with picnic tables with extended tops, raised fire grills, paved surfaces, and amphitheater. Reserve through Ticketron.

SMOKEMONT: Fully accessible sites with picnic tables with extended tops, raised fire grills, and paved surfaces. Reserve through Ticketron.

CATALOOCHEE: Moderately accessible sites with flat, natural terrain. Fully accessible comfort stations. First come first served basis.

BIG CREEK: Moderately accessible sites with flat, natural terrain. Fully accessible comfort stations. First come first served basis.

ABRAMS CREEK: Moderately accessible sites with flat, natural terrain. Fully accessible comfort stations. First come first served basis.

LODGING AND SERVICES
GATLINBURG, TN, AND CHEROKEE, NC: Full spectrum of lodging and services.

TOURS AND SPORTS
CADES COVE LOOP ROAD, CATALOOCHEE AREA, AND ROARING FORK MOTOR NATURE TRAIL: All with self-guiding booklets.

HORSEBACK RIDING STABLES At Cades Cove, Cosby, Oconaluftee, Smokemont, and Greenbrier.

AUTHORS' NOTES
We were disappointed in the lack of accessible opportunities at this beautiful mountain park. Much can be seen by auto, and the cultural history is fascinating.

When visiting Great Smoky Mountains National Park, consider driving the 469-mile Blue Ridge Parkway, which stretches along lush mountain vistas to Shenandoah National Park. Accessible highlights include, from south to north, the Folk Arts Center displaying Appalachian native crafts, Lynn Cove Information Center featuring a paved trail, and Peaks of the Otter with a partially paved trail around Abbott Lake.

Fully accessible campgrounds are at Roanoke Mountain and Peaks of the Otter. Call Park Headquarters in Asheville, North Carolina for information: 704-259-0779.

HOT SPRINGS NATIONAL PARK
Authorized 1832, Established 1921   4,854 Acres
P.O. Box 1860
Hot Springs, AR 71902
Information: 510-624-3383

The waters of Hot Springs National Park, at a constant 143°F and containing traces of minerals, have long been visited for their alleged therapeutic qualities. Buckstaff Bathhouse, currently operating on Bathhouse Row in downtown Hot Springs, is one of the eight spas still standing. Visitor center tours in Fordyce Bathhouse offer glimpses of what a turn-of-the-century lavish bathhouse provided. Hot Springs was the first land to be authorized for protection by Congress in 1832.

EASY ACCESS HIGHLIGHTS
• Fordyce Bathhouse
• Buckstaff Bathhouse
• Grand Promenade
• Hot Springs Mountain Tower

ACTIVITIES: Bathing, getting massages, hiking, fishing, auto touring.
LOCATION: In Hot Springs, 52 miles southwest of Little Rock, AR.
MEDICAL FACILITIES: AMI National Park Medical Center, Hot Springs.
TERRAIN: Park road elevations average 1,000'.
CLIMATE: Mild winters; hot, humid summers with rain showers and thunderstorms.

Averaged Daily Temperatures at 960' (°F)

	J	F	M	A	M	J	J	A	S	O	N	D
Highs	54	58	66	76	83	91	95	95	89	78	67	55
Lows	35	37	43	52	59	68	71	71	64	54	42	36

Source: Climatables™, courtesy of the National Park Foundation.

VISITOR CENTERS AND MUSEUMS
No ISA—designated parking space.

FORDYCE VISITOR CENTER: Fully accessible information desk, exhibits, and bookstore. Film and slide programs with captioning available. Fully accessible telephone and restrooms.

ACCESS GUIDES
None.

ACCESSIBLE TRAILS, VIEWPOINTS, AND SITES
FULLY: Grand Promenade.
MODERATELY: Dead Chief Trail.

ACCESSIBLE CAMPGROUNDS
GULPHA GORGE: Fully accessible ISA-designated site with nearby fully accessible comfort station.

LODGING AND SERVICES
BUCKSTAFF BATHHOUSE: Thermal mineral baths and massage.
HOT SPRINGS: Full spectrum of services.

TOURS AND SPORTS
FORDYCE BATHHOUSE: Fully accessible self-guided and conducted tours.
HOT SPRINGS OBSERVATION TOWER: Fully accessible by elevator to top.

AUTHORS' NOTES
We took the conducted tour of Fordyce Bathhouse and were fascinated by turn-of-the-century headout steam cabinets (in which a person's entire body, except the head, was enclosed),

Scotch douche therapy, needle showers, sit tubs, hot pack rooms, the electro-mechanic room, the gymnasium, and the paralysis therapy tub (which lowered bathers from an overhead track system). The bathhouse is decorated with marble, stained glass, fountains, and fine woodwork.

ISLE ROYALE
NATIONAL PARK
Established 1940   539,282 Acres
87 North Ripley Street
Houghton, MI 49931
Information: 906-482-0984

Isle Royale National Park is situated on the largest island in the world's largest and coldest freshwater lake, Lake Superior. It is accessible only by boat or by floatplane. The park is 98 percent wilderness and is famous for its moose, wolf, and fish populations. The only wheeled vehicles permitted on the island are wheelchairs.

EASY ACCESS HIGHLIGHTS
• Windigo
• Rock Harbor

ACTIVITIES: Hiking, fishing, canoeing, kayaking, powerboating.
LOCATION: Headquarters in Houghton; Isle Royale 72 miles north of Houghton.
MEDICAL FACILITIES: Portage View Hospital, Hancock, MI.
TERRAIN: Glacier-carved roadless rocky wilderness of forests and many lakes with 166 miles of foot trails. Elevations from Lake Superior (600') to Mt. Desor (1,394').
CLIMATE: Temperate. Pleasant summers with cool nights; dense fog in spring; cold, snowy winters.

Averaged Daily Temperatures (°F)

	J	F	M	A	M	J	J	A	S	O	N	D
Highs	11	20	32	45	54	62	68	69	60	52	33	18
Lows	−11	−5	9	25	36	43	50	54	47	39	17	−1

Source: Climatables™, courtesy of the National Park Foundation.

VISITOR CENTERS AND MUSEUMS

A brochure, "Disabled Visitors — Welcome," available at visitor centers.

ACCESSIBLE TRAILS, VIEWPOINTS, AND SITES

This is a wilderness park. The park advises persons with mobility problems to visit with a nondisabled companion.

MODERATELY: Paved paths to facilities at Rock Harbor. Kneutson Historic Trail to American Dock.

ACCESSIBLE CAMPGROUNDS

ROCK HARBOR: 2 fully accessible ISA-designated camping shelters with moderately accessible water, comfort stations, and amphitheater.

WINDIGO: Significant barriers to camping shelter, .25-mile to fully accessible comfort stations.

DAISY FARM: Sandy from boat dock to campsites. One fully accessible site with raised grills and picnic tables with extended tops. Moderately accessible vault toilet and amphitheater.

LODGING AND SERVICES

ROCK HARBOR: Fully accessible store and marina with gas, diesel, and oil. Moderately accessible shower, cafe, gift shop, lodge, and housekeeping rooms may require assistance from nondisabled companion. Open late June through Labor Day.

WINDIGO: Moderately accessible store and showers; fully accessible marina with gas and oil. Open late June through Labor Day.

NATIONAL PARK CONCESSIONS: Information and Reservations, 906-337-4993 during the season; 502-773-2191 during winter. HOUGHTON: Full spectrum of services.

GETTING TO THE PARK

No boats to the island are fully accessible, nor do any have accessible restrooms. Within certain limitations, boat crews will assist visitors to board tour boats. Contact operators regarding specific needs.

BOAT SERVICE FROM HOUGHTON, MI: 6.5 hours on the NPS-operated 165' *Ranger III.* Contact Isle Royale National Park (906-482-0984).

BOAT SERVICE FROM COPPER HARBOR, MI: 4.5 hours on the 81' *Isle Royale Queen III.* Contact Isle Royale Ferry Service (906-289-4437 during the season; 906-482-4950 during winter).

BOAT SERVICE FROM GRAND PORTAGE, MN: On the 63' *Voyageur II* (3 hours) or the 65' *Wenonah* (2.5 hours). Contact Grand Portage–Isle Royale Transportation Lines (715-392-2100).

SEAPLANE FROM HOUGHTON, MI: 1 hour. Contact Isle Royale Seaplane Service (906-482-8850).

TOURS AND SPORTS

CANOE AND MOTORBOAT RENTALS AND FUEL: Windigo and Rock Harbor, mid-May to late September.

THE RANGER III: Audiovisual program presented on voyages.

RANGER'S NOTES

Boat docks have narrow bridges and rough bordwalks. Island trails have rough, sandy, rocky surfaces. Assistance may be recommended. Superintendent Bill Fink told us, "Expect an adventure; it will be physically challenging, but rewarding."

MAMMOTH CAVE
NATIONAL PARK
Established 1941   51,592 Acres
Mammoth Cave, KY 42259
Information: 502-758-2251

Mammoth Cave in Mammoth Cave National Park is the long-est natural cave in the world, and to date more than 330 miles of underground passages have been explored. Water dissolving the limestone has created pits, domes, sinkholes, and underground rivers and continues to shape the cave. More than two hundred species of wildlife, including thirty that are blind (such as the blind cave crayfish, blindfish, and endangered Kentucky cave shrimp), inhabit Mammoth Cave. Sixty-nine miles of surface trails thread through forests of oak, hickory, elm, ash, and sycamore.

EASY ACCESS HIGHLIGHTS
• Cave Tour
• Heritage Trail
• Green River

ACTIVITIES: Cave touring, hiking, fishing, canoeing, boating, auto touring.
LOCATION: 48 miles northwest of Glasgow, KY; 42 miles north-east of Bowling Green, KY; 93 miles south of Louisville, KY.
MEDICAL FACILITIES: T. J. Samson Memorial Hospital, Glasgow.
TERRAIN: Park elevations below 1,000'.
CLIMATE: Temperate. Warm to hot summers with periods of rain or high humidity; cool, rainy springs; pleasant autumns; moderately cold, snowy winters. Cave temperature constant 54°F; average cave humidity 87%.

Averaged Daily Temperatures (°F)

	J	F	M	A	M	J	J	A	S	O	N	D
Highs	45	49	58	70	78	86	88	88	82	72	58	48
Lows	25	26	35	45	52	60	64	62	56	44	36	28

Source: Climatables™, courtesy of the National Park Foundation.

VISITOR CENTERS AND MUSEUMS
ISA-designated parking spaces.

VISITOR CENTER: Information desk, book sales, and audio/ visual presentation (without captioning or printed script) fully accessible. Heritage Trial audiotape available. Fully accessible restrooms. Rangers trained (not certified) in sign language; available with advance notice.

ACCESS GUIDES
Park newspaper, *Mammoth Cave, Inside Out,* and park fact sheet list facilities and programs accessible for visitors with disabilities.

ACCESSIBLE TRAILS, VIEWPOINTS, AND SITES
FULLY: Heritage Trail (audiotape available at visitor center). MODERATELY: Sloan's Crossing (with assistance).

ACCESSIBLE CAMPGROUNDS
HEADQUARTERS: 2 sites designated fully accessible, held until 6 P.M.; paved, with raised fire grills and picnic tables with extended tops. Comfort stations, campfire circle, and amphitheater, all fully accessible. Loop with designated sites closed in winter.

LODGING AND SERVICES
MAMMOTH CAVE HOTEL: ISA-designated parking; 2 rooms designated suitable for persons with disabilities (502-758-2225). Fully accessible dining room. Significant barriers to restrooms at visitor center. Laundry and camp store, fully accessible. Public shower moderately accessible. Gas station. BOWLING GREEN, CAVE CITY, AND GLASGOW: Full spectrum of services.

TOURS AND SPORTS
CAVE TOURS: Available at exertion levels from easy to strenuous. The "Disabled Tour [sic]" takes visitors in a van with a wheelchair lift (on request) to the Service Elevator Entrance.

Half-mile tour, 1.5 hours long, including Snowball Dining Room and Cleaveland Avenue, before returns to the surface by elevator.

JOPPA RIDGE MOTOR NATURE TRAIL: 2 mile dirt and gravel road with self-guiding brochure.

GREEN RIVER BOAT TOURS: 30 steps to board boat; crew will assist visitors weighing under 165 lbs. in boarding.

SHENANDOAH NATIONAL PARK
Established 1935   195,404 Acres
Route 4, Box 348
Luray, VA 22835-9051
Information and TDD: 702-999-2243

On the Blue Ridge, a part of the Appalachian Mountains in the eastern United States, Shenandoah National Park lies closer to more people in the country than any other national park. Skyline Drive extends the length of the park, affording views of the mountains and valleys. In the spring, lush flora of wild azaleas, trillium, lady's slippers, and dogwoods bloom.

EASY ACCESS HIGHLIGHTS
• Big Meadow
• Skyline Drive
• Limberlost Trail
• Crescent Rock

ACTIVITIES: Hiking, fishing, horseback riding, auto touring, wildlife and wildflower viewing.

LOCATION: 4 miles east of Luray; 14 miles northwest of Charlottesville, VA.

MEDICAL FACILITIES: Page Memorial Hospital, Luray.

TERRAIN: Road elevations from 590' to 3,680'. Highest point is Hawksbill Mountain (4,051').

CLIMATE: Temperate. Summer days warm with cool nights; springs and falls pleasant; winters cold with snow. Fog and/or cold, wet conditions anytime.

Averaged Daily Temperatures (°F)

	J	F	M	A	M	J	J	A	S	O	N	D
Highs	38	40	47	58	67	73	76	75	69	60	49	39
Lows	20	21	26	36	46	54	58	57	50	41	30	22

Source: Climatables™, courtesy of the National Park Foundation.

VISITOR CENTERS AND MUSEUMS
Both have ISA-designated parking spaces.

DICKEY RIDGE VISITOR CENTER: Information desk, exhibits, touch table, and book and map sales, all fully accessible. Moderately accessible auditorium; films with accompanying scripts. Park brochure available in German, French, Spanish, and Japanese. Park brochure, history handout, and 2 nature trail booklets on audiotape and in Braille. Fully accessible restrooms.

BYRD VISITOR CENTER: Fully accessible information desk, exhibits, touch table, and book and map sales. Moderately accessible auditorium; films with accompanying scripts. Park brochure available in German, French, Spanish, and Japanese. Park brochure, history handout, and 2 nature trail booklets on audiotape and in Braille. Fully accessible restrooms. Signed interpretation on nature walks for deaf visitors; arrange by advance notice with the park.

ACCESS GUIDES
Printed handout, "Accessibility," available at visitor centers.

ACCESSIBLE TRAILS, VIEWPOINTS, AND SITES
FULLY: Most overlooks viewable from automobile.
MODERATELY: Nature trail at Big Meadows (part way), Limberlost (part way), Betty's Rock.

ACCESSIBLE CAMPGROUNDS

MATHEWS ARM: 2 fully accessible sites with picnic tables with extended tops. Fully accessible comfort station and amphitheater. Traces Nature Trail audiotape available. Open late May through October.

BIG MEADOWS: 6 fully accessible sites with raised fire grills and picnic tables with extended tops. Moderately accessible comfort station and amphitheater. Open March through December; reservations required May through October through MISTIX (P.O. Box 85705, San Diego, CA 92138-5705; 800-365-2267; TDD 800-274-7275).

LEWIS MOUNTAIN: 1 fully accessible site has picnic table with extended top. Comfort station and amphitheater, both fully accessible. Open May through October.

LOFT MOUNTAIN: 2 fully accessible sites with picnic tables have extended tops. Fully accessible comfort station and moderately accessible amphitheater. Open May through October.

LODGING AND SERVICES

FRONT ROYAL: Fully accessible restaurant and gift shop. Wheelchair users must drive between restaurant and gift shop to avoid long flight of stairs.

ELKWALLOW: Fully accessible food service and gas station; open mid-June through October.

PANORAMA: Fully accessible restaurant and gift shop; open May through mid-November.

SKYLAND: Lodge with 4 motel rooms designed for use by persons with disabilities. Fully accessible restaurant and gift shop. Open April through mid-December.

BIG MEADOWS: Lodge with several motel rooms designed for use by persons with disabilities. Restaurant, camp store, gift shop, gas station, and laundry, all moderately accessible. Public showers may require assistance because of very narrow stalls and no seating. Open May through October.

LEWIS MOUNTAIN: Moderately accessible camp store and laundry. Public showers may require assistance because of very narrow stalls. Open May through October.

LOFT MOUNTAIN: Food service, gift shop, camp store, gas station, and laundry, all moderately accessible. Public showers may require assistance because of very narrows stalls. Open May through October.

TOURS AND SPORTS
HORSEBACK RIDING: At Skyland and Big Meadows lodges.

AUTHORS' NOTES
On wildflower weekend, in May, we took a ranger-led walk through Big Meadows. A prearranged sign-language interpreter assisted a deaf visitor on the walk with us. Big Meadows, artificially kept as open meadow by the NPS, tantalized us with its profuse blooms of violets, wild strawberries, and wild geraniums.

When visiting Shenandoah National Park, consider driving the 469-mile Blue Ridge Parkway, which stretches along lush mountain vistas to Great Smoky Mountains National Park. Accessible highlights include, from north to south, Peaks of the Otter with a partially paved trail around Abbott Lake, Lynn Cove Information Center featuring a paved trail and the Folk Arts Center displaying Appalachian native crafts. Fully accessible campgrounds are at Roanoke Mountain and Peaks of the Otter. Call Park Headquarters in Ashville, North Carolina for information: 704-259-0779.

VIRGIN ISLANDS NATIONAL PARK

Established 1956   12,910 Acres
P.O. Box 7789, Charlotte Amalie
St. Thomas, Virgin Islands of the United States 00801
Information: 809-775-6238

Rich vegetation on gentle hills and abundant marine life in warm waters create a tropical paradise at Virgin Islands National Park. For snorkelers, the park maintains an underwater self-guided nature trail where visitors can find native coral, fish, and sea turtles.

EASY ACCESS HIGHLIGHTS
- Underwater Trail
- Trunk Bay
- Cruz Bay
- Caneel Bay
- Cinnamon Bay

ACTIVITIES: Hiking, swimming, snorkeling, scuba diving, fishing, auto touring.

LOCATION: 1,100 air miles southeast of Miami; 4 miles east of St. Thomas, Virgin Islands, by ferry. Passenger ferries may be accessible with assistance; auto ferries also available.

MEDICAL FACILITIES: St. Thomas Hospital; Clinic in St. John, Virgin Islands.

TERRAIN: Road elevations from sea level to 1,277'.

CLIMATE: Tropical. Fairly constant year-round temperatures. Brief rainshowers throughout the year; summers and falls can have violent tropical storms.

Averaged Daily Temperatures at Cruz Bay, Sea Level (°F)

	J	F	M	A	M	J	J	A	S	O	N	D
Highs	82	83	84	85	86	87	88	88	88	87	86	84
Lows	71	71	72	74	75	77	77	77	76	76	74	73

Source: Climatables™, courtesy of the National Park Foundation.

VISITOR CENTERS AND MUSEUMS
All have ISA-designated parking spaces.

CRUZ BAY VISITOR CENTER: Building is enterable; moderately accessible information desk and restrooms. Park orientation video with captioning.

HEADQUARTERS AND VISITOR CENTER (RED HOOK, ST. THOMAS): Fully accessible route to ferry. Moderately accessible information desk and telephone; doorway is significant barrier to restrooms.

CINNAMON BAY MUSEUM: Sand is significant barrier.

ACCESS GUIDES
None.

ACCESSIBLE TRAILS, VIEWPOINTS, AND SITES
MODERATELY: Cinnamon Bay (with assistance), Annaberg Sugar Mill.

ACCESSIBLE CAMPGROUNDS
CINNAMON BAY: Concession operated. Four ISA-designated sites with raised fire grills; paths to sites uneven. Comfort station, showers, and amphitheater, all fully accessible. Make reservations well in advance (Caneel Bay, Cruz Bay, St. John, VI 00830; 800-223-7637).

LODGING AND SERVICES
CINNAMON BAY: Concession operated. Cabins moderately accessible.

ST. JOHN AND ST. THOMAS, VI: Various kinds of accommodations, food services, and supplies.

TOURS AND SPORTS
PACKAGE TOURS BY VEHICLE AND BOAT FROM ST. THOMAS: Available through travel agents.

VOYAGEURS NATIONAL PARK
Established 1975   131,952 Acres
P.O. Box 50
International Falls, MN 56649
Information: 218-283-9821

Voyageurs National Park is a water park of more than 30 glacier-carved lakes, named after the "voyageurs," 19th–century French-Canadian traders who paddled their canoes along this historic route. Visitors tour the park by boat, canoe, or floatplane. (See *Best Visits: Four More Parks.*)

EASY ACCESS HIGHLIGHTS
- Rainy Lake
- Kabetogama Lake
- Black Bay
- Ernst Olzoholser Nature Trail
- Kettle Falls

ACTIVITIES: Fishing, canoeing, power- and houseboating, floatplane touring, hiking, bird-watching, cross-country skiing, snowmobiling.

LOCATION: 4 entrances to the park: Rainy Lake, 8 miles east of International Falls; Kabetogama, 26 miles southeast of Rainy Lake; Ash River, 11 miles east of Kabetogama; Crane Lake, 25 miles north of Orr, MN.

MEDICAL FACILITIES: Falls Memorial Hospital, International Falls.

TERRAIN: Lake waters, covering 39% of the park, are between 1,107' and 1,126' above sea level. Land elevations to 1,322'.

CLIMATE: short, warm summers; cold, snowy winters. Lakes inaccessible during freeze-up in late fall and freeze-out in early spring. Snow will complicate any outdoor activity for persons with mobility problems.

Averaged Daily Temperatures at Rainy Lake, 1,107′ (°F)

	J	F	M	A	M	J	J	A	S	O	N	D
Highs	11	20	32	49	64	73	78	75	64	53	33	16
Lows	−11	−5	9	27	39	49	54	51	42	33	17	−1

Source: Climatables™, courtesy of the National Park Foundation.

VISITOR CENTERS AND MUSEUMS
All have ISA-designated parking spaces.

RAINY LAKE VISITOR CENTER: Information desk, exhibits, touch exhibit, book- and map-sales area, all fully accessible. Slide show with accompanying printed script. Birdcall and -song audiotape can be played in the bookstore. Fully accessible restrooms. Open year-round.

KABETOGAMA VISITOR CENTER: Small but fully accessible exhibits include folk art, photography, touch table, and comfort station. Open seasonally.

ASH RIVER VISITOR CENTER: Significant barriers to entrance. Moderately accessible ramp in rear to comfort station. Open seasonally.

ACCESS GUIDES
None.

ACCESSIBLE TRAILS, VIEWPOINTS, AND SITES
FULLY: Ernst Olzoholser Nature Trail.

ACCESSIBLE CAMPGROUNDS
WOODEN FROG STATE PARK: Near Kabetogama; the only campground accessible by automobile. Moderately accessible sites; pit toilets with significant barriers.

LODGING AND SERVICES
KETTLE FALLS: Ramp to lodge, step at threshold to dining room; all rooms upstairs. Open seasonally.

INTERNATIONAL FALLS, ISLAND VIEW KABETOGAMA, ASH RIVER, CRANE LAKE: Lodging and services.

TOURS AND SPORTS

VOYAGEURS NATIONAL PARK BOAT TOURS: Tours of Rainy and Kabetogama lakes (Rte. 8, Box 303, Dept. F-9, International Falls, MN 56649; 218-286-5470). Boat crew will assist persons with disabilities.

GUIDED CANOE TRIPS: From Rainy and Kabetogama lakes visitor centers.

AUTO TRIPS: During winter, when the lakes are frozen solid, cars drive on the 7-mile-long Rainy Lake Ice Road.

CROSS-COUNTRY SKI, SNOWSHOE, AND SNOWMOBILE: Rentals available at International Falls, Island View Kabetogama, Ash River, and Crane Lake.

AUTHORS' NOTES

We especially enjoyed our boat tour on the *Pride of Rainy Lake* and marveled at the island rookeries crowded with nesting cormorants and herring gulls. We saw many people fishing in the lakes and camping in primitive backcountry island sites by the water. (None were fully accessible.)

9·ROCKY MOUNTAINS AND GREAT PLAINS REGION

BADLANDS NATIONAL PARK

Established 1939   232,742 Acres
P.O. Box 6
Interior, SD 57750
Information and TDD: 605-433-5361

Badlands National Park, an intriguing combination of eroding barren ridges and mixed-grass prairie, holds rich deposits of mammal fossils laid down 37 million to 23 million years ago. The park's South Unit, an area rich in Sioux history, is owned by the Oglala Sioux Tribe.

EASY ACCESS HIGHLIGHTS
• Windows Trail
• Fossil Exhibit Trail

ACTIVITIES: Hiking, wildlife and flower viewing, auto touring.
LOCATION: 29 miles south of Wall, SD; 95 miles southeast of Rapid City, SD.
MEDICAL FACILITIES: Rapid City Regional Hospital, Black Hills Rehabilitation Hospital, Rapid City; Clinic 35 miles northeast in Phillip, SD.
TERRAIN: Road elevations from 2,443′ to 3,247′.
CLIMATE: Temperate. Hot summer days with possible thunderstorms; warm, wet springs, yet blizzards possible through April; autumns mild and pleasant, with blizzards possible

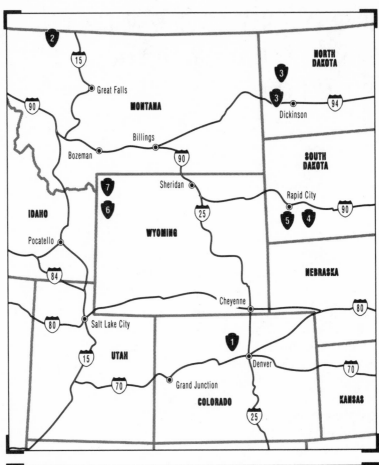

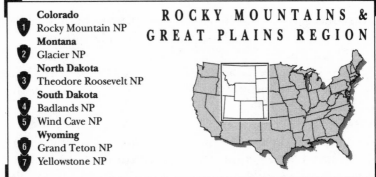

Colorado
1 Rocky Mountain NP
Montana
2 Glacier NP
North Dakota
3 Theodore Roosevelt NP
South Dakota
4 Badlands NP
5 Wind Cave NP
Wyoming
6 Grand Teton NP
7 Yellowstone NP

ROCKY MOUNTAINS &
GREAT PLAINS REGION

in late September; winter days may be mild, but with frequent blizzards and extreme cold. Exposure in the summer may cause heat exhaustion; hypothermia possible in winter, even on mild days.

Averaged Daily Temperatures at Cedar Pass, 2,443′ (°F)

	J	F	M	A	M	J	J	A	S	O	N	D
Highs	32	36	46	61	71	81	91	89	78	66	48	36
Lows	6	9	19	32	42	53	59	54	46	33	20	10

Source: Climatables™, courtesy of the National Park Foundation.

VISITOR CENTERS AND MUSEUMS
All have ISA-designated parking spaces.

CEDAR PASS VISITOR CENTER: Information desk, exhibits, touch exhibits, and book and map store, all fully accessible. Park video program with captioning available. Fully accessible telephone and restrooms open 24 hours.
WHITE RIVER VISITOR CENTER: Information desk, Oglala Sioux exhibits, captioned video, bookstore, and telephone, all moderately accessible, and fully accessible restrooms. Open 9 A.M. to 5 P.M., June to September.

ACCESS GUIDES
Some accessibility information in park seasonal handout.

ACCESSIBLE TRAILS, VIEWPOINTS, AND SITES
FULLY: Windows, Door (part way), Fossil Exhibit (part way).
MODERATELY: Cliff Shelf.

ACCESSIBLE CAMPGROUNDS
CEDAR PASS: Some fully accessible sites, others flat and usable. Comfort stations and amphitheater moderately accessible. Fires prohibited. No running water in winter, pit toilets only.

LODGING AND SERVICES
CEDAR PASS: Fully accessible restaurant and gift shop. Motel

rooms have significant barriers; open April 15 to October 15 (reservations: P.O. Box 5, Interior, SD 57750; 605-433-5460). INTERIOR: Has a few essential services.

TOURS AND SPORTS
None.

AUTHORS' NOTES
The various overlooks have views noted for their stark beauty and sharp-edged ridges, making for interesting photography. The Windows Trail gave us a closer view into the twisting canyons that inspired the French Canadian trappers to call the area *les mauvaises terres à traverser* (bad lands to travel across).

G L A C I E R
N A T I O N A L   P A R K
Established 1910   1,012,996 Acres
West Glacier, MT 59936
Information: 406-888-5441
Recorded Information: 406-888-5551

Glacier National Park in the United States and Waterton Lakes National Park in Canada form an International Peace Park in the rugged glacier-sculptured northern Rocky Mountains, with more than 50 glaciers and with large lakes, spectacular mountain passes, and abundant wildlife, including bighorn sheep, grizzly and black bears, moose, elk, and gray wolves. Some of the rocks in Glacier are more than 1 billion years old.

EASY ACCESS HIGHLIGHTS
• Going-to-the-Sun Road
• Trail of the Cedars
• Logan Pass

- Lake MacDonald
- Lake St. Mary

ACTIVITIES: Hiking, fishing, horseback riding, boating, boat cruising, cross-country skiing, snowshoeing, auto touring.
LOCATION: 20 miles northeast of Kalispell, MT; 32 miles northwest of Browning, MT.
MEDICAL FACILITIES: Kalispell Regional Hospital.
TERRAIN: Park road elevations from 3,153′ to 6,680′. Highest point is Mt. Cleveland (10,466′). Persons with respiratory and/or cardiac conditions should limit activities accordingly, and consult with a physician.
CLIMATE: Temperate. Warm, pleasant summers, cool springs and autumns; severe, cold, snowy winters. Sudden storms and extremely low temperatures possible even during summer months. Snow will complicate any outdoor activity for persons with mobility impairments.

Averaged Daily Temperatures (F°)

	J	F	M	A	M	J	J	A	S	O	N	D
Highs	27	33	39	52	63	69	79	77	66	55	39	32
Lows	11	15	20	29	36	44	47	46	39	32	22	17

Source: Climatables™, courtesy of the National Park Foundation.

VISITOR CENTERS AND MUSEUMS
All have ISA-designated parking spaces.

APGAR VISITOR CENTER: Information desk, exhibits, book and map sales, telephone, and restrooms, all fully accessible. Park relief map, park brochure on audiotape, some tactile nature, and hands-on outdoor program available.
LOGAN PASS VISITOR CENTER: Bookstore (moderately accessible) and telephone. Significant barrier (steps) to information desk and exhibits. Fully accessible comfort station. Open mid-June to early September.
ST. MARY VISITOR CENTER: Fully accessible interior, moderately steep ramp to auditorium, audiovisual program, park relief

map, park brochure on audiotape, some tactile nature, and hands-on outdoor program available. Moderately accessible, roomy restrooms.

ACCESS GUIDES
The guide "Accessibility for Disabled Visitors" has information on activities that may be accessible for persons with disabilities.

ACCESSIBLE TRAILS, VIEWPOINTS, AND SITES
FULLY: Trail of the Cedars, Apgar bicycle paths, Going-to-the-Sun Point, Goat Lick Overlook.
MODERATELY: Hidden Lake Trail (1st part), Running Eagle Trail.

ACCESSIBLE CAMPGROUNDS
APGAR: ISA-designated fully accessible site in Loop C and fully accessible amphitheater and comfort station; many other sites flat and usable.
FISH CREEK: ISA-designated fully accessible site; amphitheater and comfort station also fully accessible.
SPRAGUE: Moderately accessible sites and comfort stations.
AVALANCHE: Moderately accessible sites and comfort stations, fully accessible restroom near Trail of the Cedars.
ST. MARY: ISA-designated fully accessible site; amphitheater and comfort station also fully accessible.
MANY GLACIER: Moderately accessible sites and comfort station.
TWO MEDICINE: Moderately accessible sites and comfort station.

LODGING AND SERVICES
APGAR: Fully accessible deli. Moderately accessible store and coffee shop without an accessible restroom. Boat dock restaurant moderately accessible.
LAKE MACDONALD LODGE: Two moderately accessible cabins with fully accessible showers. Lobby fully accessible; dining

for wheelchair users in bar area. Moderately accessible camp store.

RISING SUN: Coffee shop and 3 motel rooms, all fully accessible; camp store, boat dock, and restroom moderately accessible.

MANY GLACIER: Restaurant, gift shop, and 3 guest rooms, all moderately accessible.

SWIFTCURRENT: Coffee shop, camp store, and 2 motel rooms, all moderately accessible.

TWO MEDICINE: Moderately accessible camp store.

TOURS AND SPORTS
GLACIER PARK BOATS: Tour cruises from Lake MacDonald Lodge, Rising Sun, Many Glacier, and East Glacier. Rising Sun has the only dock with moderate accessibility, and even there persons with mobility problems will need assistance boarding. Crew will help. Call park for information.

AUTHORS' NOTES
The boardwalk and asphalt Trail of the Cedars along Avalanche Creek made for a fun jaunt. In September, we encountered a snowstorm as we drove the Going-to-the-Sun Road over the Continental Divide at Logan Pass. Boat tours on the lakes at the bottom of glacier-carved valleys take visitors into pristine backcountry.

GRAND TETON
NATIONAL PARK

Established 1929   307,617 Acres
P.O. Drawer 170
Moose, WY 83012
Information: 307-733-2880
Recorded information: 307-733-2220
TDD: 307-733-2053

The most dramatic mountain range in the Rockies towers above Grand Teton National Park. For those not wanting to hike the rugged mountains, remarkably scenic overlooks provide views of glacier-cut valleys, alpine lakes, winding rivers, and the Teton Range. Moose, pronghorn, elk, and trumpeter swans appeal to wildlife observers. (See *Best Visits.*)

EASY ACCESS HIGHLIGHTS
• Colter Bay
• Jackson Lake
• Jenny Lake
• Cunningham Cabin
• Snake River

ACTIVITIES: Hiking, wildlife and wildflower viewing, horseback riding, rafting, fishing, boating, cross-country skiing, snowmobiling.
LOCATION: 7 miles south of Yellowstone National Park; 5 miles north of Jackson, WY, on the John D. Rockefeller, Jr. Memorial Parkway.
MEDICAL FACILITIES: St. John's Hospital, Jackson.
TERRAIN: Road elevations from 6,364' to 7,593'. Highest point is Grand Teton at 13,770'. Persons with respiratory and/or cardiovascular problems should consult a physician before ascending to high elevations.
CLIMATE: Temperate. Warm, pleasant summers; cool springs and autumns; cold, snowy winters.

Averaged Daily Temperatures at Moose, 6,474' (°F)

	J	F	M	A	M	J	J	A	S	O	N	D
Highs	29	34	39	50	61	69	80	78	68	56	39	31
Lows	9	13	15	25	33	40	46	44	37	29	19	13

Source: Climatables™, courtesy of the National Park Foundation.

VISITOR CENTERS AND MUSEUMS
All have ISA-designated parking spaces.

MOOSE VISITOR CENTER: Information desk, exhibits, and book and map sales, all fully accessible; park orientation video/ slide programs with large-print script and narrative audio-tape available. Telephone and restrooms, open 24 hours, fully accessible.

COLTER BAY VISITOR CENTER: Information desk, exhibits, book and map sales, telephone, and restrooms all moderately accessible. Park orientation video/slide programs with large-print script and narrative audiotape available. Open mid-May to late September.

NATIVE AMERICAN MUSEUM: Enterable from outside at north side of Colter Bay Visitor Center.

ACCESS GUIDES
Teewinot, the park information newspaper, lists information on activities that may be accessible for persons with disabilities. Park information in Braille at visitor centers.

ACCESSIBLE TRAILS, VIEWPOINTS, AND SITES
FULLY: Colter Bay Lakeshore Foot Trail, String Lake Picnic Area, Taggart Lake, Blacktail Ponds, Snake River.
MODERATELY: Cunningham Cabin, Jenny Lake, Menor's Ferry.

ACCESSIBLE CAMPGROUNDS
GROS VENTRE: Many sites flat and usable. Loop D comfort station fully accessible. Moderately accessible amphitheater.
JENNY LAKE: A few sites flat and usable. Fully accessible comfort stations.

LODGING AND SERVICES

COLTER BAY: Trailer Park open mid-May to mid-September, offering RV hookups (no provisions for persons with disabilities). Gas station, store, wagon rides, and laundromat. Showers not fully accessible; may require assistance. Restaurant has significant barriers.

SIGNAL MOUNTAIN LODGE: Fully accessible restaurant, several fully accessible motel rooms.

JACKSON LAKE: Several moderately accessible motel rooms, restaurant, gift shop, wagon rides, and gas station.

JENNY LAKE: Moderately accessible restaurant. Cabins have significant barriers.

MOOSE: Gas station and post office, moderately accessible with assistance.

DORNAN'S: Grocery, deli, bar, liquor store, gas station, and gift shop, all fully accessible.

JACKSON: Full spectrum of services.

TOURS AND SPORTS

Concessionaires will assist boarding tours when needed.

AUTOMOBILE CASSETTE TAPE TOURS: For purchase at gift shops and gas stations in park.

COLTER BAY AND JACKSON: Wagon rides in summer, assistance may be necessary for boarding.

DORNAN'S AND SIGNAL MOUNTAIN: Canoe rentals, assistance needed for launching and landing.

HORSEBACK RIDES: See *Teewinot* for listings.

SNAKE RIVER FLOAT TRIPS: More than a dozen companies offer trips. Check with park or see *Teewinot* for current listings. Boat personnel will assist at short, steep landings.

JACKSON LAKE BOAT TOURS: From Signal Mountain Marina (307-733-5470).

JENNY LAKE BOAT CRUISES: Teton Boating Co. (307-733-2703).

AUTHORS' NOTES

We visited Grand Teton when the aspens, willows, and cottonwoods were in their full autumn colors. The alpine lakes reflected the mountains with a pure clarity. Near our campground at Gros Ventre, a large herd of pronghorn grazed. We enjoyed the park's many stupendous views from roadside and other accessible vantage points.

ROCKY MOUNTAIN NATIONAL PARK

Established 1915   264,747 Acres
Estes Park, CO 80517
Headquarters: 303-586-2371
TDD: 303-586-8506
West Unit: 303-627-3471

Rocky Mountain presents spectacular scenery. High peaks, subalpine tundra, glacier-carved valleys, forests, lakes, waterfalls, and meadows accentuate the park's landscape. One-third of the park, above the tree line, hosts an ecological treasure, the tundra, which survives arcticlike winters. (See *Best Visits*.)

EASY ACCESS HIGHLIGHTS
• Sprague Lake Nature Trail
• Handicamp
• Beaver Ponds Trail
• Trail Ridge Road
• Forest Canyon Overlook
• Rock Cut Trail

ACTIVITIES: Hiking, fishing, horseback riding, wildflower viewing, auto touring.
LOCATION: Main Visitor Center — 1 mile west of Estes Park; 80 miles northwest of Denver. Grand Lake/Kawuneeche — 50 miles from Estes Park; 60 miles from Empire, CO, at Interstate 70.

MEDICAL FACILITIES: Estes Park Medical Center; St. Anthony Medical Center, Granby, CO.

TERRAIN: Park road elevations from 7,500' to 12,185'. Highest point is Long's Peak (14,255'). Glaciated granite mountains, subalpine tundra above the tree line, hilly valleys with meadows, lakes surrounded by forestlands. Persons with respiratory and/or cardiovascular conditions should consult a physician before ascending to high elevations.

CLIMATE: Temperate at lower elevations with mild summers and snowy winters. Arctic winters at highest elevations.

Averaged Daily Temperatures at Estes Park 7,500' (°F)

	J	F	M	A	M	J	J	A	S	O	N	D
Highs	27	30	36	47	50	61	75	72	66	55	40	29
Lows	01	02	08	21	30	36	42	41	33	25	15	06

Source: NPS, Rocky Mountain Park.

VISITOR CENTERS AND MUSEUMS

All have ISA-designated parking spaces.

MAIN VISITOR CENTER: Beaver Meadows entrance at Highway 36. Fully accessible information desk, large-print and Braille park brochures available at desk, book and map sales, orientation film. Moderately accessible telephone and restrooms.

MORAINE PARK MUSEUM: On Bear Lake Road. Exhibits of wildlife in park, information desk, video presentation, bookstore, moderately accessible restroom on accessible 1st floor. Slide show and exhibits on 2nd floor with significant barrier. Plans underway to remodel for more exhibit space and better access.

ALPINE VISITOR CENTER: On Trail Ridge Road about midway between east and west entrances to park. Information desk, bookstore, exhibits, large-print copies of the park brochure, phone, restrooms, all fully accessible. Cafeteria with snacks.

KAWUNEECHE VISITOR CENTER: At Grand Lake (West Unit) entrance on Highway 34. Information desk, bookstore, exhibits, orientation film (captioned), all fully accessible. Audiotape auto tour available. Moderately accessible restrooms open all the time.

ACCESS GUIDES
Available at visitor centers.

ACCESSIBLE TRAILS, VIEWPOINTS, AND SITES
FULLY: Sprague Lake Trail (1st half), Rainbow Curve, Forest Canyon Overlook.
MODERATELY: Alluvial Fan, Bear Lake, Beaver Ponds, Rock Cut, Sprague Lake (2nd half).

ACCESSIBLE CAMPGROUNDS
All amphitheaters are accessible.

MORAINE PARK: 1 moderately accessible site with extended tabletops, located near fully accessible comfort station. Reservations with MISTIX (P.O. Box 85705, San Diego, CA 92138-5705; 800-365-2267; TDD 800-274-7275).
ASPENGLEN: 1 flat ISA-designated site (#5) in Loop A with extended tabletop, raised grill; fully accessible comfort station more than 100 yards away in Loop C.
GLACIER BASIN: Many moderately accessible level sites; comfort stations have significant barriers (steps and narrow stalls). Reservations through MISTIX.
SPRAGUE LAKE HANDICAMP: Backcountry. Fully accessible with extended tabletops, flat area, and fully accessible vault toilet. By reservation only.

LODGING AND SERVICES
No lodging in park.

ESTES PARK AND GRAND LAKE, CO: Adjacent towns; full spectrum of lodging, stores, and services.

TOURS AND SPORTS
HORSEBACK RIDING: Stables at Moraine Park and Sprague Lake; accommodations available for persons with physical impairments.
SKIING: At Hidden Valley in winter.
MOUNTAIN CLIMBING: Colorado Mountain School will guide

persons with mobility, vision, hearing, and developmental problems.

AUTHORS' NOTES
Rocky Mountain has a variety of access opportunities: lakeside paths, beaver-pond boardwalk, and paved high-mountain tundra trails. We found Handicamp at Sprague Lake to be a singular backcountry experience for people with disabilities. The trail around the lake rewarded us with impressive views of mountain peaks and waterfowl. We enjoyed Beaver Ponds Trail for the opportunity to observe beaver habitats at close range. One highlight of our visit was Trail Ridge Road, the highest paved throughfare in the United States, which took us to trails in the subalpine tundra and overlooks of the Rocky Mountains.

THEODORE ROOSEVELT NATIONAL PARK
Established 1947   69,702 Acres
Theodore Roosevelt National Park, ND 58645
Information: 701-623-4466

The prairie-dog towns of Theodore Roosevelt National Park are only one kind of habitat visitors can observe in this badland region surrounded by prairie. Teeming with wildlife, flowers, and unusual rock formations, the park's South, North, and Elkhorn Ranch units commemorate the former president who ranched in the area and was one of the great conservationist leaders in the United States.

EASY ACCESS HIGHLIGHTS
• Painted Canyon
• Squaw Creek
• Maltese Cross Cabin
• Skyline Vista

ACTIVITIES: Hiking, horseback riding, wildlife and bird viewing, river floating trips.

LOCATION: South Unit — 36 miles west of Dickinson, ND; North Unit — 14 miles south of Watford City, ND; Elkhorn Ranch Unit — inquire about access.

MEDICAL FACILITIES: St. Joseph's Hospital, Dickinson; Watford City Hospital.

TERRAIN: Road elevations below 3,000'.

CLIMATE: Temperate; sudden violent storms and harsh temperatures. Hot summer days with possible thunderstorms; wet springs, yet blizzards possible through April; autumns cool and pleasant, blizzards possible in late September; winters may be cool, but frequent blizzards with extreme cold possible. Exposure to heat in the summer may cause heat exhaustion; hypothermia possible in winter, even on mild days. Snow will complicate any outdoor activity for persons with mobility problems.

Averaged Daily Temperatures at South Unit (°F)

	J	F	M	A	M	J	J	A	S	O	N	D
Highs	25	33	42	57	70	79	87	87	75	63	43	32
Lows	−1	7	16	29	40	50	54	52	41	30	17	6

Source: NPS, Theodore Roosevelt National Park.

VISITOR CENTERS AND MUSEUMS

No ISA-designated parking spaces noted. Park brochures available in French, German, and Spanish at visitor centers. North Unit Visitor Center is under construction.

MEDORA VISITOR CENTER (SOUTH UNIT): Information desk, exhibits, book and map sales, and touch exhibits, all fully accessible. Park orientation film with large-print script and volume-adjustable audio message. Fully accessible water fountain and restrooms open 24 hours.

PAINTED CANYON VISITOR CENTER (SOUTH UNIT): Information desk, exhibits, book and map sales, and touch exhibits, all fully accessible. Park orientation film with large-print script and volume-adjustable audio message. Fully accessible water fountain and restrooms and lowered telephone. Open mid-June to late August.

ACCESS GUIDES
Large-print brochure and accessibility guide available.

ACCESSIBLE TRAILS, VIEWPOINTS, AND SITES
FULLY: Maltese Cross Cabin, Painted Canyon, Skyline Vista, Squaw Creek Nature Trail.
MODERATELY: Wind Canyon (part way), Oxbow Overlook, Caprock Coulee Trail.

ACCESSIBLE CAMPGROUNDS
COTTONWOOD (SOUTH UNIT): Fully accessible site #5, not clearly designated. Fully accessible vault toilets. Many other sites flat and usable. Fully accessible amphitheater.
SQUAW CREEK (NORTH UNIT): Fully accessible site #4, not clearly designated. Fully accessible vault toilets. Many other sites flat and usable. Fully accessible amphitheater.

LODGING AND SERVICES
None in park.

MEDORA, ND: Full spectrum of services during summer; limited services in winter.

TOURS AND SPORTS
HORSEBACK RIDES: At Peaceful Valley; ramp for mounting animals (Peaceful Valley Trail Rides, P.O. Box 197, Medora ND 58645).

AUTHORS' NOTES
Maltese Cross Cabin, a historic structure relocated from the original Teddy Roosevelt Ranch to outside the Medora Visitor Center, is worth a tour. At the Edge of Glacier Pullout in the North Unit we saw a marsh hawk nab a field mouse and drop it midair to its mate.

WIND CAVE
NATIONAL PARK
Established 1903   28,295 Acres
Hot Springs, SD 57747
Information: 605-745-4600

Wind Cave National Park features the 7th longest cave in
the world (more than 53 miles), with a small area accessible
to persons with disabilities. Calcite formations, known as
boxwork, distinguish the cave. Above ground, forest and
prairie provide habitats for much wildlife.

EASY ACCESS HIGHLIGHTS
• Assembly Room in Cave

ACTIVITIES: Cave touring, spelunking, wildlife- and bird-
watching.
LOCATION: 11 miles northwest of Hot Springs; 70 miles south
of Rapid City, SD.
MEDICAL FACILITIES: Southern General Hills Hospital, Hot
Springs.
TERRAIN: 4,095′ above sea level at the visitor center; 3,835′
in cave. Persons with respiratory and/or cardiac conditions
should limit activities accordingly, or consult a physician.
CLIMATE: Summers mild to hot with cool evenings; autumn
days pleasantly warm, nights cold; severe winters; windy
springs with occasional snowstorms. Cave temperature is a
constant 53°F.

Averaged Daily Temperatures (°F)

	J	F	M	A	M	J	J	A	S	O	N	D
Highs	34	39	42	51	62	72	80	79	70	60	45	38
Lows	6	10	15	25	34	43	49	46	37	27	16	10

Source: Climatables™, courtesy of the National Park Foundation.

VISITOR CENTER AND MUSEUMS
ISA-designated parking spaces.

VISITOR CENTER: Fully accessible exhibits and book- and map-sales area; information desk not lowered. Fully accessible restrooms.

ACCESS GUIDES
None.

ACCESSIBLE TRAILS
MODERATELY: Assembly Room on Garden of Eden Tour, via elevator into cave.

ACCESSIBLE CAMPGROUNDS
ELK MOUNTAIN: Fully accessible paved site and comfort station.

LODGING AND SERVICES
No lodging in park; gift shop and lunch service in visitor center.

HOT SPRINGS AND CUSTER, SD: Lodging and services.

TOURS AND SPORTS
CAVE TOURS: Garden of Eden, Natural Entrance, Candlelight, and Spelunking cave tours given daily, infrequently during winter. Wear jackets and sturdy shoes. Tours not accessible for individuals with heart, lung, or leg problems or for wheelchair users, except by prior arrangement. The park may be able to accommodate persons with hearing impairments on tours.

AUTHORS' NOTES
Our descent by elevator to the Assembly Room revealed some views of boxwork, cave popcorn, and frostwork decorations. If asked, rangers will leave visitors in quiet for a short period to experience the cave without distraction. Though only 1 small room, the Assembly Room is a slice of what the full tours include.

YELLOWSTONE NATIONAL PARK

Established 1872   2,219,773 Acres
P.O. Box 168
Yellowstone National Park, WY 82190
Information: 307-344-7381
Emergencies: 911

Accessible geysers, wildlife, lakes, rivers, waterfalls, and mountains abound in Yellowstone, the world's first national park. Yellowstone contains the greatest array of geothermal activity on Earth. (See *Best Visits*.)

EASY ACCESS HIGHLIGHTS
- Upper and Lower Geyser Basins
- Old Faithful
- Norris Geyser Basin
- Yellowstone Falls
- Lehardy Rapids
- Mud Volcano
- Lake Yellowstone

ACTIVITIES: Hiking, fishing, boating, wildlife and wildflower viewing, cross-country skiing, snowmobiling.
LOCATION: Mammoth Hot Springs at the northwest entrance — 61 miles south of Livingston, MT; 64 miles north of Jackson, WY, via U.S. 89. West Yellowstone, MT, entrance — 60 miles east of Ashton, MT. East entrance — 53 miles west of Cody, WY, on U.S. 20.
MEDICAL FACILITIES: Lake Hospital, Mammoth, Old Faithful Clinic, all in park.
TERRAIN: Road elevations from 5,300' to 8,530'. Highest point is Eagle Peak (11,358'). Most accessible features between 6,000' and 7,800'. Persons with respiratory and/or cardiovascular conditions should consult a physician before ascending to high elevations.

CLIMATE: Temperate. Summer days warm and pleasant with cool to chilly nights; spring and autumn days cool with chilly nights; cold winters with snow. Rain or snow can fall anytime. Higher elevations tend to be colder than the average.

Averaged Daily Temperatures at Mammoth Hot Springs, 6,241' (°F)

	J	F	M	A	M	J	J	A	S	O	N	D
Highs	29	34	39	50	61	69	80	78	68	56	39	31
Lows	9	13	15	25	33	40	46	44	37	29	19	13

Source: NPS, Yellowstone National Park.

VISITOR CENTERS AND MUSEUMS
All have ISA-designated parking spaces.

ALBRIGHT VISITOR CENTER (MAMMOTH HOT SPRINGS): Moderately accessible with ramped entrance in rear. Assistance may be required to open heavy doors. Exhibits have large print mounted too high for viewing by wheelchair users. Elevator to moderately accessible restrooms on 3rd floor.

NORRIS GEYSER BASIN: Moderately accessible with assistance possibly necessary on 2 steep portions from parking lot. Small, fully accessible open-air displays. Exhibits use varying type size and height. Fully accessible comfort station.

MADISON EXPLORER'S MUSEUM: Significant barriers.

OLD FAITHFUL VISITOR CENTER: Fully accessible information desk and book and map sales. Exhibits mounted too high for children and wheelchair users. Visitor center, North Geyser, and South Geyser theaters fully accessible. Moderately accessible restrooms.

CANYON VILLAGE VISITOR CENTER: Fully accessible, but information desk and exhibits too high for wheelchair users. Moderately accessible restrooms.

FISHING BRIDGE VISITOR CENTER: Moderately steep curb and entry ramps; fully accessible book and map sales; information desk not lowered. Accessible central museum area with touch exhibits; remainder of museum, including video programs, up short flight of stairs. Moderately accessible restrooms with grab bars.

GRANT VILLAGE VISITOR CENTER: Unmarked ramp on side and entryway is moderately accessible; moderately accessible information desk and restrooms.

ACCESS GUIDES
"Guide To Accessibility for the Handicapped Visitor" available at visitor centers.

ACCESSIBLE TRAILS, VIEWPOINTS, AND SITES
FULLY: Fountain Paint Pot (except 1 section), Old Faithful, Castle Geyser, Kepler Cascades, Uncle Tom's Trail Lookout, north half of LeHardy Rapids.

MODERATELY: Liberty Cap, Upper Terrace, Norris Geyser Basin, Midway Geyser Basin, Biscuit Basin, Black Sand Basin, Geyser Hill, Artist Point, Mud Volcano, West Thumb Geyser Basin.

ACCESSIBLE CAMPGROUNDS
Inquire for seasonal openings; no sites in park are ISA-designated.

MADISON: Moderately accessible sites in Loop A with fully accessible comfort station. Amphitheater is moderately accessible with very steep trail from campground and no curb cut from parking lot.

SLOUGH CREEK (NORTHEAST ROAD): Moderately accessible level terrain; fully accessible vault toilets; water needs to be hand pumped.

CANYON: Several level sites; comfort stations have step at entry, no modified stalls.

FISHING BRIDGE RV PARK: Comfort stations have step at entry, no modified stalls. For reservations May through September, call TW Recreational Services (307-344-7311).

BRIDGE BAY: Several level sites: comfort stations have step at entry, no modified stalls. Reservations with MISTIX

(P.O. Box 85705, San Diego, CA 92138-5705; 800-365-2267).

GRANT VILLAGE: Several level sites; comfort stations have step at entry, no modified stalls.

NORRIS: Several level sites; comfort stations have step at entry, no modified stalls.

LODGING AND SERVICES

For all lodging information and/or reservations, call TW Recreational Services (307-344-7311).

MAMMOTH HOT SPRINGS: Hotel 1st-floor rooms may be enterable, but not designed for accessibility. Terrace Grill and hotel restaurant have ISA-designated parking and accessible dining and restrooms. Store not accessible. Gas station attendant will serve.

OLD FAITHFUL: Snow Lodge has 1 roomy, moderately accessible cabin; entry up steep ramp; tub and toilet have grab bars. Restaurant and gift shops, all moderately accessible, at Old Faithful Inn. Hamilton Stores and gas station in area are moderately accessible.

GRANT VILLAGE LODGE: Motel has 12 accessible rooms, each varying in degree of accessibility. Restaurants, stores, boat launch, gift shops, showers, laundry, and gas station, all moderately accessible.

LAKE YELLOWSTONE HOTEL: Sandpiper Annex has 5 moderately accessible rooms with fully accessible showers. Restaurants, laundry, store, and gas station all moderately accessible.

CANYON CABINS: All rooms have significant barriers.

ROOSEVELT LODGE: All cabins have significant barriers.

TOURS AND SPORTS

AUTO TOURS: Bunson Peak Drive and Firehole Lake Drive.

CARRIAGE RIDES: At Tower-Roosevelt; nonaccessible.

HORSEBACK: Short rides offered at Mammoth, Canyon, and Roosevelt.

SNOW COACH RIDES: In winter. Call TW Recreational Services for information and accessibility (307-344-7900).

AUTHORS' NOTES
The boardwalks through the geyser basins provide a unique exposure to geysers, hot springs, mud pots, and fumaroles. We visited the park in early fall when the cold air enhanced the visual spectacle of the steam rising from the geothermal areas. Don't miss the wildlife in Hayden Valley. Our favorite geysers were Castle, Ledge, Echinus, Beehive, and Old Faithful.

10·DESERT
SOUTHWEST REGION

ARCHES
NATIONAL PARK
Established 1929   66,344 Acres
P.O. Box 907
Moab, UT 84532
Information: 801-259-8161

The greatest density of natural arches in the world is in
Arches National Park. Ground movement and 100 million
years of erosion have formed the red-, pink-, and cream-
colored layers of sandstone into long, narrow fins. Wind and
water erosion have thinned the fins to the point of break-
through, thus creating the arches.

EASY ACCESS HIGHLIGHTS
• South Park Avenue
• The Windows
• Skyline Arch
• Delicate Arch
• Balanced Rock
• Devils Garden

ACTIVITIES: Hiking, auto touring, wildlife viewing, bicycling.
LOCATION: 5 miles north of Moab; 50 miles southeast of Green
River, UT.
MEDICAL FACILITIES: Allen Memorial Hospital, Moab.
TERRAIN: Road elevations from 4,120' to 5,280'. Highest point
is Elephant Butte (5,653'). Persons with respiratory and/or
cardiac conditions should limit activities accordingly.
CLIMATE: Semiarid. Hot summers; pleasant springs and au-
tumns, mild winters with snow and cold nights.

DESERT SOUTHWEST REGION

Arizona
1 Grand Canyon NP
2 Petrified Forest NP
Colorado
3 Mesa Verde NP
Nevada
4 Great Basin NP
New Mexico
5 Carlsbad Caverns NP
6 Chaco Culture NHP

Texas
7 Big Bend NP
8 Guadalupe Mountains NP
Utah
9 Arches NP
10 Bryce Canyon NP
11 Canyonlands NP
12 Capitol Reef NP
13 Zion NP

Averaged Daily Temperatures at Visitor Center, 4,120′ (°F)

	J	F	M	A	M	J	J	A	S	O	N	D
Highs	41	51	61	71	82	86	99	96	86	72	54	44
Lows	18	27	33	42	51	55	65	64	57	42	29	22

Source: NPS, Arches National Park.

VISITOR CENTERS AND MUSEUMS
ISA-designated parking spaces.

VISITOR CENTER: Information desk, exhibits, and book and map sales, all fully accessible. Telephone and restrooms, both fully accessible, open 24 hours; water available year-round.

ACCESS GUIDES
None.

ACCESSIBLE TRAILS, VIEWPOINTS, AND SITES
MODERATELY: South Park Avenue, The Windows, Devils Garden (part way).

ACCESSIBLE CAMPGROUNDS
DEVILS GARDEN: Many sites flat and usable. One ISA-designated site near fully accessible comfort station with running water, open April through October; fully accessible vault toilets open year-round. Moderately accessible amphitheater.

LODGING AND SERVICES
None in park.

MOAB: Full spectrum of services. Brochure (available at visitor center) lists local campgrounds and services.

TOURS AND SPORTS
None in park.

AUTHORS' NOTES
While no trails are fully accessible, the park auto tour affords views of Courthouse Towers and The Windows, Delicate,

and Skyline arches. Devils Garden Campground, among sandstone boulders and fins, is one of the most scenic. It looks east over Colorado River plateau lands to the La Sal Mountains.

BIG BEND NATIONAL PARK
Established 1944   764,608 Acres
Big Bend National Park, TX 79834
Information: 915-477-2551

Big Bend National Park is exceptionally diverse, encompassing the Chisos Mountains, parts of the Chihuahuan Desert, and 107 miles of the Rio Grande River at its great U-turn. (See *Best Visits: Four More Parks*.)

EASY ACCESS HIGHLIGHTS
• Dugout Wells
• Window View Trail
• Santa Elena Canyon
• Castolon

ACTIVITIES: Hiking, river rafting, wildlife and flower viewing, horseback riding, fishing.
LOCATION: 323 miles south of El Paso, TX; 410 miles west of San Antonio, TX.
MEDICAL FACILITIES: Paramedic Clinic, Terlingua, TX; Big Bend Memorial Hospital, Alpine, TX.
TERRAIN: Road elevations from approximately 1,800' to 5,679'. Persons with respiratory and/or cardiac conditions should limit activities accordingly.
CLIMATE: Arid desert. Hot summers with pleasant evenings; mild springs and autumns; warm winters with cool nights. Thunderstorms July through September; minimal snowfall possible in winter.

Averaged Daily Temperatures at Panther Junction, 3,750′ (°F)
Chisos Basin −10°F, Rio Grande Village +10°F from chart.

	J	F	M	A	M	J	J	A	S	O	N	D
Highs	61	66	74	82	89	94	93	91	87	79	70	63
Lows	35	38	45	53	60	66	68	66	61	54	45	38

Source: NPS, Big Bend National Park.

VISITOR CENTERS AND MUSEUMS
All have ISA-designated parking spaces.

PANTHER JUNCTION VISITOR CENTER: Moderately accessible, including restrooms. Auditorium not accessible to people with mobility problems.
RIO GRANDE VISITOR CENTER: Moderately accessible, with information desk, book and map sales, exhibits.

ACCESS GUIDES
None.

ACCESSIBLE TRAILS, VIEWPOINTS, AND SITES
FULLY: Panther Path Nature Trail, Window View Trail.
MODERATELY: Dugout Wells, Castolon, Rio Grande Nature Trail.

ACCESSIBLE CAMPGROUNDS
CHISOS BASIN: Mostly hilly area, but some moderately accessible sites, flat and usable. Nearest fully accessible comfort station at ranger station. Moderately accessible amphitheater.
RIO GRANDE VILLAGE: Many flat, grassy sites may be suitable for wheelchair users. Step and narrow stalls without grab bars in comfort stations. Full RV hookups.
COTTONWOOD: Moderately accessible sites near fully accessible pit toilets.

LODGING AND SERVICES
CHISOS BASIN LODGE: Some guest rooms and restaurant fully accessible (915-477-2251). Store and gas station.

RIO GRANDE VILLAGE: Store, laundry, showers, and gas station, all moderately accessible.
CASTOLON: Store (up steps) and gas station.

TOURS AND SPORTS
HORSEBACK RIDES: The Basin Stables (915-477-2374).
RIO GRANDE RIVER RAFT TRIPS: Big Bend River Tours experienced with visitors who have disabilities (800-545-4240). Concessionaires will assist visitors to board river rafts when needed.

AUTHORS' NOTES
Our river-raft adventure through Santa Elena Canyon had many rewarding surprises; this may be the best way to see wildlife in the park on the Rio Grande River. It was worth going out of our way, and we would eagerly do it again.

BRYCE CANYON NATIONAL PARK
Established 1923   35,833 Acres
Bryce Canyon, UT 84717
Information and TDD: 801-834-5322

Bryce Canyon National Park is noted for its fantastic colorful rock formations, called *hoodoos*. Viewpoints on the rim yield panoramic vistas of the Paria River Valley from the top tier of the southern Utah and northern Arizona plateaus. (See *Best Visits*.)

EASY ACCESS HIGHLIGHTS
• Rim Trail between Sunrise and Sunset Points
• Inspiration Point
• Far View Point
• Rainbow Point
• Bristlecone Pine Trail

ACTIVITIES: Hiking, horseback riding, auto touring.

LOCATION: 220 miles northeast of Las Vegas, Nevada; 253 miles south of Salt Lake City. Entrance from the north by Utah Route 12.

MEDICAL FACILITIES: Garfield Memorial Hospital, Panguitch, UT.

TERRAIN: Elevations on the plateau between 7,835' near the entrance and 9,105' at Rainbow Point. Hoodoos, or vertical eroded sandstone pillars, with rugged hiking and horse trails descending 2,000' below the rim. Persons with respiratory and/or cardiovascular problems should consult a physician before ascending to high elevations.

CLIMATE: Semiarid. Pleasant days with cool to chilly nights and frequent, often dramatic summer thunderstorms spring through fall; snow and many nights below freezing in winter.

Averaged Daily Temperatures at Bryce Canyon Lodge, 8,000' (°F)

	J	F	M	A	M	J	J	A	S	O	N	D
Highs	40	43	51	60	68	81	86	84	75	63	53	40
Lows	20	23	27	34	43	53	60	58	50	35	27	20

Source: NPS, Bryce Canyon National Park.

VISITOR CENTERS AND MUSEUMS
ISA-designated parking spaces.

BRYCE CANYON VISITOR CENTER: Fully accessible lowered information desk; book-, map-, and poster-sales area; exhibits; touch exhibits; foreign language versions of park brochure; lowered telephones; slide presentation with captioning available on request in an accessible auditorium. Moderately accessible restrooms: narrow toilet stalls with grab bars.

SUNRISE NATURE CENTER: Moderately accessible: small step from path to stone plaza in front of the entrance. Exhibits and book, map, and poster sales. Open during summer.

ACCESS GUIDES
Handout guide to services, naturalist activities, viewpoints, and trails for visitors with disabilities.

ACCESSIBLE TRAILS, VIEWPOINTS, AND SITES

FULLY: Sunrise to Sunset Points (via Rim Trail; fully accessible restrooms), Inspiration Point.

MODERATELY: Fairyland Point, Bryce Point, Davia View, Swamp Canyon Viewpoint, Farview Point, Natural Bridge, Agua Canyon, Rainbow Overlook, Yovimpa Point, Bristlecone Pine Loop Trail (1.2 miles).

ACCESSIBLE CAMPGROUNDS

NORTH: ISA-designated spaces near moderately accessible comfort station; held for persons with disabilities until 6:00 P.M. each day.

SUNSET: No ISA-designated sites.

LODGING AND SERVICES

BRYCE CANYON LODGE: Ramp to dining room, gift shop, snack bar, and restroom (all fully accessible) on main level. Fully accessible rooms in modern buildings separate from lodge. Open mid-May to October 1. (Contact TW Recreational Services, 452 N. Main St., Cedar City, UT 84720; 801-586-7686.) Moderately accessible store with groceries, film, and souvenirs; gas station and coin laundry. Showers may require assistance.

TOURS AND SPORTS

TOURS BY HORSEBACK: For those with adequate balance and leg strength, concession-run tours into the canyon. Inquire at visitor center.

AUTHORS' NOTES

We most enjoyed the relatively flat paved trail from Sunrise to Sunset point along the canyon rim and the moderately accessible Bristlecone Pine Trail, along which we saw a 1,700-year-old bristlecone pine tree.

CANYONLANDS NATIONAL PARK

Established 1964   337,570 Acres
125 West 200 South
Moab, UT 84532
Information: 801-259-7164

Canyonlands National Park is divided by the Colorado and Green rivers into 3 districts: Island in the Sky, The Needles, and the very primitive Maze. The confluence of the rivers is 2,000' below the canyon rims. The surreal landscape, occasionally interrupted by bizarrely eroded spires, arches, and tunnels, is a succession of plateaus stepping down to the river gorges.

EASY ACCESS HIGHLIGHTS
- Grand View Point
- Green River Overlook
- Shafter Canyon
- Upheaval Dome
- Wooden Shoe Arch
- Big Spring Canyon

ACTIVITIES: Hiking, rafting, boating, bicycling, horseback riding, auto touring, wildlife viewing.

LOCATION: Island in the Sky District — 30 miles southwest of Moab; Needles Visitor Center — 49 miles northwest of Monticello, UT; Maze District — accessible by four-wheel-drive vehicles only, is 70 miles east of Hanksville, UT.

MEDICAL FACILITIES: Allen Memorial Hospital, Moab.

TERRAIN: Road elevations from 4,880' to 6,160'. Persons with respiratory and/or cardiovascular problems should consult a physician before ascending to high elevations.

CLIMATE: Semiarid. Hot summers; pleasant springs and autumns; mild winters with snow and cold nights. Due to difference in elevation, The Needles District is warmer during the day and cooler at night than the average daily temperature.

Averaged Daily Temperatures at Islands in the Sky, 5,900′ (°F)

	J	F	M	A	M	J	J	A	S	O	N	D
Highs	47	56	63	77	87	94	96	96	92	79	65	48
Lows	8	13	19	23	30	40	54	51	43	29	17	12

Source: NPS, Arches National Park.

VISITOR CENTERS AND MUSEUMS
Both have ISA-designated spaces.

ISLAND IN THE SKY VISITOR CENTER: Fully accessible information desk, exhibits, and book and map sales. Fully accessible restrooms open 24 hours; water available year-round.
NEEDLES VISITOR CENTER: Information desk, exhibits, and book and map sales, all fully accessible. Fully accessible restrooms open 24 hours; water available year-round.

ACCESS GUIDES
None.

ACCESSIBLE TRAILS, VIEWPOINTS, AND SITES
MODERATELY: Grand View Point, Green River Overlook, Bucks Canyon, The Neck.

ACCESSIBLE CAMPGROUNDS
WILLOW FLAT: Significant barriers at all sites; no water.
SQUAW CREEK: Many moderately accessible sites, flat and usable; fully accessible vault toilet; water available mid-April through September.

LODGING AND SERVICES
None in park.

MOAB AND MONTICELLO: Full spectrum of services. Brochure available at visitor center lists local campgrounds and services.

TOURS AND SPORTS
OUTFITTERS, RIVER EXCURSIONS, AND TOUR GUIDES: Lists available from the park.

For us, Grand View Overlook, at the southern edge of Island in the Sky, rivaled the best overlooks of the Grand Canyon in Arizona. River trips on the Colorado and/or Green rivers are guided and can take from ½ to 7 days.

CAPITOL REEF
NATIONAL PARK
Established 1937   222,752 Acres
Torrey, UT 84775
Information: 801-425-3791

A 100-mile-long fold of white-and-rose sandstone cut by a few narrow, deep gorges dominates Capitol Reef National Park. This "waterpocket fold" was formed by the bending and buckling of rock layers 65 million years ago. This desert area also has a long human history; petroglyphs by the prehistoric Fremont Native Americans are easily visible. Early Mormon pioneers farmed alongside the Fremont River, and the orchards from this era are being restored.

EASY ACCESS HIGHLIGHTS
• Grand Wash
• Capitol Gorge
• Fruita
• Old Fruita Schoolhouse
• Petroglyphs

ACTIVITIES: Hiking, auto touring, fruit picking, wildlife viewing.
LOCATION: 40 miles west of Hanksville, UT; 72 miles southeast of Richfield, UT.
MEDICAL FACILITIES: Seiver Valley Hospital, Richfield.
TERRAIN: Road elevations from 5,200' to 6,200'. Persons with respiratory and/or cardiovascular problems should consult a physician before ascending to high elevations.

CLIMATE: Semiarid. Hot summers with thunderstorms; pleasant late springs and early autumns; mild winters with snow and cold nights.

Averaged Daily Temperatures at Fruita, 5,500' (°F)

	J	F	M	A	M	J	J	A	S	O	N	D
Highs	41	48	56	66	76	87	92	89	81	68	53	42
Lows	18	24	30	38	47	55	62	61	53	42	30	21

Source: NPS, Capitol Reef National Park.

VISITOR CENTERS AND MUSEUMS
ISA-designated parking spaces.

FRUTIA VISITOR CENTER: Fully accessible information desk, exhibits, slide presentation, relief map, and book and map sales. Fully accessible restrooms .75 mile south in picnic area.

ACCESS GUIDES
None.

ACCESSIBLE TRAILS, VIEWPOINTS, AND SITES
FULLY: Most overlooks viewable from automobile.
MODERATELY: Fremont River Trail (part way), Petroglyphs, Old Fruita Schoolhouse.

ACCESSIBLE CAMPGROUNDS
FRUITA: Many moderately accessible sites may be flat and usable; fully accessible comfort station in Loop C. Water shut off late fall to spring.

LODGING AND SERVICES
None in park.

TORRE AND HANKSVILLE: Limited accommodations and services listed in a brochure available at the visitor center.

TOURS AND SPORTS
OUTFITTERS AND TOUR GUIDES: List available from park.

AUTHORS' NOTES
The Scenic Drive in Grand Wash and Capitol Gorge was the highlight of our visit. An accompanying road guide explains Capitol Reef's geologic history. In a tribute to the area's pioneer heritage, the park maintains the Historic Fruit Orchards, a special treat during flowering times and harvest. The apples we picked tasted great!

CARLSBAD CAVERNS NATIONAL PARK
Established 1923   46,435 acres
3225 National Parks Highway
Carlsbad, NM 88220
Information: 505-785-2232
Recorded Information: 505-785-2107

Carlsbad Caverns National Park affords superb access to a large underground cavern with impressive natural decorations. Thousands of bats swarm from the cavern entrance every summer evening. This cave and desert mountain park in the Guadalupe Mountains of the beautiful Chihuahuan Desert, NM, has more than 75 caves. Two, including the largest known underground chamber in the Western Hemisphere (the Big Room), can be visited. (See *Best Visits*.)

EASY ACCESS HIGHLIGHTS
• Big Room
• Bat Flight
• Walnut Canyon Desert Drive
• Rattlesnake Springs

ACTIVITIES: Cave touring, spelunking, bat-watching, wildlife and desert-flower viewing.
LOCATION: 27 miles south of Carlsbad; 165 miles east of El Paso, TX.

MEDICAL FACILITIES: Guadalupe Medical Center, Carlsbad.
TERRAIN: Road elevations from 3,608′ to 4,406′ at the visitor center. Elevator from visitor center descends 750′ underground to the cave. Persons with respiratory and/or cardiac conditions should limit their activities accordingly and consult a physician.
CLIMATE: Hot summers with pleasant evening; mild springs and autumns; warm winters with cool nights. Thunderstorms in summer; minimal snowfall possible in winter. Cave temperature a constant 56°F.

Averaged Daily Temperatures at visitor center, 4,406′ (°F)

	J	F	M	A	M	J	J	A	S	O	N	D
Highs	57	60	68	78	86	93	92	91	86	77	66	58
Lows	30	33	38	48	56	69	68	66	60	50	39	33

Source: NPS, Carlsbad Cavern National Park.

VISITOR CENTERS AND MUSEUMS
ISA-designated parking spaces.

CARLSBAD CAVERNS VISITOR CENTER: Fully accessible, with information desk, theater, cave-tour tickets, exhibits, bookstore, gift shop, restaurant, child's nursery, and dog kennel. Fully accessible restrooms.

ACCESS GUIDES
The park "Access Guide" is available at the visitor center.

ACCESSIBLE TRAILS, VIEWPOINTS, AND SITES
MODERATELY: Desert Trail near visitor center may require assistance on steep slopes.

ACCESSIBLE CAMPGROUNDS
None in park.

LODGING AND SERVICES
Aside from facilities available at visitor center, none in park.

CARLSBAD AND WHITE'S CITY: Camping, lodging, and services.

TOURS AND SPORTS

CARLSBAD CAVERN: The Red Tour is a moderately accessible 1.25-mile self-guided exploration of the Big Room in Carlsbad Cavern. The Blue Tour is a strenuous 3-mile self-guided tour (1st part ranger-led in winter). Visitors on both tours can rent hand-held receivers for radio interpretive tours within the cave. Park rangers, upon request, will assist people with disabilities on the Tour.

WALNUT CANYON DESERT DRIVE: 9.5-mile one-way dirt-road self-guided auto tour with brochure.

NEW CAVE: Strenuous, ranger-led cave tour; by prior reservation at visitor center.

AUTHOR'S NOTES

On The Big Room tour (the Red Tour), we marveled at the most extensive and easy, moderately accessible path through an underground cave in the park system. We felt enchanted by the cave's wide variety of natural decorations, including stalactites, stalagmites, cave popcorn, draperies, and columns. Living Desert State Park in the nearby city of Carlsbad has fully accessible paths through exhibits of more than 100 desert native and exotic plants and 50 species of animals.

CHACO CULTURE NATIONAL HISTORICAL PARK
Established 1907   23,248 Acres
Star Route 4, Box 6500
Bloomfield, NM 87413
Information: 505-988-6727

Chaco Culture National Historical Park contains the ruins of many small villages and of thirteen large "towns," pueblos built by the Anasazi between A.D. 900 and A.D. 1150. The partially excavated dwellings offer interesting insights to a complex prehistoric Native American culture. Five of these are moderately accessible. (See *Best Visits*.)

EASY ACCESS HIGHLIGHTS
- Chetro Ketl
- Pueblo Bonito
- Kin Kletso
- Pueblo Del Arroyo
- Casa Rinconada

ACTIVITIES: Hiking, ruin viewing.
LOCATION: 80 miles south of Farmington, NM; 60 north of Thoreau, NM.
MEDICAL FACILITIES: San Juan Regional Medical Center, Farmington.
TERRAIN: Road elevations approximately 6,200'. Persons with respiratory and/or cardiac ailments should consult a physician before ascending to high elevations.
CLIMATE: Arid desert with rapid, unpredictable changes. Summer days hot with nights from pleasant to cold; winter days fluctuate between warm and cold with nights usually very cold.

Averaged Daily Temperatures at Chaco Canyon, 6,175' (°F)

	J	F	M	A	M	J	J	A	S	O	N	D
Highs	43	49	56	67	76	87	91	88	82	70	55	45
Lows	14	19	23	31	39	48	55	54	45	34	22	15

Source: NPS, Chaco Culture National Historical Park.

VISITOR CENTERS AND MUSEUMS
ISA-designated parking spaces.

VISITOR CENTER: Except for heavy entrance doors, fully accessible information desk; museum exhibits and book and gift sales. Park orientation video programs with large-print script and captioning available. Moderately accessible telephone and restrooms. Reliable potable water year-round.

ACCESS GUIDES
None.

ACCESSIBLE TRAILS, VIEWPOINTS, AND SITES
MODERATELY: Chetro Ketl, Pueblo Bonito, Kin Kletso, Pueblo Del Arroyo, Casa Rinconada.

ACCESSIBLE CAMPGROUNDS
GALLO: Many moderately accessible sites, flat and usable. Fully accessible unisex comfort station. Moderately accessible amphitheater.

LODGING AND SERVICES
None in park.

BLOOMFIELD AND GALLOP, NM: Full spectrum of services.

TOURS AND SPORTS
None.

AUTHOR'S NOTES
Pueblo Bonito's large, flat central plaza proviced us with a glimpse into the subterranean kivas, T-shaped doorways, and sandstone masonry of the Anasazi pueblos. At the great kiva of Casa Rinconada, Michael was able to climb down and experience the large circular structure's unique features while Wendy could get an overview of the kiva and the surrounding canyon.

GRAND CANYON NATIONAL PARK

Established 1919   1,179,194 acres
Grand Canyon, AZ 86023
Information: 602-638-7888
TDD: 602-638-7772
Emergency: 911

For 6 million years, the Colorado River carved the immensely vast Grand Canyon, revealing rock 2 billion years old. There are views from both the South and North rims of the Grand Canyon over the 1-mile-deep chasm, luxuriant with changing light and color. (See *Best Visits: Four More Parks*.)

EASY ACCESS HIGHLIGHTS
• Rim Trail
• Mather Point
• West Rim Drive
• Tusayan
• Hopi Point
• Desert View
• Angel View
• Cape Royal

ACTIVITIES: Hiking, biking, mule riding, river rafting, auto touring, helicopter touring.
LOCATION: Grand Canyon South Rim—77 miles north of Flagstaff, AZ; direct, accessible steam-train service from Williams, AZ (call 800-THE-TRAIN [843-8724]). The North Rim—215 miles by road from the South Rim; 81 miles south of Kanab, UT.
MEDICAL FACILITIES: South Rim Clinic; Flagstaff Medical Center; George R. Aiken/Kane County Hospital, Kanab.
TERRAIN: Park road elevations from 6,800' to 8,824'. Persons with respiratory and/or cardiovascular problems should consult a physician before ascending to high elevations.

CLIMATE: Hot summer days with frequent thunderstorms and cool nights; mild springs and falls; winters cold with snow. North Rim closed mid-October to Memorial Day because of snow.

Averaged Daily Temperatures at South Rim, 6,880' (°F)

	J	F	M	A	M	J	J	A	S	O	N	D
Highs	42	48	59	69	79	88	94	91	85	68	54	44
Lows	21	26	31	37	49	58	65	63	57	42	31	23

Source: Climatables™, courtesy of the National Park Foundation.

VISITOR CENTERS AND MUSEUMS
ISA-designated parking spaces.

PARK VISITOR CENTER: Information desk, book and map sales, exhibits, drinking fountain, volume-control lowered telephone, all fully accessible. Wheelchair-accessible auditorium; slide show about the park with accompanying printed text. Moderately accessible restrooms.

YAVAPAI MUSEUM: Good canyon views, fully accessible exhibits, book and map sales, silent film about the canyon's formation, and touch exhibits. Moderately accessible restrooms.

SHRINE OF THE AGES: During winter months, fully accessible films and slide shows with accompanying printed text.

TUSAYAN MUSEUM: Entrance with 1"-high threshold at doorway; otherwise accessible for wheelchair users. Exhibits' dim light may be problematic for persons with vision impairments. Vault toilets have significant barriers.

ACCESS GUIDES
Access for Visitors available at visitor center.

ACCESSIBLE TRAILS, VIEWPOINTS, AND SITES
FULLY: Rim Trail, Hermits Rest Viewpoint, Mather Overlook, Cape Royal.

MODERATELY: Hopi Point, Zuni Point, Tusayan Ruins, Desert View.

ACCESSIBLE CAMPGROUNDS

MATHER CAMPGROUND (SOUTH RIM): Fully accessible designated sites and comfort stations. Reserve through MISTIX (P.O. Box 85705, San Diego, CA 92138-5705; 800-365-2267).
TRAILER VILLAGE (SOUTH RIM): RV sites with full hookups (602-638-2631).
NORTH RIM CAMPGROUND: Flat, moderately accessible sites and comfort stations.

LODGING AND SERVICES

Reservations for South Rim lodging: 602-638-2401.

MASWIK LODGE: Several rooms and the restaurant are fully accessible.
EL TOVAR: Fully accessible restaurant and lobby restroom. Six moderately accessible guest rooms.
BRIGHT ANGEL, KACHINA, THUNDERBIRD, AND YAVAPAI LODGES: Varying degres of moderate accessibility.
GRAND CANYON LODGE (NORTH RIM): Several moderately accessible cabins, Restaurant, down steps, is wheelchair accessible via mechanical lift. For reservations, call 801-586-7686.
BABBITT'S GENERAL STORE: Food and camping supplies.
GRAND CANYON VILLAGE: Bank, post office, gas station and car repair, pet kennels, film processing, laundry, and public showers, all fully accessible, except for an operational barrier in the shower.
VERKAMP'S GIFT SHOP: Fully accessible.
HOPI HOUSE GIFT SHOP: 3 steps; staff will place a steep ramp over steps for wheelchair access.
NORTH RIM: Store and laundry, both moderately accessible. Showers with significant barriers. Gas station.

TOURS AND SPORTS

MULE RIDES: Check at Bright Angel Lodge tour desk.
RIVER-TRIP OPERATORS AND AIR TOURS: See park newspaper, *The Guide,* and concessionaire lists available on request.

We had hoped Grand Canyon National Park would be more accessible than it proved to be. Nevertheless, we were astounded by the awesome size and grandeur of the Canyon.

GREAT BASIN NATIONAL PARK
Established 1922   77,100 Acres
Baker, NV 89311
Information: 702-234-7331

Great Basin National Park, previously Lehman Caves National Monument and upgraded to national park status in 1986, contains one of the largest limestone solution caves in the western United States. The surface ranges in elevation from 2,000' to 13,063', with diverse ecologies from high desert to alpine tundra.

EASY ACCESS HIGHLIGHTS
• Lehman Caves
• Wheeler Peak

ACTIVITIES: Hiking; spelunking; fishing; auto touring; wildlife, wildflower, and bird viewing; cross-country skiing.
LOCATION: 70 miles south of Ely, NV.
MEDICAL FACILITIES: William B. Ririe Hospital, Ely.
TERRAIN: Park road elevations from approximately 2,000' to almost 7,000'. Highest point is Wheeler Peak (13,063'). Persons with respiratory and/or cardiac ailments should consult a physician before ascending to high elevations.
CLIMATE: Semiarid. Summer days warm to hot with cool nights, occasional thundershowers; winter days cool with many nights below freezing. Cave temperature a constant 50°F.

Averaged Daily Temperatures at Lehman Caves, 6,825' (°F)

	J	F	M	A	M	J	J	A	S	O	N	D
Highs	41	44	48	56	63	76	86	83	75	62	49	42
Lows	18	21	24	31	40	48	57	56	47	37	26	20

Source: Climatables™, courtesy of the National Park Foundation.

VISITOR CENTERS AND MUSEUMS
All have ISA-designated parking spaces.

VISITOR CENTER: Moderately accessible via back entrance; information area, exhibits, and restrooms all fully accessible.

ACCESS GUIDES
None.

ACCESSIBLE TRAILS, VIEWPOINTS, AND SITES
FULLY: 1st room only (6,825') in Lehman Cave Tour is wheelchair accessible.
MODERATELY: Wheeler Peak Campground Trail (10,000').

ACCESSIBLE CAMPGROUNDS
UPPER LEHMAN (7,800'): ISA-designated site, fully accessible vault toilet.

LODGING AND SERVICES
LEHMAN CAVE: Gift shop and cafe are moderately accessible, open April to October.
ELY: Full spectrum of services.

TOURS AND SPORTS
RANGER-LED LEHMAN CAVE TOUR: .5 mile paved trail with stairways. Allow 1.5 hours and dress warmly.

AUTHORS' NOTES
The cave room that is accessible for wheelchair users has good examples of the features found throughout the cave. We saw calcite cave decorations in delicate shapes, most

notably the thin, round "shields," or "pallettes," unique to these caves. Wheeler Peak Scenic Drive gave us a sense of the grandeur and vastness of the surrounding Great Basin valleys and mountain ranges.

GUADALUPE MOUNTAINS NATIONAL PARK
Established 1972   76,293 Acres
HC 50, Box 400
Salt Flat, TX 79847-9400
Information: 915-828-3251
TDD: 915-828-3251

Desert, canyon, and highland life zones are all found. A massive limestone fossil reef formed 250 million years ago at the edge of an ancient ocean and was later lifted and exposed by forces concurrent with the uplifting of the Rocky Mountains. In this park surrounded by desert, wildlife includes elk, mountain lions, collared lizards, rattlesnakes, willows, and Texas walnuts. (See *Best Visits: Carlsbad Caverns National Park.*)

EASY ACCESS HIGHLIGHTS
• McKittrick Canyon
• Frijole Ranch
• The Pinery
• El Capitan

ACTIVITIES: Hiking, fishing.
LOCATION: 55 miles southwest of Carlsbad, NM; 58 miles north of Van Horn, TX; 105 miles east of El Paso, TX.
MEDICAL FACILITIES: Guadalupe Medical Center, Carlsbad.
TERRAIN: Road elevations from 5,000′ to 6,293′. Highest point is Guadalupe Peak (8,729′). Persons with respiratory and/or

cardiac ailments should consult with a physician before ascending to high elevations.

CLIMATE: Hot summers with pleasant evenings; mild springs and autumns; mild winters with cold nights and occasional bitter cold. Thunderstorms in summer; minimal snowfall possible in winter.

Averaged Daily Temperatures at Pine Springs, TX, 5,500' (°F)

	J	F	M	A	M	J	J	A	S	O	N	D
Highs	53	58	63	71	78	88	87	84	78	71	61	57
Lows	30	35	38	46	55	63	63	62	57	49	38	33

Source: NPS, Guadalupe Mountains National Park.

VISITOR CENTERS AND MUSEUMS
All have ISA-designated parking spaces.

PINE SPRINGS VISITOR CENTER: New visitor center with information desk, book and map sales, exhibits, and a slide presentation with captioning and transmitters for persons with hearing impairments, all fully accessible. Shorter rear entrance also fully accessible. Fully accessible comfort station.
MCKITTRICK VISITOR CENTER: Small exhibit area and comfort station, both fully accessible.

ACCESS GUIDES
None.

ACCESSIBLE TRAILS, VIEWPOINTS, AND SITES
MODERATELY: The Pinery, McKittrick Canyon (part way).

ACCESSIBLE CAMPGROUNDS
PINE SPRINGS: Two ISA-designated sites with picnic tables with extended tops, concrete and asphalt surfaces, fully accessible comfort stations.
DOG CANYON: Moderately accessible sites; very steep path to comfort station dangerous for wheelchair users.

LODGING AND SERVICES
None in park.

NICKEL CREEK: 4 miles northeast of Pine Springs, restaurant and gas station. Lodging, restaurant and stores in White's City.
CARLSBAD: Full spectrum of services.

TOURS AND SPORTS
None.

AUTHORS' NOTES
At the Pinery little remains from the Butterfield Stagecoach stop save stone walls, but one of the nation's first transcontinental mail routes skirted the south end of the Guadalupe Mountains. We were surprised to learn that no fires are allowed in Pine Springs Campground; however, as the winds picked up to 40 mph, we understood the potential hazard.

MESA VERDE NATIONAL PARK
Established 1906   51,891 Acres
Mesa Verde National Park, CO 81330
Information: 303-529-4465

Mesa Verde National Park is world famous for its well-preserved multiroom cliff dwellings built by pre-Columbian Anasazi Native Americans. Remarkably, several of the ruins dating from A.D. 550 to A.D. 1276 are accessible to the modern-day visitor. (See *Best Visits*.)

EASY ACCESS HIGHLIGHTS
• Spruce Tree House Ruin
• Mesa-Top Loop
• Far View House

- Wetherill Mesa Overlooks
- Badger House Trail
- Step House Ruin

ACTIVITIES: Hiking, ruin viewing.

LOCATION: Park entrance in southwestern Colorado, 45 miles west of Durango, CO, and 10 miles east of Cortez, CO. Park entrance only from the north off U.S. 160.

MEDICAL FACILITIES: Southwest Memorial Hospital, Cortez.

TERRAIN: Rugged mountain elevations ranging between 6,000' and 8,572'. Persons with respiratory and/or cardiovascular conditions should consult a physician before ascending to high elevations.

CLIMATE: Pleasant spring and fall days with cool to chilly nights; summer days warm to hot with frequent and often dramatic thunderstorms; snow in winter with many nights below freezing. Summer or winter, beware of the sun and use sun protection at these altitudes.

Averaged Daily Temperatures at Chapin Mesa, 6,969' (°F)

	J	F	M	A	M	J	J	A	S	O	N	D
Highs	40	44	50	52	71	83	88	85	76	66	51	42
Lows	18	19	26	34	44	52	58	56	48	39	28	21

Source: NPS, Mesa Verde National Park.

VISITOR CENTERS AND MUSEUMS
Both have ISA-designated parking spaces.

FAR VIEW VISITOR CENTER: ISA-designated parking on service road near base of visitor center. Entrance ramp moderately steep; interior fully accessible, with information desk, exhibits, and book sales. Moderately accessible restrooms at base of entrance ramp.

CHAPIN MESA ARCHEOLOGICAL MUSEUM: Information desk, slide presentation, Braille transcription of park brochure, and bookstore with video of park highlights, all fully accessible; wheelchair for loan. Moderately accessible exhibits. Fully accessible comfort station nearby.

ACCESS GUIDES

The park's "A Guide to Accessibility at Mesa Verde National Park" helps visitors with disabilities find accessible ruins, viewpoints, trails, activities, and services.

ACCESSIBLE TRAILS, VIEWPOINTS, AND SITES

All parking areas have ISA-designated parking.

FULLY: Park Point (short paved path), Far View House, plaza area, Mesa-Top Loop (8 fully accessible surface ruins, 1 fully accessible vault toilet), Badger House Community Trail.
MODERATELY: Spruce Tree House Ruin (steep, partially paved trail), Wetherill Mesa Minitram Tour (very steep tram ramp; trails to Kodak and Long House overlooks; comfort station, snack bar, and picnic area all fully accessible), Step House Cave (steep trail to ruin).

ACCESSIBLE CAMPGROUNDS

MOREFIELD: 4 designated sites near fully accessible comfort stations.

LODGING AND SERVICES

MOREFIELD VILLAGE: Laundry, store, gift shop, snack bar, restrooms, lowered telephones, gas station, all fully accessible. Public showers with 1 fully accessible stall and other stalls with significant barriers.
FAR VIEW: Motor Lodge with 6 fully accessible rooms, 2 with wheel-in shower stalls and the other with grab-bar–equipped bathtubs. Fully accessible lodge restaurant with amplified telephone. Far View Terrace gift shop, cafeteria, gas station, all fully accessible.
CHAPIN MESA: Fully accessible gift shop and snack bar. Moderately accessible post office.
CORTEZ: Full range of services.

TOURS AND SPORTS

BUS TOURS: From Morefield Village and Far View to Wetherill and Chapin mesas; not wheelchair accessible.

CHAPIN MESA RUINS: 2 self-guided, 6-mile paved loops with brochures to surface ruins and overlooks of cliff dwellings. Buses available from Morefield Village and Far View. WETHERILL MESA RUINS: Minitram tour, moderately accessible, with very steep ramps to tram car.

AUTHORS' NOTES
We found the ranger-led tour of Spruce Tree House particularly informative and wheelchair accessible with assistance. Among our exciting and revealing experiences were peering down into a kiva at Spruce Tree and watching the sun set on Cliff Palace across the canyon from Sun Temple Overlook. The well-interpreted Badger House Community Trail on Wetherill Mesa gave us a chronological understanding of cultural development at Mesa Verde.

PETRIFIED FOREST NATIONAL PARK
Established 1906   93,533 Acres
Petrified Forest National Park, AZ 86028
Information: 602-524-6228

The Painted Desert landscape in Petrified Forest National Park features fossilized animals and petrified trees revealed by erosion. The petrified logs, with their crystalized, multicolored patterns, began slowly turning to stone 225 million years ago. Petroglyphs and ruins suggest prehistoric Native American habitation for more than 2,000 years, until about A.D. 1400.

EASY ACCESS HIGHLIGHTS
• Painted Desert Inn
• Puerco Ruin
• Newspaper Rock
• Crystal Forest

- Long Logs
- Rainbow Forest

ACTIVITIES: Hiking, auto touring.
LOCATION: 26 miles east of Holbrook, AZ; 70 miles west of Gallop, NM.
MEDICAL FACILITIES: Baptist Hospital, Holbrook; Rehoboth McKinley Christian Hospital, Gallop.
TERRAIN: Park road elevations from 5,100′ to 6,235′. Persons with respiratory and/or cardiovascular conditions should consult a physician before ascending to high elevations.
CLIMATE: Warm to hot summer days with sudden thunderstorms possible; winter days cool with cold nights. Snow can close park roads.

Averaged Daily Temperatures (°F)

	J	F	M	A	M	J	J	A	S	O	N	D
Highs	47	54	62	70	77	90	93	90	86	73	56	45
Lows	18	22	27	33	43	51	60	58	51	39	27	20

Source: NPS, Petrified National Park.

VISITOR CENTERS AND MUSEUMS
All have ISA-designated parking spaces.

PAINTED DESERT VISITOR CENTER: Information desk (not lowered), exhibits, and book and map sales, all fully accessible. Park orientation film program has large-print script. Park brochure available in Braille, Japanese, French, German, and Spanish. Fully accessible telephone and restrooms open 24 hours year-round.
RAINBOW FOREST MUSEUM: Fully accessible (via side entrance) information desk, exhibits, book and map sales, and restrooms. Park orientation film program has large-print script. Park brochure available in Braille, Japanese, French, German, and Spanish.

ACCESS GUIDES
Ask at visitor center if available.

ACCESSIBLE TRAILS, VIEWPOINTS, AND SITES
FULLY: Kachina Point, Puerco Ruins, Newspaper Rock, Long Logs (partially).
MODERATELY: Crystal Forest, Giant Logs, Blue Mesa.

ACCESSIBLE CAMPGROUNDS
No campgrounds in park.

LODGING AND SERVICES
PAINTED DESERT: Fully accessible cafeteria and gift shop.
HOLBOOK: Full spectrum of services.

TOURS AND SPORTS
None.

AUTHORS' NOTES
Although Crystal Forest is only moderately accessible and requires assistance on a few steep grades, we appreciated its beautiful and diverse petrified trees. We were distressed to see visitors collecting petrified wood and fossils, which is strictly prohibited by the service in order to protect them for everyone's enjoyment. Several dealers outside the park sell these items legally.

ZION NATIONAL PARK
Established 1919   143,040 Acres
Springdale, UT 84767
Information: 801-772-3256

The imposing cliffs and canyons of Zion National Park are bisected by the Virgin River, its canyon walls narrowing in places to only 18'. The Park contains a wealth of natural gardens with ferns and mosses. Wading pools and delicate waterfalls flow beneath towering rock spires. (See *Best Visits: Bryce Canyon National Park.*)

EASY ACCESS HIGHLIGHTS
- Gateway to the Narrows
- Emerald Pools
- Zion–Mt. Carmel Tunnel
- Checkerboard Mesa

ACTIVITIES: Hiking, fishing, horseback riding, auto touring, wildlife viewing.
LOCATION: 37 miles northeast of St. George, UT; 34 miles west of Mt. Carmel, UT.
MEDICAL FACILITIES: Dixie Medical Center, St. George.
TERRAIN: Road elevations from 4,000' to 5,700'. Persons with respiratory and cardiovascular problems should consult a physician before ascending to high elevations.
CLIMATE: Semiarid. Warm to hot summer days with cool nights and dramatic thunderstorms; spring and fall days pleasant, nights sometimes cold; occasional snow and some nights below freezing in winter.

Averaged Daily Temperatures at Springdale, 5,500' (°F)

	J	F	M	A	M	J	J	A	S	O	N	D
Highs	52	57	63	73	83	93	100	97	91	78	63	53
Lows	29	31	36	43	52	60	68	66	60	49	37	30

Source: Climatables™, courtesy of the National Park Foundation.

VISITOR CENTERS AND MUSEUMS
Both have ISA-designated parking spaces.

ZION CANYON VISITOR CENTER: Lowered information desk, book and map sales, exhibits, slide presentation with printed scripts, and unisex restroom, all fully accessible.
KOLB CANYON VISITOR CENTER: Information desk, exhibits, lowered telephone, and restrooms all fully accessible.

ACCESS GUIDES
Printed handout, "Access to Zion National Park for People with Disabilities."

ACCESSIBLE TRAILS, VIEWPOINTS, AND SITES
FULLY: Most overlooks viewable from automobile.
MODERATELY: Gateway to the Narrows Trail (to river), Emerald Pools.

ACCESSIBLE CAMPGROUNDS
SOUTH: 5 ISA-designated fully accessible asphalt-covered-with-gravel sites, water spigots, and picnic tables with extended tops. Fully accessible comfort station.
WATCHMAN: 3 ISA-designated fully accessible asphalt sites in Loops B and C; raised fire grills and picnic tables with extended tops. Moderately accessible comfort station because of 29″ narrow doorways.

LODGING AND SERVICES
ZION LODGE: Several fully accessible rooms, dining room, and gift shop (contact TW Recreational Services, 451 N. Main St., Cedar City, UT 84720; 801-586-7686).

TOURS AND SPORTS
TRAM TOURS OF PARK: Not available for our review.
HORSEBACK RIDES: Late March to early November (Bryce-Zion Trail Rides, P.O. Box 58, Tropic, UT 84776; 801-772-3967).

AUTHORS' NOTES
The paved 1-mile Gateway to the Narrows Trail has some steep drop-offs, but it was one of the first accessible trails we encountered on our journeys through the national parks. In fact, it helped inspire us to produce *Easy Access to National Parks*. The Zion–Mt. Carmel Tunnel is a dramatic drive with long views into Zion Canyon.

11 · PACIFIC STATES REGION

CHANNEL ISLANDS NATIONAL PARK
Established 1980   64,255 Acres
1901 Spinnaker Drive
Ventura, CA 93001
Information: 805-644-8262
TDD: 805-658-8090

Channel Islands National Park preserves 5 islands of the southern California coast: Anacapa, Santa Rosa, Santa Cruz, Santa Barbara, and San Miguel. Visitors reach the islands by boat and hike the islands' interior or dive offshore. This is not an easily accessible park.

EASY ACCESS HIGHLIGHTS
• Sea Lions
• Whale-Watching

ACTIVITIES: Boating, scuba diving and snorkeling, wildlife and bird viewing, fishing, swimming.
LOCATION: Ventura — 70 miles west of Los Angeles.
MEDICAL FACILITIES: Community Memorial Hospital, Ventura.
TERRAIN: No vehicles permitted on islands. Highest point is Devil's Peak on Santa Cruz Island (2,450′).
CLIMATE: Subtropical. Warm, dry summers; pleasant springs and autumns with fog, mild, occasionally rainy winters.

Averaged Daily Temperatures (°F)

	J	F	M	A	M	J	J	A	S	O	N	D
Highs	63	64	63	64	65	68	70	72	72	70	68	65
Lows	47	48	51	55	58	61	62	61	61	56	51	47

Source: Climatables™, courtesy of the National Park Foundation.

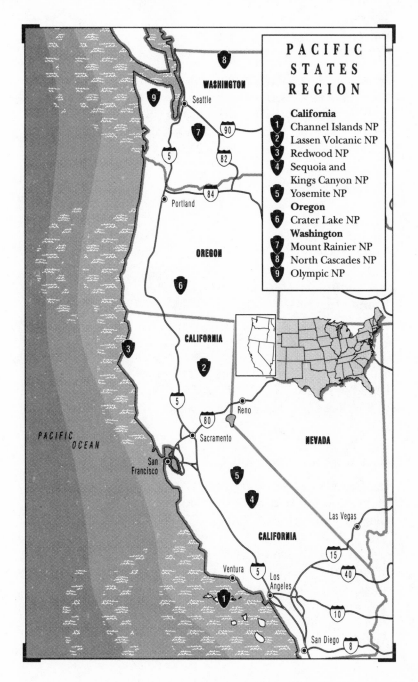

CHANNEL ISLANDS NATIONAL PARK 327

VISITOR CENTERS AND MUSEUMS
ISA-designated parking spaces.

PARK VISITOR CENTER (VENTURA): Information desk, exhibits, large relief models, tide-pool display, and book and map sales, all fully accessible. Park orientation film program fully accessible with closed captioning available on request. Fully accessible lowered telephone and restrooms.

ACCESS GUIDES
None.

ACCESSIBLE TRAILS, VIEWPOINTS, AND SITES
None.

ACCESSIBLE CAMPGROUNDS
None.

LODGING AND SERVICES
CHRISTY GUEST RANCH (SANTA CRUZ ISLAND): Room and tent accommodations with transportation and meals, Channel Island Adventures (805-987-1678).
VENTURA AND OXNARD, CA: Full array of services.

TOURS AND SPORTS
All tours with significant barriers.

EXCURSIONS TO THE FIVE ISLANDS: Half day, all day, and overnight camping trips with transportation and meals, led by Island Packers (1867 Spinnaker Dr., Ventura, CA 93001, 805–462-1393).
CHARTER BOATS AND DIVE EXPEDITIONS: Information available from park.
AIRPLANE SERVICE: From Camarillo, California to Santa Barbara and Santa Rosa islands; strong upper body or assistance may be needed to transfer into airplane. Channel Islands Aviation, 805-987-1301.

RANGER'S NOTES

None of the 5 islands is easily accessible. In fact, the most visited, Anacapa, has 156 steps from the boat dock up to the islands's facilities at the top of the cliff. Other islands have similarly significant barriers, such as sandy beaches or rocky shores. The park concessionaire, Island Packers, operates scheduled trips to the islands throughout the year. Former park superintendent William Ehorn told us that some of his best experiences in the park were boat touring around the islands, observing the marine life, and visiting a sea cave.

CRATER LAKE
NATIONAL PARK

Established 1902   183,224 Acres
P.O. Box 7
Crater Lake, OR 97604
Information: 218-283-9821

The blueness of the lake in the caldera of an ancient volcano of the Cascade Range at Crater Lake National Park astounds all who visit. Forest and peaks snowcapped for much of the year surround the isolated lake, a closed ecosystem and, at 1,932', the deepest lake in the United States.

EASY ACCESS HIGHLIGHTS
- Rim Drive
- Phantom Ship
- Wizard Island

ACTIVITIES: Hiking, fishing, auto touring, boat touring, cross-country skiing, snowmobiling.
LOCATION: 52 miles northwest of Klamath Falls, OR, 80 miles northeast of Medford, OR.
MEDICAL FACILITIES: Merle West Medical Center, Klamath Falls.

TERRAIN: Road elevations from 4,400′ to 7,850′. Highest point is Mt. Scott (8,929′). Persons with respiratory and/or cardiac ailments should consult a physician before ascending to higher elevations.

CLIMATE: Temperate and freezing temperatures anytime. Summers brief with infrequent rain showers; winters cold with much snow.

Averaged Daily Temperatures at Rim Village, 7,000′ (°F)

	J	F	M	A	M	J	J	A	S	O	N	D
Highs	36	39	42	50	56	66	77	75	68	56	44	36
Lows	17	18	20	24	30	35	40	39	34	29	24	19

Source: Climatables™, courtesy of the National Park Foundation.

VISITOR CENTERS AND MUSEUMS
All have ISA-designated parking spaces.

STEEL VISITOR CENTER: Information desk, exhibits, and book and map sales, all fully accessible. Park orientation video and movie with large-print script available. Relief map of park. Fully accessible restrooms. Open year-round.

RIM VILLAGE VISITOR CENTER: Information desk, exhibits, book and map sales, and restrooms, all moderately accessible. Open mid-June to September.

ACCESS GUIDES
None.

ACCESSIBLE TRAILS, VIEWPOINTS, AND SITES
FULLY: Corrals Overlook, Rim Village.
MODERATELY: Discovery Point Overlook Trail.

ACCESSIBLE CAMPGROUNDS
MAZAMA: Several fully accessible sites, none designated. Fully accessible comfort station and public showers.

LODGING AND SERVICES
CRATER LAKE LODGE: Under reconstruction until 1994.

RIM VILLAGE CAFETERIA: Moderately accessible serving breakfast, lunch, and dinner; has gift shop. Winter hours: 9 A.M. to 4 P.M., snow permitting.

CABINS: Near Mazama Campground; 2 units designed for wheelchair users. Open mid-May to mid-October 503-594-2511).

TOURS AND SPORTS
BOAT TOUR OF LAKE: From Cleetwood at north end of lake; departs from dock at foot of 1.1-mile steep, dirt trail not accessible by wheelchair.

AUTHORS' NOTES
Our September visit was cut short by a sudden early snowstorm. The Lake was crystal blue, reflecting the lake rim and clouds. The best view of Phantom Ship, from Sun Notch, is not easily accessible. Discovery Point and the Corrals have great views of the Lake and of Wizard Island.

KINGS CANYON NATIONAL PARK
See *Sequoia and Kings Canyon National Parks.*

LASSEN VOLCANIC NATIONAL PARK
Established 1907   106,366 Acres
P.O. Box 100
Mineral, CA 96063
Information: 916-595-4444

After many decades of dormancy, Lassen Peak in Lassen Volcanic National Park erupted in 1914. A great explosion blasted out a new crater 1 year later as a volcanic cloud rose

40,000' skyward. Quiet since 1921, Lassen still has active sulphur vents, fumaroles, boiling mud pots, and steaming hot springs. Forested valleys and large meadows surround barren lava flows.

EASY ACCESS HIGHLIGHTS
- Sulphur Works Thermal Area
- Lake Helen
- Devastated Area Trail

ACTIVITIES: Hiking, fishing, boating, swimming, auto touring, cross-country skiing, snowshoeing.

LOCATION: 32 miles northwest of Chester, CA; 46 miles east of Redding, CA.

MEDICAL FACILITIES: Seneca District Hospital, Chester.

TERRAIN: Park road elevations from 5,737' to 8,493'. Highest point is Lassen Peak (10,457'). Persons with respiratory and/or cardiovascular problems should consult a physician before ascending to high elevations.

CLIMATE: Summer days warm to hot with cool nights and occasional rain showers; winter temperatures vary from 40°F to below 0°F at night. Average annual snowfall, 400".

Averaged Daily Temperatures at Manzanita, 5,950' (°F)

	J	F	M	A	M	J	J	A	S	O	N	D
Highs	42	41	51	61	62	70	82	78	76	66	51	38
Lows	20	13	25	32	37	38	45	42	37	31	23	14

Source: NPS, Lassen Volcanic National Park.

VISITOR CENTERS AND MUSEUMS
All have ISA-designated parking spaces.

MANZANITA VISITOR CENTER: Information area, exhibits, and restrooms, all fully accessible. Indian Ways Program moderately accessible. Open summer only.

SOUTHWEST INFORMATION STATION: Information area, exhibits, and restrooms, all fully accessible. Open summer only.

ACCESS GUIDES
Accessible facilities listed in park newspaper, *Lassen Park Guide.*

ACCESSIBLE TRAILS, VIEWPOINTS, AND SITES
FULLY: Sulphur Works Thermal Area (6,970'), Devastated Area Trail (6,450'), Lake Helen (8,240').
MODERATELY: Manzanita Lake (5,950').
SIGNIFICANT BARRIERS: Bumpass Hell (8,370').

ACCESSIBLE CAMPGROUNDS
SOUTHWEST (6,540'): 2 moderately accessible sites, fully accessible comfort stations.
SUMMIT (7,000'): 1 moderately accessible site, fully accessible comfort station.
MANZANITA (5,950'): 2 fully accessible sites, fully accessible comfort stations. Moderately accessible amphitheater.
BUTTE LAKE (6,100'): A fully accessible site and comfort station.

LODGING AND SERVICES
DRAKESBAD GUEST RANCH (5,680'): Dining room, lodge, and cabin with shower fully accessible. Surrounding terrain rough; trail to hot spring pool is thick grass: (916-529-1512.)
MANZANITA (5,950'): Gas station, fully accessible store, laundromat, and public showers.
LASSEN SUMMER CHALET (6,720'): Food service and fully accessible restrooms.
CHESTER: Full spectrum of services.

TOURS AND SPORTS
HORSEBACK RIDING AT DRAKESBAD: For ranch guests only.

AUTHORS' NOTES
We found the Sulphur Works Thermal Area Trail boardwalk around the sulphur vents very convenient until we reached a set of stairs. We were, however, able to get close to the steaming and odoriferous gurgling thermal features.

Lake Helen, icy even in August, is an accessible and beautiful glacial cirque filled with water. The recently completed and fully accessible Devastated Area Trail was built by volunteers from the Telephone Pioneers of America.

MOUNT RAINIER NATIONAL PARK
Established 1899   235,613 Acres
Tahoma Woods, Star Route
Ashford, WA 98304
Information: 206-569-2211

The largest glacier system in the United States outside of Alaska graces the 14,410′ dormant volcano of Mount Rainier National Park. Below the glaciers, subalpine meadows are often filled with wildflowers, old-growth forest, and rushing snow-fed streams. (See *Best Visits: Olympic National Park.*)

EASY ACCESS HIGHLIGHTS
• Trail of the Shadows
• Nisqually Vista
• Myrtle Falls
• Box Canyon

ACTIVITIES: Hiking, wildlife and wildflower viewing, cross-country skiing, snowshoeing, snowmobiling.
LOCATION: 45 miles southeast of Eumclaw, WA; 58 miles north of Morton, WA; 90 miles southeast of Seattle.
MEDICAL FACILITIES: Community Memorial Hospital, Eumclaw; Lewis County Hospital, Morton.
TERRAIN: Road elevations from 1,716′ to 6,403′. Highest point is Mt. Rainier (14,410′). Persons with respiratory and/or cardiovascular conditions should consult a physician before ascending to high elevations.

CLIMATE: Warm, pleasant days and cold nights in summers; spring, and autumn, sometimes very cold, with snowfall until July; cold winters at low elevations and bitter cold at higher elevations.

Averaged Daily Temperatures at Paradise, 5,400' (°F)

	J	F	M	A	M	J	J	A	S	O	N	D
Highs	34	38	43	51	59	64	74	75	68	57	42	34
Lows	12	15	19	25	32	37	42	41	35	29	22	19

Source: Climatables™, courtesy of the National Park Foundation.

VISITOR CENTERS AND MUSEUMS
All have ISA-designated parking spaces; wheelchair available for loan.

LONGMIRE VISITOR CENTER: Fully accessible small museum and information station; open daily year-round.

PARADISE VISITOR CENTER: Information desk and restrooms, both fully accessible. Exhibits, movie/slide presentation/ video, and top-floor observation windows moderately accessible with moderately steep interior ramps. Fully accessible restrooms. Open daily April through December; weekends January through March.

OHANAPECOSH VISITOR CENTER: Fully accessible small exhibit area. Moderately accessible restrooms. Open summer only.

SUNRISE VISITOR CENTER: Information desk, book and map sales, and restrooms all moderately accessible. Open summer only.

ACCESS GUIDES
None.

ACCESSIBLE TRAILS, VIEWPOINTS, AND SITES
MODERATELY: Trail of the Shadows, Nisqually Vista, Box Canyon (portion of trail's east side).

ACCESSIBLE CAMPGROUNDS
COUGAR ROCK: 1 ISA-designated site with picnic table with

extended top and adjacent moderately accessible vault toilet; moderately accessible comfort station with step at entrance in Loop A; moderately accessible amphitheater.

LODGING AND SERVICES
PARADISE INN: 5 rooms designated for persons with disabilities. Dining room (open summers only), snack bar (open weekends and holidays only), and restrooms on ground floor, all fully accessible.

PARADISE VISITOR CENTER: Snack bar (summer only), moderately accessible.

NATIONAL PARK INN (LONGMIRE): Several fully accessible rooms; dining room, gift shop, and restrooms fully accessible. Moderately accessible store; gas station and cross-country ski rentals. Open year-round.

SUNRISE: Store and snack bar (open summer only), moderately accessible.

TOURS AND SPORTS
CROSS-COUNTRY SKI RENTALS: At Longmire.

AUTHORS' NOTES
The sight of the snow-covered peak of Mt. Rainier as we awoke was awe-inspiring. Touring the park by automobile yields remarkable views, but assistance is usually required for persons with mobility problems on all trails.

NORTH CASCADES NATIONAL PARK

Established 1968   504,555 Acres
2105 Highway 20
Sedro Woolley, WA 98284
Information: 206-856-5700

North Cascades National Park has more than half the glaciers and some of the finest mountain scenery in the lower 48 states. It is a large wilderness park where the NPS, the U.S. Forest Service (USFS), and Seattle City Light utility cooperate to make portions of this remote area more accessible to all. (See *Best Visits: Olympic National Park*.)

EASY ACCESS HIGHLIGHTS
• Happy Creek
• Rainy Lake
• Washington Pass
• Gorge Creek
• Trail of the Cedars

ACTIVITIES: Hiking, fishing, kayaking, canoeing, powerboating, horseback riding, cross-country skiing, snowmobiling.
LOCATION: 125 miles northeast of Seattle; 61 miles east of Sedro Woolley; 83 miles west of Twisp, WA.
MEDICAL FACILITIES: United General Hospital, Sedro Woolley.
TERRAIN: Road elevations below 3,600'. Highest point is Goode Mountain (9,206'). Washington Pass is at 5,483'. Persons with respiratory and/or cardiovascular conditions should consult a physician before ascending to high elevations.
CLIMATE: Warm summers and moderate winters, considerably colder at higher mountain elevations. Rainfall greater on western slope than on drier, warmer east slope. Higher mountain elevations receive 400" to 600" of snow each year. Temperature chart for lower elevation on west side.

Averaged Daily Temperatures at Marblemount, 353' (°F)

	J	F	M	A	M	J	J	A	S	O	N	D
Highs	37	42	48	57	66	70	78	77	70	58	45	40
Lows	26	29	32	37	43	48	52	52	48	41	34	31

Source: Climatables™, courtesy of the National Park Foundation.

VISITOR CENTERS AND MUSEUMS
All have ISA-designated parking spaces.

SEDRO WOOLLEY HEADQUARTERS: Information desk, exhibits, and book and map sales, all fully accessible. Park orientation video/slide programs. Fully accessible restrooms.

MARBLEMOUNT INFORMATION STATION (USFS): Wilderness office and restrooms, both fully accessible.

NEWHALEM VISITOR CENTER: Due for completion June 1992; plans include full accessiblity.

ACCESS GUIDES
None.

ACCESSIBLE TRAILS, VIEWPOINTS, AND SITES
FULLY: Happy Creek Forest Walk, Rainy Lake (4,800'), Shadows of the Sentinels Trail.

MODERATELY: Thunder Creek, Trail of the Cedars, Heather Meadows (1st part), Fire and Ice Trail (1st 1,800').

ACCESSIBLE CAMPGROUNDS
NEWHALEM: ISA-designated sites, comfort stations, and amphitheater, all fully accessible.

COLONIAL CREEK: No ISA-designated sites; many sites flat and usable. Comfort stations and amphitheater fully accessible.

WINNEBAGO FLATS (HOZOMEEN): Sites and comfort station moderately accessible.

LODGING AND SERVICES
NEWHALEM: Moderately accessible store and gas station.

STEHEKIN LODGE: Several fully accessible rooms; comfort station, restaurant, stores, and gas also fully accessible.

LAKE CHELAN FERRY TO STEHEKIN: 4 hours one way; concessionaires will assist visitors to board ferry when needed.

AUTHORS' NOTES
Happy Creek Forest Walk Interpretive Trail features an elevated boardwalk where we were eye level with birds and wildlife among the trees. Rainy Lake Trail, in the adjacent Okanogan National Forest, is a beautiful 1-mile hike to the lake at the bottom of a glacial cirque. Washington Pass Overlook affords stupendous views of Liberty Bell Mountain and into Canada, 35 miles north.

OLYMPIC NATIONAL PARK
Established 1909   913,051 Acres
600 East Park Avenue
Port Angeles, WA 98362
Information: 206-452-4501

Olympic National Park spans Pacific shoreline, rainforest, and glacier-topped mountains. Salmon spawn in many of the park's rivers, spotted owls nest in the virgin mixed-conifer forests, and Roosevelt elk graze the meadowlands. The park is the largest roadless wilderness area in the lower 48 states. (See *Best Visits*.)

EASY ACCESS HIGHLIGHTS
• Hoh Rain Forest
• Madison Falls
• Hurricane Ridge
• Marymere Falls
• Lake Crescent
• Sol Duc Hot Springs
• Salmon Cascades
• Mora and Rialto Beach

- Kalaloch Beach
- Staircase Rapids
- Deer Park

ACTIVITIES: Hiking, wildlife and wildflower viewing, fishing, boating.
LOCATION: 2 miles south of Port Angeles; from Tacoma, WA, 120 miles. From Seattle, 1-hr. ferry ride to Bremerton, followed by 99-mile drive to Port Angeles.
MEDICAL FACILITIES: Olympic Memorial Hospital, Port Angeles; Grays Harbor Community Hospital, Aberdeen, WA.
TERRAIN: Sea level to 7,965' at Mt. Olympus. Road elevations as high as 6,007' at Deer Park. Persons with respiratory and/or cardiovascular conditions should consult a physician before ascending to high elevations.
CLIMATE: Summer, spring, and autumn cool with many overcast days; winter brings snow to the mountains and heavy rain to the western side of the park, which receives 145" of rain annually at Hoh Rain Forest and 103" at Kalaloch. The eastern side is drier.

Averaged Daily Temperatures at Kalaloch, 39' (°F)

	J	F	M	A	M	J	J	A	S	O	N	D
Highs	45	48	50	55	60	64	69	69	67	59	51	46
Lows	33	35	34	37	42	46	49	50	47	42	37	35

Source: Climatables™, courtesy of the National Park Foundation.

VISITOR CENTERS AND MUSEUMS
All have ISA-designated parking spaces.

PIONEER VISITOR CENTER: Open information desk, book and map sales, orientation slide presentation, exhibits, touch exhibits, and restrooms, all fully accessible. Large-print booklet, *Ever Changing, Ever Green,* for visitors with vision impairments, available at the information desk.
HURRICANE RIDGE VISITOR CENTER (5,230'): For day use only. Upper level fully accessible, with information desk, exhibits,

THE AUTHORS AT OLYMPIC NATIONAL PARK.
Photo by Richard A. Roth.

viewing porch, and unisex fully accessible restroom. Lower
level, fully accessible by elevator, has cafeteria, gift and book
shop, fully accessible restroom.
HOH RAIN FOREST VISITOR CENTER: Information desk, bookstore, exhibits, and restrooms, all fully accessible.

ACCESSIBLE TRAILS, VIEWPOINTS, AND SITES
FULLY: Big Meadow Loop at Hurricane Ridge, Madison Falls,
Lake Crescent Bike Trail, Salmon Cascades, Mora/Rialto
Beach, Hoh Mini-trail, Staircase Rapids.
MODERATELY: Marymere Falls, Olympic Hot Springs, Cirque
Ridge Trail at Hurricane Ridge, Hall of Mosses at Hoh Rain
Forest, Blue Mountain Trail.

ACCESSIBLE CAMPGROUNDS
HEART 'O HILLS (LOOP A): Fully accessible ISA-designated site

with moderately accessible comfort station (flat entrance but no grab bars) and moderately accessible amphitheater.

ELWHA: Moderately accessible sites, fully accessible unisex pit toilets, moderately accessible comfort stations without wide stalls or grab bars.

ALTAIR: Moderately accessible sites, fully accessible unisex pit toilets, moderately accessible comfort stations without wide stalls or grab bars.

FAIRHOLM: Moderately accessible campsites and comfort stations.

SOLEDUCK: Loop A has an ISA-designated site, fully accessible comfort station, and accessible amphitheater.

MORA: Loop B has ISA-designated site, fully accessible comfort station.

HOH RAIN FOREST: Moderately accessible sites and comfort stations.

KALALOCH: Several fully accessible ISA-designated sites with a moderately accessible comfort station (flat entrance but no grab bars) and moderately accessible amphitheater.

STAIRCASE: Campsites, comfort stations, and amphitheater all moderately accessible.

LODGING AND SERVICES

LAKE CRESCENT: Storm King Motel (206-928-3211) West Lodge unit has 2 fully accessible units with bathtubs and 2 other rooms with level entry but with neither bathrooms nor interior doors outfitted for access by visitors with limitations. Olympic Park Institute hosts an Elder Hostel with fully accessible wheel-in showers (206-928-3720) Log Cabin Inn, Dining Room has significant barriers, fully accessible bar will serve meals. Fairholm grocery store moderately accessible.

SOL DUC HOT SPRINGS RESORT: Fully accessible restaurant and hot springs; and 2 accessible rooms (206-928-3211).

KALALOCH: Fully accessible dining room and grocery store; restrooms up stairway.

PORT ANGELES AND FORKS, WA: Many accessible services, accommodations, and stores.

TOURS AND SPORTS
None.

AUTHORS' NOTES
We enjoyed the lush rainforest and subalpine meadows in Olympic. The fully accessible Madison Falls Trail and Hoh Mini-trail were especially rewarding. Kalaloch Campground, with its sites hidden among the salal leaves, has cliff-top views out to the Pacific Ocean.

REDWOOD NATIONAL PARK
Established 1968   75,341 Acres
1111 Second Street
Crescent City, CA 95531
Information and TDD: 707-464-6101

Redwood National Park, along with Prairie Creek Redwoods, Del Norte Coast Redwoods, and Jedediah Smith California Redwoods state parks, preserves 39,000 acres of pristine ancient redwood forests, including the tallest tree in the world. Some of the few remaining herds of magnificent Roosevelt elk can be seen in the park along northern California's scenic coast. (See *Best Visits*.)

EASY ACCESS HIGHLIGHTS
- Redwood Creek Estuary
- Stout Grove
- Redwood Creek Overlook
- Lady Bird Johnson Grove
- Yurock Trail
- Gold Bluffs
- High Bluff Overlook
- Crescent and Enderts Beaches

ACTIVITIES: Hiking, whale- and bird-watching, auto touring, kayaking.

LOCATION: Orick Visitor Center is 44 miles north of Eureka, CA, and 40 miles south of Crescent City.

MEDICAL FACILITIES: Sutter Coast Hospital, Crescent City; Mad River Hospital, Arcata, CA.

TERRAIN: Park elevations between sea level and 3,082' at Schoolhouse Peak. The rugged coastal mountains can be steep, with level, open prairie along riverbeds.

CLIMATE: Mild summers and winters along coast. Summer days with fog; heavy rains October to March, with occasional snow inland at higher elevations.

Averaged Daily Temperatures at Crescent City, 26' (°F)

	J	F	M	A	M	J	J	A	S	O	N	D
Highs	53	55	55	57	60	62	64	64	65	62	58	54
Lows	41	42	42	43	47	50	51	52	51	48	45	42

Source: Climatables™, courtesy of the National Park Foundation.

VISITOR CENTERS AND MUSEUMS
All have ISA-designated parking spaces.

REDWOOD INFORMATION CENTER: Lowered information desk; book, map, and poster sales area; foreign language versions of the park brochure; exhibits; touch exhibits; lowered telephones; slide presentation with captioning available on request in an auditorium; restrooms—all fully accessible.

PRAIRIE CREEK REDWOODS SP VISITOR CENTER: Small and enterable, with book sales; Braille pamphlet and audiocassette for nearby Revelation Trail. Fully accessible comfort station.

CRESCENT BEACH INFORMATION CENTER: Book and poster sales, exhibits, and restrooms, all fully accessible.

CRESCENT CITY VISITOR CENTER: Information desk; book, map, and poster sales area; foreign language versions of the park brochure; exhibits; touch exhibits; lowered telephones—all fully accessible. Restrooms are very small, with significant barriers to wheelchairs.

HIOUCHI INFORMATION CENTER: Book and map sales area, comfort station, and lowered telephone, all fully accessible. Departure point for ranger-led kayak trips on the Smith River (see Tours and Sports for information).

JEDEDIAH SMITH REDWOODS VISITOR CENTER: Small and enterable, with information and book sales, near campground and fully accessible amphitheater.

ACCESS GUIDES
The park's guide for visitors with disabilities, *Access,* contains general information about information centers, auto tour routes, viewpoints, and trails.

ACCESSIBLE TRAILS, VIEWPOINTS, AND SITES
FULLY: Redwood Creek Estuary (ISA-designated parking, boardwalk path from Redwood Information Center), Redwood Creek Overlook (ISA-designated parking, overlook, picnic tables, and vault toilet), Redwood Creek Trail (first 1.5 miles of old dirt road fully accessible; picnic area and vault toilet with significant barriers), Lost Man Creek (1-mile old dirt roadbed, picnic tables, and vault toilets fully accessible; next 9 miles moderately accessible, some slopes may need assistance), Revelation Trail (Prairie Creek — ISA-designated parking, .5-mile fully accessible self-guided trail; portion suitable for persons with visual impairments, with Braille placards and rope and rail guides), High Bluffs Overlook (near junction of Coastal and Alder Camp roads, with overlook, picnic tables, and vault toilets), Klamath Overlook (near Requa, CA, with ISA-designated parking, overlook, extended picnic tables, asphalt path, and vault toilets), Lagoon Creek (picnic area and comfort station).

MODERATELY: Lady Bird Johnson Grove (on Bald Hills Road — ISA-designated parking, moderately steep dirt and paved trail), Yurok Trail (1-mile, self-guided, may need assistance), Crescent and Enderts beaches (Crescent Beach picnic area near the sand; Enderts Beach Trail to Nickles Creek primi-

tive campground), Stout Grove (on Howland Hills Road—
ISA-designated parking; after a moderately steep slope at
trailhead, trail is fully accessible through grove).

SIGNIFICANT BARRIERS: Tall Trees Grove (automobile permit
needed—or take free shuttle bus from Redwood Information Center; strenuous trail), Fern Canyon Trail (easy .7 mile,
though with significant barriers for wheelchairs).

ACCESSIBLE CAMPGROUNDS

All developed campgrounds in California State Parks. For
reservation information, call MISTIX (800-444-PARK [7275];
TDD: 800-444-7275.)

PRAIRIE CREEK REDWOODS: A moderately accessible ISA-designated site with limited paved area and raised fire grill, near
fully accessible comfort station and moderately accessible
showers with narrow stalls.

DEL NORTE COAST REDWOODS, MILL CREEK: Several sites not
designated may be suitable for persons with disabilities. Fully
accessible comfort station with showers.

JEDEDIAH SMITH REDWOODS: ISA-designated site near fully accessible comfort station with showers.

LODGING AND SERVICES

DEMARTIN REDWOOD HOSTEL: Moderately accessible rooms,
retrofitted and ramped for wheelchair use (707-482-8265).

KLAMATH, ORICK, AND REQUA: Small California towns along
U.S. Highway 101; many services.

CRESCENT CITY: Moderately large town; full range of lodging,
restaurants, laundry, food, and auto services.

TOURS AND SPORTS

DAVISON/FERN CANYON ROAD: 6-mile auto tour; whale and
Roosevelt elk watching.

RANGER-GUIDED TALKS, TOURS, AND PRESENTATIONS: Offered by
the park service; varying degrees of accessiblity. Inquire at
visitor centers.

RANGER-LED KAYAKING: Down the Smith River during summer months; moderately accessible with assistance and advance notice (707-464-6101).
ACCESSIBLE HORSEBACK RIDING: Call the park for information.

AUTHORS' NOTES
We were impressed by the combination of tall coast redwood groves and ocean views. Stout Grove, Lady Bird Johnson Grove, and High Bluff Overlook ranked among our favorites.

SEQUOIA AND KINGS CANYON NATIONAL PARKS

Sequoia and Grant Grove National Parks Designated 1890
Kings Canyon National Park Designated 1940
864,144 Acres Total
Three Rivers, CA 94371
Information: 209-565-3341
Recorded Road and Weather Information: 209-565-3351

Sequoia and Kings Canyon national parks are large wilderness areas in the southern Sierra Nevada offering good access opportunities through groves of giant sequoia trees, the largest living organisms on Earth. The parks also boast Mt. Whitney (14,495'), the highest mountain in the United States outside of Alaska; 2 large caves; and one of the deepest canyons on the North American continent. The latter, Kings Canyon, is easily accessible via a breathtaking auto route that ends in Cedar Grove, a high Sierran glacier-gouged valley sometimes called "the other Yosemite." (See *Best Visits*.)

EASY ACCESS HIGHLIGHTS
- Giant Forest
- Trail for All People
- Tharp's Log

- General Sherman Tree
- General Grant Grove
- Roaring River Falls

ACTIVITIES: Hiking, fishing, wildflower and bird viewing, auto touring, horseback riding, cave touring.
LOCATION: 180 miles northeast of Los Angeles; 265 miles southeast of San Francisco.
MEDICAL FACILITIES: Kaweah Delta Hospital, Visalia, CA.
TERRAIN: Park roads between 1,700' and 7,800' in elevation. Eight peaks over 14,000'. Persons with respiratory and/or cardiovascular conditions should consult a physician before ascending to high elevations.
CLIMATE: Temperate. Warm to hot summers with thundershowers; winters with snow at higher elevations. Rapid changes year-round.

Averaged Daily Temperatures at Giant Forest, 6,600' (°F)

	J	F	M	A	M	J	J	A	S	O	N	D
Highs	42	44	46	51	58	68	97	96	91	80	67	58
Lows	24	25	26	30	36	44	51	67	61	52	43	37

Source: NPS, Sequoia and Kings Canyon National Parks.

VISITOR CENTERS AND MUSEUMS
All have ISA-designated parking spaces.

ASH MOUNTAIN VISITOR CENTER: Fully accessible, with information desk, exhibits, book sales, and lowered telephone. Fully accessible restrooms.
LODGEPOLE VISITOR CENTER: Fully accessible, with information desk, theater, exhibits, book sales, and lowered telephone. Moderately accessible restrooms.
GRANT GROVE VISITOR CENTER: Fully accessible, with information desk, exhibits, book sales, and lowered telephone. Fully accessible restrooms.
CEDAR GROVE VISITOR CENTER: Moderately accessible, with book and map sales. Open summer only. Fully accessible comfort station in nearby campground.

ACCESS GUIDES
Park list of accessible facilities available at visitor centers.

ACCESSIBLE TRAILS, VIEWPOINTS, AND SITES
FULLY: Trail for All People, General Sherman Tree, Grant Grove Tree Trail.

MODERATELY: Crescent Meadow Trail to Tharp's Log, Congress, North Grove, Roaring River Falls, Zumwalt Meadow.

SIGNIFICANT BARRIERS: Sunset Rock, Moro Rock.

ACCESSIBLE CAMPGROUNDS
POTWISHA (2,100'): ISA-designated site with extended picnic table, asphalt path to fully accessible comfort stations, water fountain, lowered telephone, raised food storage bin (bear box). Open year-round.

LODGEPOLE (6,969'): 2 moderately accessible sites near moderately accessible comfort station. Sites must be reserved through MISTIX (P.O. Box 85705, San Diego, CA 92138-5705; 800-365-2267). Fully accessible public showers with wheel in shower stall designed for wheelchair users.

DORST (6,720'): Several ISA-designated sites available on first-come first-served basis, picnic tables with extended tops, and fully accessible comfort stations. Amphitheater accessible to wheelchair users only by a back road.

AZALEA (6,580'): ISA-designated site available on first-come first-served basis; flat and sunny space with extended picnic table adjacent to fully accessible comfort station.

CRYSTAL SPRINGS (6,575'): ISA-designated site available on first-come first-served basis, with picnic table with extended top. Comfort station has sloped entrance, but interiors are fully accessible.

SUNSET (6,580'): No ISA-designated site; first-come first-served basis; many sites possibly negotiable by wheelchair users. The most enterable comfort station, near site #5, has no grab bars or wide stalls inside. Men's doorway flat; 2 steps to women's side.

SENTINEL (4,730'): ISA-designated site reserved for persons

with disabilities. Picnic table with extended top near fully accessible comfort station. Public showers near Cedar Grove Lodge with wheel-in shower stall designed for wheelchair users.

LODGING AND SERVICES
GIANT FOREST: Lodge with 5 fully accessible large rooms; shower/tub with grab bars and bath bench supplied by the lodge. Fully accessible cafeteria, store, and gas station. Moderately accessible gift shop; significant barrier to restaurant at lodge.

LODGEPOLE: Snack bar, ice cream parlor, store, post office, wheel-in showers, laundromat, gift shop, and gas station, all fully accessible.

GRANT GROVE: Fully accessible restaurant, lowered telephone, and gas station. Gift shop, store, and post office moderately accessible. Significant barriers to cabins and public showers.

CEDAR GROVE: Lodge with fully accessible room and short-order food service; store with food and camping supplies; and lowered telephone. Snack bar, gift shop, market, wheel-in shower, laundromat, and gas station, all fully accessible.

MINERAL KING: Silver City store and cabins, restaurant, gas station, and showers; facilities not accessible to persons with mobility problems.

TOURS AND SPORTS
CRYSTAL CAVE TOUR: Significant barriers, including steep trail with steps and slippery surface.

HORSEBACK RIDING: At Wolverton (near Lodgepole), Grant Grove, Cedar Station, and Mineral King.

AUTHORS' NOTES
While much of the parks land is high Sierran backcountry, we delighted in our visits to find some accessible groves of giant sequoias. Getting close to these huge trees at Grant Grove was a special thrill for us. Don't miss the General Sherman Tree, the largest living tree on Earth, in the Giant

Forest. The drive into Kings Canyon gave us access to views of the sharp, steep granite slopes carved by the rushing Kings River and by glaciers in the past.

YOSEMITE NATIONAL PARK
Established 1890   759,465 Acres
Yosemite Park, CA 95389
Information: 209-372-0265
Recorded Information: 209-372-0264
TTY: 209-372-4726

Yosemite's sculptured granite formations, valleys, waterfalls, and giant sequoia groves contribute to its renowned beauty. Eight miles of bike trails and a ski program for people with disabilities distinguish the park for its accessibility. Yosemite National Park boasts the nation's highest waterfall and also Tioga Pass through mountain meadows of the Sierra Nevada. (See *Best Visits*.)

EASY ACCESS HIGHLIGHTS
• Yosemite Valley
• Yosemite Falls
• Glacier Point
• Wawona
• Mariposa Grove
• Tioga Pass Road
• Tuolumne Meadows

ACTIVITIES: Hiking, bicycling, fishing, river rafting, skiing, wildflower viewing.
LOCATION: 193 miles southeast of San Francisco via Interstate 580 and California 120; 315 miles northeast of Los Angeles via Interstate 5 and California 99 and 140.
MEDICAL FACILITIES: Yosemite Medical Group, Yosemite Valley.
TERRAIN: Road elevations from 2,127′ to 9,941′. Glacier-carved

valleys and high mountain country over 9,000' with meadows, lakes, rivers, and waterfalls. Persons with respiratory and/or cardiovascular conditions should consult a physician before ascending to high elevations.

CLIMATE: Temperate. Warm summers with thundershowers; winters with snow at all elevations. Rapid changes year-round.

Averaged Daily Temperatures in Yosemite Valley, 4,000' (°F)

	J	F	M	A	M	J	J	A	S	O	N	D
Highs	47	55	58	65	71	80	89	89	82	72	57	49
Lows	25	26	30	34	39	46	50	50	48	39	30	26

Source: NPS, Yosemite National Park.

VISITOR CENTERS AND MUSEUMS

All have ISA-designated parking spaces.

VALLEY VISITOR CENTER (YOSEMITE VILLAGE): Fully accessible information desk, large-print trail guides (available at desk), bookstore, captioned orientation film and videodisc, and fully accessible restrooms. ISA-designated parking behind the post office.

INDIAN MUSEUM AND ART GALLERY (NEAR THE VALLEY VISITOR CENTER): Fully accessible.

HAPPY ISLES NATURE CENTER (EAST END OF YOSEMITE VALLEY): Moderately accessible, with habitat exhibits especially for children. Fully accessible telephone.

PIONEER YOSEMITE HISTORY CENTER (WAWONA): Moderately accessible cultural history programs and a moderately accessible collection of early buildings from the area.

TUOLUMNE MEADOWS VISITOR CENTER (TIOGA PASS ROAD): Information desk (moderately accessible), book and map sales, exhibits, and fully accessible restrooms in lower parking lot.

ACCESS GUIDES

Available at visitor centers.

ACCESSIBLE TRAILS, VIEWPOINTS, AND SITES
FULLY: Yosemite Valley bicycle trails, Village of Ahwahnee, A Changing Yosemite Nature Trail, Glacier Point. MODERATELY: Lower Yosemite Fall, Valley View, Bridalveil Fall, Happy Isles, Mirror Lake, Soda Springs/Parsons Lodge.

ACCESSIBLE CAMPGROUNDS
LOWER PINES (YOSEMITE VALLEY): Fully accessible designated site with extended tabletops and asphalt paths to fully accessible comfort stations. Public showers at nearby Curry Village, fully accessible. Reservations through MISTIX (P.O. Box 85705, San Diego, CA 92138-5705; 800-365-2267).

UPPER PINES (YOSEMITE VALLEY): Nondesignated fully accessible sites; comfort stations with significant barriers. Reservations through MISTIX.

SUNNYSIDE (YOSEMITE VALLEY): Walk-in campground with some flat, moderately accessible sites and a fully accessible comfort station.

LODGING AND SERVICES
Information and reservations: 209-252-4848.

CURRY VILLAGE: Fully accessible tent cabins, cabins and motel-type rooms, fully accessible public showers.

YOSEMITE LODGE: 1 fully accessible motel room, several rustic cabins, restaurants, lounge.

AHWAHNEE HOTEL: Several fully accessible cottages, fully accessible restaurant, lounge.

YOSEMITE VALLEY VILLAGE: Restaurants, gas station, post office, gallery, Ansel Adams Photography Studio, gift stores, food market (Yosemite Valley Store), laundromat, sports shop, delicatessen, pizza parlor, ice cream shop, all fully accessible. Wheelchair-accessible volume-control telephone in front of Yosemite Valley Store.

WAWONA HOTEL: Moderately accessible rooms, no accessible shower. Fully accessible restaurant, gift shop, gas station.

TUOLUMNE MEADOWS: Lodge with enterable tent cabins; bathhouse up 4 steps. Fully accessible restaurants, store, and gas station.

GLACIER POINT: Moderately accessible snack bar and gift shop.

TOURS AND SPORTS
BUS AND TRAM TOURS: 209-372-1240.
WINTER SIT-SKI PROGRAM: Badger Pass Ski Area; for persons with physicial disabilities (209-372-1330).
RIVER RAFTING: Merced River in the Yosemite Valley.
HORSEBACK RIDING: Stables in Yosemite Valley, Wawona, and Tuolumne Meadows; no accommodations for persons with physical disabilities (information: 209-372-1248).

AUTHORS' NOTES
Yosemite is popular for beauty on a grand scale. We particularly enjoyed strolling along the bicycle trails of Yosemite Valley through meadows and forest. Yosemite and Bridalveil falls, while not fully accessible, delighted us. Broad vistas at Glacier and Olmsted points allowed us to appreciate the superb scenery of Yosemite. We enjoyed driving through the high Sierra over Tioga Pass to the meadows of Tuolumne.

12 · ALASKA
AND HAWAII

DENALI NATIONAL PARK
Established 1917   4,715,200
6 Million Acres
P.O. Box 9
Denali Park, AK 99755-0009
Information: 907-683-2294
TTY—Alaska Public Lands Information Centers:
   Anchorage—907-271-2738;
   Fairbanks—907-451-7439

Denali National Park is primarily a trailless wildlife preserve
with caribou, moose, Dall sheep, grizzly bears, and wolves
among its highlights. The majority of Denali lies either in
the world of tiny plants, the *tundra* ("land above the trees")
or in the area of scant tree growth, the *taiga* ("land of little
sticks"). Private vehicles are generally prohibited from the
85-mile park road, and visitors use park-provided shuttle
buses.

EASY ACCESS HIGHLIGHTS
• Mt. McKinley
• Alaska Range
• Muldrow Glacier
• Caribou

ACTIVITIES: Wildlife and wildflower viewing (June through
August, peak in end of June), hiking, fishing, bus touring.
LOCATION: 126 miles south of Fairbanks; 240 miles north of
Anchorage.

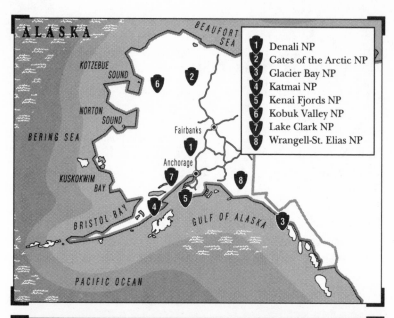

ALASKA

BEAUFORT SEA

KOTZEBUE SOUND

NORTON SOUND

BERING SEA

Fairbanks

Anchorage

KUSKOKWIM BAY

BRISTOL BAY

GULF OF ALASKA

PACIFIC OCEAN

1	Denali NP
2	Gates of the Arctic NP
3	Glacier Bay NP
4	Katmai NP
5	Kenai Fjords NP
6	Kobuk Valley NP
7	Lake Clark NP
8	Wrangell-St. Elias NP

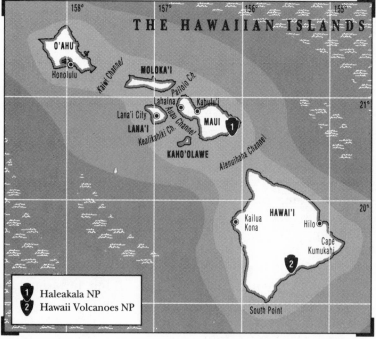

THE HAWAIIAN ISLANDS

158°   157°   156°   155°

O'AHU

Honolulu

MOLOKA'I

Pailolo Ch.

Kaiwi Channel

Lahaina   Kahului

Lana'i City

Au'au Channel

MAUI   1

LANA'I

Kealaikahiki Ch.

KAHO'OLAWE

Alenuihaha Channel

21°

Kailua Kona

HAWAI'I

Hilo

Cape Kumukahi

20°

2

South Point

1	Haleakala NP
2	Hawaii Volcanoes NP

MEDICAL FACILITIES: Fairbanks Memorial Hospital; small clinic in Healy, AK.
TERRAIN: Road elevations from 2,070′ to 3,980′. Mt. McKinley (20,320′) is the highest mountain in North America.
CLIMATE: Subarctic. Summers cool and overcast with snow or rain anytime; long, bitter, cold winters.

Averaged Daily Temperatures 2,070′ (°F)

	J	F	M	A	M	J	J	A	S	O	N	D
Highs	11	16	21	38	53	64	66	62	51	34	19	11
Lows	−7	−4	1	16	30	40	43	40	31	16	1	−6

Source: NPS, Denali National Park.

VISITOR CENTERS AND MUSEUMS
ISA-designated parking spaces at Visitor Access Center.

VISITOR ACCESS CENTER: Fully accessible information desk, book and map sales, bus-tour coupons, and backcountry registration. Fully accessible auditorium with film and accompanying printed script. Fully accessible restrooms and lowered telephone.
EIELSON VISITOR CENTER: Information desk, touch table, viewing windows, book and map sales, and restrooms, all fully accessible.

ACCESS GUIDES
Large-print handout, "Information for the Differently Abled," available at Visitor Access Center and at Denali National Park Hotel. *Denali Alpenglow,* the park newspaper, lists accessible programs.

ACCESSIBLE TRAILS, VIEWPOINTS, AND OVERLOOKS
FULLY: No trails accessible. Wildlife and sights viewable from vehicles.
MODERATELY: Path from hotel to Horseshoe Lake Overlook.

ACCESSIBLE CAMPGROUNDS
RILEY CREEK: 2 fully accessible sites with hard-packed gravel,

picnic tables with extended tops, and raised fire grills. Moderately accessible anphitheater. Fully accessible comfort stations from late May through mid-September; pit toilets inaccessible in winter.

SAVAGE RIVER: 1 fully accessible site with raised fire grill and picnic table with extended top. Moderately accessible amphitheater. Fully accessible comfort station. Open late May through mid-September.

TEKLANIKA RIVER: 2 fully accessible sites have picnic tables with extended tops. Moderately accessible amphitheater. Fully accessible vault toilets. Open late May through mid-September.

WONDER LAKE: Permit requited to drive vehicle to campground. One fully accessible site with picnic table with extended top. Fully accessible comfort station. Open June to mid-September.

LODGING AND SERVICES

DENALI NATIONAL PARK HOTEL: One fully accessible room; dining room, restrooms, snack bar, store, and gas station, all fully accessible (907-683-2215 late May through mid-September; 907-276-7234 in winter). Fully accessible auditorium presents film *Denali Wilderness,* with accompanying printed script.

CAMP DENALI: Moderately accessible rustic cabins; assistance recommended (907-683-2290 in late May through mid-September; 907-675-2248 in winter).

HEALY AND CANTWELL, AK: Minor automobile repair and limited services.

TOURS AND SPORTS

AUTOMOBILE TOUR: Limited private automobile use beyond Savage River. Persons with severe mobility problems can obtain a permit to drive a private vehicle in restricted areas.

SHUTTLE SERVICE: Free 8-hour round-trip service operated by the NPS from Visitor Access Center to Eielson Visitor Center in the summers. One van equipped with lift and wheelchair

tie-downs; reserve a day or more in advance (907-683-2294).
WILDLIFE BUS TOURS: Concession operated (907-683-2294 in
winter; 907-683-2215 in summer).
RANGER-LED DOG SLED DEMONSTRATION PROGRAM: Access infor-
mation: 907-683-2294.
SCENIC AIRPLANE FLIGHTS: 907-683-2281.

GATES OF THE ARCTIC
NATIONAL PARK
Established 1980   7,281,654 Acres
P.O. Box 74680
Fairbanks, AK 99707-4680
Information: 907-456-0281

A congressional mandate set aside Gates of the Arctic National Park and Preserve to remain an undeveloped wilderness area. Situated entirely north of the Arctic Circle, Gates
of the Arctic encompasses part of the Brooks Range, the
northern end of the Rocky Mountains.

EASY ACCESS HIGHLIGHTS
• Endicott Mountains
• Koyukuk River
• Arrigetch Peaks
• Kobuk River

ACTIVITIES: Hiking, wildlife viewing, canoeing, kayaking, river
rafting, cross-country skiing, dog-sledding, touring by airplane. No developed facilities.
LOCATION: Extremely remote; accessible by airplane or cross-
country skiing from Dalton Highway. 260 air miles north
of Fairbanks.
MEDICAL FACILITIES: Fairbanks Memorial Hospital.
TERRAIN: No roads; rugged arctic mountain area. Igikpak
(8,510') is the highest point in the park.

CLIMATE: Artic. Short, mild, cool summers (June to August) with a few warm days; mosquitoes and gnats plentiful mid-June through July; rainy in August. Freezing temperatures and rain anytime. Long, bitter, cold winters.

Averaged Daily Temperatures (°F)

	J	F	M	A	M	J	J	A	S	O	N	D
Highs	−2	8	20	37	55	68	70	64	51	30	11	0
Lows	−20	−17	−9	7	28	42	48	44	33	15	−2	−15

Source: Climatables™, courtesy of the National Park Foundation.

VISITOR CENTERS AND MUSEUMS

ALASKA PUBLIC LANDS INFORMATION CENTER (FAIRBANKS): Fully accessible information desk, museum exhibits with floor map, trip-planning room for all Alaska, captioned video programs, fully accessible restrooms.

ADMINISTRATIVE OFFICE (BETTLES, AK): Fully accessible restrooms.

COLDFOOT: Small information station operated by the NPS, the Bureau of Land Management, and the U.S. Fish and Wildlife Service. Steep, ramped access to the building; no running water; primitive outhouse.

ACCESS GUIDES
None.

ACCESSIBLE TRAILS, VIEWPOINTS, AND SITES
None in park.

ACCESSIBLE CAMPGROUNDS
No developed campgrounds.

LODGING AND SERVICES
BETTLES: Supplies and services.

TOURS AND SPORTS
AIR CHARTER AND GUIDES: List available from park.

RANGER'S NOTES

We did not visit Gates of the Arctic, but in response to our queries, Park Ranger Ron Suttan wrote:

> Gates of the Arctic National Park is 8.5 million acres of wild country. It has no roads. It has no viewpoints. It has no restrooms. It has no lodges. There are no child changing areas or even campgrounds.
>
> Gates of the Arctic was set aside as a National Park in 1980. It was the wish of Congress that Gates of the Arctic remain wild without development. We manage the park according to this mandate. There is no development for visitors anywhere in the park.
>
> Nobody just visits Gates. You don't just drop in. It isn't possible to drive up, jump out of the car, take a few pictures and head for the nearest burger stand. Everyone who visits this park has invested a lot of time in planning and preparation. Everyone! Presumably somewhere in the planning process folks take a look at their vistas and limits and plan accordingly.
>
> The typical visitor contracts with a bush pilot, gets flown into the park, hikes or runs a river for somewhere between three days and three weeks, gets picked up and is flown out. [While] in the park, [visitors] may not see another soul; they are totally on their own (this is also true of our ranger patrols). This is a big park without a lot of visitation. Gates of the Arctic can be a very, very challenging place—for everyone. But it is truly open to anyone who wants to accept the challenges it offers. . . . There are many many many persons with no disabilities who would have a horrid time at Gates just as there are many many many people with severe disabilities who would have a grand time here. It depends on the person.

GLACIER BAY
NATIONAL PARK

Established 1925   3,224,938 Acres
P.O. Box 74680
Gustavus, AK 99826
Information: 907-697-2230

Dramatic tidewater glaciers and lush temperate rainforests distinguish Glacier Bay National Park and Preserve. Brady, at Taylor Bay, is the largest of the 16 tidewater glaciers. Since the first written accounts of the area 200 years ago, glaciers have receded 65 miles, revealing Glacier Bay, where humpback, minke, and orca whales can be seen in summer.

EASY ACCESS HIGHLIGHTS
- Tidewater Glaciers
- Whales
- Bartlett Cove
- Fairweather Range

ACTIVITIES: Hiking, fishing, kayaking, wildlife viewing, canoeing, cross-country skiing, boat cruising, touring by airplane.
LOCATION: Remote; accessible only by airplane or boat; 110 air miles west of Juneau, AK.
MEDICAL FACILITIES: Bartlett Memorial Hospital, Juneau.
TERRAIN: No roads connect to park. Highest point is Mt. Fairweather (15,300').
CLIMATE: Short, cool, rainy summers (May to September) with a few warm days and many nights below freezing. Mosquitoes and gnats plentiful May through August. Moderately cold winters.

Averaged Daily Temperatures (°F)

	J	F	M	A	M	J	J	A	S	O	N	D
Highs	32	38	41	48	55	62	63	62	57	48	41	35
Lows	23	28	29	34	39	44	48	48	44	38	32	27

Source: Climatables™, courtesy of the National Park Foundation.

VISITOR CENTERS AND MUSEUMS

BARTLETT COVE CENTER: 2nd floor of Glacier Bay Lodge. Information desk, exhibits, touch exhibits, park orientation video closed-captioned with sign language introduction, restrooms, all fully accessible. Open late May through mid-September.

ACCESS GUIDES

Park accessibility brochure available at visitor center.

ACCESSIBLE TRAILS, VIEWPOINTS, AND SITES

FULLY: Forest Trail (1st .5 mile).

ACCESSIBLE CAMPGROUNDS

No accessible campsites.

LODGING AND SERVICES

GLACIER BAY LODGE: 2 rooms designated as fully accessible. Dining room, gift shop, telephone, and restrooms, all fully accessible. (Information: 206-623-7110; reservations: 800-622-2042).

GUSTAVUS: Limited supplies and services.

TOURS AND SPORTS

AIR CHARTER, CHARTER BOAT, CRUISE BOAT, RIVER RAFTING, AND OTHER GUIDE SERVICES AND OUTFITTERS: Write to the park for current list.

HALEAKALA NATIONAL PARK

Established 1961   27,487 Acres
P.O. Box 369
Makawao, Maui, HI 96768
Information: 808-572-9306
Weather: 808-572-7749
Camping and Hiking: 808-572-9177

Haleakala Volcano, dormant since 1790, is the primary feature of mountainous Haleakala National Park, home of the famous spherical shaped silversword with its daggerlike leaves. The east portion of the park, Kipahulu, is filled with coastal grasslands, valleys surrounding pools, rainforest, pictographs, and unusual birdlife. (See *Best Visits: Hawaii Volcanoes National Park.*)

EASY ACCESS HIGHLIGHTS
• Haleakala Crater
• Puu Ulaula Summit

ACTIVITIES: Hiking, bicycling, swimming, horseback riding, auto touring.
LOCATION: Headquarters — 30 miles east of Kalului, HI. The Kipahulu area — 53 miles southeast of Kalului.
MEDICAL FACILITIES: Maui Memorial Hospital, Wailuki, HI.
TERRAIN: Road elevations from 6,849' to 10,023'. Persons with respiratory and/or cardiac conditions should limit activities accordingly and consult a physician before ascending to high elevations.
CLIMATE: Tropical Mountain Zone. Hot and sunny or cold and rainy, often during the same day. At the summit, cold and freezing temperatures common.

Averaged Daily Temperatures at Park Headquarters, 7,000' (°F)

	J	F	M	A	M	J	J	A	S	O	N	D
Highs	63	63	64	65	66	68	69	69	69	68	67	65
Lows	45	45	46	47	48	50	51	51	51	50	49	46

Source: NPS, Haleakala National Park.

VISITOR CENTERS AND MUSEUMS
All have ISA-designated parking spaces.

PARK HEADQUARTERS (7,000'): Information desk, book and map sales area, exhibits, restrooms, all fully accessible.
HOUSE OF THE SUN VISITOR CENTER (9,760'): Information desk, book- and map-sales area, exhibits, restrooms, all fully accessible. Observation windows slightly high for wheelchair users and young children.

ACCESS GUIDES
None.

ACCESSIBLE TRAILS, VIEWPOINTS, AND SITES
MODERATELY: Puu Ulaula Summit (10,023'), Hosmer Grove Nature Trail (6,980').

ACCESSIBLE CAMPGROUNDS
HOSMER GROVE: Moderately accessible flat sites; comfort station with step and narrow stalls.

LODGING AND SERVICES
None in park.

KALULUI, LAHAINA, AND KAANAPALI, ALL ON MAUI: Full spectrum of services.

TOURS AND SPORTS
HORSEBACK RIDES: Pony Express (808-667-2200), Charlie Aki (808-248-8209).

AUTHORS' NOTES
We did not visit Haleakala, but one of our brothers, Dick, and his wife, Char, who uses a wheelchair, gave us a report of their experiences with the park's accessibility. The .5-mile Hosmer Grove Nature Trail proved challenging to Char, even with her athletic wheelchair abilities, but it was nevertheless a delightful forest and shrubland experience. Dick and Char found the views of Haleakala Crater marvelous and accessible.

HAWAII VOLCANOES NATIONAL PARK
Established 1916   217,298 Acres
Hawaii Volcanoes National Park, HI 96718
Information: 808-967-7311
Eruption Information: 808-967-7977

Two of the world's most active volcanoes are within Hawaii Volcanoes National Park. Some geothermal features are surprisingly accessible. (See *Best Visits*.)

EASY ACCESS HIGHLIGHTS
• Waldron Ledge
• Devastation Trail
• Halemaumau Crater Overlook
• Chain of Craters Road

ACTIVITIES: Hiking, auto touring.
LOCATION: Kilauea Crater — 29 miles west of Hilo, HI, via Hawaii Route 11.
MEDICAL FACILITIES: Hilo Hospital.
TERRAIN: Park road elevations from sea level to approximately 4,000'. Mauna Loa's summit is at 13,661'. Persons with respiratory and/or cardiovascular problems should avoid gases emitted by volcanic activity and consult a physician before ascending to higher elevations.
CLIMATE: Tropical with relatively constant temperatures year-round; rain anytime, usually afternoons.

Averaged Daily Temperatures at Kilauea, 4,000' (°F)

	J	F	M	A	M	J	J	A	S	O	N	D
Highs	66	65	66	66	68	69	70	71	71	71	68	66
Lows	50	50	50	52	53	54	55	55	54	54	53	51

Source: Climatables™, courtesy of the National Park Foundation.

VISITOR CENTERS AND MUSEUM
All have ISA-designated parking spaces.

KILAUEA VISITOR CENTER: Fully accessible exhibits and restrooms. Film without provisions for visitors with vision or hearing impairments. The park plans to remodel the visitor center as a nature center with improved access.

THOMAS A. JAGGER MEMORIAL MUSEUM: Exhibits, video captioned with large type, restrooms, and a lowered telephone, all fully accessible. High book-sales desk.

TEMPORARY VISITOR CENTER: Mobile unit at end of Chain of Craters Road; up steps, but rangers will assist with information outside unit. Vault toilets with significant barriers.

ACCESS GUIDES
None.

ACCESSIBLE, TRAILS, VIEWPOINTS, AND SITES
FULLY: Waldron Ledge, Steaming Bluff Overlook, portion of Steaming Crater Trail.
MODERATELY: Devastation Trail, Halemaumau Crater.

ACCESSIBLE CAMPGROUNDS
NAMAKANI PAIO CAMPGROUND: Flat with moderately accessible sites and comfort stations. Lowered telephone.
KAMOAMOA CAMPGROUND: Flat with moderately accessible sites in grassy area; pit toilets with significant barriers.

LODGING AND SERVICES
VOLCANO HOUSE: Guest room, dining hall, snack bar, gift shop, lowered telephone, restrooms (all fully accessible) (P.O. Box 53, Hawaii Volcanoes National Park, HI 96718; 808-967-7321).
NAMAKANI PAIO: Inexpensive primitive cabins with a step at entry. Inquire at Volcano House.

TOURS AND SPORTS
No concessionaire or park programs.

AUTHORS' NOTES
We were pleased to find the Devastation and Halemaumau

Crater trails wheelchair usable although not fully accessible and requiring care. A 1983 earthquake rendered Waldron Ledge inaccessible to automobiles; however, the remarkable view of Kilauea Caldera from it remains accessible to wheelchair users and other hikers.

KATMAI NATIONAL PARK
Established 1918   3,575,000 Acres
P.O. Box 7
King Salmon, AK 99613
Information: 907-246-3305

A remote wilderness area on the Alaska Peninsula, Katmai National Park and Preserve is a wildlife sanctuary to the brown bear, the largest land-living carnivore on Earth. Sockeye salmon spawn in the park's rivers every summer, and many become food for brown bears. Collapsing with the world's most violent explosion ever recorded, Mt. Katmai Volcano last erupted in 1912.

EASY ACCESS HIGHLIGHTS
• Valley of Ten Thousand Smokes
• Naknek River

ACTIVITIES: Hiking, wildlife and bird viewing, fishing, boating, cross-country skiing, touring by plane.
LOCATION: Extremely remote; accessible only by boat or airplane. 290 air miles southwest of Anchorage, AK.
MEDICAL FACILITIES: Clinic in Naknek, AK; many facilities in Anchorage.
TERRAIN: No roads; rugged mountain area with streams and lakes. Mt. Denison (7,606') is the highest point.
CLIMATE: Subarctic. Short, windy, rainy, cool summers (June to August) with a few warm days; long, dark, windy winters with rain and snow.

Averaged Daily Temperatures (°F)

	J	F	M	A	M	J	J	A	S	O	N	D
Highs	24	26	31	41	55	63	67	64	57	41	32	22
Lows	3	4	5	22	32	40	45	45	38	25	15	5

Source: Climatables™, courtesy of the National Park Foundation.

VISITOR CENTERS AND MUSEUMS
None.

ACCESS GUIDES
None.

ACCESSIBLE TRAILS, VIEWPOINTS, AND SITES
None.

ACCESSIBLE CAMPGROUNDS
No developed campgrounds.

LODGING AND SERVICES
BROOKS LODGE: Rustic, with dining (family style), 1 room large enough for wheelchair users, with moderately accessible toilet and shower.
KING SALMON AND NAKNEK: Supplies and services.

TOURS AND SPORTS
BUS TOUR TO VALLEY OF TEN THOUSAND SMOKES: June 1 through September 10; not wheelchair-user accessible.
AIR CHARTER: List available from the park.

RANGER'S NOTES
Ranger David Nemeth wrote to us, "Katmai is a remote wilderness area. We have a few disabled visitors each year who manage to negotiate float planes, boats, etc., to get to the park (there is no road access)."

KENAI FJORDS
NATIONAL PARK
Established 1978　　649,946 Acres
P.O. Box 1727
Seward, AK 99664-1727
Information: 907-224-3175

Fed by the Harding Ice Field, one of 4 major ice caps in the United States, 30 active glaciers dominate Kenai Fjords National Park. Moose, mountain goats, grizzly bears, wolves, and bald eagles live inland, while the intricate, mountainous coastline teems with horned puffins, sea otters, sea lions, and other marine life.

EASY ACCESS HIGHLIGHTS
• Exit Glacier
• Harding Ice Field

ACTIVITIES: Hiking, wildlife and bird viewing, fishing, sailing, sea-kayaking, boating, cross-country skiing, touring by airplane.
LOCATION: 130 miles south of Anchorage, AK; Exit Glacier is 13 miles northwest of Seward.
MEDICAL FACILITIES: Clinic in Seward; Central Peninsula General Hospital, Kenai, AK; many facilities in Anchorage.
TERRAIN: Rugged mountain and ice field. Elevation at Exit Glacier is 450'. An unnamed peak near McCarty Glacier (6,340') is the highest point in the park.
CLIMATE: Subarctic marine. Foggy, rainy, cool summers (June to August) with a few sunny warm days; long, overcast, stormy winters with rain and snow.

Averaged Daily Temperatures at (°F)

	J	F	M	A	M	J*	J*	A*	S	O	N	D
Highs	29	31	35	42	49	65	70	64	54	44	35	30
Lows	14	19	21	28	34	43	44	44	41	33	24	17

Source: Climatables™, courtesy of the National Park Foundation;
*NPS, Kenai Fjords National Park.

VISITOR CENTERS AND MUSEUMS
ISA-designated parking spaces.

SEWARD SMALL BOAT HARBOR: Fully accessible interior with exhibits, video and slide presentations, and restrooms.

ACCESS GUIDES
None.

ACCESSIBLE TRAILS, VIEWPOINTS, AND SITES
MODERATELY: Exit Glacier, to within .25-mile of glacier.

ACCESSIBLE CAMPGROUNDS
No developed campgrounds.

LODGING AND SERVICES
None in park.

SEWARD: Accommodations, supplies, and services.

TOURS AND SPORTS
BOAT AND AIR CHARTER: List available from park.

KOBUK VALLEY NATIONAL PARK
Established 1980   1,726,463 Acres
P.O. Box 1029
Kotzebue, AK 99752
Information: 907-442-3890

Surrounded by the Baird, Jade, and Waring mountains, Kobuk Valley National Park and Preserve protects more than 30 square miles of impressive sand dunes, the middle portion of the Kobuk River drainage, and the Salmon River. More than 340,000 caribou, a staple for native Eskimos, migrate yearly through the park. Human presence in the area dates back 14,000 years.

EASY ACCESS HIGHLIGHTS
- Kobuk River
- Great Kobuk Sand Dunes
- Little Kobuk and Hunt River Dunes
- Salmon River

ACTIVITIES: Hiking, wildlife and bird viewing, fishing, boating, kayaking, taking river trips, touring by airplane.
LOCATION: Accessible only by airplane. 350 miles northwest of Fairbanks, AK, by air; 75 miles east of Kotzebue.
MEDICAL FACILITIES: Maniilaq Medical Center, Kotzebue.
TERRAIN: Arctic mountains, valleys, and tundra. Highest point is Mt. Angayukaqsraq (10,197').
CLIMATE: Arctic. Summers (June through August) with cool temperatures and moderate rain. Snow or rain anytime. Long, bitter, cold winters.

Averaged Daily Temperatures (°F)

	J	F	M	A	M	J	J	A	S	O	N	D
Highs	−2	0	10	28	46	65	66	61	48	27	10	0
Lows	−20	−17	−9	7	28	42	48	44	33	15	−2	−15

Source: Climatables™, courtesy of the National Park Foundation.

VISITOR CENTERS AND MUSEUMS
No ISA-designated parking spaces.

ALASKA PUBLIC LANDS INFORMATION CENTER (FAIRBANKS): Information desk, museum exhibits with floor map, trip-planning room for all Alaska, captioned video presentations, and restrooms, all fully accessible.
NPS VISITOR INFORMATION CENTER (KOTZEBUE): Ramped entrance, video presentations, and restrooms moderately accessible.

ACCESS GUIDES
None.

ACCESSIBLE TRAILS, VIEWPOINTS, AND SITES
None.

ACCESSIBLE CAMPGROUNDS
No developed campgrounds.

LODGING AND SERVICES
None in park.

KOTZEBUE AND KIANA, AK: Limited accommodations, supplies, and services.

TOURS AND SPORTS
GUIDES AND BOAT, RIVER-FLOAT, AND AIR CHARTER SERVICES: Current list available from park.

AUTHORS' NOTES
No facilities or trails have been developed for visitors in the park. Access is primarily by air.

LAKE CLARK NATIONAL PARK
Established 1980   2,573,724 Acres
4230 University Drive, Suite 311
Anchorage, AK 99508
Information: 907-271-3751
TTY—Alaska Public Lands Information Center:
    Anchorage—907-271-2738

Lake Clark National Park and Preserve, where the Alaska and Aleutian mountain ranges join to form the Chigmit Mountains, offers a sampling of each ecosystem in Alaska. Swift rivers, active volcanoes, and jagged peaks stand out in this wilderness inhabited by humans at various times during the past 6,000 years. There are no trails in Lake Clark, and access is primarily by air.

EASY ACCESS HIGHLIGHTS
• Lake Clark

- Twin Lakes
- Iliamna and Redoubt Volcanoes
- Chigmit Mountains

ACTIVITIES: Hiking, wildlife and bird viewing, fishing, boating, kayaking, taking river trips, touring by airplane. No facilities developed for visitors with disabilities.
LOCATION: Accessible only by airplane. 200 miles southwest of Anchorage by air; 48 miles northeast of Iliamna, AK.
MEDICAL FACILITIES: Central Peninsula General Hospital, Kenai, AK; small clinic in Iliamna.
TERRAIN: Elevations from sea level to Mt. Redoubt (10,197').
CLIMATE: Subarctic. Summers (mid-May to September) with mild temperatures, windy and rainy on the coast, sunnier inland. Snow or rain anytime. Long, bitter, cold winters.

Averaged Daily Temperatures (°F)

	J	F	M	A	M	J	J	A	S	O	N	D
Highs	24	26	31	41	55	63	67	64	57	41	32	22
Lows	3	4	8	22	32	40	45	45	38	25	15	5

Source: Climatables™, courtesy of the National Park Foundation.

VISITOR CENTERS AND MUSEUMS
ISA-designated parking spaces.

PORT ALSWORTH (FIELD HEADQUARTERS): One building presenting interpretive programs; accessible in good weather. No accessible comfort station.

ALASKA PUBLIC LANDS INFORMATION CENTER (ANCHORAGE): Information desk, museum, trip-planning room for all Alaska, captioned video presentations, and restrooms, all fully accessible.

ACCESS GUIDES
None.

ACCESSIBLE TRAILS, VIEWPOINTS, AND SITES
None.

ACCESSIBLE CAMPGROUNDS
No developed campgrounds.

LODGING AND SERVICES
None in park.

ILIAMNA: Limited supplies and services.

TOURS AND SPORTS
COMMERCIAL AIRLINE SERVICE: From Anchorage.
AIR CHARTER SERVICE: From Anchorage, Homer, and Kenai,
all in Alaska.

WRANGELL-ST. ELIAS
NATIONAL PARK
Established 1978   8,095,970 Acres
P.O. Box 29
Glennallen, AK 99588
Information: 907-822-5234
Alaskan Public Lands Information Office, Tok, AK:
  907-883-5667
TTY: 907-271-2738

Wrangell-St. Elias National Park and Preserve is the largest
park in the United States and also contains the greatest collection of glaciers in the country. Known as North America's
mountain kingdom, this vast unspoiled wilderness — where
bands of Dall sheep, caribou, and moose roam — extends
from the Gulf of Alaska to dry inland foothills.

EASY ACCESS HIGHLIGHTS
• Wrangell Mountains
• Malaspina and Hubbard Glaciers
• Mt. St. Elias
• Chitina River

ACTIVITIES: Hiking, wildlife and bird viewing, fishing, river rafting, boating, horseback riding, cross-country skiing, touring by airplane.

LOCATION: Accessible by high-clearance vehicle or airplane. 189 miles by paved road east of Anchorage, AK, to Glennallen; McCarthy (central section of park) is 95 miles southeast of Glennallen.

MEDICAL FACILITIES: Crossroad Medical Center (clinic), Glennallen.

TERRAIN: Road elevations below 4,000′. Mt. St. Elias (18,008′) the second-highest peak in the United States.

CLIMATE: Subarctic. Summers (mid-May to September) cool with some warm days; warmest in July. Rain anytime. Cold, sometimes harsh winters.

Averaged Daily Temperatures (°F)

	J	F	M	A	M	J	J	A	S	O	N	D
Highs	24	26	31	41	55	63	67	64	57	41	32	22
Lows	3	4	8	22	32	40	45	45	38	25	15	5

Source: Climatables™, courtesy of the National Park Foundation.

VISITOR CENTERS AND MUSEUMS
No ISA-designated parking spaces.

HEADQUARTERS (8 MILES SOUTH OF GLENNALLEN): Moderately accessible book and map sales; short orientation film on park and road to McCarthy. Significant barrier to restroom.

ALASKA PUBLIC LANDS INFORMATION CENTER (TOK): Information desk, museum exhibits with floor map, captioned video programs, trip-planning room for all Alaska, restrooms, all fully accessible.

ACCESS GUIDES
None.

ACCESSIBLE TRAILS, VIEWPOINTS, AND SITES
None accessible.

ACCESSIBLE CAMPGROUNDS
No developed campgrounds.

LODGING AND SERVICES
SILVERLAKE LODGE: On Chitna-McCarthy Road; significant barriers.
SPORTSMAN'S PARADISE LODGE: On Nabesna Road; significant barriers.
KENNICOTT GLACIER LODGE: Use of hand-operated tram required to cross river; significant barriers.
MCCARTHY LODGE: In McCarthy; use of hand-operated tram required to cross river; significant barriers.
COOPER CENTER, AK, AND GLENNALLEN: Supplies and services.
CHITINA, AK, AND SLANA, AK: Limited supplies and services.

TOURS AND SPORTS
AIR CHARTER SERVICE: From Tok, Yakutat, Cordova, Glennallen, and Valdez, all in Alaska.

PARK RECREATION SUPPORT GROUPS

The following are groups that organize and/or have information about outdoor recreation in the parks for persons with disabilities and for seniors:

ADVENTURE ON WHEELS
1900 Ascot Parkway, No. 1822
Vallejo, CA 94591
707-557-9089

ADVENTURES IN MOVEMENT FOR HANDICAPPED CHILDREN
945 Danbury Road
Dayton, OH 45420
513-294-4611

ALL OUTDOORS (CHAPTER OF NATIONAL HANDICAPPED SPORTS AND RECREATION ASSOCIATION)
P.O. Box 1100
Redmond, OR 97756

ALTERNATIVE MOBILITY ADVENTURE SEEKERS (AMAS)
Boise State University
1910 University Drive
Boise, ID 83725

AMERICAN CAMPING ASSOCIATION
Martinsville, IN 46151
317-342-8456

AMERICAN CANOE ASSOCIATION
Disabled Persons Committee
8580 Cinderbed Rd., Suite 1900
P.O. Box 1190
Newlington, VA 22122-1190
703-550-7495

AMERICAN YOUTH HOSTELS
1434 Second Street
Santa Monica, CA 90401
213-393-1769

BILL DVORAK'S KAYAKING AND RAFTING EXPEDITIONS
17921 U.S. Highway 285
Nathrop, CO 81236
303-539-6851
800-824-3795, in Colorado

BOLD (BLIND OUTDOOR LEISURE DEVELOPMENT)
533 East Main Street
Aspen, CO 81611

BORP (BERKELEY OUTREACH RECREATION PROGRAM)
605 Eshleman Hall
University of California
Berkeley, CA 94720
415-849-4662

BRECKENRIDGE OUTDOOR RECREATION CENTER (CHAPTER OF NATIONAL HANDICAPPED SPORTS AND RECREATION ASSOCIATION)
P.O. Box 697
Breckenridge, CO 80442
303-453-6422

CANADIAN WHEELCHAIR SPORTS ASSOCIATION
333 River Road
Ottawa, Ontario, K1l 8H9
Canada
613-748-5685

CAPABLE PARTNERS
15100 Stone Road
Wayzata, MN 55391
612-475-1451

CHALLENGE ALASKA (CHAPTER OF NATIONAL HANDICAPPED SPORTS AND RECREATION ASSOCIATION)
P.O. Box 110065
Anchorage, AK 99511

CW HOG (COOPERATIVE WILDERNESS HANDICAPPED OUTDOOR GROUP)
Box 8118, Student Union
Idaho State University
Pocatello, ID 83209
208-236-3912

DEPARTMENT OF THE INTERIOR NATIONAL PARK SERVICE
Special Programs and
  Populations Branch
P.O. Box 37127
Washington, DC 20013-7127

ELDERHOSTEL
75 Federal Street
Boston, MA 02110

ENVIRONMENTAL TRAVELING COMPANIONS
Fort Mason
Building C, Room 360
San Francisco, CA 94123
415-474-7662

HANDICAPPED SCUBA ASSOCIATION
1104 El Prado
San Clemente, CA 92672
714-498-6128

NANTAHALA OUTDOOR CENTER
U.S. 19W, Box 41
Bryson City, NC 28713
704-488-2175

NATIONAL ASSOCIATION OF HANDICAPPED OUTDOOR SPORTSMEN
R.R. 6, Box 25
Centralia, IL 62801
618-532-4565

NATIONAL HANDICAPPED SPORTS AND RECREATION ASSOCIATION (NHSRA)
1341 G Street, N.W., Suite 815
Washington, DC 20005
202-783-1441

NATIONAL OUTWARD BOUND OFFICE
384 Field Point Road
Greenwich, CT 06830
800-243-8520

NATIONAL THERAPEUTIC
RECREATION SOCIETY
NATIONAL RECREATION
AND PARK ASSOCIATION
3101 Park Center Drive
Alexandria, VA 22302

NATIONAL WHEELCHAIR
ATHLETIC ASSOCIATION
1604 East Pikes Peak Avenue
Colorado Springs, CO 80909
719-635-9300

NORTH COUNTRY
REGIONAL SPORTS FOR
HEALTH OUTDOOR
RECREATION CENTER
Bemidji State University
Bemidji, MN 56601
218-755-3760

PARA PADDLERS
50 South Thirty-First Street
Boulder, CO 80303
303-444-3620
303-494-3765, evenings

PAW (PHYSICAL ACCESS
TO THE WOODS)
P.O. Box 346
Empire, CO 80438
303-569-2106

POINT (PARAPLEGICS ON
INDEPENDENT NATURE
TRIPS)
3200 Mustang Drive
Grapevine, TX 76051
817-481-0119

SEQUOYA CHALLENGE/
OUTDOOR ACCESS FOR ALL
c/o John Olmsted
Box 1026
Nevada City, CA 95959
916-432-3185

SOAR (SHARED OUTDOOR
ADVENTURE RECREATION)
P.O. Box 14583
Portland, OR 97214
503-238-1613

S'PLORE (SPECIAL
POPULATIONS LEARNING
OUTDOOR RECREATION
AND EDUCATION)
699 East South Temple,
   Suite 120
Salt Lake City, UT 84102
801-363-7130

STUDENT CONSERVATION
ASSOCIATION
P.O. Box 550
Charlestown, NH 03603
603-826-5206

TOTAL ACCESS CAMPING
10835 Ringwood Avenue
Santa Fe Springs, CA 90670
213-864-6896

VINLAND NATIONAL CENTER
Lake Independence
Loretto, MN 55357
612-479-3555

VOYAGEUR OUTWARD
BOUND SCHOOL
10900 Cedar Lake Road
Minnetonka, MN 55343
800-328-2943

WILDERNESS INQUIRY
1313 Fifth Street, S.E.
Suite 327A
Minneapolis, MN 55414
612-379-3858

EASY ACCESS
PARKS BY STATE

ALASKA
Denali National Park and
  Preserve
Gates of the Arctic National
  Park
Glacier Bay National Park
Katmai National Park
Kenai Fjords National Park
Kobuk Valley National Park
Lake Clark National Park
Wrangell-St. Elias National
  Park

ARIZONA
Grand Canyon National Park
Petrified Forest National Park

ARKANSAS
Hot Springs National Park

CALIFORNIA
Channel Islands National
  Park
Kings Canyon National Park
Lassen Volcanic National
  Park
Redwood National Park
Sequoia National Park
Yosemite National Park

COLORADO
Mesa Verde National Park
Rocky Mountain National
  Park

FLORIDA
Biscayne National Park
Everglades National Park

HAWAII
Haleakala National Park
Hawaii Volcanoes National
  Park

KENTUCKY
Mammoth Cave National
  Park

MAINE
Acadia National Park

MICHIGAN
Isle Royale National Park

MINNESOTA
Voyageurs National Park

MONTANA
Glacier National Park

NEVADA
Great Basin National Park

NEW MEXICO
Carlsbad Caverns National
  Park
Chaco Culture National
  Historical Park

NORTH DAKOTA
Theodore Roosevelt National
  Park

OREGON
Crater Lake National Park

SOUTH DAKOTA
Badlands National Park
Wind Cave National Park

**TENNESSEE-
NORTH CAROLINA**
Great Smoky Mountains
  National Park

TEXAS
Big Bend National Park
Guadalupe Mountains
  National Park

UTAH
Arches National Park
Bryce Canyon National Park
Canyonlands National Park
Capitol Reef National Park
Zion National Park

VIRGINIA
Shenandoah National Park

VIRGIN ISLANDS
Virgin Islands National Park

WASHINGTON
Mount Rainier National Park
North Cascades National
  Park
Olympic National Park

WYOMING
Grand Teton National Park
Yellowstone National Park

GLOSSARY

ACCESS GUIDES: Printed material distributed by the national parks describing facilities available for possible use by persons with disabilities.

ACCESSIBLE: A general, nonspecific term describing a park, trail, facility, or portion thereof that can be approached, entered, and used by persons with disabilities, either independently or with assistance. *See also* **Fully accessible** and **Moderately accessible**.

ADA: The Americans with Disabilities Act (ADA). Signed into law July 1990; an expansion of the rights of individuals with disabilities with regard to accessibility, employment, and services.

ASL: American Sign Language. Signed language used by deaf persons in the United States.

BARRIER-FREE ENTRY: A building entrance without obstructions to persons with mobility problems.

BLIND: Having severe or total loss of vision and light perception.

BLM: Bureau of Land Management, U.S. Department of the Interior.

BM: Bureau of Mines, U.S. Department of the Interior.

CAPTIONING: Visual text of audio portions of film, video, or slide presentations for deaf persons or persons hard of hearing.

CROSS SLOPE: A slope across the direction of travel.

DEAF: Having severe or profound hearing impairment.

DEVELOPMENTAL DISABILITY: Mental retardation.

DISABILITY: Diminished physical, mental, or sensory functions.

EDGE PROTECTION: Border prventing trail users from accidentally and dangerously leaving a path or trail.

ENTERABLE: A term used to describe a bulding having an entrance moderately accessible to persons with mobility problems.

EXTENDED PICNIC-TABLE TOP: A table top with clear space of at least 19 inches deep underneath to allow for use by wheelchair users.

FEE USE AREA: U.S. government property where visitors must pay a fee to partake in recreational activities.

FULLY ACCESSIBLE: A term used to describe trails or facilities that exceed, comply with, or nearly comply with Uniform Federal Accessibility Standards (UFAS) and recent professional studies concerning accessibility to outdoor recreation facilities for persons with disabilities, particularly those with mobility problems. *See also* **Accessible** and **Moderately accessible**.

GOLDEN ACCESS PASSPORT: For people medically determined to be blind or to have permanent disabilities. Provides complimentary admittance to federally operated parks, monuments, historical sites, recreation areas, and wildlife refuges that charge entrance fees and a 50 percent discount on federal usage fees charged for camping, boat launching, parking, and so on.

GRAB BARS: Hand rails installed to assist persons with mobility problems in transfer to and from seating situations.

HEARING IMPAIRMENT: Mild to severe loss of hearing.

INFORMATION DESKS: Visitor information service areas. Information desks noted as lowered are not higher than 34 inches.

INTERPRETIVE PLACARDS: Mounted explanatory exhibits to increase visitors' awareness of a specific park feature.

ISA: International Symbol of Access.

LARGE PRINT: Type size no smaller than 18 point used for better readability by persons with visual impairments.

LOCK-DOWNS: Secure mechanical mounting systems for wheelchairs in moving vehicles.

LOWERED TELEPHONE: Public telephones mounted at accessible height for wheelchair users.

MISTIX: A reservation system that serves campgrounds in selected national parks. For information, contact MISTIX, P.O. Box 85705, San Diego, CA 92138-5705; 800-365-2267.

MOBILITY PROBLEMS: Decreased ambulatory function as a result of physical injuries, disease, or deterioration.

MODERATELY ACCESSIBLE: Designation for trails and/or facilities that do not meet full accessibility standards and that present possible barriers to wheelchair users and persons with other mobility problems. Assistance is usually necessary. *See also* **Accessible** and **Fully Accessible**.

MODERATELY STEEP SLOPE OR RAMP: A walkway with an incline that exceeds UFAS guidelines and is more difficult than a fully accessible slope or ramp for persons with mobility problems to negotiate.

NONDISABLED: Having minor to no mobility problems; also without moderate to severe vision, hearing, or developmental disabilities.

NPS: National Park Service, U.S. Department of the Interior.

RAISED FIRE GRILL: Fire grill elevated 30 to 36 inches from the ground for increased access by wheelchair users.

RV: Recreational vehicle.

SELF-GUIDED TRAIL: Trail with accompanying interpretive information.

SIGNED INTERPRETATION: Sign language for presentations by park rangers.

SIGNIFICANT BARRIER: Natural or structural objects preventing accessibility for people with mobility problems and/or vision, hearing, and/or developmental disabilities, except for persons with extraordinary abilities or assistance.

SLOPE: Lineal rise of a walkway or ramp in the direction of travel. Sometimes described by a ratio of lineal rise over a given length of level distance; for instance, a ratio of 1:12 means a 1-foot rise over a level distance of 12 feet.

TDD: Telecommunication Device for the Deaf. Enables users to send and receive printed messages via telephone lines. *See also* TTY.

TIE-DOWNS: Mounting systems utilizing belts or ropes to secure wheelchair users in moving vehicles.

TOE BOARDS: Edge protection for ramps, bridges, and elevated boardwalks to prevent falls.

TREAD: Surface characteristics of a walkway or trail.

TTY: Teletypewriter. Enables persons with hearing impairments to send and receive printed messages via telephone lines. *See also* **TDD.**

UFAS: Uniform Federal Accessibility Standards.

USFS: United States Forest Service, U.S. Department of Agriculture.

USFWS: United States Fish and Wildlife Service, U.S. Department of the Interior.

VERY STEEP SLOPE OR RAMP: A walkway with a lineal incline steeper than 1:8; may present a significant barrier to persons with mobility problems.

VISUALLY IMPAIRED: Having mild to severe visual loss but retaining some residual sight. Such a person is said to have a vision impairment.

WHEEL-IN-SHOWER: A shower stall without barriers that is directly accessible to persons using wheelchairs.

WIDE STALL: A toilet stall that complies with UFAS and is a minimum of 48 inches wide and 56 inches long.

BIBLIOGRAPHY

In addition to conducting on-site research and interviews and utilizing park-provided brochures, newspapers, and pamphlets, the authors used the following sources in their research for *Easy Access to National Parks:*

Ambler, J. Richard. *The Anasazi: Prehistoric Peoples of the Four Corners Region.* Flagstaff, AZ: Museum of Northern Arizona, 1989.

American Automobile Association. *Campbook®: RV and Tent Sites in California and Nevada.* Falls Church, VA: AAA, 1989.

_____. *Campbook®: RV and Tent Sites in Oregon and Washington.* Falls Church, VA: AAA, 1989.

_____. *Campbook®: South Central RV and Tent Sites in Arkansas, Kansas, Missouri, Oklahoma, and Texas.* Falls Church, VA: AAA, 1989.

_____. *Campbook®: Southwestern RV and Tent Sites in Arizona, Colorado, New Mexico, and Utah.* Falls Church, VA: AAA, 1989.

Anderson, Douglas, and Barbara Anderson. *Chaco Canyon: Center of a Culture.* Tucson, AZ: Southwest Parks and Monuments Association, 1981.

Aquilar, Teresita E., and Barbara J. DeWall. "Connecting with the Accessible Outdoors." *Sports 'N Spokes,* November/December 1987, 50–53.

Architectural and Transportation Barriers Compliance Board. *Uniform Federal Accessibility Standards.* Rev. ed. Washington, DC: Government Printing Office, 1985.

_____. *Access to Outdoor Recreation Planning and Design: A Technical Paper of the Architectural and Transportation Barriers Compliance Board, Prepared by Federal Government Working Group on Access to Recreation.* Washington, DC: 1989.

Ash, Sidney. *Petrified Forest: The Story Behind the Scenery.* Rev. ed. Las Vegas, NV: KC Publications, 1986.

Barnes, F. A., and Michaelene Pendleton. *Canyon Country Prehistoric Indians: Their Cultures, Ruins, Artifacts and Rock Art.* Salt Lake City: Wasatch Publishers, 1979.

Barnett, John. *Carlsbad Caverns: Silent Chambers, Timeless Beauty.* Carlsbad, NM: Carlsbad Caverns Natural History Association, 1981.

Bendick, Robert L., Jr. "Sailing Together." *Courier*, May 1990, 21–23. Washington, DC: National Park Service, U.S. Department of the Interior.

Breining, Greg. *Voyageurs National Park.* International Falls, MN: Lake States Interpretive Association, 1987.

Brown, Dee. *The American Spa, Hot Springs, Arkansas.* Little Rock, AR: Rose Publishing Company, 1982.

Brown, Joseph E. *Monarchs of the Mist: The Story of Redwood National Park and the Coast Redwoods.* Point Reyes, CA; Coastal Parks Association, 1982.

Buchholtz, C. W. *Rocky Mountain National Park: A History.* Boulder: Colorado Associated University Press, 1983.

Collier, Michael. *An Introduction to Grand Canyon Geology.* Grand Canyon, AZ: Grand Canyon Natural History Association, 1980.

Collier, Sargent F. *Mt. Desert Island and Acadia National Park: An Informal History.* Camden, ME: Down East Books, 1978.

Cooper, Susan, ed. *A Guide to Designing Accessible Outdoor Recreation Facilities.* Ann Arbor, MI: Heritage Conservation and Recreaton Service, U.S. Department of the Interior, 1980.

Decker, Robert, and Barbara Decker. *Road Guide to Hawaii Volcanoes National Park.* 2nd ed. Mariposa, CA: Double Decker Press, 1987.

Dewitt, John B. *California Redwood Parks and Preserves: A Guide to the Redwood Parks and a Brief History of the Efforts to Save the Redwoods.* San Francisco: Save-the-Redwoods League, 1985.

Disabled Outdoors. 5223 South Laurel Ave., Chicago, IL 60638.

Dorsey, Joan. *Introducing Your Kids to the Outdoors.* Boston: Stone Wall Press, 1978.

Douglas, Marjory Stoneman. *The Everglades: River of Grass.* Rev. ed. St. Simons Island, GA: Mockingbird Books, 1974.

DREAM (Disabled Recreation and Environmental Access Movement). *Glacier Park — Flathead Valley: Accessibility Guide to Undiscovered Montana.* Kalispell, MT: DREAM, 1988.

Durant, Mary, and Michael Harwood. *This Curious Country: Badlands National Park.* Interior, SD: Badlands Natural History Association, 1989.

Ellis, W. Kay, and Susan Robbins. "Accessing Our National Parks." *Paraplegia News*, March 1990, 64–67.

Everhart, William C. *The National Park Service.* Boulder, CO: Westview Press, 1983.

Harris, Stephen L. *Fire Mountains of the West: The Cascades and Mono Lake Volcanoes.* Missoula, MT: Mountain Press, 1988.

Heliker, Christina. *Volcanic and Seismic Hazards on the Island of Hawaii.* U.S. Geological Survey. Washington, DC: Government Printing Office, 1990.

Hoffman, John F. *Arches National Park: An Illustrated Guide.* San Diego: Western Recreation Publications, 1985.

Hughes, J. Donald. *In the House of Stone and Light: A Human History of the Grand Canyon.* Grand Canyon, AZ: Grand Canyon Natural History Association, 1978.

Keefer, William R. 1971 Reprint *The Geologic Story of Yellowstone National Park.* Geological Survey Bulletin 1347, Mammoth, WY: Yellowstone Library and Museum Association.

Kinmont, Vikki, and Claudia Axcell. *Simple Foods for the Pack.* San Francisco: Sierra Club Books, 1976.

Leach, Nicki, ed. *Hawaiian National Parks.* Santa Barbara, CA: Sunrise Publishing, 1986.

Lister, Robert H., and Florence C. Lister. *Those Who Came Before.* Globe, AZ: Southwest Parks and Monuments Association, 1983.

Love, J. D., and John C. Reed, Jr. *Creation of the Teton Landscape: The Geologic Story of Grand Teton National Park.* 1st rev. ed. Moose, WY: Grand Teton Natural History Association, 1971.

Lyons, Kathleen, and Mary Beth Cooney-Lazaneo. *Plants of the Coast Redwood Region.* Boulder Creek, CA: Looking Press, 1988.

MacNielle, Suzanne. "A Guide to Eight Natural Preserves." *New York Times,* 26 May 1991, Travel Section, 14.

Malville, J. McKim, and Claudia Putnam. *Prehistoric Astronomy in the Southwest.* Boulder, CO: Johnson Publishing Company, 1989.

McGregor, John C. *Southwestern Archaeology.* 2d ed. Chicago: University of Illinois Press, 1982.

Murphy, Dan. *The Guadalupes: Guadalupe Mountains National Park.* Carlsbad, NM: Carlsbad Caverns Natural History Association, 1984.

Mutelm, Cornelia Fleischer, and John C. Emerick. *From Grassland to Glacier: A Natural History of Colorado.* Boulder, CO: Johnson Publishing Company, 1984.

National Geographic Society. *A Guide to Our Federal Lands.* Washington, DC: National Geographic Society, 1984.

National Park Foundation. *The Complete Guide to America's National Parks.* 1990–1991 ed. New York: Prentice Hall, 1990.

National Park Service, U.S. Department of the Interior. *Accommodation of Disabled Visitors at Historic Sites in the National Park System.* Washington, DC: Government Printing Office, 1971.

_____. *National Park Guide for the Handicapped.* Washington, DC: Government Printing Office, 1971.

_____. *Access National Parks: A Guide for Handicapped Visitors.* Washington, DC: Government Printing Office, 1977.

_____. Special Programs and Populations Branch. *Interpretation for Disabled Visitors in the National Park System.* Washington, DC: Government Printing Office, 1984.

_____. *The National Parks: Camping Guide 1988–89.* Washington, DC: Government Printing Office, 1988.

_____. *Design.* Alexandria, VA: National Recreation and Park Association, Winter 1989.

Noble, David Grant. *New Light on Chaco Canyon.* Santa Fe, NM: School of American Research Press, 1984.

North Carolina Department of Human Resources and Department of Commerce. *Access, North Carolina.* Raleigh, NC: Department of Human Resources and Department of Commerce, 1985.

Northern Cartographic. *Access America: An Atlas and Guide to the National Parks for Visitors with Disabilities.* Burlington, VT: Northern Cartographic, 1988.

Oppelt, Norman T. *Guide to Prehistoric Ruins of the Southwest.* 2d ed. Boulder, CO: Pruett Publishing, 1989.

Palmer, Arthur N. *An Ancient World Beneath the Hills: Wind Cave.* Hot Springs, SD: Wind Cave/Jewel Cave Natural History Association, 1988.

Pearson, John, ed. *Road Guide to Paved and Improved Dirt Roads of Big Bend National Park.* Rev. ed. Big Bend National Park, TX: Big Bend Natural History Association, 1980.

Peterson, Roger Tory. *Peterson First Guides to Wildflowers of Northeastern and North-central North America.* Boston: Houghton Mifflin Company, 1986.

Quealy, Patrica, Anthony Anderson, Eckert, Seamans, Cherin & Mellot. *Americans with Disabilities Act: A Campground Operator's Guide to Compliance.* Reston, VA: NCOA Educational Foundation, 1990.

Robertson, William B. *Everglades: The Park Story.* Rev. ed. Homestead, FL: Florida National Parks and Monuments Association, 1989.

Roth, Wendy Carol. "Taking to the Trail by Wheelchair: Vistas and Access in Canyon Country." *New York Times,* 17 April 1988, Travel Section, 14.

Schoch, Henry A. *Theodore Roosevelt National Park: The Story Behind the Scenery.* Las Vegas, NV: KC Publications, 1974.

Schreier, Carl. *A Field Guide to Yellowstone's Geysers, Hot Springs and Fumaroles.* Moose, WY: Homestead Publishing, 1987.

Shuler, Jay. *A Revelation Called the Badlands: Building a National Park 1909–1939.* Interior, SD: Badlands Natural History Association, 1989.

Sierra Club Guides to the National Parks of the Desert Southwest. New York: Stewart, Tabori and Chang, 1984.

Sierra Club Guides to the National Parks of the Pacific Southwest and Hawaii. New York: Stewart, Tabori and Chang, 1984.

Sierra Club Guides to the National Parks of the Rocky Mountains and the Great Plains. New York: Stewart, Tabori and Chang, 1984.

Sierra Club Guides to the National Parks of the Pacific Northwest and Alaska. New York: Stewart, Tabori and Chang, 1985.

Sierra Club Guides to the National Parks of the East and Middle West. New York: Stewart, Tabori and Chang, 1986.

Smithson, Michael T. *Rocky Mountain: The Story Behind the Scenery.* Las Vegas, NV: 1987.

Strong, Douglas Hillman. *Trees—Or Timber? The Story of Sequoia and Kings Canyon National Parks.* Three Rivers, CA: Sequoia Natural History Association, 1968.

Tilden, Freeman. *The National Parks.* Rev. and expanded by Paul Schullary. New York: Alfred A. Knopf, 1986.

Weiss, Louise. *Access to the World: A Travel Guide for the Handicapped.* Rev. ed. New York: Henry Holt and Company, 1986.

Wenger, Gilbert R. *The Story of Mesa Verde National Park.* Mesa Verde, CO: Mesa Verde Museum Association, 1980.

White, Randy Wayne. "Beyond the Chair." *Outside,* May 1990.

Whitney, Stephen. *A Sierra Club Naturalist's Guide: The Sierra Nevada.* San Francisco: Sierra Club Books, 1979.

Wilkerson, James A., ed. *Medicine for Mountaineering.* 3d ed. Seattle: The Mountaineers, 1985.

Willard, Bettie E., and Michael T. Smithson. *Alpine Wildflowers of the Rocky Mountains.* Estes Park, CO: Rocky Mountain Nature Association, n.d.

Williams, Jack R. *Indians of the Guadalupes.* Rev. ed. Florissant, CO: Carlsbad Caverns Natural History Association, 1979.

Wood, Robert S. *The 2 oz. Backpacker: A Problem Solving Manual for Use in the Wilds.* Berkeley, CA: Ten Speed Press, 1982.

INDEX

Mesa Verde National Park, 119,
124, 320
Redwood National Park, 145, 147
Rocky Mountain National Park,
162, 163
Yosemite National Park, 203,
206, 354
Byers, William N., 169

Cache La Poudre River, 168
California national parks
Channel Islands, 326–339, *327*
Kings Canyon, 171, 173–174,
181–184, 347–351
Lassen Volcanic, 331–334
Redwood, 140–155, *144,* 343–347
Sequoia, 171, 173, 174–181, *178,*
347–351
Yosemite, 200–215, *202,* 351–354
California state parks, 140
Big Basin Redwood, 143
Del Norte Coast Redwoods, 140,
143, 150, 152, 343, 346
Jedediah Smith Redwoods, 140,
143, 155–156, 343, 345, 346
Prairie Creek Redwoods, 140,
143, 149–150, 343, 344, 345,
346
Campfires, 13–14
Bryce Canyon National Park, 56
Carlsbad Caverns National Park,
66
Guadalupe Mountains National
Park, 318
Mesa Verde National Park, 116
Yosemite National Park, 212
Campgrounds, 240
See also specific parks
Handicamp, 162–163, 283, 284
Wilderness on Wheels, 170
Canada
support group, 379

Waterton Lakes National Park,
274
Canoeing, 22
Acadia National Park, 41, 43–44,
44–45, 46, 245
Everglades National Park, 81,
87–88, 89, 90, 250, 251
Grand Teton National Park, 101,
280
Isle Royale National Park, 259
support group, 378
Voyageurs National Park, 228,
229, 230, 270
Cantu, Ranger Danny, 64
Canyonlands National Park, 302–
304
Capek, Ranger Sonya, 189
Capitol Reef National Park, 304–
306
Captioning, 383
Badlands National Park, 273
Bryce Canyon National Park, 300
Carlsbad Caverns, 63
Chaco Canyon, 74, 309
Channel Islands National Park,
328
Everglades National Park, 83
Gates of the Arctic National Park,
360
Glacier Bay National Park, 363
Grand Canyon, 223
Guadalupe Mountains National
Park, 317
Hawaii Volcanoes National Park,
108, 367
Hot Springs National Park, 256
Redwood National Park, 344
Rocky Mountain National Park,
159
Virgin Islands National Park,
267
Yosemite National Park, 204, 352

Elderhostel, 379
Olympic Park Institute, 133, 342
Elevation considerations, 25, 239.
See also specific parks
Ellis, Ranger Janet, 189
Emergency telephone numbers. *See
specific parks*
Equipment, 9–10, 11, 12, 15
Erner, Ranger Bob, 124
Everglades National Park, 21, 23,
79–92, *82,* 248–251
Anhinga Trail, 21, 83, 84, 250,
251
Everhart, William C., 215

Fallen Monarch, 182
Federal Recreation Passport Program, 18–19
Fink, Ranger Bill, 259
Firewood, 14, 15
Fish hatchery, 148–149
Florida
Biscayne National Park, 22–23,
93, 246–248
Everglades National Park, 21, 23,
79–92, *82,* 248–251
Florida Keys. *See* Biscayne National
Park
Foreign-language materials
Bryce Canyon National Park, 300
Petrified Forest National Park,
322
Redwood National Park, 344
Shenandoah National Park, 263
Theodore Roosevelt National
Park, 285
Fountain Paint Pot Trail, 22, 191–
193
Four Corners, panoramic view of,
119
Frontcountry areas, 20–21
Fully accessible sites, 21, 30, 31–32.
See also specific parks

Gates of the Arctic National Park,
359–361
Gateway to the Narrows Trail, 5–6,
59, 325
General Grant Tree, 181, 182
General Sherman Tree, 173, 179,
350–351
Giant sequoias (*Sequoiadendron giganteum*), 141, 142, 201
in Kings Canyon/Sequoia, 173,
176, 177, 179, 181, 182, 350–351
in Yosemite, 201, 212
Glacier Bay National Park, 362–363
Glacier National Park, 274–277
Golden Access/Golden Age/Golden
Eagle Passports, 19, 384
Grab bars, 31, 32, 384
Grand Canyon National Park, 12,
23, 216, 222–227, 311–314
Grand Canyon of the Yellowstone
River, 196–197
Grand Teton National Park, 94–
103, *106,* 278–281
Great Basin National Park, 314–316
Great Smoky Mountains National
Park, 216, 217–221, 252–254
Green River, 302, 303, 304
Grouse Strut, 103
Guadalupe Mountains National
Park, 14, 69, 316–318
Guide dogs, Grand Canyon and, 224

Haleakala National Park, 113–114,
364–365
Handicamp, 162–163, 283, 284
Happy Isles (Yosemite), 206–207
Harding, Warren, 210
Hawaii
Haleakala National Park, 113–
114, 364–365
Hawaii Volcanoes National Park,
8, 14, 104–113, *106, 109,* 366–
368

Slopes, accessibility and, 31, 32, 33
Smith River, 141, 143, 156, 347
Smith River National Recreation
  Area, 156
Smithson, Ranger Michael, 128,
  135, 136, 169, 170
Snake River, 94, 101, 280
Snorkeling, Virgin Islands, 266
Snowmobiling, 22
  Grand Teton National Park, 99
  Voyageurs National Park, 228, 270
South Dakota
  Badlands National Park, 271–
    274, 272
  Wind Cave National Park, 287–
    288
Sprague Lake, 162–163, 283, 284
Stagecoach rides
  Yellowstone National Park, 195,
    197
  Yosemite National Park, 212
Standing table, 15–16, 208
Stehekin River, 24
Strollers. See Baby strollers
Support groups, 378–381
Sutton, Ranger Ron, 361

TDD/TTY, defined, 385
Tennessee, Great Smoky Moun-
  tains National Park, 216, 217–
  221, 252–255
Tent requirements, 11
Teton Range, Grand Teton National
  Park, 94–103, 106
Texas
  Big Bend National Park, 7–8,
    216, 232–236, 297–299
  Guadalupe Mountains National
    Park, 14, 69, 316–318
Tharp, Hale D., 171, 177
Theft problems, 15–16, 208
Theodore Roosevelt National Park,
  284–286

Three-wheeled scooter, 9
Tioga Pass, 215
Tioga Pass Road, 213
Toileting. See Bathroom facilities
Touch exhibits
  Badlands National Park, 273
  Bryce Canyon National Park, 53,
    300
  Chaco Culture National Historic
    Park, 74
  Denali National Park, 357
  Glacier Bay National Park, 363
  Glacier National Park, 275, 276
  Grand Canyon National Park,
    223, 312
  Kings Canyon National Park, 181
  Olympic National Park, 128, 340
  Prairie Creek Redwoods State
    Park, 149
  Redwood National Park, 145, 344
  Sequoia National Park, 180
  Shenandoah National Park, 263
  Theodore Roosevelt National
    Park, 285
  Voyageurs National Park, 229,
    230, 269
  Yellowstone National Park, 290
Trail for All People, 177–178, 178
Trail Ridge Road, 165–169, 282, 284
Tram tours
  Everglades National Park, 9, 80–
    81, 91, 251
  Mesa Verde National Park, 124,
    321
  Yosemite National Park, 212, 354
  Zion National Park, 325
Tuolumne Meadows, 214
Tuolumne River, 201

Uniform Federal Accessibility Standards (UFAS), 20, 31
U.S. Forest Service, passport program, 18–19

Utah
Arches National Park, 12–13, 294–297, *295*
Bryce Canyon National Park, 49–59, *52, 53, 55*, 299–301
Canyonlands National Park, 302–304
Capitol Reef National Park, 304–306
Kodachrome Basin State Park, 59
Zion National Park, 5–6, 59, 323–325

Vans, hydraulic lift, 11–12
in Denali National Park, 358–359
Virgin Islands National Park, 266–267
Virginia, Shenandoah National Park, 262–265
Visually impaired, 385
accessibility for, 30
alternative modes of travel for, 22
audio materials for. *See* Audio materials
Braille materials for. *See* Braille materials
Carlsbad Caverns tour for, 64–65
Everglades National Park and, 21, 83, 84–85, 250, 251
Grand Canyon and, 224
large-print materials for. *See* Large-print materials
support group for, 378
Volcanoes
Crater Lake National Park, 329–331
Haleakala National Park, 113–114, 364–365
Hawaii Volcanoes National Park, 8, 104–113, *106, 109*, 366–368
Katmai National Park, 368–369
Lake Clark National Park, 373, 374

Lassen Volcanic National Park, 331–334
Voyageurs National Park, 22, 216, 228–231, 268–270

Washington
Lake Chelan National Recreation Area, 23
Mount Rainier National Park, 138–139, 334–336
North Cascades National Park, 23–24, *28*, 138–139, 337–339
Olympic National Park, 21, 127–138, *129, 135*, 339–343, *341*
Waterton Lakes National Park (Canada), 274
Wellman, Ranger Mark, 203, 204, 206, 209, 210
Wheelchairs for loan
Everglades National Park, 83
Mesa Verde National Park, 120, 319
Olympic National Park, 133
Wheelchairs for trail use, 9–10
renting, 16
Wheelchair user(s)
bicycle paths for. *See specific parks*
Everglades tram tour for, 81
support groups for, 378–380
Whitney, Mt., 174, 207, 347
Wilderness on Wheels, 170
Wind Cave National Park, 287–288
"Windshield experiences," 18
Wrangell-St. Elias National Park, 375–377
Wyoming
Grant Teton National Park, 94–103, *106*, 278–281
Yellowstone National Park, 14–15, 21–22, 24, 185–199, *186, 196*, 289–293

Yellowstone Lake, 198–199

Yellowstone National Park, 14–15, 21–22, 24, 185–199, *186, 196,* 289–293
fire damage to, 187–188
Yellowstone River, 196, 197–198
Yosemite National Park, 200–215, *202,* 351–354
standing table theft at, 15–16, 208
Yosemite Valley, 200, 203–205
Youth hostels. *See* Hostels

Zion National Park, 5–6, 59, 323–325
Zuni, Anasazi and, 126